INTERNATIONAL HUMAN RESOURCE MANAGEMENT

Sara Miller McCune founded SAGE Publishing in 1965 to support the dissemination of usable knowledge and educate a global community. SAGE publishes more than 1000 journals and over 800 new books each year, spanning a wide range of subject areas. Our growing selection of library products includes archives, data, case studies and video. SAGE remains majority owned by our founder and after her lifetime will become owned by a charitable trust that secures the company's continued independence.

Los Angeles | London | New Delhi | Singapore | Washington DC | Melbourne

EDITED BY **MIGUEL MARTÍNEZ LUCIO** & **ROBERT MACKENZIE**

INTERNATIONAL HUMAN RESOURCE MANAGEMENT SECOND EDITION

THE TRANSFORMATION OF WORK IN A GLOBAL CONTEXT

$SAGE

Los Angeles | London | New Delhi
Singapore | Washington DC | Melbourne

Los Angeles | London | New Delhi
Singapore | Washington DC | Melbourne

SAGE Publications Ltd
1 Oliver's Yard
55 City Road
London EC1Y 1SP

SAGE Publications Inc.
2455 Teller Road
Thousand Oaks, California 91320

SAGE Publications India Pvt Ltd
B 1/I 1 Mohan Cooperative Industrial Area
Mathura Road
New Delhi 110 044

SAGE Publications Asia-Pacific Pte Ltd
3 Church Street
#10-04 Samsung Hub
Singapore 049483

Editor: Ruth Stitt
Assistant editor: Jessica Moran
Production editor: Manmeet Kaur Tura
Marketing manager: Lucia Sweet
Cover design: Naomi Robinson
Typeset by: C&M Digitals (P) Ltd, Chennai, India

Library of Congress Control Number: 2021943004

British Library Cataloguing in Publication data

A catalogue record for this book is available from the British Library

ISBN 978-1-5297-3498-0
ISBN 978-1-5297-3497-3 (pbk)

Contents

About the editors

Miguel Martínez Lucio is a Professor at the University of Manchester (Alliance Manchester Business School), UK and is involved in its Work and Equalities Institute. He researches on questions of employment regulation, the role of the state, the changing nature of worker representation and social inclusion and inequality at work. He is involved in various networks, such as Critical Labour Studies, and is an editor of *New Technology, Work and Employment*.

Robert MacKenzie is Professor of Working Life Science at Karlstad Business School, Karlstad University, Sweden. He is also an editor of *New Technology, Work and Employment*. His research focuses on the regulation of the employment relationship in the context of restructuring. His work links the social and economic experiences of workers with broader patterns of socioeconomic restructuring and the role played by multiple stakeholders, contract form, technological change and occupational identity in mediating the experience of restructuring.

About the contributors

Roland Ahlstrand is Professor of Working Life Science at Dalarna University, Sweden. His research into industrial relations and work organizations includes industrial restructuring, corporate social responsibility, digitalization, job quality, organizational change and worker participation. His research has primarily dealt with larger and global companies in the manufacturing industry, ranging from the manufacture of automobile to the steel industry.

Phil Almond is a Professor at Leicester University, UK and a comparative researcher interested in how work, management and organization are shaped by economic, social, political and geographical contexts. Most of his research focuses on multinational companies, examining both their internal coordination and the ways in which the disruptions to national and local business systems caused by corporate globalization shape the decisions of managers, social actors and policy-makers.

Lisa Berntsen is a Researcher at the Scientific Research Institute for the Dutch Labour Movement (De Burcht). Her main research interests are in employment relations, labour migration and trade union representation strategies of migrants and young workers.

Kendra Briken is a Senior Lecturer at the University of Strathclyde, Department for Work, Employment and Organization, Glasgow, Scotland. She has a background in sociology. Her research interests include new technologies, the labour process and precarity, as well as speculative futures of work.

Erka Çaro is a Researcher and Lecturer at the Department of Geography, University of Tirana, Albania. She received her PhD in Population Studies from the University of Groningen in the Netherlands. She is a member of the executive board of the Western Balkans Migration Network. Her research interests include migration, labour mobility, trade union relationships with migrants, gender studies and the Western Balkans. Her work has been published by the *Journal of Ethnic and Migration Studies, Gender, Place & Culture* and Oxford University Press, among others.

Fang Lee Cooke is Professor at Monash Business School, Monash University, Australia. Her research interests are in the area of strategic Human Resource Management (HRM), knowledge management and innovation, outsourcing, international HRM, diversity and inclusion management, employment relations, migrant studies, HRM in the healthcare sector, digitalization and the implications for employment and HRM, and low carbon growth and the future of work. Her recent research examines the tensions, challenges and implications associated with these topics for various key stakeholders, such as the state, employers' associations, trade unions, workers and labour NGOs.

Carlos J. Fernández Rodríguez is Associate Professor in Sociology at the Universidad Autónoma de Madrid, Spain. His research interests are the sociology of organizations, the sociology of labour, the sociology of consumption and industrial relations.

Betty Frino is a Lecturer in Management at the University of Wollongong, Australia with a background in HRM, employment relations and organizational psychology. Her research interests include employee engagement and voice, motivation and well-being, wage determination and labour market regulation. More recently, her work has focused on the digital economy and work health and safety, and Covid-19 and well-being at work.

María C. González Menéndez is Associate Professor of Sociology at the University of Oviedo, Spain. Her research interests are in the comparative study of labour market governance and labour management. She has researched workers' participation, women's presence at board-of-directors level, the subnational governance of multinational firms and youth employment policies. She is currently co-editing a book on trade unions and the subnational governance of industrial relations and employment.

Jennifer Hobbins is Lecturer in Leadership at the Swedish Defense College. Her research interests include the social consequences of restructurings and redundancy, unemployment policies and citizen–state relations. More recently, her research has included the role of collective memory for communities and professional ideals.

Debra Howcroft is Professor of Technology and Organization at the Work and Equalities Institute, University of Manchester, UK. She is an editor of *New Technology, Work and Employment*. Her research focuses on new technologies and experiences of work, which includes an Economic Social and Research Council-funded project on digitalization as part of the Digital Futures of Work Research Centre.

Lars Ivarsson is Associate Professor of Working Life Science at Karlstad University, Sweden. His research interest is focused on various experiences of work and work-related relations from the perspective of employees. More recently, he has been interested in the experiences and consequences of precarious work. He is an editor of the Swedish journal *Arbetsmarknad & Arbetsliv*.

Naresh Kumar is a Professor of Human Resource Management at the Faculty of Entrepreneurship and Business, Universiti Malaysia Kelantan. His research interests include employee relations, organizational behaviour and entrepreneurial competency development.

Lena Lid-Falkman is a Lecturer in Working Life Science at Karlstad University and an Associated Researcher at Stockholm School of Economics, Sweden. Her research interests are in leadership, communication and organization. She has focused the last ten years of her research on modern worklife, offices and ways of work.

Nathan Lillie is Professor of Social and Public Policy at the University of Jyväskylä, Finland. He has published books and articles on international union cooperation, migrant labour rights, union organizing and migrant integration. He is currently involved in DG Employment funded projects on the protection of labour rights for migrant workers in the EU, and in the Horizon 2020 SIRIUS project on the labour market integration of migrants, refugees and asylum seekers.

Leo McCann is Professor of Management at the University of York, UK. His research and teaching interests include the sociology of work, globalization and management history. Using qualitative methods, his research has explored the working lives of expert workers and professionals, including healthcare workers, corporate managers, university academics and uniformed personnel.

Christopher J. McLachlan is Lecturer in Human Resource Management at the School of Business and Management at Queen Mary, University of London, UK. His research focuses on the consequences of industrial restructuring and redundancy, and the associated employment relations processes. His research has also explored the impact of deindustrialization on affected workers and communities.

Stephen Mustchin is Senior Lecturer in Employment Studies at Alliance Manchester Business School, University of Manchester, UK. His research interests focus on industrial relations, changing union organization and strategies, the role of the state in work and employment, public sector employment relations and conflict at work.

Martin O'Brien is Associate Professor of Labour Economics at the Faculty of Business and Law, University of Wollongong, Australia. He is Director of the Centre for Human and Social Capital Research and has published widely in the areas of older-worker employment issues, workforce redundancy, evaluation of employment policies and learning analytics. He has also served as expert witness in a number of cases in Australia's Fair Work Commission.

David Öborn Regin is a Postgraduate Researcher in Working Life Science at Karlstad Business School, Karlstad University, Sweden. His research interests are in the field of social interactions in workplace relations and the changed role of administrators. He is currently involved in a project regarding the impact of gig platforms on the Swedish labour market.

Josef Ringqvist is a Postgraduate Researcher in Working Life Science at Karlstad Business School, Karlstad University, Sweden. His research interests include the implications of trade unions for class and employment relations, and the relationship between trade unions and the environment, specifically pertaining to the environmental attitudes of union members.

Jenny K. Rodriguez is Senior Lecturer in Employment Studies and a member of the Work and Equalities Institute at Alliance Manchester Business School, University of Manchester, UK. Her research interests include intersectional inequality in work and organizations, and the interplay between identity, work and regulation. Her current work focuses on the transnational experiences of skilled migrant women.

Óscar Rodríguez-Ruiz is a Lecturer in Human Resource Management and Organizational Theory at the Universidad Complutense in Madrid, Spain. His work focuses on people management and employment relations. He has published his research on HRM in leading academic journals.

Alexis Rydell is Senior Lecturer in Working Life Science at Dalarna University, Sweden. His research interests include industrial relations, occupational health and safety, corporate social responsibility and organizational restructuring. His research has mainly dealt with companies in the manufacturing industry and the hospitality sector.

Paul Stewart is Senior Professor of the Sociology of Work and Employment, Département Homme Organisation et Société (DFR HOS), Grenoble Ecole de Management, France. He was part of the Autoworkers' Research Network, 1993–2013. He is a non-executive director of CAIRDE Teo, an Irish-language community association in Armagh City. He is co-author of *We Sell Our Time No*

More and was editor of *Work, Employment and Society* (2001–4). He is on the editorial committee of *Capital and Class* and *La Nouvelle Revue du Travail*.

Nathaniel Tetteh is a Lecturer at the Alliance Manchester Business School, University of Manchester, UK. His research interests focus on international industrial relations, union strategies in the developing world, the role of the state in work and employment, and conflict at work.

Ines Wagner is Senior Research Fellow at the Institute for Social Research in Oslo, Norway. Her research focuses on the double mobility of capital and labour in the European single market, equal pay for work of equal value and the future of work. She has held fellowships at the American Institute for Contemporary German Studies at Johns Hopkins in Washington, United States, the Max Planck Institute for the Study of Societies in Cologne, Germany and the European University Institute in Florence, Italy.

Preface

Miguel Martínez Lucio and Robert MacKenzie

The aim of this second edition of the book is to widen further the discussion on globalization, work and multinational corporations (MNCs). The critical perspective adopted allows for a more analytical and progressive approach to the comparative and international study of such subjects. The aim is to broaden further the remit of the study of International Human Resource Management (IHRM). All with a more critical view of globalization, the chapters address issues such as: the role of technology; non-governmental organizations; migration and worker mobility (and not just management mobility); the contradictory roles of management consultancies and business schools; and the development of lean production as an ideology and problem for workers. In this edition more time is spent on questions of organizational change, sustainability and ethical issues relating to the way work is organized and regulated. The case studies within the chapters allow the reader to understand the dilemmas and real challenges globalization and MNCs bring to our lives and how they require a more ethical and informed dialogue within organizations. There has emerged a growing need to address the broader context of work and globalization in terms of ethical considerations; the importance of establishing decent forms of work and social rights related to employment; the need for a greater attention to equality and fairness; and a more socially oriented approach to questions of change and restructuring within organizations. This new edition is based on such an approach and engages with some of the dilemmas and challenges emerging from a range of changes within work and organizations, from technological changes associated with the rise of the platform economy to the growing significance of sustainability agendas. As in the first edition, the issue of teaching and learning in business schools is also a focus of the book: these institutions are often limited or problematic in their approach to the tensions that pervade globalization.

The book has a secondary purpose: to act as a bridgehead for those studying the sociology of work and industrial relations – or what is now commonly called labour and employment relations – into debates on globalization and work. The book is intended to provide a supportive resource for those wanting to take a critical approach to the teaching of IHRM, that draws upon various academic traditions to address a wide range of issues facing people working in an increasingly internationalized and globalized context. In this way, the book would be of value to those studying in universities and beyond, especially trade unionists and those employed in non-government organizations dealing with work-related issues and policy-oriented individuals.

Many people have helped us in this endeavour, and we would like to thank Jessica Moran and Ruth Stitt at Sage, who have assisted us and advised at every stage. They have been important navigators for the book. The anonymous reviewers (the army of individuals who silently guided our work and that of our colleagues) played a very important role; they were like a Greek chorus who showed the way ahead. Thanks is also due to Manmeet Kaur Tura for work on the style and layout.

We would also like to thank our colleagues who contributed to the book and had the time and energy to engage with this project and support its merits. Without them, this text would not be in your hands or, indeed, on your screen today.

Online resources

International Human Resource Management: The Transformation of Work in a Global Perspective, Second Edition is accompanied by a range of online resources designed to support lecturers in their teaching.

Visit **https://study.sagepub.com/martinezluciomackenzie** to access:

- **PowerPoint slides** that can be downloaded and adapted to suit individual teaching needs.
- **Additional case study material** providing further examples to use in class.

Introduction: an Employment Relations perspective on IHRM and the transformation of work in a global perspective

Miguel Martínez Lucio and Robert MacKenzie

The ongoing challenge of globalization

Work and employment within a globalized context requires an approach and form of study that is sensitive to the question of context. The way systems of employment and experiences of work develop is the outcome of a wide range of institutional and cultural factors, strategic and political interventions and struggles over the balance of power. The study of international human resource management (IHRM) has increasingly highlighted these issues, through a range of texts. The first edition of this book made an explicit point of ensuring that the way we understand the impact of globalization on work and employment needs to be sensitive to matters of power and politics. There have been major changes since the first edition was published, such as the way the 'gig economy' has developed, for example, and in the way many public and private organizations are increasingly calling for greater attention to 'decent work' in the face of forms of employment that are precarious, vulnerable and exposed to high levels of work intensification. This is why this edition engages with questions of ideology, politics, technology, regulation and ethical matters in relation to the global dimensions of work and employment.

The way people work, the character and nature of their workplaces, the manner in which they are managed and the mechanisms by which they are recruited into these jobs have to a great extent reflected the economic, political and cultural characteristics of their national economies and specific sectors of employment. A national economy may be more or less developed, the technologies used may vary and there may be customs and practices that have shaped the way people work and how they value or view the management of their work and themselves as workers. The laws and institutions that govern their work may also differ. For example, the rights they have may vary in terms of how they may express their views at work, may argue for a safe environment to work in and are compensated when their employment is terminated.

Within capitalist societies, workers have to sell their labour in the labour market and thus enter into a contractual relationship of some form with organizations and other individuals. While the indeterminate nature of this contract is universal, the expectations of each party regarding the contract, and the manner in which rights and obligations on either side are understood and operationalized, often tend to diverge.

The study of work and employment has become more challenging in a context where the boundaries of labour markets and national economies have been changing. There has also been a restructuring of national spaces around which work and employment are experienced, managed and regulated. These changes have brought new challenges to the ways that companies manage their workforce, be they multinational corporations (MNCs) or local firms.

One of the main sources for change has been *increasing levels of internationalization of investment*. The emergence of a greater intensity of international trade has meant that national systems of employment and management have been subject to greater instability and a range of increasingly diverse influences and pressures. Overseas competition and the ability to compete in international markets mean increasing the pressures on firms to find more productive and cost-efficient ways of employing workers and managing their work.

Globalization and the movement of people and resources across boundaries, between and within firms, bring to the fore the problems of dealing with different approaches to representation and systems of rights and customs in relation to work and employment. Operating across countries, both directly and indirectly – through subcontracting work to a range of smaller firms, for example – brings a degree of complexity, which needs ongoing attention from management to the detail of contracts and product quality. Different organizational and management approaches and the responses to them have to be taken into account.

For the workforce itself, changes are emerging from the opportunities and challenges that globalization brings in one form or another. In many industrial sectors, we may see decline in one country as a result of competition based on undermining traditional industries on labour costs. The emergence of China as a major manufacturing economy has impacted on sectors in Europe as diverse as steel and toy production. There may also be opportunities for advanced economies in newer sectors, for example information technology (IT). However, such developments have also been associated with international divisions of labour and the offshoring of routine and even more complex tasks to developing economies such as India, based on the availability of lower-cost skilled labour. Globalization also brings with it the adoption of new practices and new ways of working for some workers, such as a greater emphasis on working in teams or a greater number of people employed on new types of contingent contract. Such practices may vary in take up, but overall their impact alters general patterns of work and employment. What is more, the very boundaries of national labour markets may be challenged, as people migrate in search of better employment and work. Such changes can be seen in the high presence of overseas professionals in the medical sector in the United Kingdom (UK), or the inflow of migrant workers into the Malaysian construction industry in response to local shortages. In such cases, the dynamics of migration are shaped by state polices and employer strategies in the destination countries. MNCs also play a role, deploying managers and professionals across wider geographical areas. Globalization also effects internal migration within countries. For example, China's rise in economic power has seen internal migration on a huge scale, as workers from rural communities have moved to manufacturing jobs in urban centres. It could be argued that there is nothing new in such changes, but their intensity and regularity of movement do appear to be increasing.

Since the editing of the first edition, we have also seen a range of political and social disruptions generate further challenges to the way work is experienced, managed and regulated. There has been a political backlash to questions of globalization – or perceptions of globalization – from various quarters, which has reflected a growing concern with the impact of new global orders and influences. In addition, the Covid-19 pandemic that began in 2019 has brought to the fore a range of questions over international coordination, the way we work in relation to health and safety risks, and the general nature of how the economy is organized in different contexts. These are all challenges that highlight the transnational nature of work and accentuate the greater levels of interdependence that exist across the globe.

As a consequence of these changes during the past few decades, *governments are now under pressure to balance a new set of roles in the way they manage work and employment*. In a globalized economy, national governments need to ensure that their workforce is 'attractive' in terms of skills and/or costs to those investing or proposing to invest in their country. In turn, they may also have to deal with the after-effects of the changes outlined above, in terms of declining industrial areas, mass mobility across regions and the possible exit of key workers and professions from their labour markets.

Globalization, as Chapter 1 will outline, is therefore a complex development bringing various types of change and contradictory outcomes. It is not simply a case of there being winners and losers, because even those gaining from increasing their external trade and developing new dynamic industrial sectors face new challenges and objectives in relation to worker expectations and new social needs, such as health services and education. For example, we may see the growth of employment in the IT sector in developing economies, but with that come new ways of working and new types of control at work, which can unsettle relationships and generate new expectations that are themselves challenging to manage. New forms of inequality may emerge and existing inequalities may indeed be accelerated.

The realities of IHRM

The widening spaces within which leading firms operate globally, and their own widening remit and greater scale, mean that the question of managing and regulating work and employment generates new challenges. International human resource management (IHRM) is one area of study that has addressed these challenges by focusing on how MNCs attempt to manage the way people work in their operations across different national boundaries. Much depends on the type of MNC and whether it wishes to have – or whether it *can* have – an integrated and coherent form of management across a number of countries; much depends on the type of business and corporate strategy a company follows. Such contingencies have led to some preferring transnational corporation (TNC) as the appropriate term to capture more recent developments in the internationalization of capital (see Chapter 2).

IHRM emerged initially from a focus on the management structures of MNCs and the problems of organizational control brought by operating in different countries. The focus at first was on American multinationals during the late 20th century adapting to different national contexts and attempting to change them; sustaining a coherent management elite in personnel and strategic terms was often a priority, but this reflected an almost colonial perspective where the problem was ensuring order and supporting managers travelling overseas (Scullion, 2005: 3–21). Yet this focus on management has led to a range of limitations on the priorities of IHRM. First, the focus has been in the main 'internal'; the debate has been concerned chiefly with the internal environment of the firm and the manner in which it manages and develops its resources (especially human resources). While the external environment of different national HRM contexts, cultural factors and the challenge of creating synergies between national contexts in terms of personnel and strategies have been discussed, the focus has been primarily on the

internal structures and strategies of the firm in response to the external environment. The MNC is thus the principal focus for much of this debate, in terms of
creating effective and coherent strategies, structures and personnel deployment
across diverse operations. Second, a concern with management strategy has pre-
dominated. At the heart of this concern is the stress on management in terms of
its strategies and the ways management are rewarded, promoted and supported:
in this respect, unlike critical approaches to HRM, IHRM is more insular in its
concerns, which is ironic given that it is meant to engage with globalization. The
development of globalization and its impact on various organizational levels is
of concern primarily as a test for senior managers and executives in ensuring the
success of their MNC.

Increasingly, texts have widened the sphere of engagement by taking an interest in regulation and dealing with international concerns about the behaviour
and business ethics of MNCs. In the European context – and the British context
in particular – publications have begun to engage with these topics. However,
the subject of IHRM remains a challenge because it has no real original theory
or focus beyond that mentioned earlier. In part, this is because HRM theories
continue to focus on the internal sphere of the firm and management responses
to external factors instead of taking a broader view of the political and economic
environment. There may be perspectives which concern themselves with the
internal politics, diverse stakeholders and competing strategies and perspectives
within a firm (Beer et al., 1985; Blyton and Turnbull, 2008; Dundon and Rafferty,
2018; Legge, 2005), but these are rarely central to IHRM textbooks addressing
strategy-related issues. In the managerialist literature, the role of internal and
external stakeholders appears to be a lower priority, though the situation is different in the UK (see Edwards and Rees, 2006, and subsequent editions).

Critical approaches to HRM that locate the subject in relation to the broader
context of political economy and debates (see Thompson, 2011) do not seem to be
well reflected in IHRM textbooks. The question of a choice between control-based
or cooperation-inducing strategies for firms is not an explicit aspect of many managerial texts. Whether an MNC adopts a 'hard' or 'soft' approach in its attitude
to its workforce – with the associated ethics and challenges – is more a leitmotif
than an explicit subject of concern. Despite the ongoing concern about the 'dark
side' of HRM, such as the development of surveillance and tighter performance
management, or the ambivalent impact of MNCs on the quality of people's lives,
these issues appear to form a small part of the backdrop to the discussion in most
IHRM texts. Ultimately, Scullion's (2005) concern is correct, and the colonial heritage of management theory seems – unfortunately – to be alive and well in many
of these texts.

There is a need to introduce a broader perspective (Delbridge et al., 2011),
as IHRM is not an academic discipline with a clear theoretical basis but rather

an area that derives much from an engagement with organizational behaviour and HRM. Yet the object of IHRM is – in reality – the management of work and employment: this means that the dynamics of work and employment in terms of representation, worker development, the working environment and regulation need to move to the centre in order to provide a wider academic and teaching agenda. One area in particular that can greatly benefit this exercise is Employment Relations. Employment Relations, as a field, approaches the subject matter of IHRM from the perspective of the impact of the actions of MNCs on workers, national contexts and national systems of representation and regulation. What is more, Employment Relations scholars – broadly speaking – have been mapping these subjects in terms of their international dimension through studies on the mobility of workers internationally, and the changing nature of international systems of regulation. In many ways the aim of this book is to shift the gaze of the reader and start from 'the ground up', seeking to put MNCs in a more dynamic context and a contested space.

An Employment Relations perspective

This book therefore takes a broader approach to IHRM by drawing on the traditions of Employment Relations. The Employment Relations approach has informed much of the radical critique of HRM, drawing on the traditions of political economy and the sociology of work to problematize the nature of the employment relationship and locate Employment Relations in broader institutional settings. Aspects of this perspective are to be found in some of the leading texts on IHRM (Edwards and Rees, 2006; Harzing and Pinnington, 2011), which similarly have tried to widen the way the subject is taught and understood. First and foremost, an Employment Relations perspective offers a critical approach to the study of IHRM that goes beyond concerns over implementation failures or the challenges of managing in an international context. The aim here is to systematically ground our approach in the politics of globalization and MNCs in relation to the structured antagonisms that underpin work and employment, thus building on the insights of a range of scholars who share this agenda (Morgan and Kristensen, 2006; Edwards and Bélanger, 2009; Ferner et al., 2012).

First, an Employment Relations perspective focuses on *the inherent tensions that exist in the employment relationship*. Such tensions are seen as the outcome of the nature of the capitalist employment system, which is based on a 'market' where people buy and sell labour. It is important to acknowledge that there is an uncertainty and instability within employment relations and modes of representation (Hyman, 1975). Unlike other commodities, what is bought and sold on the 'market' is not a fixed amount; rather, it is the potential to labour. The crux of the employment relationship is turning this potential into labour itself; hence, the role of management is to entice a level of performance or effort from workers. This is a radical perspective that sees management initiatives on behalf of employers as variously focused on enticing effort from workers via mechanisms control, such as surveillance and performance management (Friedman, 1977), or by gaining the consent of workers for the purpose of productive activity by inducing worker commitment to their jobs through consensual, participative schemes. The 'hard' and 'soft' variants of HRM can be understood in such terms. This perspective assumes that there is no real common interest between employers and workers. Some see this as the conflict of interest between labour and capital, given the ownership of the means of production and the alienation of labour from its work (Hyman, 1975). Others have elaborated on this arguing that there is a 'structured antagonism' between employer and worker (Edwards, 2003: 17).

> This term is used to stress that the antagonism is part of the basis of the relationship, even though, on a day-to-day level, cooperation is also important. It is important to distinguish this idea from the more usual one of a conflict of interest. The latter has the problem of implying that the real or fundamental interests of capital and labour are opposed, and hence that any form of participation scheme is simply a new way of bending workers to capital's demands. The fact that workers have a range of interests confounds this idea. A structured antagonism is a basic aspect of the employment relationship, which shapes how day-to-day relations are handled, but it is not something that feeds directly into the interests of the parties. Firms have to find ways of continuing to extract a surplus, and if they do not, then both they and their workers will suffer. (Ibid.)

Pluralists in general argue that these tensions can be overcome – at least in the short term (see Blyton and Turnbull, 2008, for a discussion of pluralism). This can be done through the use of dialogue and mechanisms of representation that allow the different interests to find some common point of reference – for example, seeking to sustain employment activity in one particular location by developing activities such as training to enhance the skills of the workforce to the benefit of both worker and employer. Chapter 3 will provide further details with regard to the way an Employment Relations framework assists our understanding of work and employment dynamics, and their politics. So the question becomes one of how employers, managers, workers and in many cases their representatives engage with each other to further their specific interests, or reconcile them in one way or another, and what the mechanisms are for doing so.

Second, an Employment Relations perspective is one where *rights, and the propagating and management of rights, are significant*. Human resources are not just another 'resource': what is more, many workers seek fair treatment in the way they are employed and deployed. In this respect, we need to understand the question of individual rights at work and locate these within the politics of the workplace, as in the struggles between actors, shaped by the power resources available to them. Slichter (1941) spoke of systems such as collective bargaining – where managers and unions negotiate a common settlement regarding questions of pay or working hours – being an extension of democratic rights at work and the extension of the democratic space into work. Rights may not just be a question of political rights of voice and participation. In developing economies, the right to economic enhancement may be at the heart of political and organizational activities, and issues of wages and rewards more generally (Macpherson, [1965] 1992). Social rights may also be seen as important, in that the right to a working environment without serious hazards or risks in terms of individuals' health and safety may also be the basis of demands from workers, and even the interests of management. The desire to push the understanding of rights as far as the questions of *a voice at work* (political rights), *a decent type of work* (social rights) and *employment itself* (economic rights) is at the very heart of the human dimension of work and employment. In this book, various chapters deal with the question of rights and their development and meaning.

Third, an Employment Relations approach deals with the tensions and realities of work, including the importance of rights, but it also highlights *the context of their regulation*. For many, the field of Employment Relations is about the regulation of the employment relationship, and this can be developed in formal terms through written rules, contracts and agreements or through informal and unwritten rules and agreements in the form of custom and practice (MacKenzie and Martínez Lucio, 2005; see also Chapter 12). The broader institutional context is part of this, as are the formal institutions within the workplace, but beyond these are the informal processes that make up the politics of the workplace and shape the dynamic interplay that constitutes the relationship between the firm and the workforce. In terms of MNCs, regulation can involve multiple spaces and relationships as their operations criss-cross countries. These are regulatory spaces (MacKenzie and Martínez Lucio, 2005) where the representatives of workers and employers engage with each other in one way or another and establish a workable consensus on issues such as pay, working hours, work practices and other related activities necessary for production and service delivery to proceed unhindered, irrespective of the different interests that might exist. The questions of how MNCs are to be regulated, how sustainability issues are to be propagated and the way worker voice and roles are to be integrated are of growing concern within the study of work in transnational terms. Furthermore, the question of how MNCs are to be regulated is also shaped by the ideational competition and conflict between actors over defining rights at work (Morgan and Hauptmeier, 2021).

Fourth, in terms of the regulation of the employment relationship we have to *'map' the broad range of actors involved, in a national, and now international, context.* These are not just the employers and their managers, and the workforce and their representatives, vital as these are. For a complete understanding, this political map must recognize internal and external actors. Internal actors would be management and worker representatives, but these might be differentiated internally, with cohorts of managers having distinctly different professional backgrounds and networks or even organizational interests (see Edwards et al., 1999). Worker representatives may also vary in terms of their political allegiances or their relations with employers. There are also external actors who can frame the process of regulation. The state – and its various constitutive institutions – is an especially important actor, and one that is much ignored in traditional accounts of IHRM. The state may attempt to steer labour and employment relations, for example by emphasizing different forms of worker representation. Political projects may be developed to counter conflict within employment relations, albeit with variable outcomes (see Panitch, 1981). Moreover, just as the state incorporates social actors, it can also coerce them (Hyman, 1975: 144) with strategies of containment and control in the regulation of union affairs, giving rise to new tensions and new forms of worker action. Instability and uncertainty are central features of employment relations, requiring ongoing state investment in institutional processes, projects of reform and strategies of change. Yet, the role of the state is almost non-existent within mainstream IHRM texts. What is more alarming is the relative absence of any discussion of coercion and force – a major moral and ethical dilemma to which some MNCs have contributed in terms of the repression of democratic systems and worker rights in host countries.

Yet new discussions on employment relations also point to a broader set of actors including, *inter alia*: international law firms; transnational consultancy firms propagating new ideas about work; non-government organizations (NGOs) and social movements raising ethical questions in relation to issues such as child labour; new media and virtual organizations linked by the internet in organizing work-related protest; and educational bodies, particularly business schools, which are central to the propagation of approaches to HRM. Work and employment relations are influenced by many bodies, some of which may be beyond the direct remit of the employment relationship (Heery and Frege, 2006). This book opens the door to these issues, and some of these actors, in terms of the way they shape strategies and understanding of employment and IHRM.

Fifth, there is *tension over the different natures of the economic and social systems themselves.* It is important, therefore, to locate the employment relationship within the context of the broader political economy. MNCs are caught between national systems that organize and regulate work in different ways, and they support the systems they see as convenient and useful for their economic development and power. MNCs can be drawn to or deterred by the nature of national systems, and can sometimes reflect the traditions of different national systems in their own approaches to HRM. In this text, much is made of the tension between socially oriented and more coordinated systems on the one hand, and more liberal and market-facing systems on the other: the 'varieties of capitalism' debate (see Hall and Soskice, 2001: 1). Various chapters will discuss these issues and the debates that have ensued.

Sixth, there are also *issues over technological trajectories and how new forms of technology relate to the way we work and are managed.* Technology is an important factor in the way we work: how technological innovations are implemented, such as the emergence of the assembly line or the development of the platform economy, has an important impact on patterns of employment and modes of work (see Chapters 14 and 15; also see Howcroft and Bergvall-Kåreborn, 2019). What is more, the communicative dimensions of work through social media and the internet more broadly can shape both patterns of work, such as teleworking, but also forms of resistance and counterpoints that emerge. Trade unions and social movements have increasingly engaged with social media for example, to highlight problems within employment.

Seventh and finally, all of the above must be located within an appreciation of power relations. Foremost in our analysis must be the way in which power relations are articulated through class, gender and ethnicity and the intersectionality between them. The employment relationship is a class-based relationship between capital and labour and reflects the respective power resources available to each. Although inherently imbalanced to the disadvantage of labour, the balance of power is not static but rather subject to constant negotiation, whether that be through formal institutional processes, such as the work of trade unions, or through the micro politics of the workplace and worker resistance. Moreover, the employment practices of MNCs, particularly when these involve developing economies through direct investment or supply chains, must be viewed in terms of the respective power resources held by those who buy and sell labour: employers and workers. Gender relations are also central to this power dynamic. The investment decisions of MNCs, which may be informed by existing gender divides in the labour market, serve to exacerbate low pay and precarious employment. These are jobs in which women are over-represented, while women remain under-represented in the senior managerial positions of the same MNCs. Similarly, investment in the technologies of production reflects segmented labour markets in which women are over-represented in lower-paid sectors, where labour costs act as a deterrent to automation. The power relations articulated though discriminatory employment practices based on ethnicity must likewise be recognized in our understanding of international divisions of labour in MNC investment decisions, and also in the experiences of migrant labour. The power dynamics are intensified where there is intersectionality between class, gender and ethnicity. When confronted with these power dynamics, workers may be unable to resist being placed in highly vulnerable positions. *In extremis*, such power dynamics have resulted in tragedy for Chinese migrant cockle-pickers in the UK and female textile workers in Bangladesh.

Power relations are also manifest in the broader geopolitical economy in which MNCs operate. MNCs from developed economies such as the United States not only wield significant power based on their own resources, but also as reflections of the political and ultimately military power of their home nation. Historically, US foreign policy in South America, for example, did much to open up key economies to American MNCs. More recently international trade agreements have been a key means through which governments in developed economies have promoted access to foreign markets. The power disparities between developed and developing economies are such that negotiations between MNCs from the former and governments of the latter are not on a level playing field. In short, power relations permeate throughout IHRM, the recognition of which is central to an employment relations approach to the subject.

By engaging an Employment Relations perspective, we can situate IHRM in a broader environment or context, and give due respect to the nature of the employment relationship and the politics of the workplace. This allows us to locate MNCs in the real dynamic of the competing visions and politics of globalization. Perhaps the term 'IHRM' is not appropriate, given this approach, but it has become the byword for the study of transnational work and employment issues, particularly relating to MNCs. The agenda, however, is not fixed and we hope to offer an alternative approach in this book. Recurrent throughout the book is the message that there are always alternatives to the neoliberal, managerial and universalist prescriptions on IHRM, reflected in more socially oriented approaches to restructuring, transnational regulation, worker representation, equality and fairness at work and broader agendas around sustainability.

The structure of the book

This book therefore links IHRM more closely to the contribution of Employment Relations. It opens up IHRM to new influences and schools of thought engaged with its study from a less managerialist perspective.

In the first of the four thematic sections, there are three chapters exploring the *Dynamic Context of International Human Resource Management*. Chapter 1 engages with the subject of work and employment in the context of globalization. It aims to look at how we understand globalization and how it has changed the way people are employed and the way that they work. The chapter focuses on the dynamics of globalization and the competing interpretations of what it is changing in terms of the global context, the firm and the nature of work. The chapter explores the problems facing workers and organizations due to greater levels of degradation at work.

The subject of MNCs and HRM is discussed in Chapter 2. The chapter focuses on how HRM strategies are developed by MNCs, and how in many cases they attempt to change the contexts within which they are operating. MNCs use a wide range of strategies and techniques as part of their attempt to transfer their practices and broad philosophies of work to subsidiaries and host contexts. The chapter draws from a range of schools of thought, which view MNCs as micro-political organizations using an array of strategies to influence the nature of work and the employment systems in which they operate.

Chapter 3 examines employment relations by looking at the role of regulation in different contexts and how industrial relations theories – both new and old – can be used to understand the differences that exist in relation to the varied environments faced by MNCs and other transnational bodies. Different national contexts in terms of employment relations remain, and though these are changing, it is essential to understand the ways in which these differences are sustained both as systems of regulation and as traditions of representation.

The second section of the book, *Working in a Globalized Context*, consists of chapters engaging with what we could call the 'internal environment' of the firm in light of the external changes taking place. Chapter 4 focuses on pay, which is the quintessential distributive element of the employment relationship. The chapter looks at how rewards depend on national contexts and structures. MNCs often try to introduce new or organizationally specific reward systems, yet find themselves confronting not just locally embedded systems of pay but also tensions that arise in relation to questions of equity and fairness, especially in a context of growing income inequalities. This discussion leads the reader into broader questions of equality and diversity in the next chapter.

Chapter 5 expands on the theme of equality and diversity. A major development in IHRM and international employment relations is growing concern with equality and fair treatment of staff. Equality and diversity vary across countries and contexts in terms of meaning and impact. The chapter maps the development of diversity management and outlines some of the challenges it can lead to, drawing attention to the progress still needed with regards to the question of diversity management within MNCs.

Chapter 6 addresses the issues of international assignments and worker mobility within MNCs. There is a broad literature on the challenges facing workers and managers when they are deployed across different international workplaces of MNCs, related to matters of 'cultural adjustment' and 'coping with change and travel'. Beyond this, there are significant developments in terms of work intensification, work–life balance, health and safety challenges and increasingly equality issues, as more women and lesbian, gay, bisexual and transgendered workers are being deployed on international assignments.

Chapter 7 widens the discussion on international mobility, focusing on migration and the manner in which MNCs capitalize on the increasing movement of workers across boundaries more broadly, beyond international assignments. In many cases, this is managed in a way that allows MNCs to bypass regulations and laws relating to pay levels and working conditions. Migration is an important theme throughout this book. The IHRM literature often only discusses mobility issues with reference to middle and senior managers, as if the broader workforce does not exist, especially those workers who are not directly employed. The role of MNCs in manipulating such flows of labour, and in the main downgrading working conditions, is rarely a subject of discussion, yet this raises the serious issue of the unethical behaviour of many international firms.

IHRM in relation to work and employment in developing economies is examined in Chapter 8. The chapter focuses on the competing and politicized views of management and employment related issues in developing economies exposed to globalization, in which the role of the state is pivotal in terms of responses to the benefits and challenges that MNCs bring. In many cases states may help develop the infrastructure necessary to engage with international firms; however, developing economies are not always passive recipients of overseas investment. Tensions emerge because of the inherent contradiction of MNCs wanting a skilled and educated workforce on the one hand, but often a cheaper and more pliable workforce on the other. States are caught between the development of a supportive local environment in terms of workers' skills and the management of the expectations that consequently emerge within their workforce and labour markets. These national contexts also give rise to a range of debates on establishing 'decent work' standards.

A further feature of the internal environment of the firm is the question of human resource development; this is dealt with in Chapter 9. Many IHRM texts engage with how MNCs attempt to develop more consistent and integrated systems of training in light of the global requirements that emerge from the need to create increasingly 'cosmopolitan' leadership and management. Yet, local systems of training and the way they are managed remain important. Hence, this chapter points to the role of local contexts in influencing strategies related to human resource development, but also shows how these local environments emphasize the development of a workforce that is adaptable and focused on social and communication skills. The cult of 'soft skills' is discussed as a challenging feature and political dilemma in terms of development strategies.

The learning environment in relation to management is also subject to a range of dilemmas and political factors, as outlined in Chapter 10. Dominant ideas about what management *is* and what *it ought to do* have not emerged just because they are 'superior' or because of the prominence of US MNCs in the context of globalization. To a great extent, the spread of these ideas is driven by a range of 'other actors' who push the relevance and 'sale' of these models – for example, business schools and consultancy firms. Chapter 10 therefore focuses on the role of US, and US-influenced, business schools and management education in disseminating these views. This process is supported by a range of consultancy firms, which in effect sell 'fashions' and encourage a particular political view of how work and employment should be managed. These actors are central to the apparatus of the dissemination of Americanization, and especially neoliberalism, in organizational practices.

The third section of the book focuses on *Changing Ideologies and Practices of Global Production*. Chapter 11 on varieties of capitalism and IHRM focuses on the increasing role of the liberal market model and the emergence of Anglo-Saxonization and Americanization as a reference point in the global context. This approach offers a vision of globalization that is focused on short-term profitability, shareholders as dominant players and a financial and accounting view of the organization and its priorities. There has been great concern regarding these developments for some time, and the chapter updates us on many features of these shifts in IHRM through the lens of varieties of capitalism (see also Djelic, 2001).

One of the missing features of the study of IHRM has been the way particular dominant strategies have evolved within MNCs. How visions of production and employment are disseminated has been explained in terms of how MNCs develop their strategies, but not always what the politics of the strategies are. In Chapter 12, the focus is on the concept of lean production as a dominant ideology and a set of practices that have been part of the transformation of work in many sectors and national contexts. These practices are seen by many to represent a central form of labour exploitation and a dominant transnational paradigm of capitalism, which brings major issues in terms of health and safety for many workers. The discussion of lean production again brings the politics of the workplace to the fore of our attention.

Chapter 13 addresses restructuring, policy and practice. Organizational restructuring is a persistent feature of IHRM. The investment and divestment decisions of MNCs often result in redundancies that have serious negative consequences for individuals, communities and national economies. As well as addressing internal influences on management decision-making, such as corporate social responsibility (CSR) or socially responsible restructuring (SRR) agendas and the role of trade unions, the chapter locates organizational restructuring within the wider institutional context in which such decisions are made.

The chapter compares restructuring in the UK, Sweden and Australia and examines the notion of *restructuring regimes* as one way of understanding the distinctions between approaches to restructuring apparent in different national, institutional contexts.

Chapter 14 examines the relationship between technology, the organization of work and approaches to the management of people. The starting point in analysing the connection between new technologies and the organization of work is to understand the role for human labour. In this respect technology has a triple function: it is a means of enhancing the human contribution to production, but also a means of controlling labour and ultimately superseding human labour. The chapter explores these issues across four stages in the development of technology: Mechanization, Automation, Computerization and Industrie 4.0. Despite the appeal of such grand narratives, these stages did not unfold in an unproblematic, universal and linear fashion; the chapter warns against technological determinism, to stress the socially mediated nature of the introduction of technology, and the influence of worker resistance, institutional context and gender relations.

Chapter 15 continues the discussion of technology and work through a focus on the gig economy as one of the most significant developments in recent years. Many claim platform work associated with the gig economy represents a distinct challenge to our understanding of employment relations. As a variant of non-standard employment, this type of work has come to be associated with insecurity, precarity, poor levels of remuneration and limited scope for collective bargaining. The chapter examines the platform-based business model, which is supported by venture capital despite the absence of profit, and the three-sided relationship between the platform, the requester of work and the worker, in which the platform eschews the responsibility of the employer. While worker experiences and expectations are varied, promises of flexibility and autonomy are tarnished by the reality of menial work, dependency and insecurity. Ambiguities over the employment status, in which platforms claim workers are independent contractors, also shift the burden of risk from capital to labour. These issues are examined through a case study of Uber, one of the most contentious examples of platform work.

The fourth and final section of the book explores issues relating to *Regulation and the Agenda for Decent Work*. Chapter 16 develops further issues concerning employment change and initiatives that contribute to the upgrading of work in terms of rights and representation within a more globalized context. The chapter focuses on the way that transnational systems of regulation have had to be developed to create a political environment that can moderate and condition MNCs in terms of the more problematic aspects of their development and behaviour. The chapter addresses new forms of regulation, such as the use of international law and ethical codes of conduct, as ways of influencing the operations of MNCs.

These developments are discussed in the light of the debate on regulation that has emerged in the current economic context of crisis and change. The chapter also addresses concerns over the extent to which transnational regulation is developed and effective.

Such developments are picked up in the next chapter, which maps how the voice of workers has developed in the face of greater transnational coordination by firms. Chapter 17 examines the way that trade unions, as the main expression of workers' interests, have developed international organizational structures. These include both official structures and new forms of network-based organizations that exchange information about the nature and conduct of MNCs. The chapter also looks at the development of forms of international councils and committees that represent workers in specific MNCs, which can influence the nature of decision-making and its outcomes. The chapter also explores new forms of transnational agreements and codes of conduct, which have an input from trade unions and related bodies.

Chapter 18 examines how a growing awareness of sustainability agendas has impacted IHRM. The chapter examines the evolving role of HR functions, as companies – notably high-profile MNCs – come under increasing pressure to address sustainability issues. Sustainability is examined in terms of three key dimensions: economic, social and ecological. While these dimensions may overlap and be complementary, they are also shown to be potentially mutually exclusive, adding to questions regarding the possibilities of business-led ecological sustainability. The concept of decommodification is explored as a possible alternative approach to understanding sustainability in relation to both labour and the environment.

Using the book

The chapters are presented in four thematic sections: The Dynamic Context of IHRM; Working in a Globalized Context; The Changing Ideologies and Practices of Global Production; and Regulation and the Agenda for Decent Work. There is a broad sequential logic to this structure, but there are a number of ways in which this book can be used to support a critical approach to the teaching of IHRM and it is intended to serve as a flexible and non-prescriptive resource.

While each chapter stands on its own merits in terms of critical engagement with discrete issues within IHRM, the new edition has developed links between chapters through systematic cross-referencing, so that students can develop their understanding of various issues in more detail. The links between chapters work in various combinations bringing related aspects of different debates together in innovative ways, which allows chapters to be combined in novel configurations for teaching purposes. For example, Chapter 14 explores the relationship between technology and the organization of work. In combination with Chapter 15 on the gig economy, this represents a pairing around the theme of technology and provides the basis for comparing historic and contemporary developments. Alternatively, Chapter 14 on technology and the organization of work could be paired with Chapter 12, which explores lean production as a dominant ideology and a set of practices that have been part of the transformation of work in recent decades. The role of MNCs is a theme running through most chapters, but which can be systematically linked through taking Chapter 2 as a starting point and then linking this to Chapter 4 on pay, Chapter 5 on equality and diversity, Chapter 6 on international assignments and Chapter 9 on training. In turn, the issues of training explored in Chapter 9 resonate strongly with themes raised in the following chapter on the role of business schools and consultants, providing one possible pairing, while Chapter 10 also examines the promotion of dominant management ideational agendas and so couples with Chapter 12 on lean production. Chapter 6 on international assignments may be paired with Chapter 7 on broader issues of labour migration, while the role of MNCs in manipulating labour flows and downgrading working conditions raised by Chapter 7 resonate elsewhere, for example in Chapter 8 on IHRM and developing economies and Chapter 1 on work and employment in the context of globalization. Chapter 15 on transnational systems of regulation combines with Chapter 17 on international union structures and codes of conduct, which in turn can be linked with Chapter 3 on national employment systems. Similarly, Chapter 13 deals with the issue of restructuring, which in combination with Chapter 4 on pay and remuneration and Chapter 5 on equality and diversity form a cluster around issues of fairness at work. Alternatively, the international comparative approach to restructuring presented in Chapter 13 could be paired in different combinations, such as with Chapter 11 on varieties of capitalism and Chapter 3 on national employment relations systems. In turn, the themes of fairness at work could be linked in various combinations with Chapter 18 on sustainability and IHRM, as could many chapters in the book. The possible combinations are numerous, and far from limited to these few indicative suggestions; readers will form their own approach. We would encourage tutors to make the possible combinations their own resource to develop, in novel and innovative ways, in support of a critical approach to the teaching of IHRM.

Conclusion

IHRM is a broad and rich area of study and practice, which needs to be uncoupled from managerial approaches and opened up to the realities of work and employment. Balancing the study of IHRM with a more systematic Employment

Relations perspective provides a critical understanding of the nuances and richness of work and employment in a global context.

Understanding the political aspects of many of the facets of management, and the ethical traumas MNCs give rise to, needs to be given greater prominence as human beings speak to and engage with each other across the globe in new and more effective ways. The context of IHRM is changing, with agendas linked to issues of sustainability providing an additional focus on the actions of MNCs and management decision-making. We need to place MNCs in the real context of political competition and action, especially the demands of workers, national states, and a growing range of actors. The globalization of economies and labour markets brings the need to address some fundamental issues, not just with regard to the changing nature of work and employment but also how work can be improved and enriched. Globalization and factors such as the role of MNCs, new forms of technology and market-facing political views have led to fundamental anomalies and dilemmas in the way we work. How we counter increasing levels of inequalities and degradation in many aspects of our employment has been inspiring a rich debate concerning the way the behaviour of economic actors can be influenced by social and political actors with a view to generating less exploitative forms of working.

References

Beer, M., Walton, R. E., Spector, B. A., Mills, D. Q. and Lawrence, P. R. (1985) *Human Resource Management: A General Manager's Perspective: Text and Cases*. New York: Free Press.

Blyton, P. and Turnbull, P. (2008) *The Dynamics of Employee Relations*. London: Macmillan.

Delbridge, R., Hauptmeier, M. and Sengupta, S. (2011) 'Beyond the enterprise: Broadening the horizons of international HRM'. *Human Relations*, 64(4): 483–505.

Djelic, M. L. (2001) *Exporting the American Model: The Post-War Transformation of European Business*. Oxford: Oxford University Press.

Dundon, T. and Rafferty, A. (2018) 'The (potential) demise of HRM?' *Human Resource Management Journal*, 28(3): 377–91.

Edwards, P. (2003) 'The employment relationship and the field of industrial relations'. In P. Edwards (ed.), *Industrial Relations: Theory and Practice*. Oxford: Blackwell-Wiley, pp. 1–36.

Edwards, P. and Bélanger, J. (2009) 'The multinational firm as a contested terrain'. In S. Collinson and G. Morgan (eds), *Images of the Multinational Firm*. Chichester: John Wiley & Sons, pp. 193–216.

Edwards, T. and Rees, C. (2006) *International Human Resource Management: Globalization, National Systems and Multinational Companies*. Harlow: Pearson Education.

Edwards, T., Rees, C. and Coller, X. (1999) 'Structure, politics and the diffusion of employment practices in multinationals'. *European Journal of Industrial Relations*, 5(3): 286–306.

Ferner, A., Edwards, T. and Tempel, A. (2012) 'Power, institutions and the cross-national transfer of employment practices in multinationals'. *Human Relations*, 65(2): 163–87.

Friedman, A. L. (1977) *Industry and Labour: Class Struggle at Work and Monopoly Capitalism*. London: Macmillan.

Hall, P. A. and Soskice, D. W. (eds) (2001) *Varieties of Capitalism: The Institutional Foundations of Comparative Advantage*. Oxford: Oxford University Press.

Harzing, A. W. and Pinnington, A. (2011) *International Human Resource Management*. London: Sage.

Heery, E. and Frege, C. (2006) 'New actors in industrial relations'. *British Journal of Industrial Relations*, 44(4): 601–4.

Howcroft, D. and Bergvall-Kåreborn, B. (2019) 'A typology of crowdwork platforms'. *Work, Employment and Society*, 33(1): 21–38.

Hyman, R. (1975) *Industrial Relations: A Marxist Introduction*, Vol. 220. London: Macmillan.

Legge, K. (2005) *Human Resource Management: Rhetorics and Realities*. London: Macmillan.

MacKenzie, R. and Martínez Lucio, M. (2005) 'The realities of regulatory change beyond the fetish of deregulation'. *Sociology*, 39(3): 499–517.

Macpherson, C. [1965] (1992) *The Real World of Democracy*. Toronto: House of Anansi Press.

Morgan, G. and Hauptmeier, M. (2021) 'The social organization of ideas in employment relations'. *Industrial and Labor Relations Review*, 74(3): 773–97.

Morgan, G. and Kristensen, P. H. (2006) 'The contested space of multinationals: Varieties of institutionalism, varieties of capitalism'. *Human Relations*, 59(11): 1467–90.

Panitch, L. (1981) 'Trade unions and the capitalist state'. *New Left Review*, 125(1): 21–43.

Scullion, H. (2005) 'International HRM: An introduction'. In H. Scullion and M. Linehan *International Human Resource Management: A Critical Text* (eds), Basingstoke: Palgrave.

Slichter, S. (1941) 'Union policies and industrial management'. *Right to Work Law Issues*, 37: 53–95.

Thompson, P. (2011) 'The trouble with HRM'. *Human Resource Management Journal*, 21(4): 355–67.

Section 1

The dynamic context of international human resource management

1 Globalization and employment: developments and contradictions

Miguel Martínez Lucio and Robert MacKenzie

Learning objectives

- To comprehend the meaning of globalization and the different ways in which it is discussed
- To appreciate the ways in which MNCs have evolved
- To comprehend the challenges to workers that globalization brings in terms of precarious employment and work intensification
- To appreciate the tensions within work and employment brought about by globalization

Introduction

The nature of organizations and employment within them is changing. Yet debate remains over the cause, course and consequences of this change. There has been a contention for some time that stable employment and organizational structures based in national regulatory systems are increasingly outmoded within the 'new' global context. To a great extent, this may be a view that has been propagated in the more economically developed (or privileged) parts of the world, in vindication of ongoing socioeconomic changes there witnessed. The middle decades of the 20th century witnessed the rise of stable and secure systems of work and management in countries such as Japan, the United States, Sweden and Germany. Although predominantly experienced in developed economies, countries as diverse as Nigeria, Uruguay and China saw similar trends in respect of stability and security over the same period, especially in their core industrialized and modern manufacturing-based sectors. However, things have been changing since the latter decades of the 20th century, and with increasing alacrity. With the growing internationalization of business reflected in the emergence of global markets and to some extent global production and service delivery processes, and more recently the increased financialization of capitalism, we have seen a challenge to models of employment based primarily on national structures and regulation (see Chapter 10 on business schools and consultants, Chapter 11 on varieties of capitalism and Chapter 12 on lean production).

As a first step towards dealing with the nature of the changes outlined above, this chapter will discuss what is meant by the term *globalization* and will explore the different views that prevail regarding its impact. Some consider globalization to be a major challenge and catalyst for change in human resource management (HRM) and industrial relations (IR). However, this chapter will show how such developments are variable in their effects (later, Chapters 16 and 17 pick up the way such developments have led to new forms of transnational regulation). There are many contradictions inherent in globalization: for example, MNCs continue to require political and regulatory interventions and support from national states. The idea that we are seeing the emergence of omnipotent companies such as Amazon, Apple and Sony ignores the complex reality of globalization and the continuing role of national systems of regulation.

What does this all mean for work and employment? The chapter will explore the impact of globalization on work and employment in terms of the increasing level of insecurity, the question of the degradation of work and the ongoing pressure of continuous change and uncertainty. However, the chapter will also show how these developments have contradictory effects, generating new developments in the politics of work, in terms of the distribution and utilization of power, and new patterns of mobility for both workers and managers. In short, globalization is a contested process and concept.

What is globalization?

Globalization is a multifaceted concept often employed as a shorthand for the internationalization of economic activity associated with Foreign Direct Investment (FDI) flows and the operations of MNCs. Beyond this there are the ideological and ideational aspects of globalization reflected in the spread of hegemonic business practices and association with a neoliberal agendas promoted by multinational corporations and international economic institutions like the World Bank and IMF. More recently, the espoused shift towards financialization found ideational facilitation through the standardization of accounting practices that have changed approaches to investment and divestiture on an international basis, making the buying and selling of assets more important than the manufacture of products. Local firms may be bought and sold by MNCs, then restructured, or entered into internal competition with the company's production sites in other countries, based on decisions made at corporate headquarters in a distant land. Moreover, new competitive imperatives are introduced to domestic producers; local firms now face competition from producers elsewhere in the world, where lower labour costs may provide a comparative advantage, putting pressure on wages and other terms and conditions for domestic producers. High-street retailers in developed economies operate global supply chains, meaning clothing once produced in local factories is now sourced from subcontracted suppliers in developing economies. Heightened competition and the imperatives of financialization mean that workers in developed economies feel competitive pressure from distant producers. Globalization means a factory closure in South Wales may be justified on the grounds of competition from South Vietnam or based on a decision made in South Carolina.

Globalization is the subject of much political debate concerning its impact, how it evolves and at what cost. We are inhabiting a political and economic context which is no longer anchored in specific territorial spaces but is subject to movements and forces from further afield. The dominance of key MNCs and increasing levels of labour and production mobility suggest that we are now becoming part of a new global economic dynamic.

Increasingly, we see trade and economic relations organized at a more global level, reflected in growing levels of FDI (see Figure 1.1), as well as global companies increasing in size to a point where by the end of the first decade of the 21st century they accounted for a quarter of the global gross domestic product (UNCTAD, 2011). These figures illustrate the extent of the internationalization of investment and the fundamental role of multinational corporations. These are substantial changes, which are reshaping the social and economic landscape.

Culturally, we are subjected to visions of a world where nations are considered to be less significant in political terms, and global corporations organize the economic and employment spaces of our lives. Films such as Norman Jewison's *Rollerball*, which was made back in the 1970s, presented us with a cautionary tale of a world dominated by large corporations, where there are no nation-states and where a violent sport is used as an alternative to war between such organizations (see Lillie and Martínez Lucio, 2010). In Ridley Scott's film *Alien* (and in the subsequent films in the series), made a few years after *Rollerball*, the audience was presented with corporations within which dark political forces organized major space expeditions and pernicious experiments in pursuit of commercial opportunities (a theme picked up again in the film *Moon* in 2009). These represent a consistent fear of the greater power held by faceless corporations, and the way that

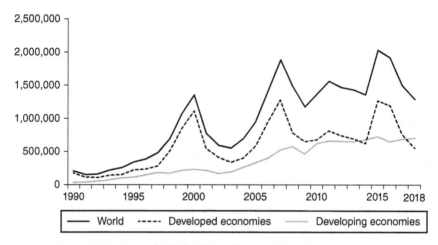

Figure 1.1   Global FDI Inflows, 1980–2018 (millions of US dollars).

Source: UNCTAD (2019)

elites dominate the economic spaces we inhabit through larger and more distant organizations, over which we have limited control and that offer very little by way of democratic checks and balances.

The consequences of the growth of powerful MNCs have seen acrimonious debate about their impact on the economy and society. Key commentators such as Naomi Klein (2000) argued that MNCs have grown in size to such an extent that they dominate political systems and nation-states by virtue of the fact that they can hold them to ransom through investment (setting up workplaces) and disinvestment (closing workplaces down). The ability of MNCs to plunder the scarce resources of the world and to drive down working conditions of many individuals who cannot counter their power means that globalization threatens to undermine the quality and social fabric of all our lives. Local communities and spaces are being undermined by such developments, leaving people with few ways in which to influence the key decisions taken in relation to the economy and employment (Monbiot, 2004) (see Chapter 2 on MNCs). In addition, this process of globalization carries with it the semblance of a new world order, managerialist in form, which privileges corporate and market-level values over social ones. For some, this represents an extension of the worst features of the American model of society in respect of its neoliberalism, while leaving the more progressive features of its liberal democratic discourse to one side.

There are opponents of such arguments, who suggest that globalization may bring upheaval and much change but that in the longer term there will be a new political space in the form of greater individuality (Friedman, 2005): this argument highlights technological and informational changes that allow individuals to communicate, move and collaborate on a much more global scale (ibid.). This is especially the case in recent waves of globalization, from 2000 to the present. Whether the power of MNCs will have such benign consequences for individuals and facilitate a new form of unhindered and accessible global networking remains to be seen, but it may not be evenly shared, with some gaining and others losing from the process of globalization and greater free trade.

However, there are other interventions that scrutinize the *meaning* of globalization, and the extent and nature of the associated impact. It is clear that the internationalization of markets and the greater breadth of corporate and economic activity are disembedding established relations within local societies, with traditional forms of social action becoming less stable (Giddens, 1990). Local political and social relations are stretched, and their ability to influence outcomes is declining, though Giddens (ibid.) would argue that this process has been ongoing throughout the development of capitalism, except that now it has a more transnational dimension. That is not to say the *local* is no longer important, in that much is produced locally and by people whose mobility remains low in relation to that of corporations (Castells, 1996). Nevertheless, as Castells argues, these local spaces are dependent on ever more distant and extensive global networks and links, including ownership structures that buy and sell local companies, which produce and organize across boundaries (ibid.). It is the 'hubs' within the global network that are the main power centres, and which create new systems of power and hierarchy (ibid.). Dickens (2007) elaborated on this point by arguing that these *flows* and *networks* were the defining features of globalization, and that these could be mapped; but they also become structures, where the participants such as states, MNCs and social organizations take part in unequal exchange relationships by virtue of the extent to which they are fixed within specific spaces. That sportswear is produced by local families in developing economies working in what are less than high-tech workplaces does not mean what they produce is not subject to globalization, because what, how and when the producers make their goods are determined by particular networks of power and interests that link these workplaces together and take the products into richer global markets. There are different experiences and engagements with the processes of change, and in effect there are also winners and losers: the latter are normally those at the end of the line or on the periphery of the network (Barrientos, 2001). The consequences of globalization are visible to many people, and so are the bitter ironies – for example, $300 sports shoes being produced in developing economies for $10.

Some observers have noted that the development of globalization benefits the winners and those already in a privileged position. Hirst and Thompson's (1999) text, for example, argued that core economic flows and activity tended to follow a traditional pattern, which privileged specific dominant and developed parts of the globe. Production and distribution remain unequally distributed and shared. Since Hirst and Thompson's book was published, the role of India and China has increased within this global space of investment flows. Within these countries there are similarly privileged internal political and economic hierarchies, and a new type of neocolonial engagement has taken place, as seen in China's role in Africa. The argument is that globalization follows specific pathways and does not include all classes and nations equally. Globalization is not something that is to be understood in terms of 'opening up economic borders' but is made and constructed in political, organizational and cultural terms – and therefore with all the tensions these imply.

There is a growing sense in the debate on globalization that while there are many negative outcomes, it is not a closed and predetermined process that will lead to a given final outcome. Instead, there are many possible outcomes. Much depends on the main players and how a language of globalization is constructed. Politically, there are greater calls for regulation and control by transnational governing bodies (see Chapter 16 on regulation). These developments may be underpinned or supported, as Monbiot (2004, 2006) argues, by new oppositional political networks as globalization processes provide new technologies of dialogue for those who desire more socially oriented outcomes.

Then there is the question of culture: if we look closely at the process of globalization in terms of international management, we are struck by the preponderance of new neoliberal American management concepts and ideologies coming from business schools and consultancy firms (see Chapter 10 on business schools and consultants, Chapter 11 on varieties of capitalism and Chapter 12 on lean production). This 'American' managerial hegemony was reinforced by the geopolitical and corporate dominance of the United States in key parts of the globe during much of the 20th century, and as Panitch and Gindin (2012: 223) have argued, this has since been reinforced:

> It was one of the hallmarks of the centrality of the American empire in the making of global capitalism that the multilateral and bilateral treaties that established the regime of free trade and investment in the final two decades of the 20th century were deeply inscribed with long standing US legal and juridical rules and practices. The wide international range of US firms, as well as the relative size and importance of US markets . . . gave rise to extensive coordination of national regulations through international institutions like the newly created WTO, the World Bank, the Bank of International Settlements and the IMF.

When the World Trade Organization (WTO) terms were presented as a fallback position in the event of a 'no deal Brexit', little attention was paid to their provenance or the influence on their provisions of a foreign political power, albeit one whose values were arguably in tune with British proponents of such an outcome.

The influence of American managerial traditions within proceses of globalization should not be underestimated. The development of Fordist models of production and the spread of the assembly-line form of mass production were a key outcome of American corporate influences, both through direct FDI and through their mimicking elsewhere by local capital. Similarly, particular models of production such as *lean production* became conflated with the new global agenda, infusing globalization with an approach to work based on labour intensification, which was influenced by specific views of economic development (see Chapter 12 on lean production and Chapter 14 on technology and the organization of production).

Multinational corporations are caught in an ambivalent relationship with local spaces, in that their power derives in part from playing one nation off against another through the politics of investment and divestment. The associated political leverage can pay dividends in terms of lower rents for factories, greater public subsidies and lower wages through labour market regulations allowing for such developments, as in so-called *special enterprise zones* (Lillie and Martínez Lucio, 2010). Yet, the global is not 'global' per se: it is about globally operating organizations manipulating the 'local'. In this respect, we need to be cautious about viewing the process of globalization as something that has emerged in a quasi-evolutionary fashion and that represents a new and superior stage of development: it is something that is manufactured and like all things that are manufactured it carries the hallmark of the makers.

The degree to which the actions of MNCs are influenced by their country of origin has long been the subject of debate. Perlmutter (1969), nearly a half a century ago, urged us to classify carefully when it comes to multinational corporations. There were, in effect, three types of company, which reflected the different ways in which they engaged with their environment. *Polycentric* firms were those that effectively fitted into their new foreign environments and would use local managers and work within the culture and working practices of the host country. This contrasts with *ethnocentric* firms, which were more focused on using management and control systems from their home environments, often insisting on a direct form of control through ethnically closed managerial networks and hierarchies. Perlmutter also began to see the emergence of firms where management practices privileged neither home nor host traditions, moreover management teams did not consist entirely of specific national groups, but were more open and cosmopolitan in culture: these were *geocentric* forms. Others, such as Bartlett and Goshal (1998), have shown how international firms have developed since the start of the 20th century, from what were in effect polycentric forms through to more geocentric ones. Beginning with what were *multi-domestic, multinational* and *decentralized* forms, but which were limited in respect of their spans of control, the 20th century witnessed more multinational forms, which were, in actuality, *global*, using expatriate managers and more centralized and coordinated systems of control. This was driven very much by the age of American capital and companies such as General Motors, Ford and IBM and other manufacturing-related enterprises that were using Taylorist forms of management based on mass and standardized production as well as bureaucratic organizational forms (see Chapter 14 on technology and the organization of production). Such organizations were seen as taking an *international* form. Subsequently, according to these authors, new *transnational* forms emerged, which were more geocentric in nature, based on networking across sites, more systematic approaches to learning by exchanging practices through these networks, and the adoption of a more cosmopolitan culture (see Bharami, 1992).

More specifically, Ferner and Edwards (1995) pointed to a range of practices or relations that could assist MNCs in changing HRM practices in any context: the use and role of resources and their strategic deployment (e.g. investment or disinvestment), the role of authority relations (e.g. the use of leadership structures and the prerogative to push for change), the importance of negotiation and exchange at key points (e.g. bargaining over questions of investment and concessions with workers in a specific site) and the overarching importance of cultural and ideological processes (e.g. establishing 'visions' and 'missions' within organizations that can legitimate change and undermine opposing views). Thus in many ways MNCs require political processes for their *sustainability*. We must not forget that, just as globalization is constructed and sustained in a variety of ways, so the organizational structures of MNCs themselves vary and engage in differing ways with local contexts (see Chapter 2 on MNCs).

Globalization and the dark side of the changes in employment and work

The end of the traditional industrial worker?

The impact of globalization has had a deep and far-reaching impact on the way people work. In relation to developed economies, there is an established debate about the way 'traditional' forms of working and employment have changed. In the 1970s we began to witness the first cracks in the system of stable employment that had been based mainly on an industrialization model. The notion of 'post-industrial society' alerted individuals to a crisis in the method of standardized and hierarchical forms of work in industrial contexts. Daniel Bell, in his book *The Coming of Post-Industrial Society* (1973), argued that the importance of innovation, a new technical and professional class, and a move away from an engineering/industrial perspective, were emerging in countries such as the United States. The factors for change were complex: social changes in the nature of the workforce and the emergence of a strong female presence in the labour market, vigorously expanding service-sector-based organizations, the emergence of the widespread use of computers; and new forms of competition from the Far East (in this context, Japan, with its newly emerging global companies such as Sony, Toshiba and Toyota). These views reflected a changing reality but they presented a binary view of change, with the industrial working class being replaced by a new technical middle class, machinery becoming subservient to computers and the traditional factory culture of work being replaced by new forms of learning. Other commentators highlighted the impact of the industrial crises and changes of the 1970s and 1980s, muting the end of the centrality of a traditional work ethic and employment based on jobs in manufacturing, and a decline in labour organizations such as trade unions (see Touraine, 1971, and Gorz, 1980). The argument was that the traditional working class was changing and in decline, though many years later others, such as Panitch and Gindin (2012), have pointed out that with the extension of American imperial globalization the size of the working class has actually expanded, if we take a world view that includes changes in developing economies.

In the 1980s, we began to see a perspective that proclaimed the decline of the Fordist model based on mass production, cost reductions through wage control, a high degree of labour standardization and mass consumption (Swyngedouw, 1986). The Fordist model began to give rise to a series of changes, purportedly marking a steady move to new forms of flexible production, smaller workplaces and flexible forms of working. Under this new 'flexible specialization' workers were deployed across various aspects of the production process: the emphasis was placed on the quality of the product and responding to more fragmented and niche-based product markets (Swyngedouw, 1986). The changes were driven by more demanding and fragmented consumers, serviced by the development of new technologies and forms of production. There are thus many other factors, such as technological developments and political upheavals that fed into narratives around the drivers of change, subsumed into some generic notion of globalization. In the case of the post-industrial narrative, as noted earlier, traditional manufacturing industries in Europe and the United States faced greater competition since the latter decades of the 20th century, initially from rapid economic development in countries such as Japan and South Korea, and subsequently India and China. Changing markets and new product-based competition in the context of what some call post-Fordism further undermined a reliance on standardized and centralized forms of production and stable employment patterns. Once more, these views were focused on developed economies and the perceived exhaustion of their traditional methods of working (see Harvey, 1989: 173–88). Hierarchical and centralized systems of management and labour regulation, which had been dominant during the middle and latter half of the 20th century, were seen not to fit this changing environment. It should be noted, however, that there are well-established critiques that proponents of such changes tended to overstate the prevalence of new, post-Fordist production regimes, as indeed there are critiques of how prevalent Fordist production regimes were themselves beyond the large American corporations of the mid 20th century. Moreover, there were ironies apparent in the respective employment conditions offered, with workers in traditional, hierarchical *Fordist* workplaces being more likely to have representation in the form of independent unions than their counterparts in workplaces pioneering *flexible specialization*.

The rise of the new worker?

Tensions at work have been exacerbated by obsessive organizational change, constant transformation in the ownership of firms and pressures from greater innovation through the 'cross-pollination' of management ideas. A greater degree of worker and management mobility brought further changes. The social and economic disruption brought about by globalization, as well as changes in their own national contexts, has increased pressure on workers for mobility in search of better employment, or indeed any employment. Pressures in managerial work from the growing internationalization of the firm meant that travel became a central feature due to the need to manage geographically distant clients and groups of workers on an ongoing basis.

Furthermore, globalization is not only a matter of employer mobility, economic change and new workplace practices, but also of a new informational economy, which brings novel spatial relations. These changes coincided with a series of technological developments, especially in information and communication technology (ICT) and the emergence and development of the internet, which as noted created new spatial and temporal bridges between groups of individuals in distinct geographical spaces (Castells, 1996). These developments break down traditional ways of balancing communication exchange and forms of working. Yet there has been a steady realization that all was not turning out as many proponents of change imagined. The utopian images of change gave rise to a growing awareness that work was becoming challenging in new and highly problematic ways. The 1990s began to see a new wave of social concerns about the new work regime in terms of its consistency and its stability.

The 1990s saw a growing debate about the problems of stress, social fragmentation and increasing risk at work. In his prophetic book *The End of Work*, first published in 1995 (and updated in 2004), Jeremy Rifkin pointed to issues of worker burnout, increasing stress and growing insecurity on a global scale as the consequences of such developments:

> The use of new information technologies are designed to remove whatever vestigial control workers still exercise over the production process by

programming detailed instructions directly into the machine, which then carries them out verbatim. The worker is rendered powerless to exercise independent judgement either on the factory floor or in the office . . . Now, an increasing number of workers act solely as observers. (Rifkin, 2004: 182)

Richard Sennett, in his text *The Corrosion of Character: The Personnel Consequences of Work in the New Capitalism* (1998), explained how new forms of flexibility and of uncertainty at work were eroding workers' sense of purpose and trust in others. Moving into the new millennia, these developments were paralleled by increasing insecurity and changes within labour markets, leading to what some have described as a new precarious class, or precariat (Standing, 2010), which emerged due to a range of factors associated with the changing nature of capitalism and its increasingly 'mobile' character.

It consists of a multitude of insecure people, living bits-and-pieces lives, in and out of short-term jobs, without a narrative of occupational development, including millions of frustrated educated youth who do not like what they see before them, millions of women abused in oppressive labour, growing numbers of criminalized tagged for life, millions being categorized as 'disabled' and migrants in their hundreds of millions around the world. They are denizens; they have a more restricted range of social, cultural, political and economic rights than citizens around them. (Standing, 2011)

While many have questioned the extent of such changes and the cohesive nature of the new 'class', let alone the nature of its politics (Conley, 2012), the reality is that globalization has led to change and crisis within labour markets.

A gendered international division of labour

In developing economies, these changes can create even greater forms of exclusion and fragmentation. An argument commonly heard is that globalization has created 'hard-to-reach' workers. For example, the high-end sports-leisure footwear industry has seen ongoing internationalization of production and outsourcing, which has resulted in reliance on a workforce in developing economies that is unprotected and easily exploited. The global system is linked by brands that invade social and private space on the one hand, yet shield the exploitative working patterns they develop on the other (Klein, 2000). The use of child labour and unpaid female work, for example, has emerged as a major transnational focus of debate because of the way the complex production networks and supply chains of many MNCs rely on such forms of labour. Globalization has brought new groups of workers into the workforce in developing economies. The extent to which this can be celebrated as offering the benefits of increasing household income must be set against the potential for exploitative practices and the gender relations within these production processes: more women have been brought into the global workforce but not on equal terms.

> For many women, unpaid work in and for the household takes up the majority of their working hours, with much less time spent in remunerative employment. Even when they participate in the labour market for paid employment, women still undertake the majority of the housework . . . When women work outside the household, they earn, on average, far less than men . . . They are also more likely to work in more precarious forms of employment with low earnings, little financial security and few or no social benefits . . . Women not only earn less than men but also tend to own fewer assets. Smaller salaries and less control over household income constrain their ability to accumulate capital. (UNICEF, 2006: 36–7)

The role of global supply chains is one of the factors that can contribute to this degradation of work, especially when there is no close monitoring and regulation through auditors and dedicated inspections (Short et al., 2016). Thus many of these workers may seem beyond the reach of regulation, working for small-scale employers, linked indirectly to MNCs through complex chains of command that are characteristic of involvement in developing economies. The main concern in many of the debates is that the current form of globalization is systematically driving down labour standards and undermining rights at work. This is a major concern for ethical and social reasons: in effect, there are many more losers than winners as we count the cost of a more unregulated context based on excessive labour intensification.

The following short case study outlines some of the social and human dilemmas that are emerging owing to globalization.

Case study: The changing nature of work in the textile sector

Montague Burton was a Lithuanian Jewish immigrant who came to the United Kingdom (UK) in 1900 to escape Russian pogroms. He went on to build a clothing company that would dominate the UK market for men's suits, at its height clothing an estimated quarter of the male population, as well as providing wartime military uniforms and the famous demobilization suit issued to war veterans affectionately known as 'The Full Monty'.

In 1921, Montague Burton opened a factory in Leeds, a city at the heart of the UK textiles industry. Specializing in clothing, Leeds offered access to a skilled workforce of tailors and machinists. The Burton's factory went on to become the largest employer in the city and the biggest clothing factory in the world, at its height employing around 10,500 workers, producing over 30,000 suits per week. Boys as young as 14 were employed as barrow boys, with the possibility of going on to apprenticeships as tailors and cloth cutters. Production was on a mass scale, with huge workrooms of machinists employing whole families. Women outnumbered men 9 to 1. Montague Burton was considered to be a *progressive employer*, providing facilities and benefits aimed at maintaining staff satisfaction. The factory boasted the largest canteen in the world, and staff had access to dentists, chiropodists and eye specialists to care for eyestrain associated with detailed needlework. There was also a health and pension scheme that pre-dated the Welfare State and trade unions were an integral part of the company's working environment (these types of company were common also in the food and drink sector: see Strangleman (2019) for an example of company with a strong social approach to work during the 20th century).

By the 1980s, UK clothing manufacturing had gone into decline. Although Burton's continued for a time as a retailer, including high-street brands such as Top Shop, clothing production at the factory in Leeds ended in 1981.The emphasis on low-cost fashion had seen production increasingly moved abroad. UK clothing retailers developed supply chains that could take advantage of lower labour costs in developing economies such as Bangladesh.

The textile sector has become an integral part of the Bangladesh economy, with a wide range of companies and a large component of the workforce being women. However, reproducing the kinds of working conditions outlined above has been a challenge. Many of the producers are part of complex supply chains working through subcontracts and other indirect mechanisms for dominant MNCs who control overseas markets. Questions have been raised about fair wages, working conditions and, crucially, the relatively limited investment in health and safety (War on Want, 2011). Tragedies such as the Rana Plaza building collapse that killed over a thousand people due to a lack of safety inspections are an example of some of the issues facing workers in such a context. There have been attempts to develop a greater degree of worker voice and safety-related enforcement mechanisms to ensure that labour standards are enhanced (Donaghey and Reinecke, 2018) but progress is at an early stage.

The absence of strong trade unions in Bangladesh is one major difference with the traditions of the textile sector in the UK in the 20th century. In addition, the local labour inspectorate faces a range of resourcing issues and problems in terms of monitoring health and safety standards generally. There is also much pressure to ensure that the country does not face a wave of disinvestment from MNCs similar to the experience that was seen earlier in the UK. However, over time alliances between a range of non-government organizations (NGOs), trade unions and transnational employers have begun to establish a consensus concerning decent work standards (ibid.). How extensive and influential these alliances will become is yet to be seen.

(Continued)

Questions

1.   What do you consider to be the main features of change in the textile sector in the case provided above?
2.   Is being considered a *progressive employer* enough to protect workers' interests?
3.   What are the commercial pressures put on producers in Bangladesh that can undermine the enhancement of working conditions?
4.   What can be done to ensure that working conditions are sustained or remain of a reasonably high standard during these periods of change?
5.   What role can bodies external to the firm such as government inspectorates, trade unions and NGOs like War on Want play in this process?

Contradiction, ironies and new agendas in the changing nature of work

As we observed earlier, there are curious ironies within the globalization debate. Globalization does not only remove barriers and boundaries, opening up spaces to competition; there are also some curious developments in the way its processes interact with *local environments* (see Chapter 9 on training). The contradictory nature of globalization is illustrated by the role of local environments in which 'traditional' models of production that were seen as antiquated in other contexts can be reconstructed: yet, as seen in the case study, there is an increasing level of interest from global bodies, consumer groups, trade unions and even various employer bodies in the question of enhancing labour standards and not focusing on 'cheap labour' as a permanent strategy (see Chapter 16 on regulation).

First, globalization works through local structures and can actually enhance differences. Many companies create complex local networks of suppliers and support firms through subcontracting (Barrientos, 2001). Products may be increasingly global, but they sometimes reflect the specificities of local circumstances, and many global networks have strong local (national and regional) hubs. This means that a manufactured good may be assembled in one MNC production site but emerge from a complex set of smaller companies that specialize within specific regional contexts in particular parts of the world. In terms of the management of employment, pressure is placed on workers to benchmark their wages locally and not look to higher levels for comparable work elsewhere in the global production process (see Swyngedouw, 2004). In one sense, this points to the power of capital to dissect and fragment as a form of control, but the irony is that capital has to work through ever more fractured systems of production and employment, which brings inevitable transaction costs and bureaucratic dilemmas around quality control and working standards (MacKenzie, 2002).

Second, the core traditional working class may be extensively changing in more developed economies but there are also developments that suggest the class dynamics left behind, according to the narrative of post-industrialism, have resurfaced in various other contexts. In countries such as China, there has been rapid growth in manufacturing and traditional industries such as shipbuilding and steel production. Ness (2016) argues that what we are seeing in such contexts are new forms of worker mobilization and campaigning that are increasingly becoming organized and linked to challenging multinational corporations and their practices.

In fact, it could be suggested that this 'return to the industrial' is not solely the case in economic and sectoral terms but is reflected in management and employment practices too. Take the case of traditional forms of direct control, standardization and surveillance – known to some as scientific management or Taylorism. These practices are a growing and persistent feature of many aspects of work in developing economies, such as manufacturing in Malaysia, but also – and hence the irony – a feature of work in the service sectors of more developed, post-industrial economies (Bain and Taylor, 2000). Surveillance, performance monitoring and direct forms of control are widely used in call centres in both India and Britain (Taylor and Bain, 2005). In other words, the idea of globalization leading to a transformation of work into some new form within a post-industrial, post-Fordist context, with associated avant garde approaches to HRM, needs to be treated with a good deal of caution; more likely we will see greater hybrids in management strategy and ongoing forms of control and work intensification.

Such developments indicate that globalization is a contested process as it gives rise to a range of concerns and political responses from individuals and organizations. The steady growth of concern with questions of dignity, decency and fairness at work is in great part driven by the negative developments outlined earlier in the chapter: for example, the use of child labour, work intensification, excessive differences in wealth exposed by the strategies of MNCs and the uneven inclusion of women in the labour market (see Chapter 16 on regulation, Chapter 17 on international employee representation and Chapter 18 on sustainability and IHRM). The shift in concerns regarding the social consequences of globalization has begun to open up the discussion in terms of the contingencies and complexities of international economic activity. As noted previously, those that suffer most from the degradations of globalization tend to be at the end of the line or on the periphery (Barrientos, 2001) but that does not mean they alone are affected. The impact of globalization may be uneven, but it is increasingly ubiquitous. While managerial jobs within MNCs may continue to be aspirational positions for many, it should be recognized that such roles have also been deeply affected by the growing intensification of work, and the social pressures placed on individual managers and core professionals (see Chapter 6 on international assignments). In another ironic turn, management have become *subject to* as well as *agents of* globalization (Foster et al., 2019; McCann et al., 2008).

Conclusion: shared miseries and possibilities

The way we work and the way we are employed changes as a result of a range of factors. Traditionally, we work within specific spaces, with specific technologies, in relation to different supervisory systems and within different cultural and organizational contexts. Work remains uneven in respect of its quality, reward and meaning within and between countries. Yet there is a sense that the way we are internationalizing – the growing presence of large corporations, the greater mobility of capital and labour between countries and the sharing of new ideas about work and employment – is fundamentally changing the realities of work. This chapter has argued that such shifts can be seen in both negative and positive terms, and that these changes bring many difficult outcomes. There is a sense that globalization is bringing as many challenges as benefits. The construction of a new global space is creating a new set of tensions that are experienced on a day-to-day basis by individuals and their families.

The once-hoped-for utopian idea that work will improve and our social condition will be enhanced through the greater convergence of humanity as a consequence of globalization is being questioned. A global order appears to be emerging framed by values and economic relations that exalt market capitalism and promulgate a particularly neoliberal and 'Americanized' view of social life that is atomized, fragmented and 'gated'. Yet these changes are unstable and complex, and rely on broad institutional networks and alliances of players and politics. Both management and workers try to prosper in this situation, but often only just survive these developments. This is a disembedding of the traditional way of working that is not necessarily leading to social and economic enhancement. This experience of globalization, the way we work and are managed within this context and the way that corporations are structured are becoming topics of increasing concern. In debating globalization, we therefore have to look carefully at the way it is defined, developed and driven and, crucially, the outcomes to which this leads: we must also follow through and see what new political and social responses emerge in local contexts affected by 'globalization'.

Reflective questions

1. What are the different elements of the optimistic and pessimistic views of globalization?
2. What main concerns has globalization given rise to in terms of the impact on work and employment?
3. Is there really an end to the industrial and manufacturing pattern of work, or are has this been overstated?
4. In what ways can labour standards be enhanced and improved in the wake of the negative impacts of globalization?

Recommended reading

- Short, J. L., Toffel, M. W. and Hugill, A. R. (2016) 'Monitoring global supply chains'. *Strategic Management Journal*, 37(9): 1878–97.
- Donaghey, J. and Reinecke, J. (2018) 'When industrial democracy meets corporate social responsibility – A comparison of the Bangladesh accord and alliance as responses to the Rana Plaza disaster'. *British Journal of Industrial Relations*, 56(1): 14–42.
- Lillie, N. and Martínez Lucio, M. (2010) 'Rollerball and the spirit of capitalism: Competitive dynamics within the global context, the challenge to labour internationalism and the emergence of ironic outcomes'. *Critical Perspectives on International Business*, 8(1): 74–93.

References

Albawaba Business (2012) 'UAE Exchange Mission Zero Suicide campaign ends on a successful note', 18 November. Available at: www.albawaba.com/business/pr/uae-exchange-mission-zero-suicide-451324 (accessed 10 March 2012).

Bain, P. and Taylor, P. (2000) 'Entrapped by the "electronic panopticon"? Worker resistance in the call centre'. *New Technology, Work and Employment*, 15(1): 2–18.

Barrientos, S. (2001) 'Gender, flexibility and global value chains'. *IDS Bulletin*, 32(3): 83–93.

Bartlett, C. and Goshal, S. (1998) *Managing Across Borders: The Transnational Solution*. Boston: Harvard Business School Press.

Bell, D. (1973) *The Coming of Post-Industrial Society*. New York: Basic Books.

Bharami, H. (1992) 'The emerging flexible organisation: Perspectives from Silicon Valley'. *California Management Review*, 34(4): 33–52.

Casciani, D. (2005) 'Morecambe Bay: One year on'. *BBC News Online*, 5 February. Available at: http://news.bbc.co.uk/1/hi/uk/4238209.stm (accessed 10 March 2013).

Castells, M. (1996) *The Rise of Network Society*. Oxford: Blackwell.

Conley, H. (2012) 'Book review symposium: Guy Standing, *The Precariat: The New Dangerous Class*, reviewed by Hazel Conley'. *Work, Employment and Society*, 26(4): 686–8.

Dickens, P. (2007) *Global Shift*. London: Sage.

DiMaggio, P. J. and Powell, W. (1983) 'The iron cage revisited: Institutional isomorphism and collective rationality in organizational fields'. *American Sociological Review*, 48: 147–60.

Donaghey, J. and Reinecke, J. (2018) 'When industrial democracy meets corporate social responsibility – A comparison of the Bangladesh accord and alliance as responses to the Rana Plaza disaster'. *British Journal of Industrial Relations*, 56(1): 14–42.

Ferner, A. and Edwards, P. (1995) 'Power and the diffusion of organizational change within multinational enterprises'. *European Journal of Industrial Relations*, 1(2): 229–57.

Ferner, A. and Quintanilla, J. (1998) 'Multinationals, national business systems and HRM: the enduring influence of national identity or a process of "Anglo-Saxonization"'. *International Journal of Human Resource Management*, 9(4): 710–31.

Foster, W. M., Hassard, J. S., Morris, J. and Wolfram Cox, J. (2019) 'The changing nature of managerial work: The effects of corporate restructuring on management jobs and careers'. *Human Relations*, 72(3): 473–504.

Friedman, T. (2005) *The World is Flat: The Globalised World in the 21st Century*. New York: Allen Lane.

Giddens, A. (1990) *The Consequences of Modernity*. Cambridge: Polity.

Gorz, A. (1980) *Farewell to the Working Class*. London: Pluto Press.

Harvey, D. (1989) *The Condition of Post-Modernity*. Oxford Blackwell.

Hirst, P. and Thompson, G. (1999) *Globalisation in Question*. Cambridge: Polity Press.

Klein, N. (2000) *No Logo*. New York: Taylor & Francis.

Lillie, N. and Martínez Lucio, M. (2010) 'Rollerball and the spirit of capitalism: Competitive dynamics within the global context, the challenge to labour internationalism and the emergence of ironic outcomes'. *Critical Perspectives on International Business*, 8(1): 74–93.

McCann, L., Morris, J. and Hassard, J. (2008) 'Normalized intensity: The new labour process of middle management'. *Journal of Management Studies*, 45(2): 343–71.

MacKenzie, R. (2002) 'The migration of bureaucracy: Contracting and the regulation of labour in the telecommunications industry'. *Work, Employment and Society*, 16(4): 599–616.

Monbiot, G. (2004) *The Age of Consent*. London: Harper Perennial.

Monbiot, G. (2006) *Heat: How to Stop the Planet Burning*. London: Allen Lane.

Ness, I. (2016) *Southern Insurgency: The Coming of the Global Working Class*. London: Pluto Press.

Panitch, L. and Gindin, S. (2012) *The Making of Global Capitalism: The Political Economy of American Empire*. London: Verso.

Perlmutter, H. V. (1969) 'The tortuous evolution of the multinational corporation'. *Columbia Journal of World Business*, 4: 9–18.

Rifkin, J. (2004) *The End of Work*. London: Penguin.

Sennett, R. (1998) *The Corrosion of Character: The Personnel Consequences of Work in the New Capitalism*. New York: W. W. Norton.

Short, J. L., Toffel, M. W. and Hugill, A. R. (2016) 'Monitoring global supply chains'. *Strategic Management Journal*, 37(9): 1878–97.

Standing, G. (2010) *The Precariat*. New York: Bloomsbury Academic.

Standing, G. (2011) 'The precariat – The new dangerous class'. *Policy Network*. Available at: www.policy-network.net/pno_detail.aspx?ID=4004&title=+The+Precariat+%e2%80%93 +The+new+dangerous+class.

Strangleman, T. (2019) *Voices of Guinness: An Oral History of the Park Royal Brewery*. Oxford: Oxford University Press.

Swyngedouw, E. (1986) *The Socio-spatial Implications of Innovations in Industrial Organisation*. Centre Européen John Hopkins.

Swyngedouw, E. (2004) 'Globalisation or "glocalisation"? Networks, territories and rescaling'. *Cambridge Review of International Affairs*, 17(1): 25–48.

Taylor, P. and Bain, P. (2005). '"India calling to the far away towns": The call centre labour process and globalization'. *Work, Employment and Society*, 19(2): 261–82.

Touraine, A. (1971) *The Post Industrial Society*. London: Wildwood House.

UNCTAD (2011) *World Investment Report*. Geneva: United Nations.

UNCTAD (2019) *World Investment Report*. Geneva: United Nations.

UNICEF (2006) *The State of the World's Children*. New York: UNICEF.

War on Want (2011) *Sweatshops in Bangladesh*. Available at: https://waronwant.org/news-analysis/sweatshops-bangladesh (accessed 15 February 2021).

2 Transnational corporations, Human Resource Management and globalization

Phil Almond and María C. González Menéndez

Learning objectives

- To understand the Human Resource Management (HRM) strategies of Transnational Corporations (TNCs)
- To comprehend the ways in which TNCs engage with their environments in terms of HRM
- To outline the nature of change and the ways in which TNCs develop HRM strategies in their operations

Introduction

This chapter looks at the role of TNCs as vehicles for change in the management of human resources. Different authors use the terms multinational corporations (MNCs) or TNCs to denote international firms, while others use 'multinational' or 'transnational' as particular corporate strategies used by different types of international firm (e.g. Bartlett and Ghoshal, 1998). Here, we simply use 'TNCs' to refer to firms that have direct employees in more than one country, through foreign direct investment (World Investment Report, 2011). However, many chapters in the book refer to them as 'MNCs' which is another way of doing so.

TNCs are actors of particular interest as, by definition, they operate across a range of national business/employment systems (Whitley, 1999), which may present them with substantially different patterns of organizing capitalism and the employment relationship in particular (see Chapter 3 on employment relations). From a managerial perspective, this produces both challenges and opportunities: challenges because features of national host systems sometimes mean that it is difficult to replicate a uniform system of HRM across the international firm, and opportunities because TNCs often have the capacity to engage in various forms of 'regime shopping' (Streeck, 1991), through which they seek to ensure that their production is conducted in countries where the labour market environment is most favourable.

From the host-country point of view, TNCs produce challenges. Foreign TNCs 'inhabit' host systems, but often 'have neither been party to nor have any real interest in the forms of social compromise that have underpinned the joint development of employment and welfare systems' (Rubery, 2011: 517). This lesser commitment to host national systems, combined with their potential mobility, makes TNCs likely to challenge those parts of host systems which they perceive as 'constraints'.

Through their presence in host economies, they participate in the reproduction and/or change of those systems, and can be seen as 'institution makers' (Streeck and Thelen, 2005), attempting to adapt or change elements of host systems to their own ends. More broadly, TNCs have been important agents in normalizing ideas about the restructuring of employment under the banner of competitiveness. How these various processes of adaptation and challenge might occur, and with what consequences for national Industrial Relations (IR) systems and patterns of HRM, is the subject of this chapter.

TNCs and strategies of change

TNCs have a number of tools which they use, to varying extents, in order to ensure that, from their perspective, the global workforce is managed as 'efficiently' and profitably as possible (see Edwards and Kuruvilla, 2005). These range from simple financial targets, through very direct prescription of Human Resources (HR) policy through bureaucratic controls, to the extensive expatriation of home-country managers in order to control foreign subsidiaries (Patel et al., 2019). In more sophisticated cases, the latter may be associated with the development of an international internal labour market for senior managers, which among other things represents an attempt to align managerial culture across the international firm. Rather than deal in detail with these and other micro-level tools, though, we concentrate here on what, broadly, TNCs are trying to achieve in their global HRM systems, and how these interact with national employment systems.

There are several schools of thought on how TNCs manage their international workforces, and International HRM (IHRM), which largely focuses on HRM within TNCs, is now a substantial field of academic endeavour with its own journals and conferences. The most orthodox approaches, based originally on transaction cost theories of the economics of the firm, try to understand the conditions under which FDI is a better strategy for the firm than trade (i.e. better than simply exporting its production or, in some cases, licensing production by third parties in foreign countries). From this perspective, which is uncritical of management, the management question in TNCs is largely one of balancing the advantages of (international) integration with those of 'responsiveness' to host-country conditions (Prahalad and Doz, 1999). 'Integration' within international HRM mostly means seeking the standardization of HR systems across the firm's different international operations. This is partly driven by the search for economies of scale: one major advantage of operating the same system globally is that the unit costs of running the system should, all other things being equal, be reduced. Integrating management across countries also aids firms to achieve standardization of production processes and facilitates bureaucratic, cultural and financial control over managers and workers in foreign subsidiaries.

On the other hand, some form of 'responsiveness' to host systems is often necessary or useful. Responsiveness can broadly be categorized in two groups, which we label as 'defensive' and 'offensive'.

(i) *'Defensive'* responsiveness occurs where there are elements of the firm's home-country HR system that are impossible or excessively expensive to replicate in a given foreign subsidiary. This may occur for one of several reasons.

First, some HR policies may be allowable in a firm's home country but illegal in specific host countries. This probably most commonly occurs in the sphere of collective industrial relations: non-union approaches to HRM are commonplace among large firms in the United States, for example (Jacoby, 1997), but are not compatible with labour law in some European countries. However, it also occurs in other spheres of HRM; for example, the performance management systems of large US TNCs have sometimes been contested in labour courts in EU countries (Muller-Camen et al., 2001).

Second, policies might also be difficult to export because the host-country employment system fails to provide the infrastructure to support them. For example, participatory forms of work organization developed in the home-country operations of German TNCs may depend on that country's system of vocational training and social partnership, and be difficult to export to countries lacking these types of institutional arrangement (Tempel, 2001).

Finally, responsiveness might also be necessary or useful because home-country practices, though legal, are seen as undesirable by host-country managers or workers. For instance, it has frequently been questioned whether Chinese managers are motivated by the performance management systems prevalent among large western firms (e.g. Gu and Nolan, 2017). It is very common, within mainstream IHRM, to ascribe firms' difficulties in achieving cross-national uniformity to 'cultural differences', typically drawing on the work of Hofstede (1980). However, this research generally has no purchase on (or interest in) the power relations inherent in either the employment relationship or the international firm. In considering processes of transfer/non-transfer of HR practices, it is clearly important to consider what actors in the TNC think of as fair, equitable or justifiable (see Chapter 5 on diversity). These 'rationalities' about what is fair are subject to national differences. However, as we will see below, the power of TNCs to overcome problems arising from different national understandings should not be underplayed.

(ii) *'Offensive'* forms of responsiveness are inspired, not by the 'constraints' presented by subsidiary workforces and employment systems, but rather by the *opportunities* that they offer. They are likely to occur where there are, from the perspective of headquarters' managers, advantages to differentiation that outweigh the advantages of uniformity.

Mainstream approaches are notably quieter on these forms of responsiveness than they are on defensive responsiveness. Work that takes more account of how national business systems shape forms of comparative advantage (e.g. Kristensen and Morgan, 2006) implies that if a particular host system presents specific advantages (e.g. Germany's strengths in engineering, derived from some of the institutional resources mentioned above), it may not make economic sense to try to impose a system designed for a workforce lacking these strengths on a German subsidiary, even if there are no particular institutional 'barriers' to doing so.

On a somewhat less benign level, critical approaches to labour markets have long explored how firms in general 'segment' labour markets, offering relatively good employment conditions to 'core' or well-organized groups of workers at the expense of 'less favoured' groups (women, ethnic minorities, etc.) (see Fagan et al., 2017: 368). Internationalization, particularly where subsidiaries are situated in significantly poorer countries, presents substantially extended opportunities for firms to act in this way. Where TNCs from the Global North choose to locate in lower-cost countries, they have opportunities not only to save on wage costs, but also to impose working conditions that would not be feasible in their country of origin.

Broad orientations of TNCs towards IHRM

Taking into account the variety of motivations for integration and responsiveness, a number of broad orientations towards the coordination and control of international workforces can be portrayed.

a) Integration through the replication of country-of-origin policies

Here, firms simply seek to export their home-country HRM policies abroad. This is characterized in the IHRM literature as an *ethnocentric* approach. The economic logic behind 'country of origin effects' (Ferner, 1997) is that TNCs compete internationally on the basis of competitive advantages that they have acquired through the resources of their domestic economies (Doremus et al., 1998). Or, from a somewhat more sociological perspective, 'firms are likely to be influenced in their international operations by the strategies, ways of doing things, and shared understandings as to appropriate behaviour that they have developed in response to the institutional constraints and opportunities of their home business system' (Ferner and Tempel, 2006: 13).

b) Integration through the creation/replication of a 'global best practices' system

In this case, firms seek to set up internationally uniform policies inspired by what senior managers believe to be global 'best practices' rather than using country-of-origin policy as the basis for global policy. This is often referred to as a 'geocentric' approach. This form of integration is increasingly common, as top corporate decision-makers are influenced by common understandings of what constitutes global 'best practice' (for a convincing argument on how good practice ideas shape managerial choices, see Woywode, 2002: 501–2). Cross-national learning on what constitute good HR strategies for international competitiveness is often derived externally to the firm. This includes models of global best practice inculcated in business schools, in the managerial literature, from consultants or from benchmarking with competitors.

TNCs also have the opportunity to engage in active cross-national learning through their internal corporate networks. In other words, some TNCs may take the 'best practices' from their various national operations and attempt where appropriate to internationalize them. Thus, if the performance management practices of the British operations of a German TNC are seen as successful (and internationalizable), then the TNC might seek to introduce a global performance management strategy, including in the home country, based on the British rather than the German system. This process is sometimes referred to as 'reverse diffusion' (Edwards, 1998).

c) Active differentiation

Active differentiation follows the logic of 'offensive' forms of responsiveness, or of strategic segmentation, introduced above. This includes approaches which attempt to exploit the better *quality* of human resources in some foreign subsidiaries. More negatively, it also includes the exploitation of low labour *costs* and/or lax labour *regulation*, particularly in the Global South.

The availability of cheap and less regulated labour elsewhere in the world is obviously one reason for establishing international subsidiaries. Not only might this lead to reduced employment in the country of origin, but the threat of relocation also weakens the bargaining power of labour. In the United States, threats to relocate to, or increase investment in, Mexico are commonplace during union organizing campaigns, for example (Logan, 2002). These threats are more realistic given Mexico's presence in the NAFTA trade bloc.

The potential for this 'whipsawing' depends on the extent to which the international division of labour within the firm's production system is fixed or changeable. Workers in TNC operations in high-cost countries are considerably more vulnerable where they are directly competing against investments in low-cost countries, rather than being involved in different parts of the production process.

d) Passive differentiation

Finally, some TNCs essentially conform to host-country patterns of management. One important facet of wider globalization in recent years has been the creation and internationalization of monopolistic regulated firms, sometimes arising from the privatization of state-owned utilities such as electricity, sometimes from the internationalization of sectors such as food retail. Such firms do not internationalize in order to integrate their production systems but to conquer new markets. They may therefore not perceive it as in their interests to internationalize much of HRM.

Strategies vis-à-vis national employment systems

This section examines what strategies TNCs employ when engaging with national employment systems. While firms that seek to integrate their management internationally probably engage more, overall, in trying to shape the host-country employment systems they face, the position of this chapter is not to draw sharp distinctions between the four approaches outlined above (in reality, the same firm may be following different broad orientations to different extents in different parts of its operations). Because of this, although some of the strategies below are a closer match to some of the orientations above than others, there is not likely to be any neat correspondence.

a) Regime shopping

The term 'regime shopping' (Streeck, 1991) relates to the leverage that mobility of investment gives to TNCs over national employment systems. Unless the location of investment is tied to markets, TNCs are likely, all other things being equal, to locate in those countries where the employment system is most amenable. Presuming sufficient quality and productivity of labour can be found in places where labour is cheap and regulation is favourable to employers, this poses a threat to more labour-friendly employment systems. First, they are likely to receive less FDI, and large national firms may export employment, with consequent effects on employment levels. Second, as governments, employers' organizations and trade unions are aware of this threat, it is one source of pressure for employer-friendly 'reform'.

A variant of this sometimes occurs where individual new FDI projects are being negotiated. Host governments and trade unions may come under pressure to develop firm-level systems that might not be so open to domestic firms, in order to secure investment. No-strike agreements in Japanese TNCs in the United Kingdom (UK) in the 1980s were an example of this 'negotiated deviation' (Ackroyd et al., 1988; Innes and Morris, 1995).

TNCs following a variety of the broad approaches above are likely to indulge in regime shopping to some extent, at least where firms have genuine choices of location. It is likely to be least prevalent in firms following the passive differentiation approach, where internationalization typically has more to do with access to product markets than to labour markets.

b) Replication through functional equivalents

Following an integration approach – whether based on the country-of-origin policies or global 'best practice' – does not always mean directly copying HRM policies in each and every host country. Where senior corporate managers have a strong belief in the superiority of a particular system of management but its details are difficult to export, they may seek to export their overall philosophy of management rather than simply reproduce individual practices.

Again, large Japanese TNCs have provided examples here. While the Japanese company union system (Watanabe, 2018) is not directly translatable into European employment systems, a number of the Japanese auto manufacturers have sought to reach single-union 'sweetheart' deals (Innes and Morris, 1995), or to engage moderate unions in multi-union systems in continental Europe. The idea here is to replicate the company union idea of providing an employee voice without the potential for industrial conflict. Equally, Elger and Smith (2005) provide examples of Japanese firms seeking to find variants of the harsher employment systems typically used in subcontractors, using aspects of the UK employment system as resources.

c) 'Buying out' national systems

Workers do not compare TNCs employment systems with an idealized, textbook presentation of the host-country system (Almond, 2011). Rather, they typically compare the wages and working conditions on offer in TNCs with those of other employers in local labour markets. As many TNCs, through their size, have the capacity to pay higher wages than their local labour market competitors, it is possible to use this labour market power effectively to buy acquiescence to elements of the firm's 'global' system that might be seen as undesirable. In particular, paying wage premiums at least partly to avoid trade unions has historically been used by some of the largest US-owned TNCs.

d) Embedded reformer/innovator

Some TNCs actively engage with host-country systems on an institutional level in an attempt to reform them, or at least try to control their perceived negative effects. IBM, for example, while retaining a strict non-union approach where possible, has historically often sought to take senior positions in host-country employers' associations. In highly internationalized sectors, foreign TNCs collectively may come to dominate host-country sectors – for example, the UK and Spanish auto sectors are almost entirely dominated by foreign-owned firms. In smaller open economies such as Ireland, the weight of TNCs in the national economy means that they become powerful institutional as well as micro-level actors.

   This type of approach is likely to be followed mainly by TNCs with substantial sunk costs in host countries, and with localized supply chains.

e) Host system rebellion

A less sophisticated practice is simply to ignore perceived negative aspects of host employment systems. It is not difficult to find examples of TNCs that are prepared to break host-country labour law, often in the expectation that any punishment is likely to be relatively trivial. Royle's (1998, 2004) work on fast-food TNCs gives a number of examples in Europe.

   Far worse has frequently occurred in the developing world, particularly regarding union organization. Aside from moral reservations, such an approach obviously carries reputational risk, not only in host countries but also in some cases among consumers. This can be seen, for example, in the pressures on Nike (Locke et al., 2007) and more recently Apple (China Labor Watch, 2017) to improve the factory regimes among their Asian subcontractors.

f)　Whipsawing

Whipsawing has several dimensions. Often, it represents a form of 'home system rebellion' as opposed to the host system rebellion above; firms threaten to invest in lower-cost countries if home-country regulations are unfavourable or if trade unions organize. This is particularly likely in US firms, partly because of the problematic nature of trade union recognition campaigns in the US industrial relations system.

Whipsawing is, however, also used as a term to describe the more general process by which TNCs play different national subsidiaries off against each other, making 'coercive comparisons' (Marginson et al., 1995) and threatening plant closures if productivity fails to reach the levels achieved elsewhere. Greer and Hauptmeier (2016), focusing on the automobile industry, identify whipsawing as a staged competition designed to elicit concessions from unions.

It is plausible to argue that whipsawing, as well as a specific strategy, is a more general leitmotif of contemporary corporate internationalization. In particular, narratives around global competitiveness within as well as between TNCs have been widely deployed as a means of justifying forms of corporate change of otherwise questionable legitimacy. Vaara and Tienar (2008) explore how plant shutdowns are justified by reference to share prices, 'overcapacity' and 'restructuring'. In many countries, widespread deployment of such narratives has led to a degree of acceptance of large firms reducing employment or closing units down completely even where they remain profitable.

Case study: Performance management and industrial relations at AJB Inc.

AJB Inc. is a US-owned TNC in the heavy engineering sector. It has manufacturing operations in the United States, Mexico, Slovakia, China and India, as well as the UK, where it has two plants. Its US operations were originally established in the north of the United States, but for some time it has been moving operations to the southern United States, owing to lower wage costs and weaker trade unions in that part of the country. More recently, it has also moved to extend its Mexican operations. The firm has a history of conflictual industrial relations in the United States. Abroad, it has a corporate guideline of attempting to follow non-union HRM strategies where possible. Within the last 10 years, it has also moved towards tougher forms of

(Continued)

performance management: individual performance-related pay makes up an increasing proportion of salaries, following a forced distribution method which forces appraisers to rank 20 per cent of their employees in a 'poor' performing group. This group is, in countries where labour law permits it, eventually liable to dismissal.

The UK operations consist of one large plant, established in 1946, and a newer 'greenfield' site opened in the late 1980s. The larger plant, which also has an R&D facility, has always been strongly unionized, and retains collective bargaining for shopfloor workers. This has been questioned by HQ managers, but has been tolerated due to relatively high productivity levels. The newer, smaller plant is non-union. Managerial employees are part of a global managerial HRM system. A number of senior UK HRM managers objected to the new performance management mechanism, and have attempted to get around it by giving low performance rankings to individuals who were in any case about to leave the firm.

The UK operations have always served the European market. For many years, the UK subsidiary was the only plant servicing this market. The Slovakian plant, launched in 1994, originally handled the assembly of a different product range. More recently, however, the UK operations have had to compete with the Slovakian plant for replacement investment; wage costs in Slovakian manufacturing are 37 per cent of those in the UK. Additionally, reduced transportation costs mean that it is now possible to undertake some production aimed for the European market in China.

Leading subsidiary managers are partly remunerated on the global performance of the firm. Additionally, the US HQ has in recent years become more open to recruiting senior managers from overseas, and subsidiary managers compete intensely for these high-profile, well paid posts. At the same time, for many managers, and all non-managers, their fortunes remain tied to those of the UK operations. The need to increase productivity levels in order to compete with other subsidiaries with lower labour costs has been a constant feature of collective bargaining for some years. An enthusiastic pursuit of lean production has led to a significant reduction in the size of the manual workforce.

Questions

1. Would you describe AJB Inc. as 'responsive' to conditions in different host countries? Why?
2. What are the potential advantages and disadvantages of the TNC having a unified global performance management system, both for managers and for workers?
3. How is the existence of the Slovakian plant likely to affect industrial relations in the UK subsidiary?
4. Why might the TNC retain any production facilities in the United States or the UK, given the existence of nearby low-cost alternatives in Mexico or Slovakia?
5. What might be the implications of the firm's global non-union guidelines on collective negotiations in the UK?

Implications for employment relations and the role of context

TNCs present a clear challenge to labour and employment relations. It is not difficult to find cases of super-exploitation in developing countries, or of pressures for work intensification and against collective worker organization under the threat of offshoring or outsourcing to cheaper and/or less regulated destinations. Equally, the substantial presence of mobile foreign-owned firms in host economies can threaten the national solidarity on which more social-democratic industrial relations systems depend. It is important to properly situate and qualify this picture though. First, we look at the relationship between corporate and other forms of globalization and national employment systems. Second, we look at factors internal to the TNC itself.

National employment relations systems

It is sometimes difficult to disentangle the specific effects of TNCs from the wider pressures of neoliberal globalization. Workers, managers and ultimately trade unions, employer organizations and the state have increasingly been subject to internationalization in the contemporary period of globalization, in ways that go far beyond the direct effects of TNCs as employers. We have seen a rapid diffusion of ideas about what constitutes global 'best practice' in management, both through business schools and global consultancies. In HRM, such ideas typically constitute a combination of individualist market-oriented management ideas originally inspired by large non-union firms in the United States, and an interpretation of the lean production ideology of Japanese manufacturers (while the latter concept originated in manufacturing, it has since expanded to the service sector, including areas of activity as far removed from auto assembly as tax collection and enforcement; see Carter et al., 2011). While one may legitimately question how closely most firms' HR systems approximate to best-practice models, elements of the current global HRM orthodoxy have clearly extended beyond TNCs to domestic firms (the spread of appraisal-based performance management systems is an example here).

This means that managers and workers are often relatively familiar with 'foreign' ideas of management, even if they have no direct experience of working for TNCs. At a macro level, it has caused pressures on national employment systems to find ways of accommodating contemporary ideas of what constitutes good practice. This can be seen in widespread pressures to modify industrial relations systems in ways that make it easier to reduce demarcations between groups of workers, and more broadly to give individual firms increased autonomy over wage determination and other areas of HR practice through the decentralization of industrial relations systems (Glassner et al., 2011).

More broadly, one of the consequences of neoliberal globalization, sometimes neglected in the conventional discussion of home- and host-country effects in international HRM, is that host-country institutions are changing in nature. While employment regulations in the older industrialized economies once had as a primary function the preservation of a sometimes fragile peace between capital and labour, the globalization of production means that the focus of national economic policies has for some time been increasingly around ensuring international competitiveness (Cerny, 2000; Jessop, 1993). This creates further pressures on national business systems to recast themselves in the image of what might best attract the lead firms in global production networks.

This should not always mean convergence, however. This is in part because national employment regimes are to some degree 'path-dependent'; that is, the possible decisions available to contemporary policy-makers and industrial relations actors are shaped by decisions made at earlier points in history (Hyman, 1999). Additionally, where nations have advantages in particular areas of production that are institutionally derived – such as institutions that create high-skilled, adaptable and participative workforces – it is not logical to erode these advantages through deregulation (Sorge, 1991). Whether social actors in individual countries can find ways of creating competitiveness that avoid a 'race to the bottom' is contingent on national politics and the power resources of social actors (Almond and González Menéndez, 2006).

Equally, a discussion on TNCs and their employment practices should not neglect the efforts of global trade union alliances and others to prevent the worst cases of 'super-exploitation' through mechanisms such as global framework agreements (Bourguignon et al., 2019) and other means by which TNCs can be encouraged to develop at least some degree of corporate social responsibility as concerns labour (see Chapter 16 on regulation, Chapter 17 on trade unions internationally and Chapter 18 on sustainability issues).

Finally, it is important to avoid exaggerating the power of TNCs in each and every case by assuming that all location decisions are primarily made according to factors relating to human resources. This is very far from being the case. First, the availability of natural resources remains key to the location of some TNCs, the energy sector being the most obvious example. Second, and equally, the presence of infrastructure such as transport and communications, while declining as a factor owing to technological advances, remains significant in many cases. Third, it often remains necessary to be physically in a particular place to serve a market. While we are familiar with the fact that even service sector markets can now often be serviced from overseas, with potentially negative consequences for labour in high-cost countries (Flecker and Meil, 2010), this is not universally the case. For example, it is often not possible to access particular segments of health or defence markets in particular countries without operations in those countries. Fourth, although no less worrying from a social point of view, location decisions are often made in response to other elements of national regulation, such as planning and environmental laws or corporate taxation. In other words, in discussing how TNCs interact with national business and employment systems, their degree of locational flexibility is a variable, not a given.

The TNC and micro-politics

Both those using orthodox economic perspectives on TNCs and their more radical critics are often guilty of treating TNCs as monolithic entities with the power to make economically rational decisions from corporate headquarters and to impose them globally. To the extent that the corporate centre retains the capacity to shift or close production in a specific national operation, subsidiaries' staff power is intuitively less than global managers. Yet, local managers and local workers retain some power to interpret, accept, reject and modify policy shaped abroad.

What is accepted, rejected or modified is likely to depend partly on domestic ideas as to what is 'good' or 'fair' practice. For example, European managers are often highly resistant to forms of performance management currently practised in many US firms, particularly where these lead to either very large pay gaps between employees at the same hierarchical level, or to the threat of dismissal for those at the wrong end of 'forced distributions' (see Blume et al., 2009). Almond and Ferner's (2006) case studies of American firms in Europe show managerial resistance to these ideas, which was sometimes successful either in modifying the policy or ensuring that its full effects were not felt in particular national subsidiaries.

Managers at corporate headquarters do not always have the information-processing capacity to know what will work, or what will be interpreted as acceptable, in different national operations. This can give subsidiary managers and workers some degree of leverage in negotiating how 'global' policies will operate within their national operations.

Equally, for many subsidiary managers, their own careers and job security are intrinsically linked to the survival and success of their own national subsidiary unit(s). They will therefore seek to ensure that the national subsidiary is successful against its 'competitors' – which may be other national operations of the TNC rather than other firms. In doing so, to the extent that the various monitoring and control tools of the corporate HQ permit them to, they are likely to do whatever they think is likely to contribute to the success of the national operations

(Kristensen and Morgan, 2006). This may well include the use of practices and policies which are outside the scope of the global system.

Conclusion

TNCs cause pressures for change in HRM both through the specific ways in which they manage their international workforces, and through the more general pressures which emerge from international firms competing within neoliberal globalization. This chapter primarily focuses on the former, arguing that it is important to look at the circumstances and strategies of individual TNCs. This is because social actors in and around TNCs need to be able to distinguish between general justificatory discourses of neoliberal globalization and the actual margins of manoeuvre available in specific cases.

While mainstream approaches are not incorrect in analysing international HRM strategies in terms of the dichotomy between 'integration' and (host) 'responsiveness', such analysis often remains fairly superficial, and tends to downplay or ignore power dynamics. The first part of the chapter attempts to go further than such work in highlighting what exactly TNCs might choose to be 'responsive' to. We would highlight that much more attention should be paid to the various forms of 'offensive' responsiveness – that is, how TNCs seek to exploit differences in host employment systems.

We then outline various broad approaches that TNCs may have towards IHRM. These include integration on the basis of country-of-origin practices, integration through global 'best practices', active (or strategic) differentiation of practices between places and more passive differentiation. While again, unlike much of the conventional literature, we are not arguing that TNCs necessarily fit neatly into only one of these categories (probably most large TNCs follow more than one of these approaches for different operations or with regard to different areas of policy), it is nevertheless important to be able to distinguish what particular TNCs are attempting to do with regard to specific policies.

When examining specific strategies concerning interactions with national employment systems, we highlight the importance of a number of corporate methodologies: regime shopping, the use of functional equivalents, 'buying out' host systems, assuming governance roles in host countries, host system rebellion and whipsawing. Again, these should not be interpreted as mutually exclusive. The chapter then examines how some of these methods play through in national employment systems and in the micro-politics of the firm itself.

Broadly, it is difficult to argue with the proposal that TNCs act, as a whole, in ways that are challenging to the more labour-friendly elements of national employment systems. However, this has to be seen alongside other pressures for change in the global political economy, and should not be seen as eliminating social and political choices at national and international levels.

Reflective questions

1. Why might TNCs try to follow uniform HR policies across different national subsidiaries? Are there circumstances in which firms are more likely to want to differentiate policies between subsidiaries?
2. What pressures does the increased internationalization of production and service provision generate for (a) workers' representatives, such as trade unions, in subsidiary operations, and (b) national industrial relations systems?
3. What options are available to high-cost countries seeking to attract foreign direct investment?
4. Consider a national business and employment system with which you are familiar. How is it likely to shape the HRM strategies of foreign-owned TNCs?
5. What managerial mechanisms might a TNC need to have in place if it wanted to learn from its overseas operations on a global basis?
6. What kinds of firms have high levels of locational flexibility, and which have less? How might this affect the employment relations strategies of local management and trade unions?
7. What is meant by 'regime shopping' and what forms might it take?
8. The internationalization of production is often used as a resource by those arguing in favour of more liberal employment systems in high-cost countries. What kinds of counterarguments can be made against this type of argument?

Recommended reading

- Clibborn, S. (2019) 'The politics of employment relations in a multinational corporation during crisis'. *Economic and Industrial Democracy*, 40(3): 560–82.
- Dupuis, M. (2018) 'Crafting alternatives to corporate restructuring: Politics, institutions and union power in France and Canada'. *European Journal of Industrial Relations*, 24(1): 39–54.

(Continued)

- Edwards, T. and Kuruvilla, S. (2005) 'International HRM: National business systems, organizational politics and the international division of labour in MNCs'. *International Journal of Human Resource Management*, 16(1): 1–21.
- Ferner, A. M., Edwards, T. and Tempel, A. (2012) 'Power, institutions and the cross-national transfer of employment practices in multinationals'. *Human Relations*, 65(2): 163–87.
- Greer, I. and Doellgast, V. (2017) 'Marketization, inequality, and institutional change: Toward a new framework for comparative employment relations'. *Journal of Industrial Relations*, 59(2): 192–208.
- Pulignano, V., Tregaskis, O., Doerflinger, N. and Bélanger, J. (2018) 'The distinctiveness of employment relations within multinationals: Political games and social compromises within multinationals' subsidiaries in Germany and Belgium'. *Journal of Industrial Relations*, 60(4): 465–91.
- Woywode, M. (2002) 'Global management concepts and local adaptations: Working groups in the French and German car manufacturing industry'. *Organization Studies*, 23: 497–524.

References

Ackroyd, S., Burrell, G., Hughes, M. and Whitaker, A. (1988) 'The Japanization of British industry?' *Industrial Relations Journal*, 19(1): 11–23.

Almond, P. (2011) 'Re-visiting "country of origin" effects on HRM in multinational corporations'. *Human Resource Management Journal*, 21(3): 258–71.

Almond, P. and González Menéndez, M. (2006) 'Varieties of capitalism: The importance of political and social choices'. *Transfer*, 12(3): 407–26.

Bartlett, C. and Ghoshal, S. (1998) *Managing Across Borders: The Transnational Solution*, 2nd edn. London: Hutchinson.

Blume, B., Baldwin, T. and Rubin, R. (2009) 'Reactions to different types of forced distribution systems'. *Journal of Business and Psychology*, 24(1): 77–91.

Bourguignon, R., Garaudel, P. and Porcher, S. (2019) 'Global framework agreements and trade unions as monitoring agents in transnational corporations'. *Journal of Business Ethics*, online advanced publication.

Brewster, C., Wood, G. and Brookes, M. (2008) 'Similarity, isomorphism or duality? Recent survey evidence on the human resource management policies of multinational corporations'. *British Journal of Management*, 19(4): 320–42.

Carter, B., Danford, A., Howcroft, D., Richardson, H., Smith, A. and Taylor, P. (2011) '"All they lack is a chain": Lean and the new performance management in the British civil service'. *New Technology, Work and Employment*, 26(2): 83–97.

Cerny, P. (2000) 'Political globalization and the competition state'. In R. Stubbs and G. Underhill (eds), *Political Economy and the Changing Global Order*. Oxford: Oxford University Press, pp. 300–9.

China Labor Watch (2017) 'A year of regression in Apple's supply chain'. Available at: www.chinalaborwatch.org/upfile/2017_05_03/20170517.pdf.

Doremus, P., Keller, W., Pauly, L. and Reich, S. (1998) *The Myth of the Global Corporation*. Princeton, NJ: Princeton University Press.

Edwards, T. (1998) 'Multinationals, employment practices and the process of diffusion'. *International Journal of Human Resource Management*, 9(4): 696–709.

Edwards, T. and Kuruvilla, S. (2005) 'International HRM: National business systems, organizational politics and the international division of labour in MNCs'. *International Journal of Human Resource Management*, 16(1): 1–21.

Elger, T. and Smith, C. (2005) *Assembling Work: Remaking Factory Regimes in Japanese Multinationals in Britain*. Oxford: Oxford University Press.

Fagan, C., Hebson, G., Tavora, I. and Grimshaw, D. (2017) *Making Work More Equal: A New Labour Market Segmentation Approach*. Manchester: Manchester University Press.

Ferner, A. (1997) 'Country of origin effects and HRM in multinational companies'. *Human Resource Management Journal*, 7(1): 19–37.

Ferner, A. and Tempel, A. (2006) 'Multinationals and national business systems: A "power and institutions" perspective'. In P. Almond and A. Ferner (eds), *American Multinationals in Europe*. Oxford: Oxford University Press.

Flecker, J. and Meil, P. (2010) 'Organisational restructuring and emerging service value chains: Implications for work and employment'. *Work Employment and Society*, 24(4): 680–98.

Glassner, V., Keune, M. and Marginson, P. (2011) 'Collective bargaining in a time of crisis: Developments in the private sector in Europe'. *Transfer: European Journal of Labour Research*, 17(3): 303–22.

Greer, I. and Hauptmeier, M. (2016) 'Management whipsawing: The staging of labor competition under globalization'. *ILR Review*, 69(1): 29–52.

Gu, F. and Nolan, J. (2017) 'Performance appraisal in Western and local banks in China: The influence of firm ownership on the perceived importance of guanxi'. *International Journal of Human Resource Management*, 28(10): 1433–53.

Hayden, A. and Edwards, T. (2001) 'The erosion of the country of origin effect: A case study of a Swedish multinational company'. *Relations Industrielles/Industrial Relations*, 56(1): 116–40.

Hofstede, G. (1980) *Cultures Consequences: International differences in Work-Related Values*. Newbury Park, CA: Sage.

Hyman, R. (1999) 'National industrial relations systems and transnational challenges: An essay in review'. *European Journal of Industrial Relations*, 5(1): 89–110.

Innes, E. and Morris, J. (1995) 'Multinational corporations and employee relations: Continuity and change in a mature industrial region'. *Employee Relations*, 17(6): 25–42.

Jacoby, S. (1997) *Modern Manors: Welfare Capitalism since the New Deal*. Princeton, NJ: Princeton University Press.

Jessop, B. (1993) *Towards a Schumpeterian Workfare State? Preliminary Remarks on Post-Fordist Political Economy*. Lancaster: University of Lancaster.

Kristensen, P. and Morgan, G. (2006) 'The contested space of multinationals: Varieties of institutionalism, varieties of capitalism'. *Human Relations*, 59(11): 1467–90.

Locke, R., Qin, F. and Brause, A. (2007) 'Does monitoring improve labor standards? Lessons from Nike'. *Industrial and Labor Relations Review*, 61(1): 3–31.

Logan, J. (2002) 'Consultants, lawyers, and the "union free" movement in the USA since the 1970s'. *Industrial Relations Journal*, 33(3): 197–214.

Marginson, P., Armstrong, P., Edwards, P. and Purcell, J. (1995) 'Extending beyond borders: multinational companies and the international management of labour'. *International Journal of Human Resource Management*, 6(3): 702–19.

Muller-Camen, M., Almond, P., Gunnigle, P., Quintanilla, J. and Tempel, A. (2001) 'Between home and host country: Multinationals and employment relations in Europe'. *Industrial Relations Journal*, 32(5): 435–49.

Patel, P., Boyle, B., Bray, M., Sinha, P. and Bhanugopan, R. (2019) 'Global staffing and control in emerging multinational corporations and their subsidiaries in developed countries: Indian IT EMNCs in Australia'. *Personnel Review*, 48(4): 1022–44.

Prahalad, C. and Doz, Y. (1999) *The Multinational Mission: Balancing Local Demands and Global Vision*. New York: Free Press.

Pudelko, M. and Harzing, A. (2007) 'Country-of-origin, localization, or dominance effect? An empirical investigation of HRM practices in foreign subsidiaries'. *Human Resource Management*, 46(4): 535–59.

Royle, T. (1998) 'Avoidance strategies and the German system of co-determination'. *International Journal of Human Resource Management*, 9(6): 1026–47.

Royle, T. (2004) 'Employment practices of multinationals in the Spanish and German quick-food sectors: Low-road convergence?' *European Journal of Industrial Relations*, 10(1): 51–71.

Rubery, J. (2011) 'Institutionalizing the employment relationship'. In G. Morgan, J. Campbell, C. Crouch, O. Pedersen and R. Whitley (eds), *Oxford Handbook of Comparative Institutional Analysis*. Oxford: Oxford University Press, pp. 497–526.

Sorge, A. (1991) 'Strategic fit and the societal effect: Interpreting cross-national comparisons of technology, organization and human resources'. *Organization Studies*, 12(2): 161–90.

Streeck, W. (1991) 'More uncertainties: German unions facing 1992'. *Industrial Relations*, 30(3): 317–49.

Streeck, W. and Thelen, K. (2005) *Beyond Continuity: Institutional Change in Advanced Political Economies*. Oxford: Oxford University Press.

Telljohann, V., da Costa, I., Rehfeldt, U. and Zimmer, R. (2009) 'European and international framework agreements: New tools of transnational industrial relations'. *Transfer: European Review of Labour Research*, 15(3–4): 505–25.

Tempel, A. (2001) *The Cross-National Transfer of Human Resource Management Practices in German and British Multinational Companies*. Munich: Rainer Hampp Verlag.

Vaara, E. and Tienar, J. (2008) 'A discursive perspective on legitimation strategies in multinational corporations'. *Academy of Management Review*, 33(4): 985–93.

Watanabe, H. R. (2018) 'The political agency and social movements of Japanese individually-affiliated unions'. *Economic and Industrial Democracy*, published online 24 January. Available at: (accessed).

Whitley, R. (1999) *Divergent Capitalisms: The Social Structuring and Change of Business Systems*. Oxford: Oxford University Press.

World Investment Report (2011) *World Investment Report 2011: Non-Equity Modes of International Production and Development*. New York: UNCTAD.

Woywode, M. (2002) 'Global management concepts and local adaptations: Working groups in the French and German car manufacturing industry'. *Organization Studies*, 23: 497–524.

3 Continuities and change in national employment relations: the role of politics and ideas

Miguel Martínez Lucio

Learning objectives

- To understand the nature of employment relations and their relevance to a discussion of work, employment and management in a global context
- To understand the different tensions that develop within employment relations
- To appreciate the different reasons why employment relations systems vary by country
- To understand the changing nature of employment relations due to the development of globalization
- To appreciate the ways that regulation continues to play a role at work

Introduction

This chapter looks at how the national level of state intervention in employment relations and its general regulation by national bodies such as trade unions is changing and with what consequences (see Chapter 17 on trade unions internationally). The way employment relations have been regulated varies by country and depends on a range of factors. These factors will be discussed in relation to some of the leading – and seminal – work in the area of employment relations. Within these contributions the term *industrial relations* is often used rather than *employment relations*, and although there may be some debate over whether these terms are directly interchangeable, the chapter will use either or both at different points as appropriate. This is an area of study with a long history. The chapter will therefore start by referencing some classic texts before it looks at more contemporary approaches.

The nature of our employment and the way we work within organizations are influenced by a range of factors such as the sector in which we work, the level or part of the organization we work in (e.g. local plant or national offices) and the type of job we do within that context. However, the place where we work and its specific geographical location also play a fundamental role in terms of the rights and regulations that govern our employment. *This chapter will outline how these differences are explained within the academic community that studies them.* National systems and contexts range from those that have more stable employment and emphasize the rights of workers in determining and influencing the nature of their work and how they are remunerated, through to those where work is more volatile and where workers are more vulnerable to being mistreated and denied basic employment, and even human, rights.

Having discussed the factors that lead to these differences, we will then move on to discuss how national systems of employment relations are being put under pressure by the process of globalization yet continue to evolve and play a role. Changes associated with globalization are placing significant pressure on the more organized and worker-oriented systems of employment relations. The ability of capital to relocate to low-cost and more 'amenable' systems places a strain on the more organized and regulated systems of employment and work. The chapter will next proceed to argue that these developments do not lend themselves to a simple interpretation, and that governments, state agencies and trade unions remain important in mediating and shaping the way that these changes take place. In addition, governments and trade unions as organizations, while having primarily been locked into national systems of employment relations, are actually creating new global links and share a range of practices across borders to engage with and challenge increasingly internationalized capitalist processes. The chapter will end by focusing on these dynamics and new forms of transnational engagement and thematic broadening by workers and the organizations linked to them.

Types of national employment relations system and state intervention at work

The way we work and are employed entails rules and obligations for both the employer and the worker. The nature, extent and effectiveness of these rules and obligations vary in relation to their context and the different legacies of struggle over worker rights. Why these rules and obligations have evolved the way they have is the subject of discussion, and the reason for their ongoing change is often the topic of significant argument. Why are some workers paid according to collective agreements agreed by trade unions and their employer when, in another sector or national context, working conditions are imposed by employers alone? What determines how working conditions are affected by the legal frameworks developed by governments and why do they vary greatly?

There is no doubt that the extent of economic development is a factor. There was once a dominant view that a strong correlation exists between the economic status and development of a country, and the role of negotiations, dialogue and state enforcement of the social features of work (Kerr et al., 1960). The process of industrialism and development was once seen as an inevitable development that would lead to a unified or homogenous model of economic activity and regulation. At the heart of these general theories is the assumption that a move to common organizational structures and processes, driven by technological developments, will lead to a homogenous set of outcomes (see Lane, 1989, for a discussion) (see Chapter 14 on technology and the organization of production).

However, the link between economic and technological development, on the one hand and the evolution of employment systems on the other, may not always be enough to explain the factors leading up to a situation where a country 'can afford' social rights. First, the manner in which a nation has developed may have involved the subjugation of rights of other nations in its imperialist past. For example, the United Kingdom (UK) developed in the 19th century not just because of its industrial progress and 'innovative' culture, but also because of its exploitation of colonies such as India and Malaysia in terms of their human and non-human resources. Many employment relations and human resource management (HRM) studies ignore this colonial and historical legacy, which explains the existence of very different sets of resources underpinning the development of countries and their systems of employment relations.

Second, there are significant levels of variation between countries with broadly similar economic levels in terms of the extent of worker rights and forms of representation in relation to their work and employment. The United States has fewer collectivist traditions and weaker trade unions than Germany, for example, yet both are located in a superior position in global economic terms. In Latin America, regulation in terms of collective bargaining is more significant in Argentina compared with its neighbour Chile (Ugarte, 2012), but both share a fairly similar economic heritage. Hence, political and historical factors, rather than purely economic considerations, may explain the differences between national systems.

Understanding regulation and rule-making: consensus and conflict in employment relations

The institutionalist and pluralist tradition of academic research in the area of employment has focused on the role of explicit rules and regulations that evolve over time and play a part in establishing a framework of expectations and behaviour. The argument here is that collective bargaining – the joint regulation through processes of negotiation between stakeholders on issues such as pay and other working conditions – is the main focus of 'industrial relations' (the term used at the time): see Poole's (1981) discussion of Clegg (1976). Variations in certain dimensions were seen to be a major influence on the substantive outcomes of industrial relations (Poole, 1981) – for example, the extent of collective bargaining (how many workers are covered), its scope (what is negotiated and dealt with), the nature of trade union involvement (the precise role of worker representatives) and the main level at which agreements are signed (at the national or local level, for example). However, in addition to state intervention, these variations are also the outcome of employer and management attitudes, which play a part in shaping the nature of employment regulation in the face of worker representation (see Clegg, 1976). Much of this tradition draws, in part, from the work of the American labour economist, John Dunlop, who emphasized the role of rule maintenance and order within industrial relations: see Rogowski (2000) for a discussion.

In Dunlop's view, the specific character of industrial relations systems derived, to an extent, from the broader forms of rule-making independent of decision-making in the economic system. While environmental factors – such as the nature of the economy, society and polity – contribute to the development of industrial relations, one must also appreciate that the processes of rule maintenance may become autonomous over time. Hence, while countries may differ in part due to the nature of economic development, the evolution, stability and complexity of rules and traditions governing the relations between unions and managers, for example, are also the outcome of political processes and influence whether the consensus between them is forged or not.

Broader political perspectives within political science and industrial relations have looked at the role of national level negotiation structures as key factors in shaping the nature of industrial relations. Such approaches have been dominant in the debates on corporatism that are concerned with macro- and national-level negotiations between governments (and their state agencies), employers and trade unions. Some of the more rule-based and negotiation-based national systems of industrial relations tend to include significant dialogue at the national level, which subsequently frames local discussions in terms of the content of bargaining and its general essence. The role of the state can be such that it is able to create a national framework or degree of coordination regarding how industrial relations are conducted locally: it does this by establishing initiatives on pay, training, and health and safety. This can be achieved to some extent through legislation, for example, but the state can also achieve its aims through some form of political exchange and bargaining that allows unions and employers' associations to be represented and to interact with governments (Schmitter, 1974).

Some of the strongest systems of industrial relations appear to be linked to and combined with extensive forms of state-level dialogue (commonly called 'societal corporatism'). Lehmbruch (1984) argued that one could detect stronger systems of corporatist engagement in Nordic European countries; in others, such as the UK, systems of corporatist engagement have been weaker, with dialogue being more sporadic and often associated with key crisis-related issues. More recently, Vandenberg and Hundt (2012) argued that corporatism, generally speaking, has remained significant in some contexts, such as South Korea and Sweden – although they point to the importance of new forms of broader alliances and types of cooperation of a more flexible and focused manner, thus suggesting changes are taking place.

From a more critical and radical perspective, Hyman (2010) argued that these institutional forms have increasingly focused on reactive responses to economic crisis and change (see also Avdagic et al., 2005), thus suggesting that we are seeing a weakening of some of the stronger corporatist traditions. Nonetheless, Marxist and other radical, critical academic strands argue that the pluralist- and institutionalist-oriented view of work and employment can ignore the fact that there may be an inherent instability within employment and industrial relations due to the nature of power and the imbalances between actors and classes. Employers and the state, it is argued, are constantly trying to limit or impose conditions on the development of trade unions and worker rights, or to contain them in a variety of ways. In citing Allen (1966), Hyman (1975: 192) argued that so-called forms of dialogue between employers and workers may result in only piecemeal gains for workers, and do not question the uneven nature of power relations between them. Hence, attempts to institutionalize and bureaucratize labour organizations, as in the case of corporatist approaches, cannot always contain the tensions between workers and management in terms of their competing interests. Panitch (1981) argued that this instability undermines the long-term incorporation of unions due to the way workplace-based trade union activists challenge constraints imposed from above on wages and working conditions generally. Thus national institutional arrangements may also lead to tensions within unions between their leaders and activists on the ground (Panitch, 1981).

The attempt to frame and institutionalize such relations is therefore never complete and stable. Even the use by employers and the state of the notion of the 'national interest' to counter industrial and class conflict and to generate a 'common interest' between workers and employers, as seen in the context of corporatist discourses, may not be able to override such structural tensions. Thus some Marxists consider such 'common interests' to be not only illusory, but also a smokescreen that conceals class conflict (see Panitch, 1981) – especially as the state, in some cases, simultaneously tries to incorporate social actors while also coercing them at certain points (Hyman, 1975: 144). Differences between national forms of employment relations may therefore be explained in terms of the nature of these ongoing struggles between capital and labour, the balance of forces between them and the way that the state intervenes and tries to control the rule-making processes by using political ideologies (e.g. through an emphasis on the notion of social dialogue or the national interest) or through coercion (e.g. the use of the police or even the armed forces during strikes). The state also frames and constrains the focus of industrial and employment relations by allowing trade unions to engage with particular worker-related issues, such as pay, but not always other deeper aspects of industrial control, for example (Hyman, 1975).

Difference and variety in employment relations: institutions in context

While we can outline the general developments and variations in terms of the balance between consensus and coercion, between union-oriented and employer- or state-led industrial relations, and between centralized (corporatist) and decentralized systems of employment relations, there is still a great deal more that defines differences in terms of the nature of employment relations. There are qualitative differences in the extent of worker influence on the social and economic systems of a society (welfare approaches versus those driven by economic or wage considerations), and in the manner in which employment relations actors have a broader social and political role. Even within what appear to be common national contexts at similar stages of development, historical factors and the nature of political development may provide different patterns of representation and regulation. Since the early 1990s – especially with the impact of the comparative research agenda and a growing realization that the British and US models are exceptional and not representative as models of industrial relations – a new focus on attempting to understand how industrial relations systems develop has emerged (hence the attempt to broaden the terminology, as we have noted in this chapter in terms of the use of 'employment relations').

A dominant stream of analysis is the 'varieties of capitalism' debate, which has been pivotal to contemporary understandings of why there is variation in systems of employment relations and regulation in general (Hall and Soskice, 2001; see Chapter 11 on varieties of capitalism). This has become an important addition to the debate on comparative approaches to the topic (for a discussion of this approach see Hyman, 2004; Wailes et al., 2011). The argument rests on the assumption that there are significant variations within capitalism, and that we need to be aware of the different dimensions constituting patterns of regulation and economic management. It is argued that history and the role of institutions are fundamental to the development of capitalist systems of regulation, and that the different dimensions of these systems link and relate to each other in ways that create a consistent system and pattern of development. The dimensions this model refers to are, for example:

- the nature of corporate governance and its structure
- how traditions of cooperation and competition have developed
- the role of voice mechanisms and regulatory processes
- the role of vocational training and education as a key feature of the labour market

These have been developed and linked in two different patterns of development: the liberal market economy (LME) and the coordinated market economy (CME). The attraction of such theories is that the nature of employment regulation is sustained by – and sustains – different ways in which capitalism is coordinated. Hence, centralized and worker-oriented systems of employment regulation with stronger trade unions tend to fit with long-term, training-oriented, participative and welfare-driven economies, of which Sweden affords a good example (see Chapter 4 on pay, Chapter 9 on training and Chapter 13 on restructuring). On the other hand, LMEs such as that of the United States tend to link a profit-driven, shareholder and low-regulation culture with a more individualized and less trade union oriented system of employment relations. Put simply:

- LMEs are, in general, market- and competition-oriented with a weaker state role and set of regulatory structures, the emphasis being on risk taking and a less regulated approach to business.
- CMEs, in general, have a greater state role and stronger culture of regulation, whether joint regulation with organized labour, association-based regulation in terms of employers' associations and similar bodies, and/or a greater role for public and quasi-public bodies in areas such as worker training.

However, while highly attractive to many commentators, some question the relevance of the model to developing economies, tending to view it as being more relevant to developed OECD countries. There is also concern with the model regarding its institutional determinism and obsession with questions of coordination and institutional relations (Kang, 2006). Furthermore, developing economies that exhibit a more coordinated set of features may, nevertheless, not systematically involve trade unions or other social organizations concerned with worker rights in state-level dialogue (see Chapter 8 on developing economies). However, the approach based on the varieties of capitalism seems to have become dominant in the comparative study of employment relations.

Similar approaches have emerged in discussions of national business systems (Whitley, 2007), which also see relations within and across organizations and broader institutions as being important. These focus on the nature of ownership structures, non-ownership relations and employment relations generally:

- *Ownership relations*: the means of ownership, the nature of ownership integration and production chains, ownership in relation to sector boundaries and the extent of coordination
- *Non-ownership relations*: the extent of alliances and coordination across and within production chains, the extent of collaboration and support between competitors, the extent of alliance coordination across sectors around common interests
- *Employment relations and the management of work*: employer–employee relations and interdependence, the extent of mutual trust and the delegation of work and decision-making

These systems will vary across countries and types of capitalism. In some cases of a more organized and state-led nature, the ownership of firms may be more coordinated, meaning they tend to be less restricted by short-term financial interests, built on a complex, mutually beneficial and sustained network of alliances and interests and engaged more fully in a dialogue with stakeholders, such as trade unions, or built on 'trust', as some would argue in the case of Germany since the end of the Second World War. One interesting point to note is that the varieties of capitalism and national business systems approaches do not solely highlight the extent of employment rights and regulation as an important set of features within any understanding of capitalism (and economic systems). Also notable are the significant role of the nature of employer cultures (that is, whether there is a proclivity towards collectivism, labour representation and an acceptance of social rights and collective welfare), the significance of training within the system and how broader stakeholders such as trade unions become involved in training.

Ideology and context: national sensitivities and politics

National systems of employment relations vary, providing a variety of constraints and possibilities in terms of those who participate in the representation and management of work. We cannot ignore the significance of specific and context-related issues, and how they evolve over time (see Hyman, 2001, and his discussion of Ross, 1981). Hyman (2001) argues that this is a major dimension that has often been ignored by analysts. The reason why some issues are significant in one context and not in another could be because political debates and national discussion viewpoints and sensitivities arise that are particular to a national or local context (Locke and Thelen, 1995). Certain issues related to work and employment may be viewed and understood as a specific constraint or challenge in one context but not in another. In France, for example, the debates on working time link to a much broader view of how workers are meant to work and live: the role of legislation and national discussion is, among other factors, important in how this issue has been framed and compared to other cases (Lehndorff, 2014). The outcomes of changes to working time may have been ambivalent in France, but it is noticeable how particular themes are central to a specific country's employment relations debates and regulations when compared to other countries. Certain reforms may be seen as 'positive' or 'negative' by different groups, given their sensitivity and importance within political discourses. Another example of a specific focus to national debates is that of Spain, where the supposed cost of dismissing workers has been a core aspect of the political concerns within employment relations. For example, employers have considered the cost of dismissals in terms of payments to their workers to be prohibitively high, and they argue it has limited their hiring of workers. However, trade unions have counterargued that such costs have not, in fact, stopped employers from creating one of the highest levels of unemployment in Europe since the early 1980s; increasingly, many workers are being put on short-term and precarious contracts, so the idea that employers cannot easily fire people is questionable (Fernández González and Martínez Lucio, 2013). These types of national sensitivity are what Locke and Thelen (1995) referred to when developing the notion of 'contextualized comparisons': in discussing national systems, we must be aware of these specific 'national concerns and debates' that frame the ways national approaches to work and employment issues develop. These specific debates and themes are the way that the underlying tensions outlined in earlier sections play themselves out within a particular national context. MacKenzie and Martínez Lucio (2014) have argued that regulation and its politics are therefore also underpinned by cultural and ideological factors. For example, the Glasgow Media Group (1976) studied the way that work-related and trade union issues were covered by the media in the UK, pointing to the bias against trade unions and their roles which was used by right-wing political interests to undermine collective worker voice.

Furthermore, it is important to recognize how political ideas and discourses concerning work and employment are developed in different ways across countries by a range of actors. Morgan and Hauptmeier (2021) argue that, along with institutional factors, we need to appreciate a range of developments in relation to ideas, and how these can shape the approaches to regulation and deregulation, for example. In a comparison of Germany and the United States, they point to the extent to which unions and employers are influential, the extent of partisanship and political positions regarding relevant knowledge on work and employment, the way expertise is mobilized, and the way ideas are represented and mobilized in relation to political leaders by a range of actors such as think tanks (Morgan and Hauptmeier, 2021). For example, the role of lobbying and specific partisan ideas about deregulation have been central to the American political approach to employment relations compared to the situation in Germany (Morgan and Hauptmeier, 2021).

It is therefore important to widen the remit of analysis by engaging with a range of representative actors (Heery and Frege, 2006) and adopting an approach to employment relations as a set of regulatory spaces (see MacKenzie and Martínez Lucio, 2005, for a discussion of the concept; see Chapter 16 on transnational regulation). There are 'direct' actors (for example, trade unions, management and government) and action-based 'indirect' actors who engage in voice-shaping in terms of influencing specific instances of participation and representation (for example, law firms engaged with assisting 'union-busting', or aiding trade unions through the provision of specific advice in relation to bargaining) and policy-facing indirect actors who attempt to frame the debates on questions of representation and voice (for a review of comparative approaches to studying worker voice in HRM and employment relations, see González Menéndez and Martínez Lucio, 2020).

Hence, in understanding why systems differ, we need to work on a range of levels. We need to be sensitive to the ways that systems are coordinated and how the different spheres link together, and how tensions in employment relations are framed. The way that interests are represented is central, and this can be done through a variety of institutional and cultural processes. The following case study on industrial democracy and the control of pension funds shows how national contexts of employment relations influence specific features of employment and HRM development: in this case, it concerns worker engagement at the corporate level in countries such as Germany and the United States.

Case study: Industrial democracy and the control of pension funds

The way workers and their representatives participate strategically within firms can vary according to the system of employment relations and the extent of worker rights as enshrined within legislation. The tendency to limit worker roles and rights in relation to collective bargaining more generally means that a voice at the level of a corporate board – for some, termed 'industrial democracy' – is tokenistic at best, but not uncommon. Foley (2014) has argued that industrial democracy reflects specific legal and historical traditions, as is seen in countries such as Germany. Germany is viewed as a more coordinated market economy in which there has been a tendency to involve worker directors as part of corporate decision-making processes, although their influence is relatively constrained – the power ultimately resting with the core shareholders and senior management. The Nordic context of Europe, and countries such as the Netherlands and Germany, have developed a strategic worker voice within their corporate business structures that reflects not just the influence of organized labour but also a belief in the importance of dialogue between employers, trade unions and the state on a range of issues (sometimes referred to as 'social dialogue').

An example of recent developments in terms of industrial participation and democracy has been the drive to extend worker influence within the managing of company pension funds. This interest has been emerging for some time due to the highly significant role of such funds within national economies. Since the 1980s, there has been a growing interest in the way pension funds are regulated so as to ensure a greater level of ethical economic investment and greater restrictions on corporate malpractice, due to the increasing abuse of such funds by senior managers and others (Clark, 1998). There has been growing interest in the European Union, for example, in the 'taming' of 'pension fund capitalism' through various legislative changes and the expanding of trade union roles within pension fund regulation. These developments are not solely visible in coordinated market economies, although differences in established forms of employment regulation do seem to be important in shaping approaches (Ebbinghaus and Wiß, 2011). Yet, historically, the attempt to extend the voice of workers and their organizations into such emerging and significant spheres of the economy has been hampered by the demands of financial regulations that exist with regard to the need to generate stable long-term investments for company-based pension schemes and the recipients of those pensions. Furthermore, ethical concerns as to where to place investments and how to use such pension funds more socially can lead to significant corporate resistance when these are seen to limit the profitability and success of such funds: hence, in some cases, the legislation may ask for a greater worker voice within such pension fund management systems while also restricting how

(Continued)

this voice can influence the use of such large investment holdings. Historically, this tension was clear in the United States, where financial regulations and corporate influence restrained the voice of labour within such structures, although this was not the case in the neighbouring North American context of Canada, where greater union control was facilitated (McCarthy, 2014).

The extension of worker voice into the corporate processes of decision-making and in the broader areas of pension fund management has become an important part of the regeneration of industrial democracy and an alternative way of managing the economy (see Chapter 18 on sustainability for a broader discussion of such ethical issues in general). However, there is a need to understand how different systems of employment relations – their coordinated versus liberal nature – may mediate the extent of worker influence in them.

Questions

1. Why has there been an interest in developing greater worker influence within pension funds?
2. What role can industrial democracy play in sustaining a more balanced form of economic system?
3. What may contribute to the variable development of such processes across countries such as the United States and Germany?
4. What are the main hurdles facing the development of a greater degree of industrial democracy and worker influence more broadly in the management of pension funds and other forms of investment?

Globalization, the crisis of employment relations at the national level and the reinvention of the state and regulation

There is a view that the regulatory capacity of national systems of employment relations is declining. According to some observers, the role of the state at the national level has been diminishing due to the impact of multinational corporations (MNCs) and the 'forces' of globalization (Hyman, 2001). Chapter 16 outlines how systems of regulation have been placed under pressure and how state-regulated employment has been steadily undermined. These changes emerge as a result of a range of developments that are challenging joint regulation, worker representation and nationally embedded systems of regulation. These changes were outlined in a seminal and prophetic text that – nearly 30 years ago – foresaw the process of disorganization confronting the once organized and regulated systems of employment relations of developed economies in the late 20th century. The nature of the changes, seen through the eyes of Lash and Urry (1987: 5–6), related to factors such as: the decline of closed national economies as they face greater internationalization, which in turn undermines the institutional processes of national systems of employment relations; the changing nature of the workforce in terms of new, individualized interests and new forms of social organization beyond traditional trade unions; challenges to collective bargaining and traditional forms of regulation; increased global competition leading to a downward effect on worker rights; and a greater number of decentralized systems of service delivery/production. Thompson (2013) has further argued that the increasing financialization of capitalism has generated a form of disconnected capitalism that leads to even greater limits on the ability of companies and their senior managers to overcome the increasing demands for short-term profits and immediate economic gains, thus limiting the space for involvement and dialogue with workers and other social stakeholders.

The argument in the current context would be that, regardless of the debate about coordinated versus liberal market economies, the pressure on coordinated and regulated systems has been increasing. Thus there has been a shift from an interventionist and collective system of capitalism to a more market-oriented, flexible and unstable context. However, the supposed march to a new market and neoliberal world was, in Lash and Urry's (1987) view, not to be seen as straightforward and without problems (something they effectively predicted). The argument they presented was premised on the view that the new, disorganized capitalism would vary, or could only make sense, if viewed in relation to how national systems had initially been organized in terms of, for example, the structure of capital, the role of the state and regulation and the nature of management systems. Furthermore, Lash and Urry (1987) argued trade unions would have a new set of opportunities presented to them: much would depend on their strategic responses and use of resources. It could be argued that trade unions have not been found lacking since then in terms of imagination and an innovative approach to renewing their roles (see Murray, 2017; see also Chapter 17 on trade unions internationally). In fact, some prophetically took the concept of disorganization to be a potentially positive development and an opportunity that had the potential to mobilize a new, open form of worker politics based on a more flexible approach (Daly, 1991). Such developments can be seen in the Occupy movements of the post-2008 crisis, and new radical voices and actors within a range of migrant and vulnerable workers who have been creating a range of networks and innovative worker organizations (Alberti and Però, 2018; Atzeni, 2010). While some have argued that current employment relations increasingly seem to be a fragmented patchwork of collective and individual systems of regulation (Bechter et al., 2019) reflecting greater deregulation and neoliberal developments (Baccaro and Howell, 2017), both established and new forms of representation within work and employment continue to play a variety of important roles. Moreover, the focus of employment relations has extended itself into a range of broader social and employment issues, as seen in the reconfiguration of health and safety issues at work, around which trade unions have mobilized extensively in many countries (see Stewart et al., 2009; Martínez Lucio, 2020).

Trade unionists are engaging in such practices as networking, benchmarking and shared learning as ways of responding to the impact of globalization and change. New practices, such as organizing workers through innovative forms of mobilization, have been disseminated by transnational union alliances and attempts have been made to create new forms of regulation within and across MNCs (see Chapter 17 on transnational forms of trade unionism). In addition, the internet has facilitated a greater degree of grassroots dialogue between trade unionists and workplace representatives across the world, and labour campaigns are being coordinated through such forms of new media and communications (Hogan et al., 2010; Geelan and Hodder, 2017; Walker, 2014). The future will be about how national systems of regulation and national social organizations such as trade unions and social movements related to work link national contexts together and create synergies and networks in an ever more globalized world.

The social role of the state and the various bodies engaged in employment relations such as unions are not the passive recipients or victims of the changes discussed above; they can, actually, reshape these changes. If anything, we have seen nation-states moving to new forms of intervention within work and employment (Martínez Lucio and MacKenzie, 2004; see Chapter 16 on regulation). The state – even when it is 'falling over backwards' to attract international investment and to 'prepare' local contexts for further involvement from MNCs – has to consider matters of social infrastructure and to ensure a regulated orderly space (Panitch, 1994). In addition, the state may reinvent itself in a variety of ways (Martínez Lucio and MacKenzie, 2006) by working alongside other 'social partners' in the processes of re-regulation of worker rights and roles to ensure that employers are compliant with regard to guaranteeing worker rights in some manner (see Chapter 8 on developing economies and Chapter 16 on transnational regulation). It is for this reason that students of the subject must constantly bear in mind the role of the political dimension of these questions (Jessop, 2002). There are various ways the state intervenes, and these suggest that globalization does not lead to any singular outcome at the national level. On the one hand, we have seen a move in some cases to what Jessop (2002: 276) called Schumpeterian workfare post-national regimes – for example, in contexts where the state uses its authority and resources to ensure that labour markets and their workforce are 'supplied' through a form of 'market mediated exploitation'. In such an approach, the state coerces workers into the labour market through 'welfare to work' programmes and other disciplinary approaches that ensure a workforce that can be utilized by employers in more coercive manner at lower wage rates (see the case study in Chapter 14 on technology and the organization of production). Yet, on the other hand, the state and regulation remain important (Ritchie, 2002), and the state's coordination of different regulatory processes is significant (Torfing, 1990) across a broader set of more socially engaged roles. The state can begin to play new roles based on coaxing organizations towards certain social or economic ends. The state may 'prompt' management into new social and worker-oriented approaches to work based on 'networking and the development of new forms of knowledge sharing and collaboration' (Martínez Lucio and Stuart, 2011: 3661–71). So, the state can play a variety of direct and indirect roles. In some cases, as in China (Cooke, 2011), the state may have a directive and centralized approach, but it is still compelled to propagate and disseminate practices and ideas about new ways of working or new forms of management. In effect, the state and regulation remain important – although in what form and for what purpose are matters of context and politics.

Conclusion

This chapter links to the book's opening discussion of globalization by focusing on the changing roles of national employment relations systems. National spaces remain an important dimension, continuing to refract and provide meaning to the processes of globalization and change as a result of the balance of forces between employers and workers, the way that institutional relations have been constructed and how practices such as collective bargaining have been established and developed.

First, we need to be alert to the basic tensions and relations that exist in the realm of work in a context where employers and workers are divided by the fact that the latter are forced to sell their labour to the former. This basic tension and how it is resolved must always be present in any analysis. Second, we need to understand how interests and organizations have evolved in terms of the extent of dialogue or conflict on various work-related issues, such as training or working hours, for example. However, how systems cope with differences and antagonisms through complex and locally specific institutional processes is an important dimension in explaining their diversity. Third, it is this history of conflict, compromises and reflection that also contributes to understandings and cultures of regulation. The role of ideas and cultural approaches to employment relations are important as well, as they can shape the way regulatory change develops.

Furthermore, the chapter has pointed to the fact that the state and regulation remain important, and that institutions and organizations can to some extent reinvent themselves significantly in a context where new economic demands are made. Even where market relations and greater employer flexibility have emerged, the state and social organizations such as trade unions or similar social bodies are still vital to sustainable and socially oriented development, and – importantly – dealing with the problems that emerge from the processes of economic disorganization outlined earlier. The nature of regulation may shift, but it will not simply disappear, especially as the state has to respond to the negative outcomes of economic crisis and change (Rubery, 2011). Globalization is not a clear trajectory which somehow dismembers all that exists in terms of national traditions. It brings new issues and new organizations into the arena of employment relations. It is also shaped by the way established institutions in the form of the state, or trade unions, social movements and even employer organizations themselves, respond and develop reflexive policies and strategies. This corresponds to the views on globalization of Hirst and Thompson (1999, 2009), who show how globalization has developed in relation to established hierarchies and power relations. Hence, the idea that globalization and increasing marketization give rise to a weaker or more neoliberal system of employment relations and work organization is not straightforward. What we see instead is a new transnational politics and re-engagement with regulation at various levels (a theme picked up in Chapter 16 on transnational regulation and Chapter 17 on international trade unionism).

Reflective questions

1. Why is there a tension between employers and workers?
2. Why do national systems of employment relations differ from each other?
3. What role do political strategies and ideas play in framing concerns at work?
4. What are the main ways in which the state and trade unions influence the conduct of employment relations and how are these roles changing?

Recommended reading

- Cooke, F. L. (2011) 'The role of the state and human resource management in China'. *International Journal of Human Resource Management*, 22(18): 3830–48.

- Hyman, R. (2001) 'Trade unions and cross-national comparison'. *European Journal of Industrial Relations*, 7(2): 203–32.
- MacKenzie, R. and Martínez Lucio, M. (2005) 'The realities of regulatory change: Beyond the fetish of deregulation'. *Sociology*, 39(3): 499–517.
- Morgan, G. and Hauptmeier, M. (2020) 'The social organization of ideas in employment relations'. *Industrial and Labor Relations Review*, 74(3): 773–97.

References

Alberti, G. and Però, D. (2018) 'Migrating industrial relations: migrant workers' initiative within and outside trade unions'. *British Journal of Industrial Relations*, 56(4): 693–715.

Allen, V. (1966) *Militant Trade Unions*. London: Merlin.

Atzeni, M. (2010) *Workplace Conflict: Mobilization and Solidarity in Argentina*. Hampshire: Springer.

Avdagic, S., Rhodes, M. and Visser, J. (2005) *The Emergence and Evolution of Social Pacts: A Provisional Framework for Comparative Analysis*, Working Paper N-05-01 (EUROGOV).

Baccaro, L. and Howell, C. (2017) *Trajectories of Neoliberal Transformation: European Industrial Relations since the 1970s*. Cambridge: Cambridge University Press.

Bechter, B., Braakmann, N. and Brandl, B. (2019) 'Variable pay systems and/or collective wage bargaining? Complements or substitutes?' *ILR Review*, 74(2): 443–69.

Clark, G. L. (1998) 'The anatomy of corruption: The practice of pension fund trustee decision making'. *Environment and Planning A*, 30(7): 1235–53.

Clegg, H. (1976) *Trade Unionism under Collective Bargaining*. Oxford: Oxford University Press.

Cooke, F. L. (2011) 'The role of the state and human resource management in China'. *International Journal of Human Resource Management*, 22(18): 3830–48.

Daly, G. (1991) 'The discursive construction of economic space'. *Economy and Society*, 20(10): 79–102.

Dunlop, J. T. (1958) *Industrial Relations Systems*. New York: Holt.

Ebbinghaus, B. and Wiß, T. (2011) Taming pension fund capitalism in Europe: Collective and state regulation in times of crisis'. *Transfer: European Review of Labour and Research*, 17(1): 15–28.

Edwards, P. K. (2018). *Conflict in the Workplace: The Concept of Structured Antagonism Reconsidered*, Warwick Papers in Industrial Relations, No. 110. Coventry: University of Warwick.

Fernández González, C. J. and Martínez Lucio, M. (2013) 'Narratives, myths and prejudice in understanding employment systems: The case of rigidities, dismissals and flexibility in Spain'. *Economic and Industrial Democracy*, 34(2): 313–36.

Foley, J. (2014) 'Industrial democracy in the twenty-first century'. In A. Wilkinson, T. Dundon, J. Donaghey and R. Freeman (eds), *Handbook of Research on Employee Voice*. Cheltenham: Edward Elgar, pp. 66–81.

Garrahan, P. and Stewart, P. (1994) *The Nissan Enigma*. London: Mansell.

Geelan, T. and Hodder, A. (2017) 'Enhancing transnational labour solidarity: The unfulfilled promise of the Internet and social media'. *Industrial Relations Journal*, 48(4): 345–64.

Glasgow Media Group (1976) *Bad News*, Vol. 1. London: Routledge & Kegan Paul.

González Menéndez, M. and Martínez Lucio, M. (2020) 'Voice across borders: Comparing and explaining the dynamics and politics of participation in a context of change'. In A. Wilkinson, T. Dundon, J. Donaghey and R. Freeman (eds), *Handbook of Research on Employee Voice*. Cheltenham: Edward Elgar, pp. 456–73

Hall, P. and Soskice, D. (2001) 'Introduction'. In P. Hall and D. Soskice (eds), *Varieties of Capitalism*. New York: Oxford University Press.

Heery, E. and Frege, C. (2006) 'New actors in industrial relations'. *British Journal of Industrial Relations*, 44(4): 601–4.

Hirst, P. and Thompson, G. (1999) *Globalization in Question*. Oxford: Wiley-Blackwell.

Hirst, P. and Thompson, G. (2009) *Globalization in Question*. Cambridge: Polity Press.

Hogan, J., Nolan, P. and Greco, M. (2010) 'Unions, technologies of coordination, and the changing contours of globally distributed power'. *Labour History*, 51(1): 29–40.

Hyman, R. (1975) *Industrial Relations: A Marxist Introduction*. London: Macmillan.

Hyman, R. (2001) 'Trade unions and cross-national comparison'. *European Journal of Industrial Relations*, 7(2): 203–32.

Hyman, R. (2004) 'Varieties of capitalism, national industrial relations systems and transnational challenges'. In A.-W. Harzing and J. Van Ruysseveldt (eds), *International Human Resource Management*. London: Sage, pp. 411–32.

Hyman, R. (2010) *Social Dialogue and Industrial Relations during the Economic Crisis: Innovative Practices or Business as Usual?* Geneva: International Labour Organization.

Jessop, B. (2002) *The Future of the Capitalist State*. Cambridge: Polity Press.

Kang, N. (2006) *A Critique of the 'Varieties of Capitalism' Approach*, Research Paper Series No. 45. Nottingham: International Centre for Corporate Social Responsibility, Nottingham University Business School.

Kerr, C., Dunlop, J. T., Harbison, F. H. and Meyers, C. A. (1960) *Industrialism and Industrial Man*. London: Penguin.

Lane, C. (1989) *Management and Labour in Europe*. Aldershot: Edward Elgar.

Lash, S. and Urry, J. (1987) *The End of Organised Capitalism*. Cambridge: Polity Press.

Lehmbruch, G. (1984) 'Corporatism in decline?' In J. H. Goldthorpe (ed.), *Order and Conflict in Contemporary Capitalism*. Oxford: Clarendon Press.

Lehndorff, S. (2014) 'It's a long way from norms to normality: The 35-hour week in France'. *ILR Review*, 67(3): 838–63.

Locke, R. M. and Thelen, K. (1995) 'Apples and oranges revisited: Contextualised comparisons and the study of labour politics'. *Politics and Society*, 23(3): 337–67.

McCarthy, M. A. (2014) 'Turning labor into capital: Pension funds and the corporate control of finance. *Politics and Society*, 42(4): 455–87.

MacKenzie, R. and Martínez Lucio, M. (2005) 'The realities of regulatory change: Beyond the fetish of deregulation'. *Sociology*, 39(3): 499–517.

MacKenzie, R. and Martínez Lucio, M. (2014) 'The colonisation of employment regulation and industrial relations? Dynamics and developments over five decades of change'. *Labor History*, 55(2): 189–207.

Martínez Lucio, M. (2020) 'Trade unions and stress at work: The evolving responses and politics of health and safety strategies in the case of the United Kingdom'. In R. J. Burke and S. Pignata (eds), *Handbook of Research on Stress and Well-Being in the Public Sector*. Cheltenham: Edward Elgar, pp. 15–32.

Martínez Lucio, M. and MacKenzie, R. (2004) 'Unstable boundaries? Evaluating the "new regulation" within employment relations'. *Economy and Society*, 33(1): 77–97.

Martínez Lucio, M. and MacKenzie, R. (2006) *Developments in Patterns of Regulation in Employment Relations: Re-appraising Views of the State in Industrial Relations Analysis*. Paper presented to Industrial Relations in Europe Conference, Ljubljana, Slovenia, 31 August–2 September.

Martínez Lucio, M., Jenkins, S. and Noon, M. (1999) 'The question of teamwork and union identity in the Royal Mail: Beyond negotiation?' In F. Mueller and S. Procter (eds), *Teamworking*. London: Macmillan.

Martínez Lucio, M. and Stuart, M. (2011) 'The state, public policy and the renewal of HRM'. *International Journal of Human Resource Management*, 22(18): 3661–71.

Morgan, G. and Hauptmeier, M. (2021) 'The social organization of ideas in employment relations'. *Industrial and Labor Relations Review*, 74(3): 773–97.

Murakami, T. (1997) 'The autonomy of teams in the car industry: A cross-national comparison'. *Work, Employment and Society*, 11(4): 749–58.

Murakami, T. (1999) 'Works councils and teamwork in a German car plant'. *Employee Relations*, 21(1): 26–44.

Murray, G. (2017) 'Union renewal: What can we learn from three decades of research?.' *Transfer: European Review of Labour and Research*, 23(1): 9–29.

Panitch, L. (1981) 'Trade unions and the capitalist state'. *New Left Review*, 125 (January–February): 21–43.

Panitch, L. (1994) 'Globalisation and the state'. In R. Miliband and L. Panitch (eds), *Socialist Register 1994: Between Globalism and Nationalism*. London: Merlin.

Poole, M. (1981) *Theories of Trade Unionism*. London: Routledge & Kegan Paul.

Ritchie, B. K. (2002) *Foreign Direct Investment and Intellectual Capital Formation in Southeast Asia*. Paris: OECD Development Centre.

Rogowski, R. (2000) 'Industrial relations as a social system'. *Industrielle Beziehungen*, 7(1): 97–126.

Ross, G. (1981) 'What is progressive about unions?' *Theory and Society*, 10: 609–43.

Rubery, J. (2011) 'Reconstruction amid deconstruction: Or why we need more of the social in European social models'. *Work, Employment and Society*, 25(4): 658–74.

Schmitter, P. C. (1974) 'Still the century of corporatism?' *Review of Politics*, 36(1): 85–131.

Stewart, P., Murphy, K., Danford, A., Richardson, T., Richardson, M. and Wass, V. J. (2009) *We Sell Our Time No More: Workers' Struggles against Lean Production in the British Car Industry*. London: Pluto Press.

Thompson, P. (2013) 'Financialization and the workplace: Extending and applying the disconnected capitalism thesis'. *Work, Employment and Society*, 27(3): 472–88.

Torfing, J. (1990) 'A hegemony approach to capitalist regulation'. In R. B. Bertramsen, J. P. Thomson and J. Torfing (eds), *State, Economy and Society*. London: Unwin Hyman.

Ugarte, S. (2012) *Women's Relative Position in the Labour Market Segment of Argentina and Chile*. Paper presented at the Fairness at Work Research Centre Conference, University of Manchester, 6–7 September.

Vandenberg, A. and Hundt, D. (2012) 'Corporatism, crisis and contention in Sweden and Korea during the 1990s'. *Economic and Industrial Democracy*, 33(3): 463–84.

Wailes, N., Bamber, G. J. and Lansbury, R. D. (2011) 'International and comparative employment relations: An introduction'. In G. J. Bamber, R. D. Lansbury and N. Wailes (eds), *International and Comparative Employment Relations: Globalization and Change*. London: Sage, pp 1–35.

Walker, S. (2014) 'Media, new union strategies and non-government organizations as global players: The struggle over representation and work'. In M. Martínez Lucio (ed.), *International Human Resource Management: An Employment Relations Perspective*. London: Sage, pp 277–92.

Wergin, N. E. (2003) 'Teamwork in the automobile industry – An Anglo-German comparison'. *European Political Economy Review*, 1(2): 152–90.

Whitley, R. (2007) *Business Systems and Organizational Capabilities: The Institutional Structuring of Competitive Competences*. Oxford: Oxford University Press.

Section 2

Working in a globalized context

4 Pay and remuneration in multinationals

Óscar Rodríguez-Ruiz

Learning objectives

- To understand the nature of payment systems and their development
- To comprehend the development of payment systems in the context of MNCs
- To engage with the problems and challenges of reward systems in relation to IHRM
- To explain some of the ongoing issues in relation to globalization

Introduction

Pay is a central element in labour relations and one of the most important human resource management (HRM) activities. It plays a key role in organizational functioning, determining the success of the whole human resources (HR) system. The effectiveness and fairness of the management of people is dependent to a great extent on reward policies. The wage relation significantly affects attitudes, work behaviours and organizational events. For employees, compensation is a source of monetary value, benefits and job satisfaction. For employers, it is a payment for a service delivered and a cost of doing business in emerging global markets.

Decisions on pay also have political and social implications. In this context, payment systems that define small differences in earnings have been considered egalitarian. Conversely, systems that fix a hierarchy of wages based on large differentials are labelled inegalitarian. With the globalization of markets and the development of multinational companies (MNCs), it is increasingly necessary to understand pay in an international context (Tsai, 2017). Governments compete hard to attract foreign direct investment (FDI), and global firms play an important part in this, being a source of capital, employment and managerial philosophies. According to Fenwick (2004: 308), international compensation is 'the provision of monetary and non-monetary rewards, including base salary, benefits, perquisites, long- and short-term incentives, valued by employees in accordance with their relative contributions to MNCs' performance'. International reward policies must be adapted to the 'needs and expectations of very different groups of subsidiaries and employees located in different countries with different legal systems' (Hiltrop, 2002: 330). Thus, pay is administered differently in organizations, depending on business strategy, economic environments and institutional and cultural frameworks.

MNCs manage an international workforce from different cultural backgrounds and deal with multiple employment relations models. Their location in different national business systems leads to different attitudes towards pay. As a result, international operations can generate differences in the levels and types of compensation provided in each country or region. The challenge of creating a fair pay system in countries with different cultures and legal frameworks raises serious issues in terms of internal and external equity. Internal equity demands consistency regarding the way that employees doing equal jobs are paid. External equity requires the matching of the organization's pay rates with those of other firms.

This chapter provides a general view of the main frameworks, controversies and shortcomings of the compensation policies of MNCs. It attempts to cover the diverse developments that are affecting global wage relations at the beginning of the 21st century. The next section of this chapter presents the general background of payment systems and pay determination. It looks at the different approaches to determining compensation in the countries in which international companies operate. The third section discusses inegalitarian and egalitarian systems as competing forms of pay regulation. Specifically, it explores how wage bargaining in MNCs can take place at different levels. The fourth section describes recent developments in payment systems, noting that the pressures towards standardization and cost reduction can undermine equality and labour standards. Some final thoughts are discussed in the last section.

To paint a comprehensive picture of global compensation issues in MNCs, some preliminary observations are necessary. Historically, the vast majority of international compensation literature has been marked by three characteristics: emphasis on the debate about the centralization or localization of pay in international companies, disregard of the study of reward policies for non-managerial workers and lack of attention to equality and fairness issues.

The first major characteristic is that, traditionally, *the central debate about compensation in MNCs has been focused on the influence of national factors and strategic alignment in the design of pay systems.* As Bloom et al. (2003) point out, managers have a

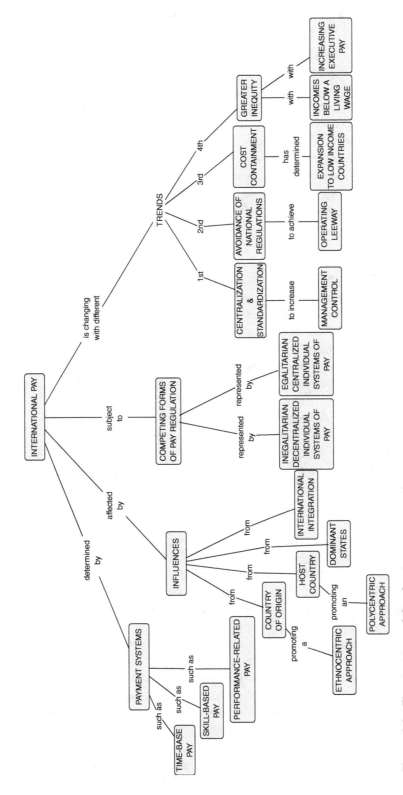

Figure 4.1 The structure of the chapter as a concept map.

strong preference for aligning the design of compensation criteria with the organizational context. The companies that follow this approach look for the reproduction of headquarters' remuneration schemes in all locations ('one pay system all over the world'). Conversely, other businesses try to create as many compensation systems as the host contexts in which they compete ('many countries, many compensation systems'). This controversy reveals a confrontation between markets and nations as competing forms of determination of the compensation system. MNCs such as IBM judge that aligning pay policies with business strategy and corporate culture is more important than adapting to local customs and idiosyncrasies. However, practices regarding pay levels and forms of pay differ across countries. For example, while European firms have a long tradition of offering non-cash benefits, American companies use more intensively cash-based compensation. Unlike Japanese MNCs, which link pay to seniority, US international firms trust firmly in pay based on individual performance. These facts reinforce the idea that international compensation must be tailored to fit national cultures and variations in contextual factors. Nevertheless, in recent years, with shifts in the power of capital relative to states, many MNCs only adapt themselves to the national structures of collective bargaining after being compelled to do so. As a consequence, friction between company practices and local prevailing conditions in terms of national culture and business systems is growing all over the world. Local institutions, such as governments, trade unions and consumer groups, are warning about the dangers that globalization entails for labour standards and industrial relations traditions (Martínez Lucio, 2009).

Second, *international HRM has concentrated mainly on remuneration for international managers, disregarding non-managerial workers* (Almond et al., 2006; Tsai, 2017). However, compensation in MNCs is more than merely fixing sophisticated remuneration packages for expatriate elites isolated in upper-class dwellings. The study of reward management of the entire workforce reveals that MNCs today use pay determination systems that differ significantly between manual and managerial job holders. A thorough analysis of international compensation and remuneration needs to take into account the full range of workers employed by international businesses, distinguishing between the compensation schemes of managerial and non-managerial employees. This is a key distinction, as there is great variety in the amount of compensation offered by MNCs to their employees. In fact, strong criticism has arisen about the overpayment of executives in comparison to rank-and-file employees. For example, in Switzerland, where managers are the highest paid in Europe, different groups collected signatures to call for a national vote to change Swiss law to increase transparency and accountability in executive pay. Lower wages and poorer working conditions often seem to be associated with blue-collar positions, while upper-level managers benefit from individualized packages ('cafeteria approach') which include a company car, club membership, insurance, educational tuition and so on (Tsai, 2017).

The current landscape of international compensation is characterized by an increasing variety and complexity (Bonache and Zárraga, 2017). Issues such as *fairness and equality are not sufficiently addressed*. In the context of international business, the application of the principle of equal pay for work of equal value is especially complex. Reward policies cannot be 'informed by business strategy in isolation from considerations of internal and external equity' (Perkins and White, 2008: 364). This means that consistency and fairness have to influence reward management within and across the organizations. Apparently, the MNCs' expertise allows them to pay higher wages than local competitors in many countries (OECD, 2008). Equality of pay could be an insurance against worker turnover and industrial unrest. Nevertheless, some research shows that higher wages benefit foreign affiliates but not domestic firms (Javorcik, 2015).

The general background of payment systems and pay determination

To address the complexities of pay in MNCs, it is necessary to clarify the differences between the concepts of pay structure and pay systems. The *pay structure* is the pattern of pay relations in a company that is determined by both internal factors (values, strategy and structure) and external factors (national culture, legislation, market characteristics, etc.). It involves an ordering of pay rates for jobs or groups of jobs and deals with issues of internal equity of the salary. The processes involved in remunerating employees within the pay structure constitute the pay form or *pay system* (Lowry, 2002). There are four types of system: time-based pay, competence- and skills-based pay, individual performance-related pay and organizational performance-related pay. The first type rewards employees for the amount of time they spend at work. In this case, compensation is based on the job position. Competence-based remuneration is not based on the job but rather on the skills of the individual. The third category rewards individuals according to some measure of their performance such as output or service quality. Finally, the fourth type consists of group-based pay systems that reward teams or organizational subunits or entire organizations according to the firm's performance.

The design of the structure and systems of pay in MNCs is a central issue affected by a wide range of influences. Among these influencing factors, Edwards and Ferner (2002) have identified country-of-origin effects, host-country effects, dominance effects and pressures for international integration. *Country-of-origin effects* can be perceived in the extension of the basic principles of work organization of the MNC's home country to its international operations. Japanese companies follow this form of reward strategy, 'transplanting' the HR system of the parent company into the subsidiaries. There are also *influences of the destination country on the pay policies of global companies*. For example, McDonald's included overtime pay in its reward system to adapt to Japanese regulations (Royle, 2010). At the same time, the determination of pay can be affected by the *imitation of the HRM practices of the dominant states*. American firms are perceived as being innovative in their management of pay, introducing forms of rewards that have become commonplace in other industrialized countries (Muller-Camen et al., 2001). This trend has led to an Americanization of compensation schemes, considered to be global best practices. Thus companies such as Toshiba are abandoning traditional Japanese reward forms and increasing pay for performance. Finally, it is possible to note *pressures for international integration* when MNCs apply similar pay systems across their subsidiaries to reinforce uniformity and control. This is the case with Walmart and its low-wages policy.

Country-of-origin and host-country pressures have generated two methods of compensation: home-country-based or host-country-based. The first involves exporting the pay schemes of the nation of the parent company, with minimal adjustment, to the destination country. For instance, Uber uses its incentive pay system as the first tool for labour control. Host-country-based compensation attempts to adapt reward practices to the destination country's culture and standards. The underlying philosophy of this view is that 'differences in national cultures call for differences in management practices' (Newman and Nolen, 1996: 753). According to this perspective, cultural norms 'of fair treatment within countries act as foundations for employee expectations for their pay' (Graham and Trevor, 2000: 136). Thus, we can observe that, in cultures with high individualism, there is a greater use of performance-related pay linked to formal appraisals of individual effort (Cleveland et al., 2000). In general terms, the companies that follow the host-country approach are adapters that try to design pay systems matching as closely as possible the local cultural preferences, economic conditions and social constraints. In this vein, it is curious that sometimes even local competitors set the institutional parameters for employment relations in multinational subsidiaries (Tsai, 2017). For example, the Spanish-owned retail store El Corte Inglés has used its power and influence to fix pay and working conditions in the Spanish supermarket sector, which also determines the behaviour of the French MNC Carrefour in Spain (Royle and Ortíz, 2009).

Obviously, there are hybrid systems combining elements of home and host approaches in many MNCs. For example, regional approaches are applied when an expatriate makes a commitment to work within a particular region of the world. Then a benchmark of wages is fixed for the operations throughout this cluster of countries with similar values. In line with this approach, the EU as a whole can be considered as a destination country for MNCs. In any case, whether or not MNCs develop global HR policies is shaped by the extent and nature of their international integration (Edwards, 2011). There is a great variety of MNCs, and each has different incentives for implementing homogeneous pay practices. Companies that provide standardized goods and services, such as UPS, enjoy benefits from making their HR practices uniform. Conversely, firms with an internationally fragmented production process, such as the leading American information technology (IT) companies, do not need major common-alities in their employment relations. Following Perlmutter (1969) (see Chapter 1 on globalization and employment), it is possible to distinguish three types of MNC: ethnocentric, polycentric and geocentric. Ethnocentric MNCs have a cen-tralized structure, and subsidiaries follow the practices of the parent company. Their business approach is global, providing standardized goods and services. Polycentric MNCs develop a local adaptation strategy based on decentralization and autonomy for affiliates. In these firms, the management practices of the sub-sidiaries conform to the local practice of the destination country. Finally, geocen-tric MNCs combine characteristics of both global and multi-domestic companies, balancing global efficacy and national responsiveness. Logically, each category of MNC has a different approach to compensation and benefits. For example, polycentric companies show the greatest interest in localizing pay policies.

The pressures to develop globally standardized pay policies are strong. However the diversity of socioeconomic paradigms and the heterogeneous nature of MNCs cause convergence and divergence in reward practices. While internationalization has become a driver towards greater consistency (Chiang, 2005: 1548), differences are unavoidable among culturally sensitive areas. The duality of home country–host country reflects the need to achieve a balance in MNCs between global integration and local responsiveness. The first studies of this issue supported the idea that international firms tend to adapt to local practices rather than exporting their own HRM policies (e.g. Marginson and Sisson, 1994). However, in recent times many international companies such as Colgate Palmolive (Briscoe et al., 2012) have adopted a global element in the way they manage their international workforces. They make important invest-ments in technology to standardize reward management practice and want to follow a common recipe for compensating workforce members irrespective of the operating environment (Perkins and White, 2008). Many of them have adopted a 'quick-fix' philosophy, moving, hiring, paying and firing people around the world without much advance reflection. A few are concerned with the implementation of 'global compensation systems that allow the organization to maintain the flexibility and ease of transfer between countries and regions while providing employees a just wage' (Watson and Singh, 2005: 33). It is sig-nificant that, in the past, global pay programmes for executives were defined at the corporate level, while strategies for other employee groups were determined either regionally or locally. But now, as employers want to facilitate mobility and reinforce organizational culture, they are attempting to globalize reward schemes to a greater extent.

Competing forms of pay regulation

As Bloom et al. (2003: 1364) point out, 'compensation is embedded in many nations' social contracts'. The national realities of industrial relation systems condition the salary structures (Lloyd and Payne, 2018). There are national business systems that differ in terms of labour relations, regulation and patterns of education and training (see Chapter 3 on employment relations, Chapter 9 on training and Chapter 11 on varieties of capitalism). Thus, in liberal market economies such as the United States or the United Kingdom (UK), the weakness of the institutions of wage determination above the firm level has led to a consolidation of inegalitarian/decentralized/individual systems of pay. Conversely, in countries such as Sweden or Denmark, where there are social market economies, government regulations have standardized employment conditions, thus promoting more egalitarian/centralized/collective systems of pay (Sánchez Marín, 2008; see Chapter 13 on restructuring and Chapter 18 on sustainability and HRM for outlines of the more regulated systems of employment and their HRM effects).

Inegalitarian and egalitarian systems represent competing forms of pay regulation in MNCs. The former are associated with large differentials in earnings. The emphasis is on variable pay and external equity. Compensation administration is flexible, and parties are allowed great freedom to settle working conditions. Government intervention is minimal. By contrast, egalitarian systems promote shared incentives and small differences in wages. Pay is based on professional categories, and internal equity is important. Compensation procedures are formal, and control is exerted by collective bargaining and the state. In recent years, international companies seem to be moving from 'paying the job' to 'paying the person'. Nations with an individualistic culture have emphasized inegalitarian/decentralized/person-based pay and their MNCs have tried to customize executive salaries at the individual level. This vision is coherent with the American ideal of 'employment at will', in which pay determination involves only agreement between the firm and the wage earners.

The emphasis on individual employee contributions, usually associated with a lean workforce constantly adapted to changing markets, does not work well in many countries (Newman and Nolen, 1996). It seems clear, for example, that the use of 'forced distributions' in MNCs to rank employees according to their level of performance has been a failure in some European nations. By the same token, the consideration of Deliveroo riders as self-contractors paid through the piece-rate system has been considered inappropriate by courts in countries such as Spain.

In countries with egalitarian/centralized/collective systems, the politics of wage distribution involves negotiation between unions and employers, and firms and sectors are included in a single wage settlement. The governments usually extend union-negotiated wage contracts to non-union members. Within these systems, collective sectoral bargaining has a number of effects on the management of pay. This is the case in Germany, where work councils co-determine bonus rates and performance-related remuneration. Traditionally, pay systems were 'collectivistic in nature', involving 'natural incremental progression along the pay structure' (Lowry, 2002: 158). Nevertheless, this collectivistic approach has been steadily replaced in recent decades by a more individualized focus in which moving up the corporate ladder allows for the negotiation of customized compensation packages. The extension of individual performance-related pay for managers and non-unionized workforces has been widespread. In this process, Western Europe's stronger labour regulation and more influential trade unions represent a major challenge for MNCs (Royle, 2010).

Developments in payment systems

It is possible to identify different trends in the compensation policies of MNCs in recent years. The concentration of capital has stimulated the centralization of pay and the implementation of cost-reduction initiatives. At the same time, international companies have adopted avoidance strategies to promote control of their workforces. The asymmetric development of globalization has also provoked wage dispersion and a growth in inequities. The main features of these developments are explained below.

Centralization and standardization

Headquarters' managers perceive a centralized approach to reward management as being more effective (Tekieli et al., 2018). With the aim of achieving internal consistency, international firms are defining rules and procedures for uniform salary decisions and applying them throughout their organizations. The main purpose is to establish compensation systems based on the principle of flexibility for the employer (Milkovich and Bloom, 1998) rather than matching local conditions. This flexibility is conceived as the ability to change wage conditions arbitrarily while allowing some 'cherry-picking' approaches for top executives who are sent overseas. The centralization of pay practices is particularly strong considering the autonomy that headquarters permit among subsidiaries in other areas of HRM (Almond et al., 2006). Key strategic salary decisions are taken in the home country by nationals of the home country which determine the behaviour of the firm at the international level.

Thus corporate HR specialists 'impose uniform practices avoiding the need to analyse each location on a case-by-case basis. Obviously, this orientation towards standardization does not mean an exactly identical approach in all the company's subsidiaries, but rather the adoption of a firm-based system of pay with uniform grading policies and similar criteria for measuring individual performance and bonus payments. Indeed, as Pudelko and Harzing (2008) remark, the standardization of personnel practices in general, and of compensation in particular, can gravitate towards two different poles: towards headquarters and towards global best practices. In the latter case, it must not be forgotten that corporate HR is the department responsible for collecting examples of best practice and disseminating them from its central position. The degree of centralization varies over time and is subject to negotiation at the subsidiary level, though subsidiaries have to justify deviations from central policies.

The central administration of the reward and incentive system has a number of advantages. First, it makes the determination of salaries a simpler process defined by the global labour market (Phillips and Fox, 2003). This simplicity mitigates the risks derived from operating in multiple and diverse economic environments and employment and taxation regimes. Second, the centralization of data enables headquarters to gain a global view of pay across the organization. Processes can be benchmarked to the industry and cutting costs is easier because compensation packages are seen in a company-wide context. Under these circumstances, differential compensation strategies are deemed unnecessary, and companies can concentrate on the definition of common job descriptions to achieve economies of scale. In general terms, the development of a centralized policy has brought more management control and pressures for efficiency.

In conclusion, it seems that while the HRM function is under pressure to adapt to local labour markets, pay policies in MNCs are increasingly centralized in corporate HR departments. A culture-free approach to compensation is being promoted and applied almost universally. A good example of this trend is Compaq, a company that has been a pioneer in introducing corporate global pay.

Avoidance of national regulations

MNCs are political systems in which different organizational actors seek to extend the application of global policies (see Chapter 2 on MNCs). They develop a number of avoidance strategies to overcome the national regulations that make the implementation of homogeneous practices difficult. Since the 1980s, there has been extensive evidence of the progressive growth of these avoidance strategies (Helfen et al., 2016). National tax and employment relation systems are deemed by MNCs to be an impediment to the globalization of pay criteria. To achieve flexibility, they try to avoid mandatory and customary pay practices, seeking alternatives in terms of response to governmental action. Thus salary conditions are often presented as something non-negotiable, reducing the claims of both workers and states. For instance, the clients of the platform for microtask labour mediation Amazon Mechanical Turk are free to withhold payment without explanation for any work they find unsatisfactory (Kuhn and Maleki, 2017).

The avoidance of national regulations is reinforced by the 'structural bargaining power' of MNCs (Phillips and Fox, 2003: 465) that allows them to place workers and countries in competition for the available jobs on offer. This power has increased as MNCs have the 'weapon of offshore investment' (McMichael, 1999: 31). Global firms exploit the internal heterogeneity of national business systems by locating units in less developed areas with low union organization (Royle, 1998: 1042).

Over the years, some MNCs have moved their production lines to developing countries with non-unionized workforces to take advantage of low wages. This is a strategy aimed at extracting value by underpaying workers in environments that can easily be entered and exited. McDonald's represents another example of an MNC that has been able to avoid local conformance pressures by taking advantage of weaknesses in regulations. In recent times, MNCs such as Uber, Deliveroo or Just Eat have been promoting low labour regulation approaches to impose management prerogatives. International compensation within these large organizations represents an attempt to move away from systems of internal labour markets and collective bargaining. The general 'anti-union animus' of some firms (Almond et al., 2006; Logan, 2019) reveals a desire to avoid the pay constraints of the standard sectoral system of collective agreement. Obviously, overriding local norms has consequences such as penalties or losing the goodwill of the local actors. Nevertheless, some MNCs carry on improving their profits by extracting concessions from the workforce.

Cost containment

MNCs have been putting a great emphasis on cost control in recent years. Managing populations across borders is a big investment, and there is a need for 'doing more with less and better people' (Swaak, 1995: 21). The first manifestation of the cost containment trend has been *MNCs' business expansion, motivated to a great extent by the cost of labour*. Developing countries have generally been considered as sources of cheap workers (Narula, 2019). In many low-income economies, wages are insufficient to cover the needs of workers and their families (ILO, 2019a). This is the case among Asian-Pacific states that do not mandate pay increases. Their productivity and low wages have provoked an exodus of industrial companies to enclaves of low-cost manufacturing.

Simultaneously, *the mobility of the international workforce has brought 'increased capabilities and often lower costs to multinationals'* (Lowe et al., 2002: 46). It is interesting that companies are curtailing sharply the high costs associated with expatriate compensation packages. Foreign assignments are increasingly considered to be part of a normal course of career development for the employee (Watson and Singh, 2005) and a cost-sensitive investment for the company. Consultants are hired to design compensation solutions, and expatriates are recommended to use 'efficient shopper indexes'. The intensive scrutiny of accommodation and education expenses and a reduction in the use of cost of living allowances are some of the measures oriented towards cost containment.

There has also been an *intense movement towards variable pay*. This means a subtle introduction of pay at risk, because an important portion of the employees' compensation is uncertain and depends on individual, group or organizational performance. Muller-Camen et al. (2001) mention as an example IBM's attempt to introduce a worldwide bonus system which reduced guaranteed monthly salaries and increased flexible pay.

The standardization of pay policies is also justified for reasons of cost and economies of scale (Almond et al., 2006). As getting timely information about each country's employment laws, tax regulation and market conditions is difficult and expensive, MNCs provide elements that are uniform around the world. By using easily available enterprise software, companies can track and compare labour costs, facilitating the role of managers who have bonuses tied to their success in cutting the personnel payroll. The following case study outlines some of the issues that emerge in relation to how MNCs use workers in developing countries with low labour standards.

Case study: A decent minimum wage after the Rana Plaza disaster?

The collapse of the Rana Plaza building killed more than a thousand textile workers in Dhaka, Bangladesh, in 2013. The tragedy called world attention to the working conditions of the garment industry. After the disaster, brands promised to pay a living wage to workers in their whole supply chain. However, it seems clear that firms have failed to meet their commitments. In 2018, the Fair Labour Association developed a study of 18 Bangladeshi factories. Not a single one of the 6,000 garment workers studied was earning an income close to a living wage (FLA, 2018).

A recent analysis of 20 global fashion companies by the University of Sheffield (Edwards et al., 2019) finds similar results. The retail sector is still based on the labour of millions of workers who are not paid enough to provide for themselves. It has been estimated that in 2018, 8 per cent of the world's workers lived in extreme poverty despite having a job (ILO, 2019b). In Bangladesh, wages are tied to the legal minimum wage which is near the World Bank Poverty

Level. After the rises in 2013 and 2018, the monthly minimum wage for garment workers is 8,000 takas (95 USD), not enough to meet basic needs such as food, housing, health and schooling.

The problem of the lack of compliance with labour standards can be explained by several reasons. First of all, there is a lack of consistency among corporations over the definition of living wage. In addition, the pricing practices of MNCs remain opaque and it is difficult to know whether brands are fulfilling their commitments. Firms argue that they cannot unilaterally raise wages because they do not own the factories that make their clothes. Yet fashion companies persistently pressure suppliers to keep prices low.

At the same time, labour standards are rarely a priority for governments of developing countries in comparison to attracting FDI (Narula, 2019). Although national institutions and regulation shape pay policies, economic goals seem to be the primary issue. Firms can choose from a large low-skilled labour supply without bargaining power. Some brands are doing more than others to improve the working conditions, but today it is not possible to say that living salaries are being paid in the whole supply chain. It is interesting to note that higher wages correlate strongly with factories with good production planning and adequate worker representation (FLA, 2018). All these issues are an indication that negotiations on a country and industry level with full representation of workers and unions are key to settle decent minimum wages.

Questions

1. What is the role of MNCs in improving labour standards in apparel global value chains?
2. Do you think that the bad reputation associated with low wages can reduce the attractiveness of a host country for MNCs?
3. What is the responsibility of governments and suppliers in remediating working conditions that result in low wages?
4. What kind of wage reform would you suggest in countries such as Bangladesh to guarantee that compensation is sufficient to meet the workers' basic needs and some discretionary income?

Growth of inequities

The rule of fair and effective remuneration has been considered a basic principle of the design of compensation systems. However, *the inegalitarian effects of international compensation are growing in the global context* (see Chapter 5 on diversity). Preserving equality in MNCs is difficult because of geographical and cultural differences and the mix of home-, host- and third-country nationals (Fenwick, 2004). To promote fairness, employees at the same organizational level and performing an identical level of tasks must have similar rewards. Nevertheless, 'disparity in compensation is unavoidable' (Chen et al., 2002: 807) because international businesses operate across nations at different levels of economic development. The increasing contact between employees from different countries has made salary and grading differences more obvious, leading to problems of internal equity. These problems show that *traditional forms of compensation are required to change*. The balance sheet approach, based on a salary in line with compensation in the home country, results in clear inequities between local and expatriate employees (Bonache and Zárraga, 2017). In the host-country approach, there can be notable differences in pay between workers performing similar jobs in different countries.

Paradoxically, the recent trend towards the standardization of pay has increased inequality, provoking a loss of work arrangements and social standards. At the same time, *the sky-high growth of executive compensation has also exacerbated the lack of equity*. Egalitarian systems of pay are being replaced progressively by the American model, which promotes large differences in compensation between top managers and average workers. In a context where pay levels trend downwards, exceptional treatments are eroding employees' perceptions of fairness.

Conclusion

This chapter has reviewed the key topics and emerging issues that are shaping the compensation polices of MNCs in the global economy of the 21st century. It has explored the complexities of the pay systems of international firms and their major implications in terms of inequality and erosion of the national basis of the wage relation. We round off with some final considerations.

In theory, ethnocentric exporting of reward practices and the 'locally responsive' response are considered extreme positions in the management of pay in MNCs. The *long debate around centralization–local responsiveness cannot be resolved by declaring one position more important than another* (Pudelko and Harzing, 2008). Nevertheless, some global firms have a 'strong interest in establishing common reward structures worldwide where possible' (Almond et al., 2006: 126). They try hard to develop common elements in pay policies with the aim of reinforcing their original national base. The motor company Toyota, for example, has used compensation policies to emphasize its Japanese identity.

Many international firms regard compensation as an essential element of HR practice and try to prevent host-country effects imposing a global reward strategy in local markets. This involves a certain standardization of work, grade of jobs and appraisals. For the managers of large corporations, a global mindset creates cross-border comparability and the consolidation of an internal labour market. In this sense, we can say that *international compensation has been 're-centralized' in recent years*. For instance, companies such as Unilever, which have traditionally had a decentralized structure, are no longer allowing autonomy to subsidiaries to develop their

HR policies. Basically, the home-pay management system is conceived as an organizational capability that can be replicated in other places. Because of this, reverse knowledge transfer from the affiliates to the corporate office barely occurs in the area of pay. The 'one size fits all' approach eventually shapes the nature of institutional frameworks (Edwards and Kuruvilla, 2005).

However, if we take into account the importance of local pay drivers, 'it would be impossible to pretend that pay globalization is ever purely global' (Gross and Wingerup, 1999: 29). For this reason, in some circumstances, MNCs do not impose a homogeneous set of practices in all their foreign subsidiaries. The home-country influences, therefore, cannot be automatically assumed. As a general rule, MNCs export their compensation practices in countries with weak legislation and unorganized unions (Cleveland et al., 2000). When union affiliation is low, global companies can operate outside of national agreements and determine pay at the individual level. However, if there is a high level of regulation, they implement host-country schemes. It seems that MNCs only accommodate national arrangements when institutions set limits on what is feasible on the part of actors. If firms are not able to avoid collective bargaining, they initiate cooperative relations in an attempt to improve their image and reflect the norms of the host country. Thus, in strong institutional contexts, international firms are pragmatic in following the legal requirements to negotiate wages with trade unions. However, when local norms are broad and diffuse, large firms find room to manoeuvre. The standardization towards head office and global best practices is limited by differences in national, cultural and institutional characteristics, which force MNCs to localize pay management.

In other cases, MNCs do not derive benefits from standardizing HR policies. This happens in international companies that follow a local adaptation strategy with employees from very diverse cultural backgrounds. When the workforce presents multiple cultural influences, a local responsiveness strategy is justified. Conversely, the use of this strategy is deemed a 'waste of resources' when there is cultural similarity. In the end, *the balance between globalization of pay and local responsiveness is mediated by pressures for the minimization of costs.*

As mentioned earlier, *the management of the international workforce is contingent on the nature and form of the international integration of the firm.* Different types of MNC will have different incentives to build global HR policies. Edwards (2011) has distinguished four types of MNC with different approaches to HRM. With respect to compensation, we can say, first, that MNCs looking for financial economies through unrelated diversification are not likely to implement global reward policies because they have a wide range of different goods and services. Second, the division of labour between subsidiaries can generate another exception to the principle of global pay. There are MNCs that carry out different aspects of their production across their various sites.

If there is segregation between labour-intensive locations and knowledge-based locations, firms have little incentive to implement homogeneous pay policies (Edwards and Kuruvilla, 2005). Frequently, policies focused on cost minimization are applied in countries that do not constitute a source of competitive advantage, while more sophisticated approaches to pay are used in other places. A third category of global firms is formed by MNCs diversified into related areas. This is the case, for example, where pharmaceutical companies replicate the production process at different sites. These businesses have significant scope to implement a global pay policy, but this is constrained by the need to adapt to the different host countries. Finally, there are MNCs with a high level of international integration that are producing standardized goods and services – such as Starbucks. These kinds of companies develop a common element in relation to how they pay their workforce across countries. Within these global industries, forces for worldwide integration are strong and subsidiaries have little room to shape specific HRM practices.

As a final reflection, it is essential to consider that often corporate decisions about pay are not the product of rational calculations but rather the result of political factors. Political behaviour complements the economic behaviour of MNCs. In this vein, actors at corporate headquarters see global policies as a way of extending their influence and authority within the firm. At other times, corporate priorities around the rationalization and standardization of pay cannot be implemented because subsidiary management has considerable power because of their knowledge of local markets. Different subsidiaries are exposed to different pressures to conform to parent practices. As Edwards (2011) admits, the form of international integration shapes the firm's approach to HRM, but it is 'the ideological commitment on the part of senior management' that ultimately determines the management of people.

In recent decades, the managerial strategy of 'minimizing differences' seems to have been adopted by many global companies. While in the past, subsidiaries had scope to influence pay policies, now headquarters impose their reward programmes increasingly across the different operating environments. However, MNCs' power to execute their strategies can be moderated by governments and regulatory bodies.

Reflective questions

1. What are the main factors that form the basis of national payments systems?
2. In what way are such systems different?
3. What are the major changes taking place and why?
4. What are the consequences of such developments and what new tensions may they bring?

Recommended reading

- Bonache, J. and Zárraga-Oberty, C. (2017) 'The traditional approach to compensating global mobility: Criticisms and alternatives'. *International Journal of Human Resource Management*, 28(1): 149–69.
- Lloyd, C. and Payne, J. (2018) 'Hard times in latte land? Analysing pay and working time in the café industry in France, Norway and the UK'. *Economic and Industrial Democracy*, 42(3): 805–827.
- Nuti, M. D. (2011) 'Industrial relations at FIAT: Dr Marchionne's class war'. *European Review of Labour and Research*, 17(2): 251–4.

References

Almond, P., Muller-Camen, M., Collings, D. G. and Quintanilla, J. (2006) 'Pay and performance'. In P. Almond and A. Ferner (eds), *American Multinationals in Europe: Managing Employment Relations across National Borders*. Oxford: Oxford University Press, pp. 119–45.

Bloom, M., Milkovich, G. T. and Mitra, A. (2003) 'International compensation: Learning from how managers respond to variations in local host contexts'. *International Journal of Human Resource Management*, 14(8): 1350–67.

Bonache, J. and Zárraga, C. (2017) 'The traditional approach to compensating global mobility: criticisms and alternatives'. *International Journal of Human Resource Management*, 28(1): 149–69.

Briscoe, D., Schuler, R. and Tarique, I. (2012) *International Human Resource Management*, 4th edn. London: Routledge.

Chen, C. C., Chui, J. and Chi, S. (2002) 'Making justice sense of local–expatriate compensation disparity: Mitigation by local referents, ideological explanations and interpersonal sensitivity in China–foreign joint ventures'. *Academy of Management Journal*, 45(4): 807–17.

Chiang, F. (2005) 'A critical examination of Hofstede's thesis and its application to international reward management'. *International Journal of Human Resource Management*, 16(9): 1545–63.

Cleveland, J. N., Gunnigle, P., Heraty, N., Morley, M. and Murphy, K. R. (2000) 'US multinationals and human resource management: Evidence on HR practices in European subsidiaries'. *Journal of the Irish Academy of Management*, 21(1): 9–27.

Edwards, R., Hunt, T. and LeBaron, G. (2019) *Corporate Commitments to Living Wages in the Garment Industry*. SPERI and University of Sheffield.

Edwards, T. (2011) 'The nature of international integration and HR policies in multinational companies'. *Cambridge Journal of Economics*, 35(3): 483–98.

Edwards, T. and Ferner, A. (2002) 'The renewed "American challenge": A review of employment practices in US multinationals'. *Industrial Relations Journal*, 33(2): 94–111.

Edwards, T. and Kuruvilla, S. (2005) 'International HRM: National business systems, organizational politics and the international division of labour in MNCs'. *International Journal of Human Resource Management*, 15(1): 1–21.

Fenwick, M. (2004) 'International compensation and performance management'. In A. Harzing and J. Van Ruysseveldt (eds), *International Human Resource Management*. London: Sage.

FLA (2018) *Toward Fair Compensation in Bangladesh: Insights on Closing the Wage Gap*. Geneva: Fair Labor Association.

Graham, M. E. and Trevor, C. O. (2000) 'Managing new pay program introduction to enhance the competitiveness of multinational corporations'. *Competitiveness Review*, 10(1): 136–54.

Gross, S. and Wingerup, P. L. (1999) 'Global pay? Maybe not yet'. *Compensation and Benefits Review*, 31(4): 25–34.

Helfen, M., Schüßler, E. and Dimitris, S. (2016) 'Translating European labor relations to the US through global framework agreements? German and Swedish multinationals compared'. *Industrial and Labor Relations Review*, 69(3): 631–55.

Hiltrop, J. M. (2002) 'Mapping the HRM practices of international organizations'. *Strategic Change*, 11(6): 329–38.

ILO (2019a) *Global Pay Report 2018–2019*. Geneva: International Labour Office.

ILO (2019b) 'The working poor or how a job is no guarantee of decent living conditions'. *Spotlight on Work Statistics*, 6. Available at: www.ilo.org/wcmsp5/groups/public/---dgreports/---stat/documents/publication/wcms_696387.pdf.

Javorcik, B. S (2015) 'Does FDI bring good jobs to host countries?' *World Bank Research Observer*, 30(1): 74–94.

Kuhn, K. M. and Maleki, A. (2017) 'Micro-entrepreneurs, dependent contractors, and instaserfs: Understanding online labor platform workforces'. *Academy of Management Perspectives*, 31(3): 183–200.

Lloyd, C. and Payne, J. (2018) 'Hard times in latte land: analysing pay and working time in the café industry in France, Norway and the UK'. *Economic and Industrial Democracy*, 42(3): 805–827.

Logan, J. (2019) 'The new union avoidance internationalism'. *Work Organisation, Labour and Globalisation*, 13(2): 57–77.

Lowe, K. B., Milliman, J., De Cieri, H. and Dowling, P. J. (2002) 'International compensation practices: A ten-country comparative analysis'. *Human Resource Management*, 41(1): 45–66.

Lowry, D. (2002) 'Reward management'. In J. Leopold (ed.), *Human Resources in Organizations*,. Harlow: Pearson Education, pp. 147–60.

McMichael, P. (1999) 'The global crisis of wage labour'. *Studies in Political Economy*, 58: 11–40.

Marginson, P. and Sisson, K. (1994) 'The structure of transnational capital in Europe: The emerging Euro-company and its implications for industrial relations'. In R. Hyman and A. Ferner (eds), *New Frontiers in European Industrial Relations*. Oxford: Blackwell, pp. 15–51.

Martínez Lucio, M. (2009) 'The organization of HR strategies: Narratives and power in understanding labour management in a context of fragmentation'. In S. Clegg and C. L. Cooper (eds), *The Sage Handbook of Organisational Behaviour*. London: Sage, pp. 323–39.

Milkovich, G. T. and Bloom, M. (1998) 'Rethinking international compensation'. *Compensation and Benefits Review*, 30(1): 15–23.

Muller-Camen, M., Almond, P., Gunnigle, P., Quintanilla, J. and Tempel, A. (2001) 'Between home and host country: Multinationals and employment relations in Europe'. *Industrial Relations Journal*, 32(5): 435–48.

Narula, R. (2019) 'Enforcing higher labor standards within developing country value chains: Consequences for MNEs and informal actors in a dual economy'. *Journal of International Business Studies*, 50: 1622–35.

Newman, K. L. and Nolen, S. (1996) 'Culture and congruence: The fit between management practices and national culture'. *Journal of International Business Studies*, 27(4): 753–779.

OECD (2008) 'Do multinationals promote better pay and working conditions?' *In OECD Employment Outlook report*. Paris OECD.

Perkins, S. J. and White, G. (2008) *Employee Reward: Alternatives, Consequences and Contexts.* London: CIPD.

Perlmutter, H. (1969) 'The tortuous evolution of the multinational corporation'. *Columbia Journal of World Business*, 4(January–February): 9–18.

Phillips, L. and Fox, M. A. (2003) 'Compensation strategy in transnational corporations'. *Management Decision*, 41(5/6): 465–76.

Pudelko, M. and Harzing, A. W. (2008) 'The golden triangle for MNCs: Standardization towards headquarters practices, standardization towards global best practices and localization'. *Organizational Dynamics*, 37(4): 394–404.

Royle, T. (1998) 'Avoidance strategies and the German system of co-determination'. *International Journal of Human Resource Management*, 9(6): 1026–47.

Royle, T. (2010) 'Low road Americanization and the global "McJob": A longitudinal analysis of work, pay and unionization in the international fast-food industry'. *Labor History*, 51(2): 249–70.

Royle, T. and Ortíz, L. (2009) 'Dominance effects from local competitors: Setting institutional parameters for employment relations in multinational subsidiaries – a case from the Spanish supermarket sector'. *British Journal of Industrial Relations*, 47(4): 653–75.

Sánchez Marín, G. (2008) 'National differences in compensation: The influence of the institutional and cultural context'. In L. Gómez-Mejia and S. Werner (eds), *Global Compensation: Foundations and Perspectives (HRM)*. London: Routledge, pp. 18–28.

Swaak, R. E. (1995) 'Expatriate management: The search for best practices'. *Compensation and Benefits Review*, 27(2): 21–29.

Tekieli, M., Festing, M. and Baeten, X. (2018) 'Centralization and effectiveness of reward management in multinational enterprises: Perceptions of HQ and subsidiary reward managers'. *Journal of Personnel Psychology*, 17(2): 55–65.

Tsai, C.-J. (2017) 'International pay and compensation'. In T. Edwards and C. Rees (eds), *International Human Resource Management: Globalization, National Systems and Multinational Corporations*. Harlow: Pearson, pp. 230–51.

Watson, B. W. Jr and Singh, G. (2005) 'Global pay systems: Compensation in support of a multinational strategy'. *Compensation and Benefits Review*, 37(1): 33–6.

5 Equality, diversity and inclusion in multinational corporations

Fang Lee Cooke

Learning objectives

- To understand the notions of equality, diversity and inclusion (ED&I) in the context of human resource management (HRM)
- To identify individual, organizational and institutional barriers to implementing equal opportunity (EO) regulations and diversity and inclusion (D&I) initiatives in an international environment for multinational firms
- To highlight tensions and the politics of ED&I initiatives at the organizational and national level
- To familiarize readers with organizational practices in different parts of the world
- To prepare readers for designing ED&I initiatives in multinational operations

Introduction

The notion of fairness and justice is central to the academic debate and organizational policy and practice related to ED&I. The meaning of ED&I is socially constructed and embedded in a specific politico-historical context. Equal opportunity (EO) and diversity and inclusion (D&I) have emerged as two related and important elements in HRM. This is largely owing to the changes in the demographic make-up of the workforce and the internationalization of firms. The emergence of *equality* and *diversity* policies in international HRM reflects not only the importance of a more transnational and multinational/cultural dimension to the workforce, but also the complex role of multinational corporations (MNCs) as political and economic actors and the opportunities and constraints they face in the global economy. In this chapter, we assess the equality and diversity policies and practices of MNCs by examining the internal management of these issues as well as the role of the broader institutional environments in shaping organizational practices.

This chapter consists of four main sections in addition to the Introduction, Case Study and Conclusion. The first main section highlights the societal contexts in which equality and diversity issues manifest themselves. Within this broader context, the second section examines challenges facing MNCs in managing a diverse workforce. The third section contemplates sources of political pressure on equality and diversity management (DM) from the macro level, including national regulations and international regulations and initiatives. In the fourth section, we analyse discourses of ED&I, their competing meanings and the role of the institutional and organizational actors through a critical lens.

ED&I in the international context

The term *equal opportunities* is associated with employment equity legislation related to discrimination as a result of individuals' characteristics, such as gender, age, ethnicity, religion, physical ability and sexual orientation. Many national governments have promulgated EO-related legislation over the last three decades, although what 'equal opportunities' means and who may be included in the category for protection vary from country to country. The focus on and pressure to introduce EO legislation is not the same across nations, and its introduction is often a response to the changing political, socioeconomic, labour market and employment relations environment.

The concept of *managing diversity* has its origin in the United States and emerged as a human resources (HR) intervention in the mid 1980s. It is primarily a response to the demographic changes (e.g. more immigrants and women) in the workplace as well as in the customer base (Agocs and Burr, 1996). It is also a response to the corporate discontent with the affirmative action approach imposed by the US government. Organizations are searching for an alternative to broaden the perceived narrow scope of affirmative action legislation that focuses primarily on recruitment. DM is seen as a way to address retention, integration and career development issues (Agocs and Burr, 1996). The growing demands from the ethnic minority, women, older, disabled, gay and lesbian groups for equal rights and the consequent human rights legislation in the 1990s and 2000s gave further momentum to the need to recognize, accept and value individual differences at workplaces and in society more generally (Mor Barak, 2005).

The concept of DM began to be propagated in countries outside of North America during the late 1990s (e.g. Süß and Kleiner, 2007). It is suggested that the objectives of DM are for organizations to increase awareness of cultural differences, develop the ability to recognize, accept and value diversity, minimize patterns of inequality experienced by those not in the mainstream and modify organizational culture and leadership practices (Cox, 1993; Soni, 2000). DM is regarded as a better approach than what is regarded as its predecessor EO because DM adopts an inclusive approach that 'focuses on valuing people as unique individuals rather than on group-related issues covered by legislation' (Chartered Institute of Personnel and Development, 2007: 6).

The transition from a focus on EO to DM signals a move away from an emphasis on procedural justice to a utilitarian approach that views DM as a means to an end to be managed strategically (Maxwell et al., 2001). However, Ferner et al. (2005: 309) pointed out that, despite growing academic interest, DM is a poorly understood, increasingly slippery and controversial concept that is used 'in an all-embracing fashion to include not just the social categories of AA [affirmative action] such as race and sex but a wide range of personal characteristics'. Consequently, the concept and moral soundness of DM remains a contentious issue (see below for further discussion; also see Lorbiecki and Jack, 2000, for an overview of the conceptual premises and a critique of DM). At the policy level, Özbilgin and Tatli (2011: 1247) have also observed that there is a discernible trend where key actors in the EO and DM field are turning away from 'regulation- and collectivism-oriented approaches'; instead, 'voluntaristic and individualistic discourses' are increasingly adopted and 'dominate the public debates on workplace equality and diversity' (also see Kramar, 2012).

Since the 2000s, the term *diversity management* has been replaced by *diversity and inclusion* or *inclusion* as the new rhetoric in the popular HRM literature (Roberson, 2006), and to a lesser extent academic studies (e.g. Donnelly, 2015). Although the terms are used interchangeably, Roberson's (2006: 233) study found that there is 'a conceptual distinction between the concepts of diversity and inclusion as well as the attributes that support each in organizations'. The Society for Human Resource Management (n.d.), the US-based largest international HRM professional association, officially uses the term 'ED&I'. It provides practical guides to assist organizations to develop ED&I initiatives to promote quality for disadvantaged social groups and to create an organizational environment in which all individuals can fulfil their potentials and organizations can maximize their performance. While practical literature tends to use the terms 'D&I', 'ED&I' or 'inclusion', the bulk of the academic literature, however, still uses the terms 'DM' and 'managing equality and diversity'.

It is important to note that the practice of DM may not necessarily lead to enhanced productivity. Academic studies on diversity–performance relationships have so far yielded inconclusive results. While some researchers argue that diversity leads to better group and ultimately organizational performance (e.g. Cox et al., 1991), others contend that diversity leads to a negative organizational performance outcome in part due to intra- and inter-group conflicts and communication deadlock derived from differences (e.g. Lau and Murnighan, 1998; Tsui et al., 1992). Moreover, there may be tensions between a collective approach to managing diverse employee groups and a more individualized approach focusing on individual needs and abilities which may actually increase, rather than decrease, inequalities (e.g. Agocs and Burr, 1996; Liff, 1996). Ali et al.'s (2011) study also suggests that an industry-specific approach is required to manage a gender-diverse workforce to capture the benefits of diversity.

In addition, the utility of this US-originated concept in other societal contexts has been questioned by many researchers (e.g. Agocs and Burr, 1996; Ferner et al., 2005; Healy and Oikelome, 2007; Nishii and Özbilgin, 2007). A number of country-specific studies have revealed unique societal contexts in which diversity issues are embedded. For example, Hennekam et al.'s (2017: 459) study that examined 'the clash between diversity policies as designed in the west and the challenges in implementing these' in MNCs in the Middle East and North Africa region' revealed that the HR managers' understanding of the complexity of the DM contexts and strategy is vital. The same study accentuates the importance of adopting a sensitive approach that takes into account local context in transplanting the DM policy and strategy from the west to the African subsidiaries. In African countries, politics assumes supreme importance in DM, and ethnicity dominates 'most national debates on diversity' as the central issue (Healy and Oikelome, 2007: 1923). This is because some disadvantaged ethnic groups have been oppressed historically, and there are now increasing demands for radical remedial actions to address racial grievances. By contrast, ethnic groups in Japan and Korea are relatively homogenous, and as a result, gender, women's marital status and their related employment status may be the key source of workforce diversity and inequality (Cooke, 2010).

In the United States and the United Kingdom (UK), workforce diversity may cover: gender, race, ethnicity, religion, age, disability, immigration status, social class, political association, marital status, parental status, sexual orientation and ex-offenders, among other categories. Many of these differences are accepted by western societies, protected by law and acknowledged in company policy. Some of these characteristics, however, may not be acceptable socially or legally in Asian countries such as China and India. Furthermore, significant differences may exist within Asian countries. For example, caste, ethnicity, religion and gender are the main sources of diversity in India, whereas age, gender, disability and place of origin (e.g. rural versus urban background) are the main causes of social inequality in China. India is a democracy in which 'inclusiveness' is the major politico-economic discourse at present. In furtherance of this thinking, talk of empowerment of socially disadvantaged groups is emerging as a powerful weapon for political parties to connect with their constituencies. By contrast, China is a socialist regime with centralized control by the communist party. Elimination of social inequality is intended to be achieved by introducing government policies and regulations through a top-down interventionist approach (Cooke, 2019).

Managing an aging workforce is an issue in developed economies, whereas this is largely not the case in developing countries where the population is relatively young as is the workforce. In many developing countries, employment insecurity is relatively high and the provision of social security benefits is extended to few. Large groups of poor people are fighting for the very right to a basic living through low-paid employment with long working hours and poor conditions. The fact that they are treated unfairly is much less of a concern for some, and inequality in the workplace and in society generally is often accepted, internalized and unchallenged due to historically deep-rooted discrimination and the evident absence of remedial prospects. For example, Cooke and Saini's (2012) comparative study of DM in China and India revealed that as a strategic HRM concept, DM had been rarely heard of and featured even less in management discussions and presentations. In addition, management's indifferent attitude to DM may well be linked to the lack of voice and bargaining power of the disadvantaged groups in these countries (see Chapter 8 for a general discussion on developing economies).

In the European continent, the dissolution of the former communist countries such as the Soviet Union and Czechoslovakia and the increasing level of inter-country migration among Central and Eastern European Countries (CEECs) have led to heightened tensions and sensitivities regarding the issues of national and ethnic identity, employment rights and protections. This is partly a consequence of the different policies adopted by the CEECs in granting citizenship to the former Soviet Union citizens and the immigration status of migrants, with some governments being more inclusive than others. National or ethnic identity is thus based on the value attached to the membership of one or another national group. For Russian speakers in the Baltic republics, this is a rather complicated issue (Vedina and Vadi, 2008). These enduring cultural heritage, social and political identities manifest themselves in the workplace through organizational policies, managerial preference and peer relationships. This poses further difficulties for foreign MNCs operating in CEECs because ethnic minority employees not only have to identify themselves with the host country's culture but also that of the MNCs (for a broader discussion on migration and posted workers, see Chapter 7).

Managing diversity and inclusion in MNCs

MNCs face a diverse set of incentives and pressures to adopt diversity and inclusion initiatives in their parent as well as host-country operations (see Chapter 6 on international assignments). These incentives and pressures exist at the macro and micro level, and emanate from home and host countries (see Figure 5.1 below and more discussion later). Efforts to manage D&I are often marred by institutional challenges and societal tensions, as described in the previous section. In this section, we look at some of the tensions and challenges encountered by MNCs in managing a diverse workforce at the organizational level.

Existing studies on DM in MNCs have found that attempts to roll out US domestic diversity programmes globally often fail to achieve their objectives and/ or meet with strong resistance in the host-country operations (e.g. Ferner et al., 2005; Nishii and Özbilgin, 2007). This is mainly because the US-specific programmes fail to reflect the specific demographic profile and the legal, historical, political and cultural contexts of equality in the host countries. Many US-owned MNCs studied in fact made little attempt to adapt their US-designed diversity programmes to capture local characteristics (Nishii and Özbilgin, 2007). As a result, MNCs may encounter 'regulatory, normative and cognitive challenges' when designing and implementing their global DM initiatives (Sippola and Smale, 2007: 1895). While the diversity philosophy may be accepted globally within the corporation, a more multi-domestic approach has been found necessary to implement the diversity initiatives, as was revealed in Sippola and Smale's (2007) study.

Company-based case studies of DM in various countries have further revealed the gap between the reality and the corporate aspiration projected in the rhetoric of DM. For instance, Kirton et al.'s (2016) study of a UK-based multinational information technology (IT) company showed that despite the implementation of numerous DM initiatives, most managers have little exposure to gender diversity in this white, male-dominant industry. They are indifferent to DM policy and hold an 'identity-blind reasoning about managing teams' (Kirton et al., 2016: 334). Kirton et al. (2016) argued that managerial autonomy (e.g. team selection) at the line management level typical of the team-based structure of the IT industry prevents messages of DM commitment from the top leadership getting through to the lower level and sustains rather than bridges gender equality gaps. Similarly, Dhar-Bhattacharjee and Richardson's (2018: 578) study of the Indian IT industry revealed that the IT MNCs in India offer 'opportunities for middle- and upper-class women professionals' with little cultural or identity barriers as found in the western IT firm. However, gendered relations remain the norm, in addition to influences of regional, class and caste differences, which contribute to inequality in the IT workplaces.

The deployment of expatriate employees poses another DM challenge to MNCs whose subsidiaries span across western and eastern geographic and cultural boundaries (see Chapter 6 on international assignments). Existing studies have highlighted the tension created by differential remuneration packages awarded to expatriates and local managers in developing countries (e.g. Bonache et al., 2009; Chen et al., 2011). An attractive compensation package is often a key mechanism to entice expatriate talent from developed home countries to work in host countries where both working and living conditions may be less favourable than in the former. However, such expatriate–local compensation disparity not only causes resentment from local managers leading to organizational conflicts, but also raises broader issues regarding fairness and distributive justice (Chen et al., 2011; see also Chapter 4 on payment systems).

A multicultural workforce brings linguistic diversity to the workplace. Language in MNCs plays an important role in knowledge transfer (Peltokorpi and Yamao, 2017) and in shaping the level of power and influence of the different social groups in the organization (Tenzer and Pudelko, 2017). Gaibrois and Nentwich's (2020) study found that while having a strong command of English may bring perceived privileges to native English-speaking management and administrative staff and non-native English-speaking management and administrative staff over and above the non-English speaking local service staff and migrant service staff, this hierarchy of privilege is contested. Where employees are multi-lingual, some companies actually impose on an official corporate language. However, such a policy may bring more problems than it solves, not least because it goes against the spirit of ED&I.

In Muslim countries, the gender norms and other cultural values may differ fundamentally from those prevalent in western societies. The transplantation of the Anglo-Saxon originated DM concept to Muslim majority countries may be met with strong challenges and require adaptation (Syed and Özbilgin, 2009). For example, according to Paetkau (2009), a large US-owned MNC set up a joint venture in Saudi Arabia and strongly encouraged certain employees to relocate there for three to four years. This expatriation was promoted as a smart career move providing enriching professional and personal experience. The Saudi government, however, refused to issue work visas for young single women, those openly homosexual, Jews, the disabled and employees over the age of 50. As a result, the 'Congress created a "foreign laws" defence or exception, which permits a covered US employer to participate in otherwise discriminatory action to avoid violating the laws of a foreign country' (Paetkau, 2009: 93).

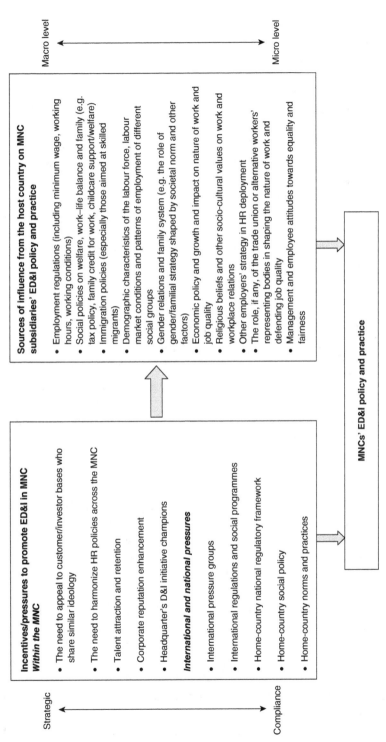

Figure 5.1 Factors influencing the ED&I policy and practice of MNC subsidiaries.

Source: Author

Equality politics and international and national regulation

Two driving forces motivate firms to adopt ED&I policies: legal and moral obligations and competitive advantage (the business case). Commitment to ED&I is an important indication of a firm's commitment to its corporate social responsibility (CSR). Legal compliance and social justice are the primary concerns of employment ethics (see Chapter 16 on transnational regulation). The business case perspective, which appears to be the dominant discourse of CSR and diversity, advances the argument further by suggesting that implementing labour standards, EO legislation and ED&I programmes not only fulfils firms' legal and social justice obligations but also creates business benefits through ethical behaviour and valuing people (Cooke, 2019). These two lines of argument reflect two distinct perspectives and different levels of politics at play (see Table 5.1).

Table 5.1   The politics of managing D&I

Level	Focus/Approach	Mechanisms	Actors
Macro-politics	Socially driven (social justice and workforce well-being)	Social policies and regulations	Institutional (e.g. policy-makers, employers, trade unions, NGOs, international regulatory bodies and pressure groups)
Micro-politics	Managerially driven (business case)	Organizational initiatives	Organizational (managers, employees, trade unions and ED&I consultants)

Source: Author

The political ideal of equality may be hijacked by politicians to serve their purposes. In democratic countries, it is not uncommon for politicians to adopt DM language to appeal to voters (e.g. in India). In China, where the political regime is less challenged, the notion of equality conforms to its ideological rhetoric: enhancing social harmony. By contrast, Australia, a country that relies heavily on the immigration of skilled labour, has witnessed a 'multicultural roll back', 'despite official rhetoric about the business benefits of cultural diversity' (Syed and Kramar, 2010: 99). Organizations are given freedom as to how they manage the cultural diversity of their ethnically diverse workforce. In situations where the coverage of local/national laws is not extended to foreign workers, employers may take advantage of this legislative loophole to avoid compliance. Moreover, host-country governments are faced with the dilemma of creating favourable conditions to attract foreign direct investment for development on the one hand, and the pressure to create jobs that offer decent terms and conditions on the other.

Where national labour regulation is weak in protecting the disadvantaged groups of workers, international regulations and global initiatives provide the needed intervention, albeit that they are largely voluntary and have limited enforcement power. These include, for example, the International Labour Standards and Decent Work initiative issued by the International Labour Organization (ILO), the Fair Trade International Framework Agreement and the United Nations Global Compact (see Chapter 16 on transnational regulation with regard to such bodies). Although led by different international organizations and pressure groups, a common objective of these initiatives is to raise the labour standards and therefore living standards in the developing world, especially in the poorest countries (see Chapter 16 on transnational regulation). Employers are required to provide decent working conditions, fair wages and freedom of association for workers. An emphasis of these regulations and initiatives is human rights through the elimination of discrimination and unfair practices. MNCs from the developed world are urged to take the lead and participate in the programmes associated with these regulations and initiatives – for example, through paying sustainable prices for products purchased from poor farmers and producers. Despite the high-profile campaigns of these organizations and some positive results, the effects of these initiatives are not universal and are not always positive. MNCs may join the programmes for reputational reasons and to avoid sanctions rather than to make a genuine effort. Their site inspection trips may actually add costs for the local suppliers. Local employers may find ways to overcome the constraints of international inspection, for example through subcontracting (e.g. Cooke, 2012).

Case study: ED&I in practice at PharmaCo (India)

The Indian pharmaceutical industry is one that is heavily populated, and in fact was dominated until the 1980s by foreign-owned MNCs. Owing to India's large population, low-cost production and research base and the enormous scope for medical development, the pharmaceutical market in India not only offers strong growth potential but also triggers fierce competition between foreign-owned and domestic pharmaceutical firms.

PharmaCorp, a Fortune 500 US-owned MNC, first entered the Indian market in the mid 1990s and subsequently set up its subsidiary PharmaCo (India) in 1997. PharmaCo (India) has several manufacturing plants in India and enjoys a high level of operational autonomy from the headquarters (HQ). Most of the senior managers are Indian nationals, as are the majority of

(Continued)

the workforce. As a result, the culture of PharmaCo (India) is heavily influenced by the Indian ethos, and the management practices are a blend of international practices that emphasize performance on the one hand and an Indian approach to handling HR issues discreetly on the other.

PharmaCo (India) adopts a rigorous recruitment process to ensure that only top performers are hired. According to the managers, PharmaCo (India) adopts an innovative '11 by 11' strategy to recruit managerial and professional/technical staff. That is, recruiting from the top 11 companies in the pharmaceutical sector for the top 11 regions in India. The intention is to ensure that the new recruits are already trained and possess the skills needed by the company. At the graduate recruitment level, PharmaCo (India) mainly targets the second-tier higher-education institutes because it cannot afford the employment packages expected by graduates from the top-tier colleges.

In some of the PharmaCo (India) plants, a large proportion of female employees are employed. They are recruited mainly from the tailoring institutes/sewing schools because these students have the precise hand movements and accurate eye–hand coordination that are required for certain production processes. Since these institutes/schools tend to have more female than male students, the company ended up recruiting more female than male employees. The high proportion of female employees enables PharmaCo (India) to satisfy the minimum gender ratio in the workforce imposed by the HQ.

Interestingly, most of the heavy manual work that is traditionally done by male workers is outsourced. Though strongly denied by management, it is believed that the reason for employing a female-dominant workforce is to avoid unionization and union demands on behalf of its members. Traditionally, female Indian workers do not get involved in a union and its politics. By contrast, manual male workers are more heavily unionized or demand unionization and collective bargaining on terms and conditions.

Despite the existence of high-profile DM propaganda at the HQ, there is no formal ED&I policy in PharmaCo (India). Its management believes that the country has a diverse population and the Indian workforce is tolerant in general. There is, therefore, no need for a formal ED&I policy. Instead, any issues raised can be addressed at the monthly management meeting. In addition, the company is said to have an established culture which encourages employees to discuss their problems with their line managers. In general, employees feel that the work environment is free from discrimination as all employees are treated alike.

The company does have a number of policies in place that are aimed at accommodating the work–life commitment of its (female) employees. For example, in general, women are allocated the day shifts whereas men work the night shifts. Crèches, maternity leave and career breaks are available to help female employees meet their child-rearing responsibilities. It is reported that the crèche facilities are seldom used by the working mothers because the high workload makes it impossible for them to visit their children during the working hours. They prefer to use domestic childcare support drawn from family networks, which is believed to be more reliable.

Like many other firms in India, PharmaCo (India) suffers from a high staff-turnover rate. In order to combat retention problems, a flexibility policy, together with other HR initiatives, has been introduced to accommodate the diverse needs of the workforce. For example, shift adjustments are made to enable young employees to study part-time at the college. At times when the staffing level is low on the shopfloor, managers may physically fill the staffing gaps to maintain the production level.

Apart from the gender ratio in the workforce and the accommodation of women workers' childcare needs, there are no specific practices regarding caste, creed, colour and religion beyond the legal requirements.

Source: Compiled based on data from a research project on ED&I led by the author.

Case study questions for discussion

1. What are the characteristics of the approach to ED&I in PharmaCo (India)?
2. In what ways may the HRM practices adopted by the company clash with the principles espoused in the American approach to ED&I, at least in rhetoric?
3. What are the politics at play?
4. How would you recommend PharmaCo to adopt a more effective ED&I policy that will be accepted by the workers and help improve staff retention?

Tensions and issues of D&I research

Studies on ED&I can be categorized into two broad strands. One comes from policy circles, professional association outlets, consultancy promotions and elementary strategic management textbooks. These publications focus on the perceived benefits of ED&I programmes and provide practical advice on effective implementation. They are often prescriptive in advice and simplistic in analysis. Presuming consensus, they focus primarily on the cognitive ability of individuals and organizations rather than on the nuances of organizational politics and the hegemonic power of certain groups over other groups of actors (Zanoni and Janssens, 2004). The other body of literature on ED&I consists of the more scholarly studies published in academic journals and research volumes. They are more critical in analysing the tensions and issues that exist on both the conceptual and practical fronts of ED&I as well as methodological challenges (e.g. Boxenbaum, 2006; Ferner et al., 2005; Healy et al., 2010; Kamenou, 2007; Roberson, 2006). Some of these studies have been discussed in the previous sections. In this section, we devote more space to this second strand of the literature to understand the role of managers and consultants as micro-institutional actors in shaping the D&I agenda at the organizational level (see Table 5.1).

Critics of the rhetoric of ED&I and the array of ED&I programmes in the HRM context have pointed out a number of tensions and issues. First, DM is seen as a managerialized discourse, the language of which is constructed in ways 'that are functional to maintaining [the managers'] privileged rights at the expense of other organizational actors' (Zanoni and Janssens, 2004: 58). In particular, '[all] employees are solely constructed as members of a group, to which a certain work attitude is ascribed' (Zanoni and Janssens, 2004: 65). According to Zanoni and Janssens (2004: 57), the rhetoric of valuing individual 'differences' in DM masks the presence of power in diversity and portrays organizations 'as arenas where differences and competences are valued and individuals receive the same opportunities'. In a similar vein, Mahadevan and Kilian-Yasin (2017) challenged the narrow, stereotypical conceptualization of Muslim as 'the inferior Muslim others' in the international HRM literature. The authors called for a more constructive and reflexive approach to examining issues related to managing migrant Muslim talents as (different) individuals instead of being a collective group.

Empirical research on the implementation of ED&I in different parts of the world revealed that ED&I was primarily used to fulfil organizational goals. As such, socially disadvantaged groups, such as migrants and women, may be used strategically to curtail the power of traditionally dominant groups, such as male workers, rendering them powerless vis-à-vis management and disadvantaged in the labour market (see Chapters 6 on international migration and Chapter 7 on migration). For example, Zanoni and Janssens' (2004: 65) study in Belgium found that 'migrant workers are valued for their willingness to take jobs that require great flexibility, are badly paid, and socially devalued'. In the case study of PharmaCo in this chapter, women are preferred for their skills, mentality and obedience. Flexible working time is only implemented for retention purposes.

Second, key organizational actors, such as managers and trade unions, are political actors in the organizations who manipulate the ED&I initiative to defend and advance their own interests, as was observed by Ferner et al. (2005) and Poster (2008) in the parent–subsidiary negotiations among key groups of organizational actors in the MNCs they studied. Similarly, Boxenbaum's (2006) study revealed how subsidiary managers in Denmark strategically reframed diversity policy from the United Sates to appeal to regional funding agencies for support.

Third, managers are not the only political actors who shape the diversity agenda. In North America, where DM has become a 'fashionable' business, independent consultants and their associations play a crucial role in shaping the diversity agenda and the perceived outcome for their client organizations (Prasad et al., 2010). Prasad et al.'s (2010: 703) study of six firms in the Canadian petroleum and insurance sectors found that these firms 'were manipulated by an institutional field of consultants and experts into adopting relatively superficial initiatives that lacked local relevance, and produced a high level of organizational cynicism regarding diversity'. For example, American-based consultants were providing DM workshops to their Canadian corporate clients based on the American history of discrimination against African Americans and professional white women rather than tailoring the workshops to reflect the local diversity issues. However, these organizations gained legitimacy for their DM programme by remaining fashionable, which 'mostly implied hiring the reputed US-based consulting firms and regularly changing diversity initiatives at the work-place' which involves the same group of strongly connected DM consultants and practitioners (Prasad et al., 2010: 715).

Conclusion

This chapter has examined the conceptual ambiguity of the notion of ED&I, and the practical challenges in the implementation of ED&I programmes. We have explored the diverse national contexts in which equality and diversity issues arise. We have also discussed tensions and dynamics related to the politics of some of the regulations that are aimed at enhancing equality and social justice at the national and international level on the one hand, and the manipulation of the managerialized diversity discourse at the organizational level on the other.

For organizations, issues related to ED&I are manifold. One is that the concept of ED&I is subject to the interpretation of organizational actors, often in ways that advance their interests. As Poster argued, 'the term *diversity* in organizations implies a commitment to social justice and respect for disadvantaged workers, yet it can be interpreted in different ways by corporate actors' (2008: 307 [emphasis in original]). The discourse of diversity is socially constructed and embedded in power relations that serve to entrench the power imbalance across class, gender, race and organizational positions (Ferner et al., 2005; Zanoni and Janssens, 2004). Inequality at workplaces is an outcome of unequal power relations at the individual, group and business unit levels. So is the design and implementation of ED&I initiatives that are aimed at dealing with inequalities. As we have seen, management may choose to employ certain socially disadvantaged groups of workers not because of the former's commitment to equality and social justice, but precisely because of the lack of voice and power of the latter. Disparity of power also exists between HQ and the subsidiaries. The very fact that the former is able to set the agenda of ED&I for the latter reveals this uneven relationship (e.g. Ferner et al., 2005; Poster, 2008).

Another issue is that the internationalization of firms and the greater mobility of labour associated with it have led to a rising level of ambiguity, and on some occasions conflicts, with regard to the applicability of host-country labour regulations to expatriates. Host-country regulations and other labour market conditions may discourage MNCs from deploying local workers, and instead they may choose to export workers from their home country. This staffing strategy may cause political and organizational problems, adding another set of challenges (e.g. language, culture and hierarchy) to ED&I.

A third issue is the utility problem of ED&I. For MNCs, initiatives designed within the North American context, which tend to be more business case-driven, may not be well received in European countries whose ideology of diversity may be more informed by social values and expectations and is underpinned by public policy such as parental leave and benefits. Similarly, European-based ED&I programmes that aim to provide a better work–life balance for the workforce may not be adequate in developing countries like China where for many workers the need to enhance their purchasing power outweighs their desire to have a more balanced family life. In addition, authoritarian management may not entertain the notion of flexible working time to accommodate workers' work–life demands (Xiao and Cooke, 2012). Although the notion of EO informed by the Marxist perspective is well understood if less practised, in the politically unitarist China the concept of ED&I premised on a pluralistic view of society remains novel to most Chinese managers and workers who are unaccustomed to a pluralistic view, despite the increasingly liberal political environment of the country.

For ED&I professionals from consultancy firms or professional associations, there may be a vested interest in the way they promote equality and diversity. For policy-makers, commitment to upholding the ideology of fairness and social justice may be undermined by the need to provide a 'business-friendly' environment for economic growth. The enforcement of national laws is by no means guaranteed, whereas soft regulations and voluntary initiatives developed at the international level that are aimed at providing extra sanctions in the weaker states may lack appeal or enforceability at the local level.

In short, ED&I is a contentious area underpinned by macro- and micro-politics through the involvement of institutional and organizational actors (see Table 5.1). Issues related to equality and diversity for MNCs are made even more complicated owing to the pressures from home and host countries and the involvement of a diverse range of actors at various levels, with some being more powerful than others. When contemplating ED&I issues, it is therefore important to adopt a broader and multi-level analytical framework (see Figure 5.1; also see Syed and Özbilgin, 2009, for their relational analytical framework of DM) informed by political and social perspectives as well as that of strategic management.

Reflective questions

1. Imagine that you are the EO officer of an American-owned international law firm that is expanding its operations in the Middle East. A small number of US-based single female lawyers who have strong career potential raise their concerns with you that they are being discriminated against by

the Middle Eastern host country's working visa restrictions that may disadvantage foreign single women. What solutions would you propose to the firm to (a) prevent the firm from being sued for discrimination by the female lawyers; (b) provide an international development opportunity for the female lawyers which will benefit their career advancement; and (c) take broader action to avoid incidents like this in the future?

2. You are the chairperson of a trade union in the mining industry in an African country where Chinese mining firms are bringing in their own miners from China in order to maintain control of the workers to secure productivity at the expense of local jobs. What would you do to persuade the Chinese firms to abandon the labour-import practice and hire local workers instead? How would you work with other institutional actors, such as the government and (international) NGOs, to achieve this goal? How would you engage the local workers in the process?

3. You are the HR Director of a UK-based MNC in the telecommunication industry. You have been asked by the CEO to develop a global work–life balance programme as part of the corporation's ED&I initiative. The aim of the programme is to attract and retain talent in the corporation's various subsidiaries in Europe, North America and Asia. What are the key factors you would be considering when designing such a programme?

Acknowledgement

A small part of this chapter draws from Cooke, F. L. (2019) 'Equal opportunity and diversity management in the global context'. In Reiche, S., Harzing, A. and Tenzer, H. (eds), *International Human Resource Management*, 5th edn. London: Sage, pp. 529–62.

Recommended reading

- Bonache, J., Festing, M., Kornau, A., Frerichs, I. M. and Sieben, B. (2020) 'An empirical analysis of research paradigms within international human resource management: The need for more diversity'. *German Journal of Human Resource Management*, 34(2): 148–77.
- Boyraz, M. (2019) 'Faultlines as the "Earth's crust": The role of team identification, communication climate, and subjective perceptions of subgroups

(Continued)

for global team satisfaction and innovation'. *Management Communication Quarterly*, 33(4): 581–615.

- Donnelly, R. (2015), 'Tensions and challenges in the management of diversity and inclusion in IT services multinationals in India'. *Human Resource Management*, 54(2): 199–215.
- Ely, R. J. and Thomas, D. A. (2001) 'Cultural diversity at work: The effects of diversity perspectives on work group processes and outcomes'. *Administrative Science Quarterly*, 46(2): 229–73.
- Moeller, M. and Maley, J. F. (2018) 'MNC considerations in identifying and managing LGB expatriate stigmatization'. *International Journal of Management Reviews*, 20(2): 325–42.

References

Agocs, C. and Burr, C. (1996) 'Employment equity, affirmative action and managing diversity: Assessing the differences'. *International Journal of Manpower*, 17(4–5): 30–45.

Ali, M., Kulik, C. T. and Metz, I. (2011) 'The gender diversity-performance relationship in services and manufacturing organizations'. *International Journal of Human Resource Management*, 22(7): 1464–85.

Bonache, J., Sanchez, J. I. and Zárraga-Oberty, C. (2009) 'The interaction of expatriate pay differential and expatriate inputs on host country nationals' pay unfairness'. *International Journal of Human Resource Management*, 20(10): 2135–49.

Boxenbaum, E. (2006) 'Lost in translation: The making of Danish diversity management'. *American Behavioral Scientist*, 49(7): 939–48.

Chen, C. C., Kraemer, J. and Gathii, J. (2011) 'Understanding locals' compensation fairness vis-à-vis foreign expatriates: The role of perceived equity'. *International Journal of Human Resource Management*, 22(17): 3582–600.

Chartered Institute of Personnel and Development (2007) *Diversity in Business: A Focus for Progress*. London: Chartered Institute of Personnel and Development.

Cooke, F. L. (2010) 'Women's participation in employment in Asia: A comparative analysis of China, India, Japan and South Korea'. *International Journal of Human Resource Management*, 21(10–12): 2249–70.

Cooke, F. L. (2012) *Human Resource Management in China: New Trends and Practices*. London: Routledge.

Cooke, F. L. (2019), 'Equal opportunity and diversity management in the global context', in Reiche, S., Harzing, A. and Tenzer, H. (eds), *International Human Resource Management*, 5th edn. London: Sage, pp. 529–62.

Cooke, F. L. and Saini, D. (2012) 'Managing diversity in India and China: Implications for western MNCs'. *Journal of Chinese Human Resource Management*, 3(1): 16–32.

Cox, T. (1993) *Cultural Diversity in Organizations: Theory, Research and Practice*. San Francisco: Barrett-Koehler.

Cox, T., Lobel, S. and McLeod, P. (1991) 'Effects of ethnic group cultural differences on cooperative and competitive behaviour on a group task'. *Academy of Management Journal*, 34(4): 827–47.

Dhar-Bhattacharjee, S. and Richardson, H. (2018) 'A tour of India in one workplace: investigating complex and gendered relations in IT'. *Information Technology & People*, 31(2): 578–94.

Donnelly, R. (2015) 'Tensions and challenges in the management of diversity and inclusion in IT services multinationals in India'. *Human Resource Management*, 54(2): 199–215.

Ferner, A., Almond, P. and Colling, T. (2005) 'Institutional theory and the cross-national transfer of employment policy: The case of "workforce diversity" in US multinationals'. *Journal of International Business Studies*, 36(3): 304–21.

Gaibrois, C. and Nentwich, J. (2020) 'The dynamics of privilege: How employees of a multinational corporation construct and contest the privileging effects of English proficiency'. *Canadian Journal of Administrative Science*, 37(4): 468–82.

Healy, G., Kirton, G., Özbilgin, M. and Oikelome, F. (2010) 'Competing rationalities in the diversity project of the UK judiciary: The politics of assessment centres'. *Human Relations*, 63(6): 807–34.

Healy, G. and Oikelome, F. (2007) 'A global link between national diversity policies? The case of the migration of Nigerian physicians to the UK and USA'. *International Journal of Human Resource Management*, 18(11): 1917–33.

Hennekam, S., Tahssain-Gay, L. and Syed, J. (2017) 'Contextualising diversity management in the Middle East and North Africa: a relational perspective'. *Human Resource Management Journal*, 27(3): 459–76.

Kamenou, N. (2007) 'Methodological considerations in conducting research across gender, "race", ethnicity and culture: A challenge to context specificity in diversity research methods'. *International Journal of Human Resource Management*, 18(11): 1995–2010.

Kirton, J., Robertson, M. and Avdelidou-Fischer, N. (2016) 'Valuing and value in diversity: The policy-implementation gap in an IT firm'. *Human Resource Management Journal*, 26(3): 321–36.

Kramar, R. (2012) 'Diversity management in Australia: A mosaic of concepts, practice and rhetoric'. *Asia Pacific Journal of Human Resources*, 50(2): 245–61.

Lau, D. and Murnighan, J. (1998) 'Demographic diversity and faultlines: The compositional dynamics of organizational groups'. *Academy of Management Review*, 23(2): 325–40.

Liff, S. (1996) 'Two routes to managing diversity: Individual differences or social group characteristics'. *Employee Relations*, 19(1): 11–26.

Lorbiecki, A. and Jack, G. (2000) 'Critical turns in the evolution of diversity management'. *British Journal of Management*, 11 (Special Issue): S17–S31.

Mahadevan, J. and Kilian-Yasin, K. (2017) 'Dominant discourse, orientalism and the need for reflexive HRM: Skilled Muslim migrants in the German context'. *International Journal of Human Resource Management*, 28(8): 1140–62.

Maxwell, G., Blair, S. and McDougall, M. (2001) 'Edging towards managing diversity in practice'. *Employee Relations*, 23(5): 468–82.

Moeller, M. and Maley, J. F. (2018) 'MNC considerations in identifying and managing LGB expatriate stigmatization'. *International Journal of Management Reviews*, 20(2): 325–42.

Mor Barak, M. (2005) *Managing Diversity: Towards a Globally Inclusive Workplace*. Thousand Oaks, CA: Sage.

Nishii, L. and Özbilgin, F. (2007) 'Global diversity management: Towards a conceptual framework'. *International Journal of Human Resource Management*, 18(11): 1883–94.

Özbilgin, M. and Tatli, A. (2011) 'Mapping out the field of equality and diversity: Rise of individualism and voluntarism'. *Human Relations*, 64(9): 1229–53.

Paetkau, T. (2009) 'When does a foreign law compel a U.S. employer to discriminate against U.S. expatriates? A modest proposal for reform'. *Labor Law Journal*, 60(2): 92–103.

Peltokorpi, V. and Yamao, S. (2017) 'Corporate language proficiency in reverse knowledge transfer: A moderated mediation model of shared vision and communication frequency'. *Journal of World Business*, 52(3): 404–16.

Poster, W. (2008) 'Filtering diversity: A global corporation struggles with race, class, and gender in employment policy'. *American Behavioral Scientist*, 52(3): 307–41.

Prasad, A., Prasad, P. and Mir, R. (2010) '"One mirror in another": Managing diversity and the discourse of fashion'. *Human Relations*, 64(5): 703–24.

Roberson, Q. M. (2006) 'Disentangling the meanings of diversity and inclusion in organizations'. *Group and Organization Management*, 31(2): 212–36.

Sippola, A. and Smale, A. (2007) 'The global integration of diversity management: A longitudinal case study'. *International Journal of Human Resource Management*, 18(11): 1895–1916.

Society for Human Resource Management (n.d.) *How to Develop a Diversity, Equity and Inclusion Initiative*. Available at: https://www.shrm.org/resourcesandtools/tools-and-samples/how-to-guides/pages/how-to-develop-a-diversity-and-inclusion-initiative.aspx (accessed 13 September 2020).

Soni, V. (2000) 'A twenty-first-century reception for diversity in public sector: A case study'. *Public Administration Review*, 60(5): 395–408.

Süß, S. and Kleiner, M. (2007) 'Diversity management in Germany: Dissemination and design of the concept'. *International Journal of Human Resource Management*, 18(11): 1934–53.

Syed, J. and Kramar, R. (2010) 'What is the Australian model for managing cultural diversity?' *Personnel Review*, 39(1): 96–115.

Syed, J. and Özbilgin, M. (2009) 'A relational framework for international transfer of diversity management practices'. *International Journal of Human Resource Management*, 20(12): 2435–53.

Tenzer, H. and Pudelko, M. (2017) 'The influence of language differences on power dynamics in multinational teams'. *Journal of World Business*, 52(1): 45–61.

Tsui, A., Egan, T. and O'Reilly, C. (1992) 'Being different: Relational demography and organizational attachment'. *Administrative Science Quarterly*, 37(4): 549–79.

Vedina, R. and Vadi, M. (2008) 'A national identity perspective on collectivistic attitudes and perception of organisational culture'. *Baltic Journal of Management*, 3(2): 129–44.

Xiao, Y. C. and Cooke, F. L. (2012) 'Work–life balance in China? Social policy, employer strategy and individual coping mechanisms'. *Asia-Pacific Journal of Human Resources*, 50(1): 6–22.

Zanoni, P. and Janssens, M. (2004) 'Deconstructing difference: The rhetoric of human resource managers' diversity discourses'. *Organization Studies*, 25(1): 55–74.

6 Here, there and everywhere: work on international assignments for multinational corporations

Jenny K. Rodriguez and Miguel Martínez Lucio

Learning objectives

- To understand the challenges of working on international assignments (IAs)
- To identify the questions of fairness and equality raised by working on IAs
- To understand well-being and work–life balance issues that emerge during IAs

Introduction

International assignments (IAs) are an important part of the operations of multinational corporations (MNCs). IAs highlight the complexity of the 'human' factor in contemporary global work and the nuanced nature of management and decision-making across the local/global spectrum, which presents a number of challenges for individuals and organizations. Debates about IAs are central to international human resource management (IHRM) as they incorporate many aspects relevant to different actors operating across borders and highlight the porosity and relative vulnerability of MNC structures and processes. IAs span organizational, cultural and spatial boundaries, exposing – often in unintended ways – the challenges of operating across different national contexts.

Increasingly, the study of IAs has pushed away from the stereotypical and archetypal vision of an 'American' or 'European' manager abroad facing 'alien' contexts and customs. The debate is increasingly honing in on broader problems around employment rights, fairness of treatment, questions of stress and work–life balance and the way these different dimensions intersect to impact workers' experiences of IAs. It is also widening its remit by studying the experiences of diverse groups of workers on IAs, such as women, ethnic minorities and members of the lesbian, gay, bisexual and transgender (LGBT) community. Hence the chapter starts by addressing general questions and issues related to IAs and then looks at issues of organizational support, compensation and fairness. The chapter then finishes by addressing broader issues of gender and well-being among others. The chapter tries to highlight the wider experiences of IAs and the way these relate to the need to adopt an approach with greater sensitivity to a more critical perspective on work and employment.

The question of IAs and mobility

IAs have become a key point of discussion in debates about IHRM. Their relevance is linked to MNCs' move to more global and transnational forms of organization, which require a greater degree of coordination and interaction among staff (e.g. home- or parent-country, host-country and third-country nationals) in home and host national contexts (see Bartlett and Ghoshal, 2002, and Jain et al., 1998). The complexity of IAs is first captured in the form these assignments take: long-term or expatriate assignment, short-term assignment, international-commuter and frequent-flyer assignments (Fenwick, 2004a; Mayerhofer et al., 2004; Meyskens et al., 2009), which we discuss further below. For the theory and practice of IHRM, an important consideration is the framing of discussions about IAs, which tends to address organizations and employees separately. There are three main approaches to these discussions. Some focus on the financial implications for organizations, for instance cost/benefit analysis of resourcing issues, such as adequately managing the flow and mobility of international talent, the cost and implications of brain drain/gain, as well as relocation costs (Baruch et al., 2007; Carr et al., 2005; Reiche and Harzing, 2011). Some focus on the process from a human resources (HR) perspective, discussing the selection of international assignees, pre-departure support, professional and personal integration in host settings and repatriation (Chiang et al., 2018; Collings et al., 2011; Sánchez Vidal et al., 2008). Finally, some focus on individual assignees, addressing issues such as motivation, career, family/spousal adaptation and well-being (Dickmann et al., 2008; Kanstrén and Mäkelä, 2020; Sarkiunaite and Rocke, 2015). This distinction shows a tension in academic interventions on the question of IAs between whether to focus on the needs of the organization or on the needs of the international assignee. While systematic organizational structures within MNCs are fundamental, the reality is that a combination of factors, such as personal relations, networks, capabilities and approaches of employees to IAs, could be pivotal to the success of the activities of an MNC in a host country. As such, the smooth operational running of activities through an effective IA programme is clearly of importance but, in part, relies on the support provided to those travelling and working abroad.

A major challenge to academics and practitioners is to accurately measure both the costs and benefits of IAs (Collings et al., 2007: 202). This is, in effect, the main concern for much of the traditional literature as it moves between a focus on 'getting the job done' and ensuring that the employee is supported and retained as an employee. Collings et al. (2007: 202) quote Tahvanainen and Suutari (2005), who pointed out that less emphasis has been placed on the implementation of strategy than on strategy formulation, with human resources (HR) policies being treated as secondary. Aspects of the debate hinge on the extent of failure experienced by employees on IAs in their work, which is difficult to measure (Harzing and Christensen, 2004; Johnson, 2005). Furthermore, there is no agreement in relation to who is ultimately responsible for IA failure; some work (e.g. Huang et al., 2005) alludes to family pressures and assignees' inability to adapt, while other work (e.g. Cole and Nesbeth, 2014) has found evidence of a lack of organizational support. In some sense, much may hinge on the nature of the IA, the alternatives that exist and the alignment between the situation and the type of assignment. Part of the challenge facing IAs and their organizations may be that the wrong form of IA has been allocated in terms of the project and a worker. To this extent, organizations must be wary of issues of length and location related to an IA.

In addition, experiences are not uniform; for example, while operational aspects may be less successful, there may be other intangible and positive outcomes related to the development of knowledge and organizational culture, as argued by Boyle et al. (2012). So, while one part of the discussion seems to be focused on the reasons why MNCs arrange IAs and deploy them internationally, there is a deeper HR question and set of concerns regarding the role of individuals on IAs, the nature of their work and the nature of the support they receive. It is not sufficient to focus on the macro and organizational levels of global staffing. Rather, there is often a need to focus on whether a long-term assignment – which requires a significant amount of cultural and social embedding – is the best choice (see Collings and Isichei, 2017: 168–9). This is increasingly the case, given alternatives that can be used that may alleviate some of the core problems that emerge from feeling alienated, experiencing cross-cultural dissonance and the personal and operational challenges of 'not fitting in or getting on'. In a review of the alternatives, Collings and Isichei (2017: 170–7) point to the use of three types of alternative to IAs, drawing on a range of debates and interventions by those researching the subject: short-term assignments, international business travel and commuter and rotational assignments. Short-term assignments of a few months sustain the extant reward systems and avoid long-term challenges emerging from organizational and social assimilation in a host country. The international business-traveller approach requires constant travel between sites and has emerged due to the acceleration of an extensive travel industry (and in the context of the pandemic creates further tensions and uncertainties). Commuter and rotational assignments are based on regular travel between the employee's home location and the overseas location in which they are required. Each of these options brings different issues and challenges, some related to how these arrangements can shape worker perceptions of a fragmented employment relationship due to the inherent dispersion across time and space. Other commonly reported experiences are fatigue and stress, to which we will return later on.

An important dimension missing from discussions about IAs is fairness and equality. For example, some (see Dabic et al., 2015: 332–3, and Kawai and Strange, 2014) note the lack of universal theorizing regarding expatriate management and support; there is a tendency to focus on adjustment issues and affective commitment and to pay less attention to key questions of fairness and equality –see also Bonache et al. (2001) as quoted in Dabic et al. (2015). To a certain extent, the focus on the individual is related more to the matters of insertion and to questions of culture, and less to the human resource management needs of the person assigned. Furthermore, it could be seen to take away the scrutiny from MNCs' responsibilities as employers. Much of this may derive from the initial 'gaze' of the study of IAs, with its focus on the challenges facing executive or strategic-level males from 'western' cultures in non-western contexts (Black et al., 1991; Suutari, 1998). This neo-imperialist set of assumptions within the debate on IAs is somewhat dated, but rarely have the reviews or discussions of the debates systematically mapped these issues – that is, until recently, when a wave of work has emerged from researchers with an interest in the nuanced experiences of groups largely under-represented in dominant discussions, such as women, ethnic minorities and LGBT employees (see, for example, Gedro et al., 2013; Rodriguez and Ridgway, 2019; and Salamin and Hanappi, 2014). In this literature, matters about international assignees' identities, location and the diverse challenges that they face are beginning to be approached in a manner that is alert to the costs of this type of work to the individual and their relationship to the organization, rather than simply focusing on the costs to the organization deploying them. Part of the challenge is that new forms of assignments continue to emerge and more diverse groups increasingly engage in this type of work, including migrants and other types of mobile worker (see McNulty and Brewster, 2017; see also Chapter 7 on migration).

Compensation, control, equality and well-being: recasting the debate in terms of the employment relationship

The debate on IAs is broad, as it overlaps with the very identity and question of IHRM. It covers the human dimension of the way MNCs manage across borders and expand their realm of influence. The debate, as can be seen, addresses broad questions related to IAs in terms of their typologizing, changing aspects and developments and in terms of the major challenges to assignees once in host settings. However, growing attention has been paid to the challenges faced by international assignees across a much broader set of employment issues, such as change in employment status. In this respect, there is a substantive part of the debate that, directly or indirectly, addresses questions of workplace control, personal development, compensation and, increasingly, matters of equality, fairness, well-being and health and safety. The debate is increasingly mirroring the concerns of many sociologists of work who have, in other areas, been drawing our attention to matters related to increasing levels of exploitation at work (see Chapter 12 on lean production) and increasingly levels of inequality (see Chapter 5 on equality and diversity), in addition to questions of well-being and health and safety (Giorgi et al., 2016).

While cast normally as a concern of international human resource management or organizational culture and cross-cultural relations, due to the emergence of studies focusing on gender, race and work–life balance, the debate can be recast as an employment relations issue. Most international assignees are not at the higher strategic level – their position is much more ambivalent and contradictory, something not uncommon for a range of managers and leading professionals within organizations more generally. For example, managers and key professionals in areas such as information technology and project management are, let us not forget, employees – workers, even – who have variable control over their work and also face challenging working conditions; for a deeper discussion of such contradictory class locations and others, see Wright (1985). Often, the managerially oriented nature of the debate on IAs misses this aspect. In doing so, problems are seen as purely technical or operational in nature and, therefore, matters that can be resolved by the organization and individuals by simply readjusting in organizational, cultural and personal terms. This approach has led to specific attention being placed on recruitment and selection, especially assignment fit: getting the 'right' person with the right skills and levels of adaptability (Cerdin and Pargneux, 2009). This keeps the discussion within more traditional approaches that do not reflect the current realities of IAs. More importantly, the positioning as a 'global talent management' problem reinforces the technical/

operational framing that sees it as a concern of HR practice and not an employment relations issue. Ultimately, fundamental questions of fairness and equality that cut across explicitly or implicitly require more insight.

Rewarding and compensating IAs 'fairly'

First, we need to address the question of compensation and reward. This is not solely a technical matter based on how levels of compensation and reward are 'set'. How international assignees are paid in relation to the tasks and challenges of international deployment, how they are paid in relation to local host staff doing similar work, how their accommodation and subsistence is covered and at what level and how any extra demands are supported how effectively an HR 'minefield'. To that extent, questions of compensation and reward need to consider these broader dimensions and activities (Vernon, 2006), and a range of challenges related to compensation disparities have been identified (Chen et al., 2002; Duvivier et al., 2019; Harzing and Christensen, 2004). For instance, McNulty (2016) argues that home-based compensation is an outdated concept and compensation should not be determined by home-country status but instead based on the role in the host setting. In addition, compensation packages must be contextualised in relation to global mobility – for instance, groups like self-initiated expatriates: individuals with a more independent approach who have left their home context out of their own volition and have forged their careers and work through international travel (McKenna and Richardson, 2007) – will likely use global comparators to shape their compensation expectations (Kim et al., 2018).

Another specific challenge that MNCs may face pertains to the relationship between compensation and performance management, which some (Claus and Briscoe, 2009; Fenwick, 2004b) argue has received little theoretical attention. There are several points of complexity related to host-country preferences as well as more HR-based considerations, such as goal-setting structures. In a study of expatriate performance management at Nokia, Tahvanainen (2000) reports on the challenges of personal goal-setting given the nature and structure of projects. One participant reported that 'we put a goal on the wall that the network has to be operating by such and such a date. It's usually much clearer that way' (Tahvanainen, 2000: 271). While it could be argued that there is implicit flexibility, ultimately, there is ambiguity that could lead to unfairness in compensation given that goal-setting is collective in a way that makes it challenging to link performance back to a specific individual in a meaningful way. In addition, individual expectations regarding compensation and support will also vary due to background and regulatory and cultural customs in national contexts (Warneke and Schneider, 2011). Similarly, there is contextual variability in the types of financial compensation that are of key significance to organizational HR strategy. Moreover, there may be cultural differences in relation to performance management and measurement among employee groups from diverse national backgrounds (Caligiuri, 2006). This sits at the heart of questions of reward and evaluation, which are always complex in HRM and are enhanced across borders in relation to different views about how performance management is to be conducted and by whom, ultimately raising concerns of equity and fairness.

Questions of fairness and how employees perceive fairness in rewards can influence aspects of employee loyalty (Hareendrakumar et al., 2020). Ensuring that reward systems are fair across borders and reflect the activities of those being rewarded will always be a challenge due to contrasting national sets of regulations that determine issues such as fairness across genders and ethnicities, as well as levels of organizational transparency and communication (see Shortland and Perkins, 2016; see also Chapter on 4 on payment systems). As those on IAs operate across different national boundaries, they may experience the tension of being located within the context of their employer's payment cultures and structures, while also experiencing cultural and national expectations that may not sit clearly with these corporate approaches. In their comparative study of Indian and Irish employees, Ramamoorthy et al. (2005) outlined how various individualist and collectivist approaches to work related to HR systems and expectations varied across both settings. This raises a seemingly unresolvable question of equity; on one hand lies the importance of equitable processes and outcomes, and on the other, the variations in terms of how different groups of workers expect to be treated and rewarded. The IA literature has focused mainly on the problems this brings with regard to 'getting the job done' but, as we will explore below, questions of fairness and equality require discussions that engage with broader understandings and expectations about the relationship between MNCs and national contexts, and policies and rules on diversity and fairness. Positioning the cultural and regulatory context of individuals and the way they frame fairness within the debate is therefore essential.

Support and control within IAs

By their very nature, IAs have organizational support (cooperation) and general control at the heart of their existence; however, it is important to understand how these relate to employment relations issues. One of the most testing aspects of the relationship between IAs and employment relations is the notion of 'IA failure'. Cole and Nesbeth (2014) summarize much of the discussion on failure, and identify job and work environment, lack of family support, lack of organizational support and the contextual features of the host country as the key factors linked to IA failure. The first set of factors includes things such as lack of development, lack of fit and clarity and problematic selection procedures. These matters speak to limitations with the HR approach to recruitment, reward and development (Thoo and Kaliannan, 2013). Lack of family support comprises, for example, partner and family adjustment (Copeland and Norell, 2002; McNulty, 2012). Lack of organizational support is also significant (Kraimer and Wayne, 2004), as organizations are typically unable to extend their core staff support programmes effectively across the range of host countries in which they operate. Finally, Cole and Nesbeth (2014) found that the contextual factors of the host country were the least important in terms of cultural and spatial context. The authors also found that the lack of organizational support in the field and the impact on family – these matters being very much linked to the social dimensions of the HR function – were the top two challenges that led to IA failure. This suggests that the social dimensions within the work environment and beyond should be viewed as key challenges – something to which we shall return when discussing gender and difference.

What appears to be less present in the core debate on the question of IAs is the issue of organizational control. Employees on IAs seek organizational support but may also seek a degree of autonomy. Indeed, there may be myriad reasons that will make IAs attractive (for a systematic survey of the literature on motives for taking on IAs, see Hippler (2009)). Working in particular environments or locations may be a necessity of one's contract or a step encouraged with the promise of career progression, but the decision to work in these circumstances may also emerge from the specific choices an employee makes – when options are available – that are linked to other social and personal objectives and needs. The most common reasons for pursuing and accepting international assignments have traditionally been related to creating a personal life-oriented experience that allows the individual to experience other cultures and national contexts and develop their own social capital and networks (see Collings, 2014). Other works (see Stroppa and Spieß, 2011, and Tung, 1998) have linked motives for travel to 'escape': from a head office, from home-based social networks, from difficult organizational relations – in some cases IAs are organized to separate staff from each other and from management in the event of a problematic workplace. This could resemble what we have seen with individuals in relation to homeworking and teleworking being used as a way of managing one's autonomy as well as escaping perceived organizational politics (Fonner and Roloff, 2010). A particular factor that both IAs and teleworking share is that they enable new forms of organizational control through the employer's use of information and communication technology (ICT) and greater forms of reporting to management. While geographical distance – whether nationally or internationally based – can allow for greater autonomy, advances in terms of how surveillance and control are organized by employers can limit this autonomy, even in the furthest reaches of the globe: this is another employment relations issue that should be explored as a key dilemma facing people working on IAs.

The question of diversity and IAs

Until the end of the 20th century, discussions about IAs had been traditionally characterised by gender and race blindness (Adler, 2002). More recently, IA debates have taken a greater interest in questions of gender, race, sexuality and identity yet there is need for more work that expands on these issues (Dabic et al., 2015: 333). In early research in this area, Forster (1999) outlined the challenges women face on IAs due to cultural factors and the way gender roles are viewed in different contexts, also pointing out that, typically, women were primarily locked into lower- and middle-ranging positions. Evidence continues to show these disparities; in a review of women in IAs, Altman and Shortland (2008) map out evidence that suggests that gendered stereotypical views of women have been the primary explanations used for their under-representation in IAs. These are reproduced transnationally; for instance, in their study of Chinese female expatriates, Shen and Jiang (2015: 312) point out, among other things, that culture and traditions in a host country with hostile attitudes may lead to a negative and challenging experience for this group of women. Similar findings have been reported by others (see Fischlmayr and Puchmüller, 2016, and Hutchings and Michailova, 2014).

New research approaches have emerged in this area to include the interaction of gender, race, sexuality and other social categories of difference (see, for example, Paisley and Tayar, 2016). Rodriguez and Scurry (2019) have pointed to the importance of drawing on theories of intersectionality – a sensitivity to the multiple identities of workers in their employment and social context. In their work, not only did skilled migrant women in the Saudi Peninsula have to deal with negative perceptions related to their gender, but also with their 'foreignness' as a marker of their identity, leading to multiple forms of exclusion and marginalization. Work in this area (see Bader et al., 2018; Harrison and Michailova, 2012; and Tung, 2008) brings to the fore the complexities of national contexts, where LGBT expatriates might experience threats to their safety and physical well-being (see McPhail and McNulty, 2015) or where women expatriates experience dualities, such as being part of 'elite' expatriate communities while also being subjected to patriarchal cultures that undermine them (Rodriguez and Ridgway, 2019). Other work explores institutional and legal dimensions relevant to the experiences of workers on IA, such as LGBT expatriates in host settings where homosexuality is deemed legally and socially unacceptable by locals or single-parent households in contexts with traditional understandings of the idea of family (see McNulty and Hutchings, 2016, and McPhail et al., 2016). These works highlight the imperative for HR departments to be alert not only to questions of equality but also to understandings of intersectional difference and safety of IAs within national contexts. In the particular case of LGBT on IAs, some authors (see Moeller and Maley, 2018) speak of a duty of care within organizations to prioritise their well-being and safety in different national locations, with others (see McPhail and McNulty, 2015) arguing that it is more than a matter of formal support and the legal status of LGBT expatriates, but also a matter of the 'comfort factor' in a host country when assessing risks to this group. Therefore the recruitment, selection, preparation and support of LGBT employees on IAs comprise an important issue that HR departments need to address.

Well-being and work–life balance

The previous discussions overlap with a set of critical questions related to well-being and work–life balance. Generally speaking, work–life balance issues are multilayered and can emerge from a range of sources: from work pressures, to contextual challenges, to social and family demands. Against this backdrop, questions of health – especially mental health – are an important issue in the study of work and employment that must also be considered in relation to certain developments, such as work intensification, greater travel, absence from home and the impact of ICT and teleworking. These impact on the quality of employment and negatively shape the experience of work (Vanroelen, 2019). While these are issues relevant to a large constituency of employees, those on IAs may experience them in very specific ways, which must be appreciated if a fuller picture of the challenges of IAs is to be understood. Balancing various roles across the boundaries of work and family and social life may be a challenge that varies in intensity across different national contexts, especially for those with broader social, personal, family or support roles (Caligiuri and Lazarova, 2005). Balancing such roles may also affect spouses and partners of employees on IAs who also confront the challenges of different national environments. This can lead to an overall picture of conflict where IAs struggle to manage both the workspace as well as their own boundaries with and within the personal sphere (Shaffer and Harrison, 2001; Starr and Currie, 2009). Evidence (see Meyksens et al., 2009) suggests that both long-term and short-term assignments have the potential to lead to problems and challenges related to work–life balance. Mäkelä et al. (2011) note that greater attention needs to be paid to the views of those on IAs, especially the way openings and opportunities made available to female employees from such forms and locations of work may be made positive, even if the challenges and social hardships are significant. As previously noted, despite considerable changes since the late 1990s, women still face a range of hurdles linked to their deployment on IAs. An important consideration is the choices and calculations women on IAs make, as longer career development and a more settled family context may be the outcome of dealing with challenging contingencies in the short term, and much may depend on support and national context (Shortland, 2016). This calls for closer scrutiny of the benefits and costs of IAs in work–life balance and social terms, especially with a broader range of employee groups engaging in IAs. In addition, as mentioned earlier, working in different environments may also allow for a degree of 'escape' or 'autonomy' in terms of established working and social relationships and this speaks to the complexity of motives for staying on IAs despite challenging experiences (Reiche et al., 2011).

Another issue to consider is travel, which adds to the complexity of dealing with a host context, and sustaining and supporting partners, families and others close to IAs. Challenges associated with travel for IAs include schedule disruption, jetlag, working on the move, responding to work demands from different time zones and also 'dead time', such as time in the air or between locations. In this respect, travel has a strong 'behind-the-scenes' nature that has significant implications for stress and overall well-being. Dimitrova et al. (2020) note that job resources (e.g. job decision latitude and supervisory support) are fundamental to offset the negative impact of travel on the work experiences of IAs. In their special issue on 'International Business Travel', Beaverstock et al. (2009) call for a broader approach and location of business travel as part of discussions about the corporate ecologies of work. We would argue that a broader approach should also include travel in the context of the reformulated notions of spaces of work and their implications for employment relations. For example, what is the quality of employment of those having catch-up meetings in the waiting area of an airport or on a train journey? And what is the impact of parenting or solving caring arrangements in such circumstances?

Finally, reflecting on work–life balance issues, we could draw on Noon et al.'s (2013) discussion; they outline challenges to work using Greenhaus and Beutell's (1985) argument that overlapping spheres of work and non-work can lead to three different forms of conflict: time-based, strain-based and behaviour-based. Framing the challenges to IAs using these three dimensions, we can identify that: (i) due to working long hours and lengthy travelling, IAs have reduced time for personal obligations, which results in *time-based conflict*; (ii) with strain emerging from one sphere, be it work or social life, the pressures of accommodating a challenging host-nation context can lead to *strain-based conflict* in the other sphere; and (iii) certain *behaviour* in one sphere, such as methods of socializing at work in different countries, can lead to tensions and contradictions in personal and family life. Against this backdrop and its implications and consequences, issues of mental health and stress require vital attention in the study and management of work. Rosenbusch et al. (2015) argue that stress can emerge from the challenges of balancing work, family and related spheres, and note that its roots may not only be in organizational change and the way shifts take place in operations and organizational relations across countries, but also from a lack of communication and support related to them. This goes back to the idea we discussed before about the challenges facing IAs of straddling different national boundaries and organizational structures. Rosenbusch et al. (2015) also point to the problems emerging from cultural stress, as well as having to deal with different ways of working and living. In this context, isolation has been discussed both as an important part of cross-cultural adjustment that affects IAs but also as an important barrier facing their partners and families. For example, reporting on the experiences of German expatriated spouses of MNC employees, Kupka and Cathro (2007) showed that lack of support and response had a direct impact on their solitary and fractured experiences. This raises an important point about the framing of HR support for IAs, which must consider them as individual employees, but also their families as central stakeholders for the success of the IA. These issues are of increasing complexity due to new forms of IA where an IA may not be directly employed by the firm for which they are working, or may not have a long-term relationship with a firm, e.g. as a result of being on a project-based IA. Collings and Isichei (2017: 178–9) draw together research on atypical work and arrangements, and suggest that more needs to be done to understand the even greater complexity of individuals on IAs – and interrogate how and whether they sit within traditional corporate HR support systems.

Case study: Mobility and work – expectations and reality

(Rodriguez and Scurry, 2014; Scurry et al., 2013)

Researcher: What were your reasons for becoming an expat?

Participant: I wasn't intending to go international, but an opportunity came up and I accepted. It was a combination of multiple things, it was traveling, the money . . . it was double my salary in the UK and tax free.

Researcher: What were your reasons for coming to Qatar?

Participant: It was by accident really because I was due to go back to the UK after Russia, but my manager said there was a job open in Qatar. I thought it would be good because it was in a part of the world I'd never been to before, and I always wanted to visit and learn the culture there. I should have gone back to London because I wanted to be near my family back together again after being away so long. My family never lived with me abroad because after we had our first child my wife didn't want our children to move around and have an unsettled life. She wanted them to be brought up in the UK with a stable life, stable house, stable friends, and I knew my international assignments were going to be long term and various. Living abroad never appealed to her.

Researcher: Did you think working abroad would advance your career?

Participant: Yeah, that wasn't the primary reason, though. It's a completely different work ethic, working at home and overseas. Things move a lot quicker, people who are sent overseas tend to be of the best, and you become an expat commodity sent to use your expertise elsewhere. You are tested, you have to work hard, and you have to deliver. I didn't primarily take it for the opportunity to develop. I took it because of the opportunity abroad and for the money. I did develop, though. I was exposed to things that I hadn't been back home. I was attending to operating meetings world-wide, dealing with things with such meaning, you get hands on experience to the actual production of oil that I would never have obtained staying in the UK. That was something to build upon in terms of career development. I realized after my first few years away from the UK, that this was an opportunity to learn a lot and be promoted, and that has happened. This sort of keeps you abroad and motivates you to keep working overseas. It becomes a point that you have been overseas so long that you cannot go back. You become a different animal. I don't think they would have me back either because you don't fit in. You handle situations different here, and I know I would be frustrated back there. I don't think I will ever go back, and I don't want to.

Researcher: How long are you planning to stay here?

Participant: I'm actually moving at the end of month. I am taking a really great job in Syria; I don't know how long I will stay there. But I am planning to stay overseas as long as I can. I can retire at 55, but it depends on my liabilities. The older you get, the more short-term you look, so I have savings to get me through financially. I don't need to worry what happens in ten years, I can survive very nicely if I left today. But I'm staying because I enjoy the work, and when I stop enjoying the work, I can do something else, like farming.

Questions for case study

1.   What does the case study tell us about some of the choices that individuals make on IAs?
2.   What are the problems outlined with regard to returning to their initial workplace and why do you think they exist?
3.   What kinds of pressures may someone like this face as they spend more time on IAs?
4.   What could go wrong with regard to this case and how can the positive features of an IA be sustained by organizational support?

Conclusion

In some sense, IAs represent an exotic part of the experience of working for an MNC. The idea of international travel, a cosmopolitan lifestyle and a more diverse set of cultural experiences at work and in its surroundings leads to this being an attractive feature of being employed by such organizations. However, as the chapter shows through its discussion of a broad range of studies, considerable challenges remain for IAs.

There are traditional challenges in the form of support for travel and physically adjusting to a new working and cultural environment – although how much of that is due to the lack of preparation and openness of individuals and organizations has preoccupied much research. However, a range of broader employment issues emerges given the way IAs are changing. First, there is growing awareness that fairness issues and transparency become extremely sensitive as workers on IAs traverse national boundaries and questions of comparison become central. Moreover, compensation across a range of activities becomes the subject of intense debate within the employment relationship – for example, compensation for accommodation, subsistence and costs of repatriation. Second, the question of well-being and stress – issues that are now central to any discussion of contemporary work – is also integral to any discussion about IAs. The consequences of alienation, isolation, overwork, lack of social support and the challenges of travel have generated concerns about well-being. Finally, the question of diversity has gained prominence as a key feature of IAs as more research efforts are made to understand the variability of experiences of particular groups of workers on IA and the challenges they face. To this extent, we need to view these issues as shaping a distinct picture of work and employment that needs attention and nuanced discussion, and not simply as questions of organizational accommodation and cultural dissonance. Globalization is stretching and broadening the challenges of work within MNCs in novel ways. The issues we have discussed are central and call for organizations to consider how the employment relationship unfolds transnationally and to develop fairer and more supportive structures in terms of employment policies and practices.

Reflective questions

1. What are the main challenges you identify working on international assignments?
2. Why are questions of equality and equity relevant to the understanding of international assignments?

3. Why and how have work–life balance issues emerged in relation to international assignments?
4. What policies and practices should HR departments improve or develop to address unresolved problems related to international assignments, such as cultural adjustment, mental health, and work–life balance?
5. In what ways can the use of teleworking and virtual working assist or facilitate international assignments? What challenges do they create for working internationally?

Recommended readings

-   Boyle, B., Nicholas, S. and Mitchell, R. (2012) 'Sharing and developing knowledge of organization culture during international assignments'. *International Journal of Cross-Cultural Management*, 12(3): 361–78.
-   Hareendrakumar, V. R., Subramoniam, S. and Hussain, N. (2020) 'Redesigning rewards for improved fairness perception and loyalty'. *Vision*, 24(4): 481–495.
-   Rodriguez, J. K. and Ridgway, M. (2019) 'Contextualizing privilege and disadvantage: Lessons from women expatriates in the Middle East'. *Organization*, 26(3): 391–409.

References

Adler, N. J. (2002) 'Global managers: No longer men alone'. *International Journal of Human Resource Management*, 13(5): 743–60.

Altman, Y. and Shortland, S. (2008) 'Women and international assignments: Taking stock – a 25-year review'. *Human Resource Management*, 47(2): 199–216.

Bader, B., Stoermer, S., Bader, A. K. and Schuster, T. (2018) 'Institutional discrimination of women and workplace harassment of female expatriates: Evidence from 25 host countries'. *Journal of Global Mobility*, 6(1): 40–58.

Bartlett, C. A. and Ghoshal, S. (2002) *Managing across Borders: The Transnational Solution*. Boston: Harvard Business Press.

Baruch, Y., Budhwar, P. S. and Khatri, N. (2007) 'Brain drain: Inclination to stay abroad after studies'. *Journal of World Business*, 42(1): 99–112.

Beaverstock, J. V., Derudder, B., Faulconbridge, J. R. and Witlox, F. (2009) 'International business travel: Some explorations'. *Geografiska Annaler: Series B, Human Geography*, 91(3): 193–202.

Black, J. S., Mendenhall, M. and Oddou, G. (1991) 'Toward a comprehensive model of international adjustment: An integration of multiple theoretical perspectives'. *Academy of Management Review*, 16(2): 291–317.

Boyle, B., Nicholas, S. and Mitchell, R. (2012) 'Sharing and developing knowledge of organization culture during international assignments'. *International Journal of Cross-Cultural Management*, 12(3): 361–78.

Caligiuri, P. M. (2006) 'Performance measurement in a cross-national context'. In W. Bennett, C. E. Lance and D. J. Woehr (eds), *Performance Measurement: Current Perspectives and Future Challenges*. London: Psychology Press, pp. 227–43.

Caligiuri, P. M. and Lazarova, M. (2005) 'Work–life balance and the effective management of global assignees'. In A. Y. Poelmans (ed.) *Work and Family: An International Research Perspective*. London: Lawrence Erlbaum, pp. 121–45.

Carr, S. C., Inkson, K. and Thorn, K. (2005) 'From global careers to talent flow: Reinterpreting "brain drain"'. *Journal of World Business*, 40(4): 386–98.

Cerdin, J. L. and Pargneux, M. L. (2009) 'Career and international assignment fit: Toward an integrative model of success'. *Human Resource Management*, 8(1): 5–25.

Chen, C. C., Choi, J. and Chi, S. C. (2002) 'Making justice sense of local-expatriate compensation disparity: Mitigation by local referents, ideological explanations, and interpersonal sensitivity in China-foreign joint ventures'. *Academy of Management Journal*, 45(4): 807–17.

Chiang, F. F., van Esch, E., Birtch, T. A. and Shaffer, M. A. (2018) 'Repatriation: What do we know and where do we go from here'. *International Journal of Human Resource Management*, 29(1): 188–226.

Claus, L. and Briscoe, D. (2009) 'Employee performance management across borders: A review of relevant academic literature'. *International Journal of Management Reviews*, 11(2): 175–96.

Cole, N. and Nesbeth, K. (2014) 'Why do international assignments fail? Expatriate families speak'. *International Studies of Management and Organization*, 44(3): 66–79.

Collings, D. G. (2014) 'Integrating global mobility and global talent management: Exploring the challenges and strategic opportunities'. *Journal of World Business*, 49(2): 253–61.

Collings, D. G. and Isichei, M. (2017) 'The shifting boundaries of global staffing: Integrating global talent management, alternative forms of international assignments and non-employees into the discussion'. *International Journal of Human Resource Management*, 29(1): 165–87.

Collings, D. G., Doherty, N., Luethy, M. and Osborn, D. (2011) 'Understanding and supporting the career implications of international assignments'. *Journal of Vocational Behavior*, 78(3): 361–71.

Collings, D. G., Scullion, H. and Morley, M. J. (2007) 'Changing patterns of global staffing in the multinational enterprise: Challenges to the conventional expatriate assignment and emerging alternatives'. *Journal of World Business*, 42(2): 198–213.

Copeland, A. P. and Norell, S. K. (2002) 'Spousal adjustment on international assignments: The role of social support'. *International Journal of Intercultural Relations*, 26(3): 255–72.

Dabic, M., González-Loureiro, M. and Harvey, M. (2015) 'Evolving research on expatriates: What is "known" after four decades (1970–2012)'. *International Journal of Human Resource Management*, 26(3): 316–37.

DeNisi, A. S. and Sonesh, S. (2016) 'Success and failure in international assignments: A review and a proposed multi-dimensional model'. *Journal of Global Mobility*, 4(4): 386–407.

Dickmann, M., Doherty, N., Mills, T. and Brewster, C. (2008) 'Why do they go? Individual and corporate perspectives on the factors influencing the decision to accept an international assignment'. *International Journal of Human Resource Management*, 19(4): 731–51.

Dimitrova, M., Chia, S. I., Shaffer, M. A., and Tay-Lee, C. (2020) 'Forgotten travelers: Adjustment and career implications of international business travel for expatriates'. *Journal of International Management*, 26(1): 1–15.

Duvivier, F., Peeters, C. and Harzing, A. W. (2019) 'Not all international assignments are created equal: HQ-subsidiary knowledge transfer patterns across types of assignments and types of knowledge'. *Journal of World Business*, 54(3): 181–90.

Fenwick, M. (2004a) 'On international assignment: Is expatriation the only way to go?' *Asia Pacific Journal of Human Resources*, 42(3): 365–77.

Fenwick, M. (2004b) 'International compensation and performance management'. In A. W. Harzing and J. V. Ruysseveldt (eds), *International Human Resource Management*. London: Sage, pp. 307–32.

Fischlmayr, I. C. and Puchmüller, K. M. (2016) 'Married, mom and manager – how can this be combined with an international career?' *International Journal of Human Resource Management*, 27(7): 744–65.

Fonner, K. L. and Roloff, M. E. (2010) 'Why teleworkers are more satisfied with their jobs than are office-based workers: When less contact is beneficial'. *Journal of Applied Communication Research*, 38(4): 33–61.

Forster, N. (1999) 'Another "glass ceiling"? The experiences of women professionals and managers on international assignments'. *Gender, Work and Organization*, 6(2): 79–90.

Gedro, J., Mizzi, R. C., Rocco, T. S. and van Loo, J. (2013) 'Going global: Professional mobility and concerns for LGBT workers'. *Human Resource Development International*, 16(3): 282–97.

Giorgi, G., Montani, F., Fiz-Perez, J., Arcangeli, G. and Mucci, N. (2016) 'Expatriates' multiple fears, from terrorism to working conditions: Development of a model'. *Frontiers in Psychology*, 7: 1571.

Greenhaus, J. H. and Beutell, N. J. (1985) 'Sources of conflict between work and family roles'. *Academy of Management Review*, 10(1): 76–88.

Hareendrakumar, V. R., Subramoniam, S. and Hussain, N. (2020) 'Redesigning rewards for improved fairness perception and loyalty'. *Vision*, 24(4): 481–95.

Harrison, E. C. and Michailova, S. (2012) 'Working in the Middle East: Western female expatriates' experiences in the United Arab Emirates'. *International Journal of Human Resource Management*, 23(4): 625–44.

Harzing, A.-W. and Christensen, C. (2004) 'Expatriate failure: Time to abandon the concept?', *Career Development International*, 9(6–7): 616–26.

Hippler, T. (2009) 'Why do they go? Empirical evidence of employees' motives for seeking or accepting relocation'. *International Journal of Human Resource Management*, 20(6): 1381–401.

Huang, T. J., Chi, S. C. and Lawler, J. J. (2005) 'The relationship between expatriates' personality traits and their adjustment to international assignments'. *International Journal of Human Resource Management*, 16(9): 1656–70.

Hutchings, K. and Michailova, S. (2014) 'Women in international management: Reviewing past trends and identifying emerging and future issues'. In *Research Handbook on Women in International Management*. Cheltenham: Edward Elgar.

Jain, H. C., Lawler, J. J. and Morishima, M. (1998) 'Multinational corporations, human resource management and host-country nationals'. *International Journal of Human Resource Management*, 9(4): 553–66.

Johnson, L. (2005) 'Measuring international assignment return on investment'. *Compensation and Benefits Review*, 37(2): 50–4.

Kanstrén, K. and Mäkelä, L. (2020) 'Expatriate partners' subjective well-being and related resource losses and gains'. *Community, Work and Family*, 1–28.

Kawai, N. and Strange, R. (2014) 'Perceived organizational support and expatriate performance: Understanding a mediated model'. *International Journal of Human Resource Management*, 25(17): 2438–62.

Kim, K., Halliday, C. S., Zhao, Y., Wang, C. and Von Glinow, M. A. (2018) 'Rewarding self-initiated expatriates: A skills-based approach'. *Thunderbird International Business Review*, 60(1): 89–104.

Kraimer, M. L. and Wayne, S. J. (2004) 'An examination of perceived organizational support as a multidimensional construct in the context of an expatriate assignment'. *Journal of Management*, 30(2): 209–37.

Kupka, B. and Cathro, V. (2007) 'Desperate housewives – social and professional isolation of German expatriated spouses'. *International Journal of Human Resource Management*, 18(6): 951–68.

Mäkelä, L., Suutari, V. and Mayerhofer, H. (2011) 'Lives of female expatriates: Work-life balance concerns'. *Gender in Management: An International Journal*, 26(4): 252–74.

Mayerhofer, H., Hartmann, L. C., Michelitsch-Riedl, G. and Kollinger, I. (2004) 'Flexpatriate assignments: A neglected issue in global staffing'. *International Journal of Human Resource Management*, 15(8): 1371–89.

McKenna, S. and Richardson, J. (2007) 'The increasing complexity of the internationally mobile professional'. *Cross Cultural Management: An International Journal*, 14(4): 307–20.

McNulty, Y. (2012) '"Being dumped in to sink or swim": an empirical study of organizational support for the trailing spouse'. *Human Resource Development International*, 15(4): 417–34.

McNulty, Y. (2016) 'Why expatriate compensation will change how we think about global talent management'. In *Global Talent Management and Staffing in MNEs*, (International Business and Management series), Vol. 32. Emerald Group Publishing, pp. 125–50.

McNulty, Y. and Brewster, C. (2017) 'Theorizing the meaning (s) of "expatriate": Establishing boundary conditions for business expatriates'. *International Journal of Human Resource Management*, 28(1): 27–61.

McNulty, Y. and Hutchings, K. (2016) 'Looking for global talent in all the right places: A critical literature review of non-traditional expatriates'. *International Journal of Human Resource Management*, 27(7): 699–728.

McPhail, R. and McNulty, Y. (2015) '"Oh, the places you won't go as an LGBT expat!" A study of HRM's duty of care to lesbian, gay, bisexual and transgender expatriates in dangerous locations'. *European Journal of International Management*, 9(6): 737–65.

McPhail, R., McNulty, Y. and Hutchings, K. (2016) 'Lesbian and gay expatriation: Opportunities, barriers and challenges for global mobility'. *International Journal of Human Resource Management*, 27(3): 382–406.

Meyskens, M., Von Glinow, M. A., Werther Jr, W. B. and Clarke, L. (2009) 'The paradox of international talent: Alternative forms of international assignments'. *International Journal of Human Resource Management*, 20(6), 1439–50.

Moeller, M. and Maley, J. F. (2018) 'MNC considerations in identifying and managing LGB expatriate stigmatization'. *International Journal of Management Reviews*, 20(2): 325–42.

Noon, M., Blyton, P. and Morrell, K. (2013) *The Realities of Work*. London: Palgrave Macmillan.

Paisley, V. and Tayar, M. (2016) 'Lesbian, gay, bisexual and transgender (LGBT) expatriates: An intersectionality perspective'. *International Journal of Human Resource Management*, 27(7): 766–80.

Ramamoorthy, N., Gupta, A., Sardessai, R. M. and Flood, P. C. (2005) 'Individualism/col-lectivism and attitudes towards human resource systems: A comparative study of American, Irish and Indian MBA students'. *International Journal of Human Resource Management*, 16(5): 852–69.

Reiche, B. S., Kraimer, M. L. and Harzing, A. W. (2011) 'Why do international assignees stay? An organizational embeddedness perspective'. *Journal of International Business Studies*, 42(4): 521–44.

Reiche, B. S. and Harzing, A. W. (2011) 'International assignments'. *International Human Resource Management*, 3: 185–226.

Rodriguez, J. K. and Ridgway, M. (2019) 'Contextualizing privilege and disadvantage: Lessons from women expatriates in the Middle East'. *Organization*, 26(3): 391–409.

Rodriguez, J. K. and Scurry, T. (2014) 'Career capital development of self-initiated expatri-ates in Qatar: Cosmopolitan globetrotters, experts and outsiders'. *International Journal of Human Resource Management*, 25(7): 1046–67.

Rodriguez, J. K. and Scurry, T. (2019) 'Female and foreign: An intersectional exploration of the experiences of skilled migrant women in Qatar'. *Gender, Work and Organization*, 26(4): 480–500.

Rosenbusch, K., Cerny, L. J. II and Earnest, D. R. (2015) 'The impact of stressors during international assignments'. *Cross Cultural Management*, 22(3): 405–30.

Salamin, X. and Hanappi, D. (2014) 'Women and international assignments: A systematic literature review exploring textual data by correspondence analysis'. *Journal of Global Mobility*, 2(3): 343–74.

Sánchez Vidal, M. E., Sanz Valle, R. and Barba Aragón, M. I. (2008) 'International workers' satisfaction with the repatriation process'. *International Journal of Human Resource Management*, 19(9): 1683–702.

Sarkiunaite, I. and Rocke, D. (2015) 'The expatriate experience: The factors of international assignment success'. *Transformations in Business and Economics*, 14(1: 34): 20–47.

Scurry, T., Rodriguez, J. K. and Bailouni, S. (2013) 'Narratives of identity of self-initiated expatriates in Qatar'. *Career Development International*, 18(1): 12–33.

Shaffer, M. and Harrison, D. (2001) 'Forgotten partners of international assignments: Development and test of a model of spousal adjustment'. *Journal of Applied Psychology*, 86: 238–54.

Shen, J. and Jiang, F. (2015) 'Factors influencing Chinese female expatriates' performance in international assignments'. *International Journal of Human Resource Management*, 26(3): 299–315.

Shortland, S. (2016). 'The purpose of expatriation: Why women undertake international assignments'. *Human Resource Management*, 55(4): 655–78.

Shortland, S. and Perkins, S. J. (2016) 'Long-term assignment reward (dis)satisfaction out-comes: Hearing women's voices'. *Journal of Global Mobility*, 4(2): 225–50.

Starr, T. L. and Currie, G. (2009) '"Out of sight but still in the picture": Short-term interna-tional assignments and the influential role of family'. *International Journal of Human Resource Management*, 20(6): 1421–38.

Stroppa, C. and Spieß, E. (2011) 'International assignments: The role of social support and personal initiative'. *International Journal of Intercultural Relations*, 35(2): 234–45.

Suutari, V. (1998) 'Problems faced by Western expatriate managers in Eastern Europe: Evidence provided by Finnish expatriates in Russia and Estonia'. *Journal for East European Management Studies*, 3(3): 249–67.

Tahvanainen, M. (2000) 'Expatriate performance management: The case of Nokia Telecommunications'. *Human Resource Management*, 39(2–3): 267–75.

Thoo, L. and Kaliannan, M. (2013) 'International HR assignment in recruiting and selecting: Challenges, failures and best practices'. *International Journal of Human Resource Studies*, 3(4): 143–58.

Tung, R. L. (1998) 'American expatriates abroad: From neophytes to cosmopolitans'. *Journal of World Business*, 33(2): 125–44.

Tung, R. L. (2008) 'Do race and gender matter in international assignments to/from Asia Pacific? An exploratory study of attitudes among Chinese'. *Human Resource Management*, 47(1): 91–110.

Vanroelen, C. (2019) 'Employment quality: An overlooked determinant of workers' health and well-being?' *Annals of Work Exposures and Health*, 63(6): 619–23.

Vernon, G. (2006) 'International pay and reward'. In T. Edwards and C. Rees (eds), *International Human Resource Management: Globalization, National Systems and Multinational Companies*. Harlow: Prentice-Hall, pp. 217–41.

Warneke, D. and Schneider, M. (2011) 'Expatriate compensation packages: What do employees prefer?' *Cross Cultural Management*, 18(2): 236–56.

Wright, E. O. (1985) *Classes*. London: Verso.

7 Migration and human resource management

Nathan Lillie, Erka Çaro, Lisa Berntsen and Ines Wagner

Learning objectives

- To understand the background of labour migration
- To understand the contemporary context of migration and varieties of mobility
- To understand the role of multinational corporations (MNCs), the state and trade unions in the regulation of migrant work
- To raise issues related to rights and decency at work in relation to migrants and their employment

Introduction

This chapter sets the scene for understanding labour migration and mobility and its challenges from the perspective of international human resource management (HRM). Migration is the temporary and/or permanent territorial movement of people. Migration presents opportunities and challenges to managers and policy-makers. For multinational firms, migrants represent an important source of skills, diversity and labour power. MNCs may have, or recruit, employees who are immigrants and post employees internally to other countries. They may also engage multinational work groups from abroad through subcontractors or work agencies. The aim of this chapter is to give an understanding of what the unique management challenges presented by migration and labour mobility are, to introduce some of the concepts used by migration scholars and to illustrate how they apply in selected real-world examples.

People are 'pushed' or 'pulled' to migrate for a variety of reasons. Push factors include difficulties in the country of origin that create incentives to leave, such as war, persecution and famine. Pull factors are incentives to go to a new location, such as good jobs, free farmland or the discovery of valuable resources such as gold. Labour migration can help alleviate poverty and unemployment in depressed regions, while providing manpower and skills in regions of labour shortage. It can be a vehicle for transferring skills and practices internationally within firms, and between societies. Migration also causes social friction. It can create downward pressure on wages for native workers and threaten national cohesion and security. Government attempts to control the quality and quantity of immigrants usually translate into policies favouring skilled migrants to minimize pressure on social welfare systems.

We start with a brief history of migration since the late Middle Ages. Next, we focus on migration in the contemporary world. First, we give an account of major migration flows around the world. Second, we describe different types of labour migration. We then present some important policy and HRM issues raised by migration, such as diversity and multiculturalism (especially in the workplace): its causes, consequences and management. This section aims at detailing and understanding the experiences of labour migration in an increasingly mobile world (see Chapter 5 on diversity in MNCs and Chapter 6 on international assignments). After sketching various migration scenarios, we end by describing ways in which vulnerable migrants' rights are protected, focusing on the role of trade unions.

Labour migration in history

This section gives an appreciation of the complex history of migration and how it has shaped and been shaped by the development of modern capitalism. Migration has been around as long as there have been humans. From prehistoric times, people have moved in search of better hunting grounds or farmland, or because of competition and conflict with other groups. International migration in the modern definition is connected with the rise of the nation-state and the global economy, which developed from the end of the Middle Ages. This section will review selected historical examples, to set the current situation in historical context. Push and pull factors are visible throughout history. On the one hand, people have fled wars and persecution. On the other, people have sought economic opportunities, such as available farmland or industrial jobs at higher wages than those at home. The cultural and ethnic make-up of modern-day societies reflects mass population movements of the past.

The early modern period from about 1500 to 1800 was characterized by migration during Europe's initial colonial expansion. Europeans moved to North and South American colonies fleeing religious prosecution, often with the intention of settling and farming new land, usually after pushing out, exterminating or enslaving the previous occupants. Africans were enslaved and brought to work in plantations, mines, industry and as servants to the wealthy in the New World. Europeans settled areas such as South Africa and Australia in this period. Immigration was often forcibly resisted by people living in the colonized areas. Europeans who immigrated in this period usually did so as part of a colonial project by supplanting and/or dominating the native societies they encountered.

Over the course of the 19th century, emigration from Europe continued, although many of the colonies became independent countries (such as the United States or Argentina), while others became established 'white' settler dominions (such as Australia). Under French dominion, French and other Europeans settled in Algeria, becoming an important minority group (which, on independence in 1962, was largely pushed out). Germans moved to German East Africa (present-day Namibia) and British settlers established themselves in Kenya, Rhodesia and South Africa. Migration occurred within colonial empires – and between the subject peoples under colonial rule. For example, under the British Raj, many Indians moved to the British colony in South Africa to work. In the 19th century, Chinese established enclave communities throughout SouthEast Asia (Vandenbosch, 1947), and in the United States (Lee, 2006). The vast colonial empires of the major European powers required administrators from the colonizing power. Business entrepreneurs frequently followed or preceded the flag into the colonial holdings of the European powers (for an account of colonialism in Africa, see, for example, Parkham, 1992).

Nineteenth-century industrialization brought millions of workers from rural areas to industrial centres in Western Europe. Railroads and other infrastructure improvements made mass migration possible (Bade, 2003). Destinations included centres of coal and steel production and rapidly expanding urban industrial zones. For example, the industrial revolution in Britain required an ever-growing labour force that could not be met by the local population. British employers recruited workers from Ireland for the textile mills and building trades in cities such as Liverpool and Manchester (Castles and Kosack, 1985).

In France, immigration was spontaneous and uncontrolled, and by 1886 there were more than a million migrants working mostly in agriculture and mining companies. In Germany, Polish and Italian workers came to work in construction and in the mines, often recruited by private agents. Apart from low-skilled labour migration, high-skilled craftsmen and merchants also migrated, contributing to technology and skill transfer (Bade, 2003). The First World War disrupted these migrations as men were called back home for military service or munitions production. Owing to political tensions, many countries enacted tight immigration legislation, causing a halt to the free movement of workers throughout Europe. In the 20th century, countries began instituting controls on who could cross their borders, settle and work. Passports and visas became increasingly important.

The First and Second World Wars, and the various conflicts between the wars, caused considerable migrant flows in the form of refugees and displaced people, but during Europe's post-war reconstruction and subsequent economic growth labour migration rose again. This prompted substantial inflows, often from the former colonies which became independent after the Second World War. France experienced immigration from francophone countries, particularly in Africa. Britain saw immigration from the Indian subcontinent, Africa and the Caribbean, and the Netherlands experienced repatriation and immigration of Moluks and Indonesians from its former Indonesian colony and, in the 1970s, immigration from its former colony Surinam. Sweden hosted substantial numbers of Finnish work migrants. Many European countries made use of migrants and guest workers in the post-Second World War period to fill jobs which the increasingly prosperous Western Europeans were no longer willing to do (Castles and Kosack, 1985).

West Germany's guest-worker programme shows how these programmes of the 1960s and 1970s functioned. The state and employers in West Germany imported temporary labour to solve growing labour shortages during the post-war *Wirtschaftswunder* (economic miracle). Rapid industrial expansion and a shift to mass production (conveyor-line work, piecework and shift-work) required a large unskilled labour force (Kindleberger, 1967). The Federal Labour Office (*Bundesanstalt für Arbeit – BfA*) signed recruitment agreements for temporary employment with Italy, Spain, Greece, Turkey, Morocco, Portugal, Tunisia and Yugoslavia. These provided employers with relatively cheap, flexible and mobile labour. Employers paid a fee to the *BfA* and provided accommodation for the workers. Recruitment was based on a rotation system where mostly male migrants worked in Germany for one or two years and were then required to leave. Migrants were expected not to bring their families, not get involved in labour struggles and make few demands on social welfare systems (Castles, 1986). The number of foreign workers increased from 95,000 in 1956 to 2.6 million by mid 1973 – the greatest labour migration anywhere in post-war Europe (Castles, 1986). In 1973 the oil crisis caused a period of economic stagnation, high unemployment and an official halt to migrant entry to Germany. The German government expected migrants to leave after stopping recruitment, but many stayed and sought to bring their families to Germany. Employers, fearing labour shortages and upward wage pressure, opposed mass repatriation. The former guest workers had become an integral part not only of the labour force but also of society.

Such immigration was not limited to Europe. In the United States, in the 20th century, immigration was subject to increasing regulation compared to the 19th century. In 1942, the US and Mexican governments organized a guest-worker programme called the Bracero Program, which allowed Mexicans to enter the United States for work and continued until 1964. The significant overheads involved in the programme often resulted in Mexican workers seeking illegal employment instead. With the ending of the Bracero Program, migration from Mexico and Latin America continued, often in irregular form, with poorly paid (irregular) immigrants making up a large part of the US workforce in certain industries, such as construction, meatpacking and agriculture.

Contemporary migration

In recent years, the scale of international migration has increased. The number of international migrants is estimated to be almost 272 million globally (United Nations (UN), 2019). Most international migrants originate from India, followed by Mexico and China (International Organization for Migration (IOM), 2020). The top destination country for migrants in absolute numbers is the United States followed by Germany, Saudi Arabia, Russia and the United Kingdom (UK), while the main immigration countries relative to their total population are the United Arab Emirates, Kuwait, Qatar, Saudi Arabia and Bahrain (UN, 2019). The largest migration corridor in the world is the Mexico–United States corridor and the emerging second largest is the Syria–Turkey corridor, with an estimated 3.7 million Syrians residing in Turkey (IOM, 2020). Within Europe the end of the communist regimes in the early 1990s, there has been a surge of migration towards Western Europe from Eastern Europe; this accelerated with the accession of most of Eastern Europe to the European Union (EU) in 2004 (2007 for Romania and Bulgaria and 2013 for Croatia) (de Haas et al., 2019).

Migration flows emerge within and between specific world regions following patterns. To give a sense of how and why some particularly important flows have emerged, how they have been regulated and the emerging policy issues, we present the exemplary cases of regional migration in the EU and in South East Asia.

Regional migration in the EU: the case of posted work

HRM across Europe is influenced by EU regulation and in particular the EU principle of free movement of labour. The EU's founding Treaty of Rome introduced free movement of workers in 1957 to encourage cross-border mobility. Subsequent treaty revisions, directives and European Court of Justice (ECJ) rulings added to the supranational legal regulation of employment in the EU. Since the accession of the Eastern European and Mediterranean island states in 2004, 2007 and 2013, transnational labour mobility from east to west accelerated. Workers move to take up work themselves, or may be sent by a firm as 'posted workers' to another EU member state. The rights of individual and posted workers are organized via different EU regulatory channels (see Chapter 16 on regulation). Individual migrants are entitled to equal treatment with natives at work when undertaking labour mobility. Posted workers are regulated via a complex system of host, sending and EU level rights. Individual labour migrants may benefit from social security provisions in the host state and many EU citizens have taken advantage of their right to work, live and enjoy social benefits in other EU states.

Posted workers remain insured in their sending country; sometimes this saves on labour costs and encourages the employment of relatively inexpensive posted labour from underdeveloped regions. In principle, posted workers are granted key labour rights through the Posting of Workers Directive (PWD), passed in 1996 and revised in 2018, which aims to guarantee free movement while ensuring that unions and goverments can enforce local labour standards. The PWD seeks to ensure that posted workers enjoy the wages and working conditions in either the country they are sent from or the host country they are sent to, whichever is higher. Not every country has minimum wages or collective agreements that apply to every worker, so legal struggles over precisely which host-country standards apply, who can enforce them and how have gruadually defined how posted work is regulated (Arnholtz and Lillie, 2020). Because of the uncertainty, complex laws, enforcement difficulties and transnational corporate constructions such as shell companies allow unscrupulous employers to exploit posted workers (Cremers, 2020). Political disagreements over labour standards resulted in the 2016 Enforcement Directive, which facilitates enforcement of the PWD provisions, and the Revised PWD in 2018, which strengthens wage regulation, among other things. Posting employers and sending states continue to maintain that free movement rights are more important than worker and union rights, while critics regard posting as an employer strategy to avoid regulations and recruit cheap labour. The polarized nature of the political debate, however, conceals the fact that much posting is unproblematic and has little to do with avoiding labour standards: many employers find it useful for moving workers around Europe without labour costs necessarily being a part of that calculus (De Wispelaere and Pacolet, 2020).

Regional migration in South East Asia

South East Asia also exemplifies a regional guest-worker migration system with many similarities to the EU. Uneven development in the region means that some countries (Singapore, Malaysia and Thailand) have become significantly wealthier than others, motivating migration from less wealthy labour supplier countries such as Indonesia and the Philippines (see Chapter 8 on developing economies). As is typical elsewhere, migrant jobs are usually in agriculture, domestic work (i.e. childcare and housework), construction and sometimes manufacturing. SouthEast Asian states' migration programmes are strictly regulated, with permission to reside tightly tied to employment, with restricted length of stay so that workers must rotate back home frequently and high administrative costs mostly borne by the migrant workers themselves. Recruitment agencies often charge high fees for placements. Some restrictions go quite far in terms of limiting personal freedom. For example, Singapore restricts unskilled foreign work migrants from marrying Singaporean nationals. Irregular migration is also popular as a way of avoiding costs and restrictions, although the legal risks are high for migrants and employers alike. The situation, both for regular and irregular domestic work migrants, increases the risk of exploitative situations, such as forced labour, wage theft and physical and sexual abuse, attracting criticism from human rights groups. Because it occurs in the private sphere, it is difficult to regulate through public enforcement.

Labour migration

People who move to new places looking for a job or better employment conditions are called *labour migrants*. Labour migration has always been an important type of migration, but it has acquired greater importance over time because of advances in transportation and communication. These days, there are estimated to be more than 168 million migrant workers, constituting around 18.5 per cent of the workforce of industrialized countries, and between 1.4 to 2.2 per cent of the labour force of developing economies (International Labour Organisation (ILO), 2018). Globally, 58 per cent of migrant workers are male and 42 per cent are female (IOM, 2020). Labour migrants are often divided into high-skilled and low-skilled migrants.

High-skilled labour and low-skilled labour migration

High-skilled migrants are migrants who possess at least a university degree or equivalent training and skills (Martin, 2003). According to Regets (2007), attracting high-skilled migrants is an important element of national economic policies. Developing economies try to retain the highly skilled, while developed economies try to attract them. Migration motivations may differ between high- and low-skilled migrants. Although both push and pull factors are important, high-skilled migrants are attracted to destination countries by better employment prospects, higher salaries and opportunities to gain international experience, while low-skilled migrants are more often also pushed from their countries of origin by low wages or unemployment. The out-migration of skilled and educated professionals from developing economies is known as *brain drain*. Brain drain is a concern in Africa, India and Eastern Europe (Cohen, 2008), because it negatively impacts the economic development of sending countries, especially where these are developing economies. One consequence of brain drain is the shortage of qualified manpower in key sectors such as health, education, science and technology. Brain drain can cause wastage, since the skills of migrants tend to be undervalued in host societies, because of discrimination, or through lack of recognition of foreign certifications. Some high-skilled and educated migrants end up in unskilled jobs after migrating.

Labour market segmentation and migrant-worker integration

Migrants in host countries are often 'target earners' (Piore, 1979). Target earners perceive their temporary jobs instrumentally – that is, solely as a way to earn money quickly. This is different from an understanding of work as a source of identity and social status, or as a rung on a career ladder (migrants' jobs and social positions in their home countries serve that purpose). They seek to save a certain amount of money to invest back home, whether in a business, a house or to pay for their children's education. However, as migrants stay longer, their perspective tends to change; they become more *integrated*. *Migrant integration theory* holds that over time migrants identify more with the host country and become more socially connected. They often integrate into the labour market, which sometimes means moving from more to less precarious work (Danaj et al., 2018).

However, integration is not always possible, and migrants are sometimes caught in 'mobility traps', or situations which discourage integration (Caro et al., 2015). These workers continue to be 'target earners' and lack motivation to improve their conditions in foreign labour markets. In these situations, firms treat low-skilled migrants as substitutable, disposable labour by employing them under exploitative conditions. According to segmentation theory, native workers refuse to accept such employment conditions and migrant workers are therefore seen as complementary to, rather than as substitutes for, native workers: migrant workers simply realize a certain unfulfilled demand for labour. On the other hand, the existence of an exploitable source of labour erodes conditions for native and migrant workers alike.

For a variety of reasons, migrants are often unable to enter employment on similar terms to native workers – even if they have a similar profile in terms of skill, experience and work ethic to native workers, they tend to be shunted into certain kinds of jobs. Low-skilled migrant workers are regularly found in precarious jobs, where they are underpaid, forced to work long hours and face hazardous conditions (see Chapter 4 on general payment issues). Lower segments of the labour market become the prerogative of migrant workers and other marginalized groups (Gordon et al., 1982; Piore, 1979). This phenomenon is explained by *labour market segmentation theory*, which holds that institutional barriers such as race and migration status segment labour markets, granting certain groups access only to specific labour market segments.

Segmentation theory assumes a dual labour market structure consisting of a capital-intensive, secure primary segment and a labour-intensive, insecure but flexible secondary segment. The conditions under which many low-skilled migrants work are characteristic of the secondary labour market segment. This segmentation is driven by employers' demand for different types of labour: low-skilled and substitutable labour for the secondary segment, and workers with a certain level of training, skills and commitment for the primary segment. Over time, the 'need' for migrant labour in particular low-segment jobs becomes institutionalized, with recruitment practices based on national sterotyping and few employer incentives to improve pay and working conditions (McCollum and Findley, 2015; Ruhs and Anderson, 2010). The segmentation of labour markets can induce migrants to accept work in slavery-like conditions (Kara, 2017). For example, in recent years, because of the tightening regulation of posted work in the EU, many employers have started looking to 're-post' migrants who come from outside the EU as intra-EU postings; this creates a new segment of Ukrainan, African or Balkan workers 'below' intra-EU posting subject to extremely low wages, precarity and abuse (Krilić et al., 2020).

Migration policy issues

Migration is dynamic, requiring diversified policy intervention to maximize its benefits and minimize the ill effects for countries both of origin and of destination as well as migrants themselves (IOM, 2020).

National governments seek to control border access and residence rights of foreigners in order to minimize the number of people drawing on government services and social security, to ensure cultural coherence, to keep out people who are thought to present security threats (such as criminals) and to regulate access to the labour market. Immigration policies often seek to attract people with wealth or rare skills, while making it more difficult for those whose skills are in oversupply. Often, labour market access comes with the caveat that the migrant cannot draw on public funds (e.g. in case of unemployment). Sometimes, such as the H1B visa programme in the United States for high-skilled migrants or the Kafala system in the Gulf states for low-skilled labourers, visas are tied to a particular employer, and if that job is lost the visa holder must leave the country.

Marriage and family reunification form a major channel for migration. Because of public perceptions that this avenue is often expoited (e.g. via sham marriages), it is usually subject to controls, tests and limitations. Another avenue is a blood tie with the country in question – Germany, Finland, Ireland and Israel, for example, all grant citizenship to people with ancestors with provable claims to that country's ethnicity.

Countries have made various reciporical migrant agreements. For example, there has been free movement between the Nordic countries (Sweden, Norway, Finland, Denmark, Iceland and the Faroe Islands) since the 1950s. Particularly notable is the freedom of movement within the EU, which allows citizens of any EU member state to take up residence in any other member state. Intra-EU migrants' access to social rights such as pensions, health insurance and unemployment insurance is partially assured, although there are gaps in access in the system (Simola and Lillie, 2016).

Migration has a major economic impact in both origin and destination countries/ regions. Remittances, or money sent by migrants back to their home country/region, are important. The top remittance-recipient countries in 2018 were India, China and Mexico while the top remittance-sending countries are the United States followed by the United Arab Emirates and Saudi Arabia (IOM, 2020).

HRM issues raised by migration

For HRM managers, migration presents challenges in coping with immigration rules, international recruitment and recognition of diverse national educational and certification systems, diversity management and managing relationships between different nationalities in multinational work environments (see Chapter 5 on diversity in MNCs). In the international HRM literature, labour mobility is almost exclusively analysed in terms of expatriate managers, focusing on why firms use expatriates, which selection procedures are best and how to support expatriates and make use of the skills they acquire in their international assignments (e.g. Harzing, 2004) (see Chapter 6 on international assignments). This focus on expatriate managers ignores the fact that most migrant employees are not managers. More important are the challenges of diversity management and managing relationships between multinational groups of workers.

Diversity and multiculturalism

With the number of international migrants increasing, workplaces around the world have become more diverse. Flows of migrants transform societies, fueling an ongoing public and political debate (Ruhs and Anderson, 2010). From the societal perspective, diversity offers benefits in terms of a variety of lifestyles, languages, ideas, styles and cultural norms. The acceptance and appreciation of cultural diversity is referred to as multiculturalism (Pharek, 2000). Multiculturalism in business, education, social policy and culture is seen as a way of reducing intra-group conflict in diverse societies and harnessing the advantage diversity can bring (see Chapter 5 on diversity).

Diverse, multicultural and multilingual workplaces and the challenges of managing these have become increasingly important. Diversity management can be a legislative necessity, yet many organizations also realize its benefits in terms of diverse forms of knowledge and skills (Egan and Bendick, 2003). A diverse and multicultural workplace can bring better decision-making, greater creativity and innovation and more successful marketing to different types of customer (Cox, 1991). Diversity also raises challenges such as interpersonal conflict and communication breakdowns (Anjorin and Jansari, 2018), and, if managed improperly, also leads to racism, sexism and ageism, creating a hostile and non-productive environment leading to loss of innovative potential and undermining an organization's effectiveness. In many countries, anti-immigration political parties and right-wing groups favour stricter immigration laws.

Managing multinational work environments

It is not uncommon to encounter work environments segmented by ethnicity, nationality and/or language. Certain types of job may be dominated by a certain national or ethnic group. At work sites where many different national groups of workers work side by side, management is often obliged to organize work groups according to language groupings. Issues related to the segmentation of labour markets resulting from migration have long been understood from a sociological perspective (Piore, 1979), but rarely from business and management studies on how to manage in such an environment.

Industries such as construction, shipbuilding, agriculture, domestic services and building maintenance, where subcontracting is common, use large numbers of migrant workers and experience ethnically segmented labour markets. Commonly, workers are recruited via agencies or personal networks with contacts to their home countries. Workers speaking the host society language are an interface point with management, taking on the foreman role. These types of worker often progress into management or go into the labour-supply business, using personal contacts and local knowledge of home country and host society to match workers with available jobs. This type of recruitment is known as 'ganging' because migrants from a particular country work together, obviating the need to learn the local language or embed themselves in the local culture. In this way, it is possible to manage and coordinate diverse groups of workers who do not share a common language.

Protecting migrant rights at the workplace

The fact that migrants are often not well integrated into host societies makes protection of migrant worker rights a matter of special concern. The fact that they often work in jobs where pay, conditions, job security and respect for worker rights are not always respected places them in precarious positions.

Efforts to protect migrant rights focus on making enforcement of immigration rules more humane, promoting access of migrants to host-state services, fighting discrimination and racism and ensuring decent treatment in the workplace. State agencies enforcing immigration laws often take little account of the migrants' situation and the consequences of enforcement actions for them, their families and their employers. For example, a deportation can break up a family and leave dependants without means of support. There are many non-governmental organizations which help migrants access legal and other services; these sometimes represent any migrant needing assistance or in other cases represent particular migrant communities. An example of the first is Migrar, in Germany, which provides legal assistance and advice to illegal migrant workers. An example of the second type is the Federation of Poles in Britain, which has a cultural, social and community-binding function and represents the interests of Polish-born people living in the UK.

At the international level, the IOM and ILO are UN-associated agencies working to promote migrant worker rights, through advocating for good practices in the treatment of migrants, conducting research on migration, and providing technical assistance to countries in developing practices to protect migrants' rights (see Chapter 16 on regulation). Despite their efforts, there is no international consensus to protect migrant worker rights. States tend to treat domestic economic interests and security policy as a higher priority than the protection of migrant rights.

Case study: The slaughterhouse industry, Germany

Germany's meat industry is a valuable part of its economy. It is highly concentrated with, for instance, more than half of Germany's pigs being slaughtered in four slaughterhouses: Tönnies, Vion, Danish Crown and Westfleisch. It is also an industry dominated by low-wage migrant labour. According to the German government, 50 per cent of the workers in slaughterhouses did not hold German passports in 2018, although trade unions estimate this number is closer to 80 per cent. Workers are rarely hired directly by the company owning the slaughterhouse, but rather by subcontractors who serve as labour intermediaries. These subcontractors hire workers in Romania, Hungary or Bulgaria and send them to work in Germany. Workers receive time-limited, labour-specific contracts, which means they receive fewer employment rights than long-term employees. The workers communicate with their foreman and colleagues in their native language, and the foreman communicates with management and other work groups in German, if necessary. Officially, workers must be paid the minimum wage, but trade unions maintain they often are not paid this much. Employers use deceptive means such as charging the workers for housing, travel or other costs to reduce the workers' net pay. The German government has recently taken steps to outlaw the use of subcontractors due to the outbreak of Covid-19 in these facilities. The Occupational Safety and Health Inspection Act (*Arbeitsschutzkontrollgesetz*) was adopted in December 2020 and encompasses a comprehensive set of provisions, with many new regulations requiring amendments to existing legislation. The new legal framework bans contract and temporary agency work. This is important in overcoming a divided workforce in the slaughterhouses. Trade unions might now be able to regain organizational strength at the workplace and to put pressure on the companies for better labour regulation. However, it will not be sufficient to ensure decent conditions across the sector. Companies are only obliged to provide the legal minimum requirements, such as the statutory minimum wage, instead of the industry-level collective bargaining standards.

Questions

1. Why is it more profitable to hire migrant workers via a subcontractor than to directly recruit domestic workers?
2. Are employment practices in the slaughterhouse industry an example of good multicultural workplace practices? Why or why not?
3. Would the management practices in slaughterhouses benefit from multicultural management?
4. Apply the three dilemmas for trade unionism (see below) to the slaughterhouse industry case.

Unions and migrants

Trade unions usually start from an ideological basis of worker solidarity. Their actual functioning as organizations is often closely tied to local communities, national identities or even ethnic backgrounds. These organic identities can be a source of strength, but also can drive them to promote insular discourses in response to migration. According to Marino et al. (2017), unions face three main dilemmas in dealing with immigrant labour. First, unions need to decide whether to accept or oppose migration politically. Second, when migrant workers have arrived, unions must decide whether to actively recruit and organize the migrants as full members or to exclude them partly or completely from full union membership and not organize them. Virdee (2000) shows that over time, unions have evolved from policies of racist – sometimes even overt – exclusion of migrants to proactive inclusion. However, the degree of inclusion differs, especially in terms of equal access to social and legal rights. Moreover, the degree of protection they offer is often strongly related to a migrant's duration of stay, as unions are more inclined to protect permanent immigrants than temporary labour migrants. Third, if unions opt for inclusion, they must decide whether to advocate and implement special measures for (im)migrant workers or to maintain equal treatment for all workers. Trade union stances regarding the EU enlargement in 2004 differed: whereas Swedish, Irish and British unions supported immediate open access of workers from the newly accessed member states, Austrian, German and Dutch unions opted for transitional measures to alleviate the inflow of cheaper migrant workers (Marino et al., 2017).

Many unions, especially in countries where immigration is a relatively new phenomenon, struggle internally with racism and whether to include foreign-born workers as members (Lillie and Sippola, 2011). For unions in countries with a longer immigration history, the question is usually what strategies are best for recruiting migrants, and whether there should be proactive policies favouring recruitment of minorities into leadership positions. Immigrant workers are, on average, more likely to perform lower-paid jobs in sectors where unions have little or no influence. This complicates effective union action to change these workers' employment conditions. The most successful union campaigns targeting immigrant workers combine the strategic pressuring of employers by union officials with bottom-up rank-and-file mobilization. Bottom-up rank-and-file mobilization involves active agitation by the migrant workers themselves, often in the form of strikes and public demonstrations (Milkman, 2006). The 'Justice for Janitors' campaign is regarded as one of the most successful immigrant organizing drives of the US. The campaign started in Los Angeles, spread to other US cities and went global, with 'Justice for Cleaners' in the UK, 'Clean Start' in Australia and New Zealand, and 'Clean Enough' in the Netherlands (see Chapter 17 on international worker representation). Through these campaigns unseen, often irregular, immigrant cleaners demanded better working conditions. Key to these campaign's successes were the effective rank-and-file mobilization combined with the strategic professional union assistance that led to industry-wide organizing strongly embedded in and publicly supported by the broader community (Milkman, 2006). Employing staff from 'target' migrant groups is a common way to make a visible commitment to that minority, while also ensuring needed linguistic and cultural skills to organize and represent those workers. Some unions in the UK have had success with reserving elected seats for minority groups to ensure a minimum level of representation in the union leadership. Seeking broad alliances has proved to be one of the more successful strategies used by unions to create a lasting change in working conditions of (im)migrant workers (see Wills, 2009, and Fitzgerald and Hardy, 2010, for interesting examples in the UK). Unions often are able to integrate 'settled' immigrant groups into their membership, but still struggle with more highly mobile migrants who have no intention to settle (Berntsen, 2016).

Conclusion

In this chapter, we have highlighted some of the issues, challenges and opportunities which labour migration presents for IHRM. We have shown that labour migration is not a new phenomenon and has always played an important part in the capitalist world economy. In the past, as now, it has been motivated by a combination of push factors – factors which make the migrants' home location undesirable – and pull factors – factors which make the destination country desirable. Labour migrants are strategic in their migration, and often behave as 'target earners', particularly when they are temporary and less skilled. They are most often employed in secondary labour markets.

Employers find migrants useful either because less skilled migrants are less expensive than locals, or because they possess scarce skills, as in the case of high-skilled migrants. National migration policies tend to favour high-skilled migrants. Many countries make use of guest-worker policies, which allow migrants access to that country's labour market, but only in restricted ways, and seek to prevent the migrant from settling. The idea is to keep migrants in the secondary labour market, allowing them access to jobs which locals cannot fill (on the high-skill end) or do not want (on the low-skill end).

The challenge for managers is to take advantage of the skill and labour power of migrants and the different perspectives they bring, while minimizing the tensions created by a diverse workforce and avoiding falling foul of state policies designed to restrict migration. For unions, and others concerned with migrant rights and the effects of migration on labour markets, the challenge is to balance the interests of native members with the rights and interests of migrants.

Reflective questions

1. How has labour migration developed through history and what are the main economic factors affecting these changes? How has labour migration affected macroeconomic developments in the contemporary world?

(Continued)

2. What are the main characteristics of high-skilled and low-skilled labour migrants? Describe the main differences in terms of motivations and the integration process among these groups.
3. What are the main challenges and benefits of multicultural work environments for migrants? Describe and explain some effective ways to manage diversity in the workplace (to maximize its benefits).
4. What is meant by the terms 'push' and 'pull' factors in migration studies?
5. What are the three dilemmas trade unions face in dealing with immigrant labour? Explain why these are dilemmas.
6. Based on the history of migration described in the chapter, do you think migration today is different from migration in the past, or is it just more of the same? Why?

Recommended reading

- Arnholtz, J. and Nathan L. (2020) *Posted Work in the European Union: The Political Economy of Free Movement*. New York: Routledge.
- Haakestad, H. and Friberg, J. H. (2017) 'Deskilling revisited: Labour migration, neo-Taylorism and the degradation of craft work in the Norwegian construction industry'. *Economic and Industrial Democracy*, 41(3): 630–51.
- Regine, P. (2015) *The Political Economy of Border Drawing: Arranging Legality in European Labor Migration Policies*. New York: Berghan.

References

Anjorin, R. and Jansari, A. (2018) 'Managing cultural diversity at the workplace'. Dissertation. Jönköping International Business School.

Bade, K. (2003) *Migration in European History*. Malden: Blackwell.

Berntsen, L. (2016) 'Reworking labour practices: On the agency of unorganized mobile migrant construction workers'. *Work, Employment and Society*, 30(3): 472–88.

Caro, E., Berntsen, L., Lillie, N. and Wagner, I. (2015) 'Posted migration and segregation in the European construction sector'. *Journal of Ethnic and Migration Studies*, 41(10): 1600–20.

Castles, S. (1986) 'The guest-worker in Western Europe – An obituary'. *International Migration Review*, 20(4), (Special Issue: 'Temporary Worker Programs: Mechanisms, Conditions, Consequences'): 761–78.

Castles, S. and Kosack, G. (1985) *Immigrant Workers and Class Structure in Western Europe*. London: Oxford University Press.

Cohen, R. (2008) *Global Diasporas: An Introduction*. London and New York: Routledge.

Cox, T. Jr (1991) 'The multicultural organization'. *Academy of Management Executive*, 5(2): 34–47.

Cremers, J. (2020) 'Market integration, cross-border recruitment, and enforcement of labour standards: A Dutch case'. In J. Arnholtz and N. Lillie (eds), *Posted Work in the European Union: The Political Economy of Free Movement*. New York: Routledge.

Danaj, S., Çaro, E., Mankki, L., Sippola, M. and Lillie, N., (2018) 'Unions and Migrant Workers'. In V. Dollgast, N. Lillie and V. Pulignano, (eds) *Reconstructing Solidarity: Labour Unions, Precarious Work, and the Politics of Institutional Change in Europe*. Croydon: Oxford University Press, pp. 207.

de Haas, H. Czaika, M., Flahaux, M.-L., Mahendra, E., Natter, K., Vezzoli, S. and Villares-Varela, M. (2019) 'International migration: Trends, determinants and policy effects'. *Population and Development Review*, 45(4): 885–922.

De Wispelaere, F. and Pacolet, J. (2020) 'The benefits of posting: Facts and figures on the use and impact of intra-EU posting'. In J. Arnholtz and N. Lillie (eds), *Posted Work in the European Union. The Political Economy of Free Movement*. New York: Routledge, pp. 31–49.

Egan, M. L. and Bendick, M. Jr (2003) 'Workforce diversity initiative in U.S. multinational corporations in Europe'. *Thunderbird International Business Review*, 45(6): 701–727.

Fitzgerald, I. and Hardy, J. (2010) '"Thinking outside the box"? Trade union organizing strategies and Polish migrant workers in the United Kingdom'. *British Journal of Industrial Relations*, 48(1): 131–50.

Gordon, D. M., Edwards, R. and Reich, M. (1982) *Segmented Work, Divided Workers: The Historical Transformation of Labor in the United States*. Cambridge: Cambridge University Press.

Harzing, A.-W. (2004) 'Composing an international staff'. In A.-W. Harzing and J. van Ruysseveldt (eds), *International Human Resource Management*, 2nd edn. London: Sage.

ILO (2018) *Global Estimates on International Migrant Workers – Results and Methodology*, 2nd edn., ILO.

IOM (2020) *World Migration Report 2020*. Available at: https://publications.iom.int/system/files/pdf/wmr_2020.pdf (accessed May 2020).

Kara, S. (2017) *Modern Slavery: A Global Perspective*. New York: Columbia University Press.

Kindleberger, C. C. (1967) *Europe's Postwar Growth –The Role of Labor Supply*. Cambridge: Harvard University Press.

Krilić, S. C., Toplak, K. and Vah Jevšnik, M. (2020) *Posting of Third Country Nationals: A Comparative Study*. Report of Con3Post Project. Ljubljana: ZRC SAZU.

Lee, E. (2006) *At America's Gates: Chinese Immigration during the Exclusion Era, 1882–1943*. Chapell Hill: University of North Carolina Press.

Lillie, N. and Sippola, M. (2011) 'National unions and transnational workers: The case of Olkiluoto 3, Finland'. *Work, Employment and Society*, 25(2): 1–17.

McCollum, D. and Findlay, A. (2015) '"Flexible" workers for "flexible" jobs? The labour market function of A8 migrant labour in the UK'. *Work, Employment & Society*, 29(3): 427–43.

Marino, S., Roosblad, J. and Penninx (eds) (2017) *Trade Unions and Migrant Workers: New Contexts and Challenges in Europe*. Cheltenham: Edward Elgar and International Labour Office.

Martin, P. (2003) *Highly Skilled Labor Migration: Sharing the Benefits*. Geneva: ILO.

Milkman, R. (2006) *L.A. Story: Immigrant Workers and the Future of the U.S. Labor Movement*. New York: Russell Sage Foundation.

Parkham, T. (1992) *The Scramble for Africa*. London: Abacus.

Pharek, M. (2000) *Rethinking Multiculturalism: Cultural Diversity and Political Theory*. Cambridge: Harvard University Press.

Piore, M. J. (1979) *Birds of Passage: Migrant Labor and Industrial Societies*. Cambridge: Cambridge University Press.

Regets, M. C. (2007) *Research Issues in the International Migration of Highly Skilled Workers: A Perspective with Data from the United States*. National Science Foundation Working Paper, SRS 07-203. Division of Science Resources Statistics.

Ruhs, M. and Anderson, B. (eds) (2010) *Who Needs Migrant Workers?* Oxford University Press.

Simola, A. and Lillie, N. (2016) 'The crisis of free movement in the European Union'. *Mondi Migranti*, 2016(3): 7–19.

UN (2019) *International Migration 2019: Report* (ST/ESA/SER.A/438), Department of Economic and Social Affairs, Population Division.

Vandenbosch, A. (1947) 'The Chinese in South East Asia'. *Journal of Politics*, 9(1): 80–95.

Virdee, S. (2000) 'A Marxist critique of black radical theories of trade-union racism'. *Sociology*, 34(3): 545–65.

Wills, J. (2009) 'Subcontracted employment and its challenge to labor'. *Labor Studies Journal*, 34(4): 441–60.

8 Developing economies: globalization, politics and employment relations

Naresh Kumar, Robert MacKenzie and Miguel Martínez Lucio

Learning objectives

- To understand the limitations of the discussion on developing economies and to appreciate the greater complexity of such countries in terms of work and regulation
- To engage with the way a broad range of actors including the state intervene in relation to multinational corporations (MNCs) in such contexts
- To outline some of the challenges in terms of employment relations and the way worker rights and worker representation are developed

Introduction

The activities of MNCs and their impact on host countries are understandably dominant themes within the international human resource management (IHRM) literature, but there is a tendency for the emphasis being on international capital as the proactive agent and the host country as a largely passive recipient of change. This tendency is particularly notable in relation to the impact of MNCs on developing economies. This problematic engagement is perhaps partly related to the difficulty of defining what is meant by the notion of 'developing'. In some cases, China is presented as developing, which is not always plausible given the extent of its social and economic development. Similarly, the language of 'developing' and 'developed' is problematic when categorizing countries with rich and often ancient cultures; hence, the term *developing economies* is preferred to *developing countries* throughout this chapter (apart from direct quotes), although in turn this term could be seen as reductionist. Such terminology also suggests a natural process of economic growth and advancement, with associated pejorative implications that ignore the historic role of European colonial powers – and latterly American neo-colonialism – in fettering economic development within their imperial spheres of influence. Moreover, there is a concern that the use of binaries such as 'developing' and 'developed' ignores the complex realities of the world in terms of the crises among developed economies and the emergence of economic powers such as India and Brazil. However, the term *developing* still has relevance for a number of reasons: ongoing income differentials, the dominance of specific types of MNC and the nature of their activities in low-income countries, the ongoing economic hierarchy between the Global 'North' and 'South' and problematic issues in relation to the nature of trade union and participatory systems in various developing contexts.

Many IHRM discussions may, in fact, conceal the challenges and dilemmas facing countries and their workforces as a consequence of the rapid and often uneven economic and social changes that are taking place. What is more, much of the debate remains silent on, or disengaged with, political issues and questions of human rights. This silence may be driven by a particular view of management and economic development dominated by neoliberal, managerialist understandings of organizational change and social context (see Chapter 10 on management education and the role of consultancies).

This chapter aims to outline some of the debates concerning developing economies in relation to HRM and broader employment relations. It will show how such debates have been structured, and how changes since the 1990s, resulting from developments in foreign direct investment (FDI) and the role of MNCs, have introduced a new set of issues and dynamics. The chapter will then focus on the impact of FDI and the way this has influenced both management and labour through the development of new forms of working and new groups of workers. However, the chapter also aims to question the passivity implied in many of the dominant views of regulation, politics and participation in developing economies by arguing that a range of actors such as trade unions, non-government organizations (NGOs), public agencies and others are highly significant in the development of the local economic context, albeit within specific, normally marketized frameworks. The chapter will also show how the impact of FDI has contributed to new sets of debates and issues concerning the management of work and employment. Changes in the composition of the workforce have created new regulatory challenges as well as raising social and ethical questions over balancing international elite interests with those of local populations, as economies and societies undergo 'development'. This chapter therefore looks at two very different features of how HRM and employment relations systems are affected by the internationalization of capital and by state responses to it. We highlight the stereotypes that tend to be propagated in relation to the regulation of work in developing economies. We also focus on the array of actors that contribute to the way initiatives for enhancing labour standards are engaged with and developed. A review of Malaysian employment policy is provided as a case-study example, through which we explore of some of the tensions that exist when governments develop 'decent work' initiatives without any social underpinning.

Understanding employment relations and the management of labour in developing economies

Beyond stereotypes: rethinking what is meant in terms of developing economies

The question of development has been less central to the study of HRM and industrial relations (IR) than might be expected. The focus of many discussions has, until the past decade or so, been on so-called developed economies. The conceit that developments in countries such as the United States or the United Kingdom need to be privileged rests on a series of assumptions about the dominance of the liberal market economy within management texts (see Chapter 10 on management education and the role of consultancies). First, these are economies that have developed market-oriented social and political structures, and where competition has led to a greater investment in management development and strategic innovation, albeit uneven. Second, within the mainstream HRM literature there has been a key concern with identifying best practice for the sake of emulation, and an assumption this is likely to be found within such 'developed' contexts. Third, where new forms of organizational innovation and change are seen in other contexts (see Chapter 12 on lean production), this can be attributed to the application of 'western' management thought, albeit within a distinct mediating context. Yet the problem with this approach and set of assumptions is that it supposes that employment practices and management strategies in developing economies can best be improved by mimicking and integrating those of developed economies, and that such practices are potentially transferable. Hence, there is a view of developing economies that stresses their passivity and fundamentally recipient status in organizational development and HRM change. Developing economies are seen as receivers and accommodators of international developments in terms of markets and organizational processes.

Historically, developing economies were often viewed in terms of the dominance of particular industrial sectors such as mining, agriculture and the public sector, with highly immobile bureaucracies and command-style management processes shaped by colonial traditions and involving direct forms of supervision or results-related payments (Blunt and Jones, 1992). Jackson (2004: 229), in an important synthesis of the study of developing economies, tried to widen this view and explore a broader range of factors that constitute the core characteristics of developing economies, and which inhibit development and change. These factors include: authoritarian management, which can be explained by the political context in many developing economies; a strong bureaucracy that emerges because of the importance of the state and formal interventions resulting from weak civil societies; a tendency to put the emphasis on inputs and direct control by management, rather than on outputs and quality, because of the limited nature of production processes and markets; the importance of informal and family links because of an absence of principles of equity in the labour market; a lack of worker involvement and a restrictive view of human resources; and a fundamental lack of management skills related to the absence of extensive education, among other factors. Many studies have focused on such features, seeing them as representative of the 'primitive' state of affairs within such countries. Moreover, they do so in many cases without explaining the colonial history of such contexts: for example, the role of the British and Belgian empires in sustaining underdevelopment, or the impact of neocolonial actors such as the United States in focusing investment support on limited, often primary, sectors in which US corporations held interests. There is also the ongoing problem that many developing economies, in Africa for instance, are studied in relation to European and North American exemplars, as if development in Asia had not taken place, or offers alternative points of reference (Kamoche, 2002).

Politics or culture? The question of context

The political background is normally downplayed in the study of work and employment. For example the manner in which authoritarian settings can systematically suppress or inhibit the development of democratic voice mechanisms within employment relations and therefore inhibit social dialogue. The study of management and work in such circumstances is normally skewed, partly because of the need to sanitize and neutralize political discussion in the management classroom, placing the focus on matters of technique and 'best practice'.

Some try to remedy this by invoking the role of culture as a means to gain a broader understanding of a country's context and the possible influence this may have on HRM. Within management and organizational studies, aspects of Hofstede's work, such as *Culture's Consequences* (2001), continue to be invoked as a means of understanding the differences between cultures and countries in organizational terms, and so they remain a point of entry for the comparative study of HRM (Marchington and Wilkinson, 2008). Differences are measured in terms of the acceptance of hierarchy, risk aversion, individual and collective identity and masculine versus feminine approaches. The accepted norm is that developing economies in the main are more hierarchical (or accepting of hierarchy), more masculine and in some cases more collectivist. That these terms are highly problematic is clear; however, the developing context is often seen as being locked into a particular cultural perspective, in which political and regulatory traditions are rarely accounted for. In approaches inspired by Hofstede (2001) the focus is on the individual more than the regulatory or political contexts. Such explanations risk making social development seem difficult: they may make the process of social change, such as the emergence of social and worker rights, appear to be less achievable. Harvey (2002), for example, warns us that the organizational and employment complexity of African nations was exacerbated by the impact of colonization and imperial control, which disrupted ethnic communities and led to uneven urbanization and change. Hence, culturalist analysis might have limitations in explaining such contexts and understanding that cultures may be shaped by repression, resistance and change and are not static entities deeply embedded in general traits.

Others have tried to move away from characterizing cultural traits or economic customs and practices through simple stereotypes, and studied newly emerging centres of power in regions as diverse as Latin America or the Arabian Peninsula with a greater awareness of context and the challenges of change (Vassolo et al., 2011). There is an increasing sensitivity – relatively speaking – in these attempts to understand a more diverse set of factors, such as the role of economic and political networks, the impact of new forms of multinationals and NGOs, and changing generational expectations. In particular, greater attention is being paid to the way the state plays a key role, even when still reliant on MNCs in many respects, and to how societal expectations regarding employment and social rights are changing. In Saudi Arabia, for example, the state regulation of employment quotas for foreign nationals has a significant influence over hiring practices and the organization of work; this intervention also serves to both challenge traditional views on hiring women while also reinforcing gender segregation at work (Basahal et al., 2021). In addition to national state activity, inter- and intra-regional collaboration between governments and social actors has emerged as being of growing importance. In such approaches, developing economies appear to be more complex and more dynamic and changeable spaces than traditionalist views would indicate. The way developing economies interact with the global context is therefore deeper and richer than might be imagined from quasi-colonialist, managerial readings of countries bound by tradition and characterized by passivity.

The Impact of MNCs and FDI

International economic investment continues to transform recipient economies and the regulatory structures within them, and the sheer scale of this investment has been remarkable. Debates in the 1970s that expressed concerns over the development of an international division of labour were challenged in the 1990s on the basis that FDI was dominated by investment flows between developed economies. The trend shifted: the *World Investment Report 2013* by the United Nations Conference on Trade and Development (UNCTAD, 2013) revealed that developing and transition economies absorbed more than half of global FDI inflows from 2010 to 2012, against a notable decrease in FDI inflows to developed economies. MNCs can bring significant political pressure on the state of a developing economy regarding the way working conditions can be altered to suit investors (see Chapter 2 on MNCs), or in combination with institutions such as the World Bank, place pressure on host governments to privatize or commercialize nationalized industries and open them up to FDI. MNCs may also generate highly complex supply chains that involve a range of providers whose coordination may be a challenge in relation to worker rights (Donaghey and Reinecke, 2018).

What is also becoming clear is that there is a need to go beyond the view of MNCs as simply depositors of investment and developers of technical and organizational knowledge: even more critical representations of MNCs as organizations that simply seek cost advantages, and do so with very little engagement with local states and social actors, also need to be rethought with regard to the role of local and nationally based actors. The image of MNCs as being able to enter and leave economies at will – exploiting cost advantages in terms of both physical and human resources – is highly questionable given the difficult and expensive processes involved in investing and divesting. Moreover, nation-states can be more responsive than is often assumed in terms of strategies to attract and sustain inward investment by MNCs (Lillie and Martínez Lucio, 2012) (see Chapter 2 on MNCs and Chapter 9 on training and development strategies): they can develop proactive workforce training programmes and invest in industrial and business parks, for example. In some cases, MNCs find themselves being forced to operate in contexts that are also changing in various ways, as their impact and that of globalization broadly speaking may unsettle established social and political hierarchies. For example, one development as a consequence of, or response to, globalization has been greater international engagement by cohorts of workers and professionals through educational networks and associations. Such developments have contributed to an increasing awareness of worker and social rights due to greater international communication on a range of social issues (see Chapter 17 on international trade unionism). What is more, civil servants working for the state and dealing with economic and transnational issues can forge their own links between similar bodies and individuals in neighbouring countries: for example, there is collaboration between the elements of the Malaysian and Indonesian states on various matters related to inward investment. Therefore, the education and training agendas in developing economies have shifted from the approach seen in the 1960s–80s, when the aim was to attract foreign capital and when investment was dominated primarily by a set of specific MNCs from developed economies. The politics of investment is more complex, as there is a more diverse set of interactions socially and politically between MNCs and the states and societies of developing economies, as well as a greater interface between the states of developing economies themselves. Developing economies can no longer be characterized as passive recipients of FDI, with various associated HRM practices introduced by MNCs submissively accommodated by a compliant state or local actors.

Enter the state

The role of the state is an important and diverse factor in the question of HRM and employment relations in developing economies. Although often abstracted to a monolithic unity, the state is made up of a multiplicity of ministries, agencies and other bodies, many of which may be involved in activities pertaining to the agenda of development or attracting FDI. The state is, therefore, a complex entity with various organs representing dominant interests in the pursuit of economic development but also having to engage socially and be seen as politically legitimate (Jessop, 1990, 1995).

The potential for power imbalances between the states of developing economies and large MNCs has been a cause for concern for some time (Klein, 2001). The politics of investment promises and divestment threats places international capital in a strong position vis-à-vis local political actors, potentially reducing their capacity for decision-making that may be contrary to the interests of MNCs in terms of social and labour market policy. Such *dependent states* may struggle to determine policy independently of the interests of MNCs (Bhopal and Rowley, 2002), but the role of the state can also create a degree of mutual dependency. The state in such contexts has used highly interventionist agendas promoting economic development through attracting FDI, as well as investment in infrastructure and education, plus taxation and labour policies favourable to MNCs to further underpin such investment. However, such approaches tended to focus primarily on attracting FDI rather than systematically developing local capital or an extensive state-led public sector. Rather than local state actors remaining the passive facilitators of MNC access to local resources – human, material and market – over time these dynamics have become more complex and interactive: we see a greater degree of state intervention in relation to MNCs on questions of training, infrastructure development and local business support (Ritchie, 2002: 32). It is for this reason that the state, and other social and economic actors within the national setting, are important to any attempt to understand how developing economies engage with international capital, develop their political space in relation to change, and establish a range of 'supportive' practices and institutions. When discussing the state in a developing context, we see these more strategic roles emerge: 'Rather than simply retreating to the sidelines to function as the game's referee, the state must strategically co-ordinate the interaction between key economic actors in a way that will stimulate deep and crosscutting developmental linkages' (Ritchie, 2002: 32).

The interaction between local institutions and processes of globalization is therefore complex and diverse. This proactive role of the state is often seen in facilitating human resource development and training support, so as to engage MNCs on the basis of an available skilled workforce, for example in Turkey through the role of local public colleges and apprenticeships (Tasli-Karabulut and Keizer, 2020). However, state actors may also take advantage of the new technologies or working arrangements MNCs may introduce to build a broader culture of 'human resource development' (ibid.) (see Chapter 9 on training and development). Much depends on the way the state assuages long-term dependence on MNCs by extending these initiatives into the realm of local businesses. These interventions can often be mainly supply side in orientation and limited in their ability to create a longer-term culture of training and development locally.

The state in countries as diverse as Tanzania, Malaysia and Indonesia, among others, are also beginning to engage with the need to ensure a sustainable workforce: one that is able to develop educational and skills-based capabilities over time and also work in an environment that is oriented towards a greater sensitivity to health and safety regulations and well-being. There is a sense in which, longer term, states need to build more capable workforces, with greater attention to the need for worker voice and rights (see Chapter 16 on transnational regulation and Chapter 17 on international trade unionism). This is not driven by some notion of altruism but from real pressures from such things as trade arrangements that insist on forms of fairness at work and socially oriented treatment of the workforce, or the need to conform to the codes of conduct and labour standards developed by the International Labour Organization (ILO) (see Chapter 16 on regulation). Increasingly the narrative of economic development has been supplemented by one based on social and welfare development. However, the state in many cases is still caught by the relative dominance of capital networks and interests – especially when there remains a dependence on investment by MNCs – such that challenges remain in developing social and economic rights for workers and society more widely.

Case study: The state, 'decent work' and postcolonial legacies in Malaysia

This case study will outline some of the ways in which the state and the industrial relations system engage with internationalization and also with related indigenous developments. We look here at some of the formal strategies and rhetoric of states in developing economies, followed by an alternative reading of the way that the state and employment relations strategies serve to develop yet constrain both workers' opinions and participation. There are various interpretations of how employment and HRM systems have developed. Readers need to be alert to the different narratives and interpretations that may exist.

Inward investment and economic development are engineered as much through local state policies as they are through external global economic trends and processes. Malaysia is an example of a nation that has begun to build a framework of skills development and 'national progress' which has helped to create a political and regulatory context that interacts with capital flows. As MNCs seek environments with cost benefits – for example, in terms of labour – or access points to new markets, they interact with the institutions of the host country in which they are investing. In many cases, these interactions are framed in a negative way in that they create a context where MNCs may not be challenged by workers and their representatives, or where development zones are constructed in which worker rights are limited or suspended. Hence, in the case of Malaysia, there are other narratives that are more critical of the way the state has prioritized inward investment at the expense of local labour standards.

However, increasingly the state has seen it as important to link economic growth to a decent work agenda, very much allied to the narratives and soft regulation of ILO labour standards (see Chapter 16 on regulation). The ILO has established a set of standards and reference points for developing economies that aim to create sustainable labour markets and work. The 'decent work' agenda has also been increasingly a point of reference for the Ministry of Human Resources (MOHR) under its list of 'deliverables' within national developmental policies. The MOHR's 'decent work' agenda in 2009 was as follows (MOHR, 2009) (it uses the term 'industrial relations' to refer to collective worker rights and systems of regulation, and it links rhetorically at least to the statements of the ILO in terms of working conditions).

1. To develop a workforce that is productive, informative, *disciplined*, caring and responsive to the changing labour environment towards increasing economic growth and hence creating more job opportunities.
2. To encourage and maintain conducive and *harmonious* industrial relations between employers, employees and trade unions for the nation's economic development and well-being of the people.

(Continued)

3. To uphold social justice and ensure *harmonious* industrial relations by solving industrial disputes between employers and employees.
4. To ensure that trade unions practise democracy, are *orderly* and responsible for helping to achieve the objective of industrial *harmony*.
5. To be the leader in the development of the nation's human resources.
6. To ensure the health and safety of the workforce.
7. To develop a skilled, knowledgeable and competitive workforce in an environment of *harmonious* industrial relations with social justice.

The text in italics (added by the authors) highlights the promotion of 'harmony' and order as cultural norms within the political discourse. The development of this approach and discourse has continued, and now forms a key part of the activities of various work and human resource-related state agencies and ministries (ILO, 2019).

The development of a 'decent work' agenda has attempted to create a 'progressive' counter-space within the state, running alongside a narrative on training led by the Ministry of Higher Education that emphasizes that both technical and soft skills are to be included in education and training programmes. These include communication skills, critical thinking and problem-solving skills, life-long learning and information management, teamwork, entrepreneurship, professional ethics and morals and leadership skills. The 'decent work' agenda also appears, however, to be linked to a more functional goal of worker flexibility based on cultural and social pliability, reflecting new employer demands from forms of inward investment fitting the more job-loading dimensions of lean production. Much of the agenda is tied to a specific hierarchical and controlled view of work. In addition, there are concerns about access and equality issues across the different constituent populations of Malaysia; it is a country with strongly embedded and large minority-ethnic groups, notably Indian and Chinese communities, raising issues about the political dominance and exclusion of particular ethnic groups in different spheres. Recent forms of migration have also brought to the fore fairly restrictive and uneven approaches to migrant worker rights, although there is growing interest in enhancing labour enforcement mechanisms on aspects of worker rights (see Chin, 2017, for a discussion on the response of the state in Malaysia). Migration is a key issue forcing the state to engage around worker rights, although the outcomes are variable (Anderson, 2021) (see also Chapter 7 on migration).

The politics of industrial relations and worker rights in Malaysia has historically been more restrictive than pluralistic (Kuruvilla and Arudsothy, 1995), based on a system of state–employer domination (Kuruvilla and Venkataratnam, 1996) and repressive confrontation rather than accommodation and cooperation (Sharma, 1996). Todd and Peetz (2001) maintain it is a 'controlled' rather than a 'commitment-based' structure, established by the early British colonial government and maintained by Malaysia since independence. Deficiencies in the democratization of labour legislation have apparently worked against the achievement of collaborative workplace relations. Anantaraman (1997) and Suhanah (2002) argue that cooperative industrial relations were undermined by Malaysian labour policies from 1958 to 1970. Thus the nature of IR policies appeared to have been a form of 'controlled pluralism' based on significant state control, aimed at avoiding industrial conflict in the interests of accelerating the industrialization process (Jomo, 2007a, b; Kuruvilla and Arudsothy, 1995).

Hence the way that the industrial relations environment has been constructed, and the way unions have been constrained, means that the positive features of social dialogue, mutual gains and more inclusive human resource strategies may not be developed easily (for overviews of these issues, see Bhopal and Todd, 2000; Jomo and Todd, 1994; Parasuraman, 2004). The development of a fair and inclusive workplace may also be hampered by the limits on trade union renewal and the lack of external support for unions from the state and employers (for a more developed discussion of these issues, see the source for this case: Kumar et al., 2013). In addition, the ongoing focus on a form of engagement by the state that accommodates business associations but limits the voice and rights of trade union organizations can create an unbalanced system of political inclusion (Jomo, 2014). The emphasis has been on creating a dialogue among elites in the various ethnic communities but not its workforce (ibid.).

In a leading intervention on the state in Malaysia, Bhopal and Rowley (2002: 1181-2) argue that the nature of state-capital relations is a key mediating factor that is central to the narrative of investment, HRM and labour-related issues in developing economies:

> The oppression of labour is not simply something desired *per se* by dependent states in all circumstances. The State has other considerations, which can give rise to concessions to labour. Yet, the degree of dependence on capital may determine the ability of the State to pursue a policy designed to meet its internal needs. If dependent states are less able to determine their labour policies owing to MNCs, the implication for those advocating trade/aid and labour rights links is that they need to address the fact that labour suppression may be the result of the actions of MNCs and inactions of states. The complicity of capital and its home state needs to be at the centre of any discussion on human rights and trade. A failure to do this not only leaves dependent developing countries caught between a 'rock and a hard place' (economic sanctions and failure to attract FDI), but fails to identify the role of home and dependent host states in the inherent contradictions between capital and labour.

Questions

1. In the case of Malaysia, how has the state attempted to shape industrial relations in different ways?
2. What impact might the 'Decent Work' agenda have on the character of industrial relations and trust within the workplace?
3. What are the challenges of supporting worker rights and voice given the ongoing reliance on ILO, inward investment and MNCs?
4. What can be done to enhance worker voice and the input of the population into the development of better working conditions?

Regulation and the diversity of actors

When we discuss national and regional contexts of HRM and employment relations in terms of the regulation and management of work, we need to account for an array of actors and relationships. We need to see how the social and economic agendas at work are contested, and in turn how these issues can go beyond the workplace to be pushed to the forefront of the policy agenda. There is an increasing awareness of the different and diverse historical approaches to economic development and the regulation of employment (Howell, 2005: 31–3). It is also important to recognize the role of the different *actors*, and the *spaces* they operate within, that make up the regulatory landscape (MacKenzie and Martínez Lucio, 2005, 2014) (see Chapter 16 on regulation). Trade unions, NGOs, management constituencies and various parts of the state compete within a variety of regulatory spaces, creating alliances and campaigns to shape the nature of regulation and rights. Developing economies often face a tension between the imperative to economically advance, on the one hand, and the different ways in which economic advancement can be understood and socially framed on the other. There are growing tensions as to how social rights, and worker rights more specifically, are developed (see Cooke et al., 2019). Increasingly, both government and non-government actors, including trade unions, are trying to ensure that economic development also links – to a greater or lesser extent – with social rights. Hence, we see a growing interest in decent work campaigns in terms of wages, working hours and questions of health and safety; although how effective these campaigns are is another matter, given established patterns of privilege and economic domination.

Much depends on the level of autonomy and power of civil society, and groups such as trade unions or social movements. There remain enormous differences and disparities in the manner in which organized labour influences workplace relations and broader political agendas. Traditions of labour regulation vary greatly in developing economies. There are examples where independent and free labour organization has been minimal, such as Saudi Arabia. There are also systems that, while being politically repressive, put in place a semblance of minimal labour regulation to avoid the need for independent unions, as in Chile under the dictator Augusto Pinochet in the 1970s and 1980s. Then there are the countries where labour representation and regulation is quite extensive but under the tutelage of a centralized one-party state that dominates labour representation, as in China or Vietnam. There are also countries as diverse as Malaysia and Ghana, where employment relations systems and trade union roles have been shaped by a colonial heritage; these are models of employment relations where, while the influence of unions may be limited, they do have a degree of independence and liberty. In other cases, trade union movements have long histories of engagement, demonstrating innovative responses to employer strategies and state intervention: the Arab Spring in 2011 in Morocco and Tunisia was highly influenced by trade unions and broader forms of worker organizations (Feltrin, 2019).

The Impact of social actors and social movements

The role of NGOs is increasingly important in both developing and developed economies. NGOs often lead agendas around labour standards, inclusive strategies at work, equality measures for women and minority groups, and health and safety issues. In developing economies, they have become a major voice and exponent of a range of issues related to decent working conditions (Donaghey and Reinecke, 2018). Regardless of the positive impact on poverty generated by some aspects of FDI (Dollar and Krayy, 2001), issues have emerged as a result of the rapid and uneven nature of economic change and its social consequences. For example, the impact on women and children through their inclusion in the labour market, often within unstable patterns of employment, has generated increasing interest in health and safety issues and a broad concern for both human and employment rights. Outsourcing to supply chains dependent on labour in developing economies has had a disproportionate impact on women as they attempt to combine traditional roles with new employment roles, often within hidden parts of the economy (Pyle and Ward, 2003). Although the increasing concern with rights varies greatly, it has led to a more complex set of debates over international corporate and political interests in which NGOs have played a key part in bringing these issues to light. These organizations have emerged as major players with substantial funding streams based on individual donations from both the private sector and the public sector of mainly developed economies.

The country of origin and funding source for NGOs is an important issue as this can be reflected in their approaches to the regulation of work and employment, with some being more oriented towards collective rights and trade union roles than others. For example, the Ethical Trading Initiative (https://www.ethicaltrade.org) tries to establish labour standards on a range of issues for both MNCs and local businesses in developing economies. This organization works mainly with businesses, promoting a range of good employer practices on issues as diverse as employee participation and safety standards at work; they also offer training and consultancy. Barrientos and Smith (2007) and Ruwanpura's (2016) discussions of various ethical trading initiatives suggest that while tending to focus on certain working conditions, they place less emphasis on workers' collective representation and voice. This organization is more oriented towards employers, while others of a more social orientation such as OXFAM (https://www.oxfam.org.uk) or War on Want (https://www.waronwant.org) work more closely with social organizations, local bodies and trade unions in developing more systematic worker-led campaigns on issues such as women's rights and child labour. These organizations are oriented to building alliances across different groups and creating a greater degree of public awareness of key challenges for workers employed in developing economies.

The impact of NGOs is becoming more substantial and they are increasingly important actors in the regulatory space of employment relations and human resource management in developing economies. They vary significantly between NGOs with a tendency towards mobilization and campaign-oriented practices to those with a greater interest in consultancy and advice. Many key campaigns have had an impact on local government policy as well, and have created an increasing level of interest in broader social questions. However, as suggested above, they can sometimes crowd out local trade union voices or create a privileged dialogue at policy level, which does not necessarily engage and include workers. Nevertheless, the regulatory space is changing, with a range of actors engaging with employment relations and workers rights issues in developing economies.

The Changing role of management

It is not solely in relation to worker representation that we may see considerable variety within developing economies. There have also been interesting changes in management circles within MNCs. Change has been driven partly by the increasing transnational orientation of MNCs' policies and staffing, reducing the dependence on management from the home country. Yet globalization and the role of MNCs have a series of indirect effects on the broader body of management. In addition, there are local developments and new sets of professional and managerial classes emerging which, alongside increasing levels of management education, lead to rising expectations in terms of career development, earnings, living standards and social status. Elsewhere, new managerial cohorts are emerging, promoting new ideational agendas. Zahra (2011) argues that, in the Saudi Peninsula for example, the growing clash between new and more internationalized organizational cultures and traditional informal and hierarchical customs – coupled with major political change within both the state and society – is leading to new sets of political and social agendas, as well as competing management views and values. For example, there is a greater push to open debate on a range of previously closed employment issues, such as the role of women at work. Hence, MNCs and 'globalization', broadly speaking, may have contradictory effects and can lead to changing expectations and political interventions on matters related to worker rights. We need to appreciate this dual effect of disruption and change resulting from development agendas driven by FDI, among other factors. It unsettles communities in their local contexts but also creates new communities and new struggles. Legacies of inward investment and mobility by capital can have a disruptive effect and create tensions between not just labour and capital but also between multinational and domestic capital and managerial constituencies, with regards to the agendas of the state (Lillie and Martínez Lucio, 2012: 77).

Conclusion

What is becoming clear is that the regulation of work and employment in developing economies is a highly complex reality, involving a range of voices and actors with competing political agendas. Governments, trade unions, NGOs and changing management cohorts are all attempting to interpret globalization and the challenges of development through different sets of narratives and viewpoints. The agenda of establishing 'decent work' and developing a greater body of rights for workers is something that is accelerating, and within this process there will be an increasing range of economic and civil society actors presenting different views and strategies. Furthermore, the state is not simply a passive recipient of overseas FDI. The state has to deal with contradictory outcomes and the manner in which expectations and the understanding of rights transform as a result of economic development and social change. The state has to balance a range of competing interests and social developments as foreign investment impacts on, and changes, the way that people work and live. Policies aimed at attracting FDI and accommodating the interests of MNCs have to be balanced against growing demands and expectations of their populace, in terms of social rights and the distribution of wealth, that may be driven by economic development. It is a dynamic and constantly shifting terrain. Even where advances are made, it is not uncommon for social agendas such as minimum wages or welfare support to be put under increasing pressure from the pursuit of economic objectives.

Reflective questions

1. What opportunities may MNCs bring to a context of economic development?
2. How can governments and social actors ensure that these benefits are built upon and consolidated in relation to work and employment for a larger part of society?
3. What tensions may emerge between different groups and organizations regarding establishing decent work initiatives and a greater commitment to improved working conditions?

> **Recommended reading**
>
> - Reinecke, J. and Donaghey, J. (2015) 'After Rana Plaza: Building coalitional power for labour rights between unions and (consumption-based) social movement organisations'. *Organization*, 22(5): 720–40.
> - Jomo, K. S. (2014) '"Malaysia Incorporated": Corporatism a la Mahathir'. *Institutions and Economies*, 6(1): 73–94.
> - Tasli-Karabulut, V. and Keizer, A. (2020) 'Multinational corporations as institutional entrepreneurs: The dynamic interplay between automobile firms and the Turkish vocational education and training system'. *Industrial Relations Journal*, 51(3): 153–68.

References

Anantaraman, A. (1997) *Malaysian Industrial Relations: Law and Practice*. Serdang: Universiti Putra Malaysia Press.

Anderson, J. T. (2021) 'Managing labour migration in Malaysia: Foreign workers and the challenges of "control" beyond liberal democracies'. *Third World Quarterly*, 42(1): 86–104.

Arudsothy, P. (1990) 'The state and industrial relations in developing countries: The Malaysian situation'. *ASEAN Economic Bulletin*, 6(3): 307–28.

Barrientos, S. and Smith, S. (2007) 'Do workers benefit from ethical trade? Assessing codes of labour practice in global production systems'. *Third World Quarterly*, 28(4): 713–29.

Basahal, A., Forde, C. and MacKenzie, R. (2021) 'Labour market localisation policies and organizational responses: an analysis of the aims and effects of the Saudi Nitaqat reforms'. *International Journal of Organizational Analysis*, published online 21st September.

Bhopal, M. and Rowley, C. (2002) 'The state in employment: The case of Malaysian electronics'. *International Journal of Human Resource Management*, 13(8): 1166–85.

Bhopal, M. and Todd, P. (2000) 'Multinational corporations and trade union development in Malaysia'. In C. Rowley and J. Benson (eds), *Globalisation and Labour in the Asia Pacific Region*. London: Frank Cass, pp. 193–213.

Blunt, P. and Jones, M. L. (1992) *Managing Organisations in Africa*. Berlin: Walter de Gruyter.

Budhwar, P. (ed.) (2004) *Managing Human Resources in Asia-Pacific*. London: Routledge.

Budhwar, P. and Debrah, Y. A. (eds) (2001) *Human Resource Management in Developing Countries*. London: Routledge.

Chin, L. C. (2017) 'A strategy of attrition through enforcement: the unmaking of irregular migration in Malaysia'. *Journal of Current Southeast Asian Affairs*, 36(2): 101–36.

Cooke, F. L., Xu, J. and Bian, H. (2019) 'The prospect of decent work, decent industrial relations and decent social relations in China: Towards a multi-level and multi-disciplinary approach'. *International Journal of Human Resource Management*, 30(1): 122–55.

Dollar, D. and Krayy, A. (2001) *Trade, Growth and Poverty*. Washington, DC: World Bank.

Donaghey, J. and Reinecke, J. (2018) 'When industrial democracy meets corporate social responsibility – A comparison of the Bangladesh accord and alliance as responses to the Rana Plaza disaster'. *British Journal of Industrial Relations*, 56(1): 14–42.

Feltrin, L. (2019) 'Labour and democracy in the Maghreb: The Moroccan and Tunisian trade unions in the 2011 Arab uprisings'. *Economic and Industrial Democracy*, 40(1): 42–64.

Harvey, M. (2002) 'Human resource management in Africa: Alice's adventures in wonderland'. *International Journal of Human Resource Management*, 13(7): 121–34.

Hofstede, G. (2001) *Culture's Consequences: Comparing Values, Behaviors, Institutions, and Organizations Across Nations*, 2nd edn. Thousand Oaks: Sage.

Howell, C. (2005) *Trade Unions and the State*. Princeton: Princeton University Press.

ILO (2019) *Malaysia to Adopt a Decent Work Country Programme*. Geneva: ILO. Available at: www.ilo.org/asia/media-centre/news/WCMS_710966/lang--en/index.htm (accessed 12 October 2020).

Jackson, T. (2004) 'HRM in developing countries'. In A. W. Harzing and J. V. Russeveldt (eds), *International Human Resource Management*. London: Sage.

Jessop, B. (1990) *State Theory*. Oxford: Polity.

Jessop, B. (1995) 'The regulation approach, governance and post-Fordism: Alternative perspectives on economic and political change?' *Economy and Society*, 24(3): 307–33.

Jomo, K. S. (2007a) 'Industrialization and industry policy in Malaysia'. In K. S. Jomo (ed.), *Malaysian Industrial Policy*. Singapore: NUS Press, pp. 1–34.

Jomo, K. S. (2007b) *Malaysian Industrial Policy*. Singapore: NUS Press.

Jomo, K. S. and Todd, P. (1994) *Trade Unions and the State in Peninsular Malaysia*. Kuala Lumpur: Oxford University Press.

Jomo, K. S. (2014) '"Malaysia Incorporated": Corporatism a la Mahathir'. *Institutions and Economies*, 6(1): 73–94.

Kamoche, K. (2002) 'Introduction: Human resource management in Africa'. *International Journal of Human Resource Management*, 13(7): 993–7.

Klein, N. (2001) *No Logo*. London: Flamingo.

Kumar, N., Martínez Lucio, M. and Rose, R. C. (2013) 'Workplace industrial relations in a developing environment: barriers to renewal within unions in Malaysia'. *Asia Pacific Journal of Human Resources*, 51(1): 22–44.

Kuruvilla, S. (1996) 'Linkages between industrialisation strategies and industrial relations/ human resource policies: Singapore, Malaysia, the Philippines, and India'. *Industrial and Labour Relations Review*, 49(4): 635–57.

Kuruvilla, S. and Arudsothy, P. (1995) 'Economic development strategy, government labour policy and firm-level industrial relations practices in Malaysia'. In A. Verma, T. A. Kochan and R. D. Lansbury (eds), *Employment Relations in the Growing Asian Economies*. London: Routledge, pp. 158–93.

Kuruvilla, S. and Venkataratnam, C. S. (1996) 'Economic development and industrial relations: The case of South and Southeast Asia'. *Industrial Relations Journal*, 27(1): 9–23.

Lillie, N. and Martínez Lucio, M. (2012) 'Rollerball and the spirit of capitalism: Competitive dynamics within the global context, the challenge to labour transnationalism, and the emergence of ironic outcomes'. *Critical Perspectives in International Business*, 8(1): 74–92.

MacKenzie, R. and Martínez Lucio, M. (2005) 'The realities of regulatory change: beyond the fetish of deregulation'. *Sociology*, 39(3): 499–517.

MacKenzie, R. and Martínez Lucio, M. (2014) 'The colonisation of employment regulation and industrial relations: Dynamics and developmnents over five decades of change'. *Labor History*, 55(2): 189–207.

Marchington, M. and Wilkinson, A. (2008) *Human Resource Management at Work*. London: CIPD.

MOHR (2009) *Realizing Decent Work for Decent Life*. Malaysia: Ministry of Human Resources.

Parasuraman, B. (2004) *Malaysian Industrial Relations: A Critical Analysis*. Kuala Lumpur: Pearson Prentice Hall.

Pyle, J. and Ward, K. (2003) 'Recasting our understanding of gender and work during global restructuring'. *International Sociology*, 18(3): 461–89.

Ritchie, B. K. (2002) *Foreign Direct Investment and Intellectual Capital Formation in Southeast Asia*. Paris: OECD Development Centre.

Rowley, C. and Warner, M. (2004) 'Big business in Asia'. *Asia Pacific Business Review*, 10(4): 485–96.

Ruwanpura, K. N. (2016) 'Garments without guilt? Uneven labour geographies and ethical trading – Sri Lankan labour perspectives'. *Journal of Economic Geography*, 16(2): 423–46.

Sharma, B. (1996) *Industrial Relations in ASEAN: A Comparative Study*. Kuala Lumpur: International Law Book Services.

Suhanah, S. S. A. (2002) 'Law and labour market regulations in Malaysia: Beyond the new economy policy'. In S. Cooney, T. Lindsey, R. Mitchell and Y. Zhu (eds), *Law and Labour Market Regulation in East Asia*. London: Routledge.

Tasli-Karabulut, V. and Keizer, A. (2020) 'Multinational corporations as institutional entrepreneurs: the dynamic interplay between automobile firms and the Turkish vocational education and training system'. *Industrial Relations Journal*, 51(3): 153–68.

Todd, P. and Peetz, D. (2001) 'Malaysian industrial relations at century's turn: Vision 2020 or a spectre of the past?' *International Journal of Human Resource Management*, 12(8): 1365–82.

UNCTAD (2011) *Global Investment Trends Monitor*. Geneva: UNCTAD.

UNCTAD (2013) *The World Investment Report*. Geneva: UNCTAD.

Vassolo, R. S., De Castro, J. O. and Gomez-Mejia, L. R. (2011) 'Managing in Latin America: Common issues and a research agenda'. *Academy of Management Perspectives*, 25(4): 22–36.

Zahra, S. A. (2011) 'Doing research in the (new) Middle East: Sailing with the wind'. *Academy of Management Perspectives*, 25(4): 1–16.

9 Training in the context of 'globalization': politics and symbolism in skill formation

Miguel Martínez Lucio and Stephen Mustchin

Learning objectives

- To outline the reasons why training varies across countries
- To understand the changing approaches to skill formation
- To comprehend the impact of multinational corporations (MNCs) on the development of a nation's skills
- To appreciate the economic and political significance of the development of soft skills
- To understand the role of soft skills in management development
- To outline the role of trade unions in such matters as skills in a global context and describe new progressive ways of approaching training and learning

Introduction

The aim of this chapter is to outline the subject of training and development in relation to the growing internationalization of the firm and the changing nature of employment relations. The development of work-related skills is a vital feature of economic and social development. It is seen by many to be pivotal to the resources of a firm and a country in relation to their strategic market position. The ability to work within certain organizational environments, with specific technologies and within a climate of continuous innovation is held to be one of the defining features of leading-edge competitors. A range of developing economies emphasize the need to develop a nation's skills, especially those of its core workforce and its management. These countries set targets for their education systems; alongside a desire to promote economic growth is an obsession with meeting education and learning targets, from higher education through to workplace qualifications.

However, the question of skills and the development of skill formation is political (Heyes and Stuart, 1998; Lloyd and Payne, 2002). The level of resources and the level of political commitment to skills formation and vocational education are key factors in this political process, along with the role and capacity of governments and their broader public bodies. Much also depends on the commitment of employers and their representative associations (and the effectiveness of these associations), alongside the role of workers' organizations in their involvement and commitment to training. In addition, the political focus of skill formation can vary: in some cases, training can be a matter of providing new technical abilities that are essential to particular jobs, but on the other hand, training may focus on attitudinal issues and on changing the 'mindsets' of workers in relation to new forms of work. Certain 'skills' may also be developed with a view to enhancing the further exploitation of workers, as we discuss later. There is therefore the fundamental question of what types of skill are being focused on in any one context.

The reality is that nation-states develop different approaches to the resourcing, organizing and development of training programmes for their workforce and the first part of this chapter will discuss this: the difference between coordinated and liberal market approaches in terms of regulated and state-led approaches in the former and more market- and employer-oriented approaches in the latter. This is not just about the difference between developed and developing economies; there are also differences within the 'developed' world, where we see that there is a tension between two different views of skills formation which are central to the future paths others take. MNCs engage with, and can shape and influence, these regimes and approaches; hence, their own role will be discussed. While they can provide new job opportunities, they do not always provide consistent and meaningful processes of skills development.

Central to these discussions are notions of 'soft skills'. These skills are seen as important for dealing with a greater level of organizational change and continuous improvement and innovation. For some, this is central to the new, post-bureaucratic age; however, for others this represents a move to greater exploitation of workers (see Chapter 1 on globalization and employment). The chapter will also focus on the question of alternative and more emancipatory views regarding skills and training. Trade unions have begun since the late 20th century to develop a more engaged approach to worker education – although some would argue that this was always the case in terms of supporting free education and accessible learning. However, we have seen a greater interest in workplace learning and the ongoing development of workers that builds not just those features of the workforce that are relevant to their job and employer, but the broader capacities of individuals (Cornelius et al., 2008) as both workers and as active citizens within society. The chapter focuses on the broader workforce and not just a select elite minority of managers, which is often the way international human resource management (IHRM) approaches the subject.

Context of skills: national systems and different approaches

In a classic study of management and labour in Europe, Lane (1989: 63–4) pointed to the importance of recognizing differences in emphasis in terms of public policy and employment relations and how they influenced the way management and employers responded to the question of skills. In Germany, general and vocational education have been equally developed, through a strong role for the state, the establishment of a system of social dialogue and highly structured approaches to skill formation. This contrasts with Britain, where there has been a more decentralized approach with an unclear – if not confusing – set of bodies dealing with learning. There has been a move to systematically create national vocational standards, but the level of investment and engagement remains uneven. The United Kingdom (UK) contrasts with the more centralized, institutionally embedded German system where the extent of coordination and regulation is higher (Busemeyer and Schlicht-Schmälzle, 2014) and where poaching staff that are already trained by other companies is comparatively limited (Mohrenweiser et al., 2019).

This fundamental difference between the more voluntarist and market-based learning contexts of the UK on the one hand and state-oriented and social-dialogue-based systems on the other hand, such as in Germany, has been explored in studies on the redesign of work: 'Workplace innovation has come to mean a broader process of organizational renewal consistent with high quality, high skill, high trust, business approaches. An important question is the extent to which publicly supported programmes aimed at supporting and resourcing this kind of development are able to achieve success' (Payne and Keep, 2005: 148). This is also the case with the way new skills are developed through the support of the state in relation to the adoption of new technologies as in Norway with its more proactive public policy and trade union influence (Lloyd and Payne, 2019).

In a study of Finland and Norway on the one hand and the UK on the other, Payne and Keep (2005) argued that while changes to skills and worker roles were not always that easily measurable in the former two countries as a consequence of such developments, in the case of the UK the decline in bargaining, the lack of state regulation and resourcing and the absence of a high trust relation between workers and managers meant that workplace redesign and change were often concerned with cutting labour costs and a tokenistic approach to re-skilling workers. Grugulis (2007: 36–9; Martin, 2017) sees such differences in training – in terms of resourcing, coordination and creating a culture of worker involvement, among other factors – as depending on the nature of state intervention with some relying more on public funding and intervention and worker participation while others rely more on voluntarist employer-led systems.

Much of the employment relations literature is therefore concerned with how skills and their development vary greatly according to the nature of the employment system and its regulation (see Chapter 3 on national systems of employment relations in different countries and Chapter 11 on varieties of capitalism). The level of state resourcing may also vary, as will the role of employer organizations and worker representatives in participating in training systems and their input into work. In some cases, one may see a more organized and bureaucratic approach to skills with clear definitions in terms of skill differences, classifications and their development from, for example, an apprentice level through to a qualified full-time employed worker.

In the past 10 years, such an approach to the study of training has been further underpinned by a deeper interest in the *nature* of capitalist systems. This work, pioneered by Hall and Soskice (2001), looks at capitalism more broadly and not solely at systems of regulation in terms of who drives training and skill formation. By focusing on the nature of relations between different sets of capitalist interests and the role of ownership structures, this approach locates training in the nature of political and economic relations that exist in any one context (see Chapter 3 and Chapter 11 on national systems of employment relations for a discussion of coordinated market economies (CME) and liberal market economies (LME)). According to Kaufman (2011: 49–50), this approach has become a major pivot of the study of labour and employment relations. It allows for different approaches to capitalism to be wedded to an understanding of the nature of training and learning across different contexts. In LMEs, the emphasis is on lowering costs, less government intervention and a more flexible approach to skills: this is linked to a short-term approach to investment and the pursuit of higher profitability with skills developed in a more ad hoc manner. Within this context, employers are a clear driver with less state and union involvement. The UK and the United States are seen as examples of LMEs. CMEs are different as there is a greater attempt to organize skill formation through longer-term apprenticeships and more systematic and technical approaches to skills, based on a labour-relations system driven by dialogue and trust, with unions and government sometimes even leading discussions. The focus is on the long term and investment in deeper skill formation, in part due to there being less of an emphasis on short-term profits among shareholders. Germany is seen as an example of a CME. Analysis of how training opportunities are distributed within the relatively liberal context of the United States indicates that those with a higher level of educational attainment are more likely to get further opportunities to train (Lillard and Tan, 1992: 46), thus limiting opportunities to access training among a significant part of the population.

In terms of management development, we can also see such differences reflected in the way managers are trained. Handy et al. (1988), in a dated but highly significant and pioneering report on the way managers were trained and developed during the latter half of the 20th century, pointed to similarities and differences between countries such as Japan, the UK, France, Germany and the United States. (This was a period when management development and related standards or accreditation were becoming a significant area of debate; see Winterton and Winterton (1997)). There were many similarities: (a) it was large firms that tended to set the management development agenda; (b) university-based education was pivotal in the early stages (apart from the UK); (c) continuous management education was common; and (d) greater levels of organizational change were requiring and bringing forth a broader approach to management learning based on understanding different types of management. However, there were differences that reflected some of the features outlined earlier. Continuous learning in relation to managers was more structured and formal in Germany and Japan compared with the relatively opportunistic approach of the United States and the UK. Management and business education was more pronounced in the United States, whereas in Germany, the sciences, engineering, law and economics were the basis of management background. In Japan, the company and its internal practical spaces were important for on-the-job training, while the French and British tended to recruit from elite educational institutions for their management elites with less emphasis on internal progression. In the UK, accountancy has been a more dominant route into management compared to Japan or Germany. Evans et al. (2002) pointed to how German firms emphasized having stable development programmes based on strong internal labour markets, while the UK and Dutch models were driven by a market-based approach and less internal development (see also Pilz, 2009). Many management studies are replete with simplistic stereotypes of nations so caution is needed with such generalizations but the point we need to consider is that regardless of such typologies, and how they evolve, differences between the more coordinated and liberal market approaches in general terms tend to hold even for these types of study on management even if the cult of the Anglo-Saxon business school has become extended into almost all national contexts (see Sisson and Story, 1988; see also Chapter 10 on management education and Chapter 11 on varieties of capitalism).

MNCs are confronted with very different contexts in terms of the countries in which they operate, of training in terms of how it is financed, how skills are classified and how managers and workers are involved in the development of learning agendas. Nevertheless, MNCs can have an influence on these contexts, as we discuss later. The increasing pace of globalization and the greater movement of capital in order to exploit labour costs and skills have placed increasing pressures on systems with a high resource investment level. In a wide-ranging study of the European context, Stuart (2007) argued that there were pressures to shift to new approaches given ongoing restructuring and the demand for flexibility.

In addition, there has been a growing emphasis on new types of skills and learning – commonly called soft skills (see below). At the heart of this approach is a supply-side emphasis which highlights flexibility and adaptability as key features of the learning agenda (Stuart 2007), which is problematic as this may represent a more neoliberal and liberal market approach involving changes in policy in more coordinated economic contexts (Greenwood and Stuart, 2006) although whether this leds to any 'upskilling' or greater levels of discretion is questionable as Vidal (2019) argues. Implementing these changes when systems of skills regulation remain focused around complex relations and traditions, and involving actors such as employer bodies and trade unions to implement and sustain developments, is difficult (Martínez Lucio et al., 2007), especially when in the key nation-states within the European Union (EU), training budgets have been challenged in the past few years. However, in Europe political and social dialogue around learning and training remains a major feature of policy involving public bodies, employers and trade unions, although this varies in intensity across countries (Busemeyer and Thelen, 2020; Heyes, 2007).

These complex dynamics and changes are apparent in developing- or emerging-state and economic contexts. In such contexts, the role of the state is central in distributing funding for training and its implementation (see Chapter 8 on developing economies). Governments play a key role; however, their limited resources, the problem of a fragmented employer class, reliance on lower labour costs and limited or constrained social dialogue on such issues with employers and unions means that they cannot adopt the CME approach with consistency. The relationship between the state and employers, and the extent to which they involve unions, varies and often reflects ideology, power structures and traditions: even at the local regional level (Almond et al., 2017). Further problems arise when MNC demand for higher skills is mainly met by those within developing economies with enough wealth to access the education system, potentially reinforcing existing inequalities (Kapstein, 2002: 10). However, the state remains one of the few actors capable of sustaining a vocational training strategy in the absence of strong national capitalist enterprises and effective 'peak' organizations such as employer associations and trade unions: there are many cases as in Turkey where the local vocational educational system interacts in a collaborative manner with MNCs so as to ensure a more systematic approach to training (Tasli-Karabulut and Keizer, 2020). The state is therefore an active player in drawing in and attracting more dynamic interventions from MNCs:

> Rather than simply retreating to the sidelines to function as the game's referee, the state must strategically co-ordinate the interaction between key economic actors in a way that will stimulate deep and crosscutting developmental linkages. These linkages are necessary to facilitate information flow,

increase vested interests through participation (as opposed to simply consultation), and improve cross-checked monitoring and implementation . . . But this new role for the state is also dramatically different from the theoretical role of the developmental state. Instead of simply directing investment and ameliorating risk, the state must now encourage, facilitate, and co-ordinate the formation of *intangible* assets, which often requires more private-sector leadership. (Ritchie, 2002: 32)

Training in both developed and developing economies therefore can be measured across various dimensions: we may find some countries tending to emphasize formal skills and a more industrial, state-driven agenda, while others may emphasize the service sector and new understandings of skills (as discussed later).

Globalization and change in training and skills: the example of soft skills

The question of MNCs and their roles

An important view within many international bodies and governments is that MNCs are keenly attracted to areas where there are high levels of human capital and a strong infrastructure of technological capabilities (Noorbakhsh et al., 2001, cited in Ritchie, 2002). This is one reason why governments see their education strategies as essential to the development of their countries through greater foreign direct investment (FDI). Hence, MNCs can in many cases be free-riders by 'shopping around' not just for cheaper labour costs but for a workforce that has already been trained up for their organizational needs. Yet this would be only one side of what MNCs do. The counterargument suggests that MNCs in developing economies in South East Asia such as Malaysia have added to the skills stock by providing more training than local employers (Abdullah, 1994, cited in Ritchie, 2002); however, the comparison may not be a fair one as local firms may not have a strong training tradition or access to state resources to start with and the voice of labour and employment regulation may not be as integrated into the state-level decision-making processes leading to a weaker approach to skill formation (for policy-making and 'social partners' in Malaysia, see Jomo, 2017 and Chapter 8). The focus of such inward investment is often on relatively low-skilled manufacturing processes, and thus the types of skill needed may be of a routine, assembly-oriented nature, centred on short-term commitments based on 'kit' production – putting manufactured components together but not actually making them. In a classic study of MNCs and FDI in the UK during a period of de-industrialization, Knell (1993) argued that overseas companies may just bring specific low-skill aspects of their work, exploit lower wage costs and take a narrow view of training. In addition, the introduction of new platform technologies may lead to a greater informalization of the economy and labour markets as they exascerbate the fragmentation of labour conditions and the use of non-standard employment systems, especially in the absence of strong worker voice and regulations (Edward, 2020), although others may point to the potential over the long term for a degree of formalization and economic stability to emerge through such uses of platform-based systems (Lakemann and Lay, 2019).

Much depends on the industrial sector which is being discussed, as some will lend themselves to a lower-skills approach (as in much manufacturing and many service industries), while others (such as medical research, engineering and information technology (IT)) may not. However, one thing that does emerge from these studies is that the interaction between national state bodies and MNCs is a key factor in enhancing longer-term development in terms of skill. The way the state intervenes in a wide manner of ways – not just in terms of resourcing but also in terms of creating alliances between firms and public bodies, creating spaces for dialogue about training and in creating benchmarks and best practices – is of fundamental importance (Martínez Lucio and Stuart, 2011).

The age of 'soft skills'?

Hence, while we see very different approaches to skill formation and its context, there is a view that soft skills are crucial to the way workers are developed. The dominant skills models of LMEs are framing the development of global 'skill sets' at work in the form of soft skills (Shakir, 2009). What are soft skills and why are they seen as being fundamentally important to training for future forms of work? Grugulis (2007: 72–9) draws together a range of positions and argues that there are various factors that constitute and drive the development and use of soft skills:

1. There are sectors such as hospitality and retail that require a type of employee with certain social and communication skills.
2. This links to a more positive attitude to work and life – working as a team and behaving socially towards an economic end.
3. This in effect is based on a range (and sometimes complex understanding) of personal traits and attitudes which are seen as being cohesive and engaged with a market approach.
4. Hence technical skills have to be supplemented by soft skills that engage the customer and place an emotional element within the relationships between workers and their clients. This is relevant for dealing with external customers but also for seeing your own work colleagues as internal customers.

5.   This has led to a growing debate about 'emotional labour' – a new type of labour based on the use and portrayal of one's emotions in a positive light.

In addition, the development of the platform economy pushes the interface between the customer and the worker further into the spotlight in sectors such as transportation and home delivery, such that the need for communication and personal skills is key to managing exchanges and potential conflict. It is not hard to see the ideological dimension of these characteristics and preferred skills as they are clearly linked to a market economy and a focus on customer relations as a primary concern for HRM. They are about sustaining a more adaptable workforce which is positive in their engagement with organizational change rather than sincerely deepening their actual skills and abilities (Lloyd and Payne, 2009). In some respects, it is an extension of the 'Americanization' of workplace relations (see Chapter 10 on management education and consultancy and Chapter 11 on varities of captialism). The aim is to continuously engage in a positive manner: not to exhibit criticism at work (Hughes, 2005), and to be conformist with organizational needs in terms of appearance and even dress code, which is a feature of aesthetic labour (Nickson et al., 2005). In addition, much of the soft skills agenda is also about basic self-management and creating a vision of a reliable and manageable individual which in some contexts is seen as vital even for national development (Baharun et al., 2012).

However, the idea that we need to view each other as customers can ironically undermine open discussion and genuine and authentic interaction (Ritzer, 1997). There are concerns that the development of soft skills can be a conduit for a new form of exploitation and work intensification.

First, the increasing emphasis on the needs of the customer creates new forms of labour control and further pressures on workers (Bain and Taylor, 2000). In viewing students as customers and trying to satisfy their needs, academics, for example, may lower standards and change the way they assess students so that more pass their modules. Student complaints and student surveys can be used to humiliate and even discipline academics. In various call centres in India, workers have to tolerate a range of bullying behaviour from UK callers, given the imperative to engage positively with such callers (Taylor and Bain, 2005). There are various studies of bullying in such sectors in India due to a range of performance management issues (D'Cruz and Rayner, 2013). In some cases, such behaviour may be racist; this puts the worker in a difficult position as they have to 'please the customer'.

Second, call-centre customer interactions may be scripted, with workers having to follow certain protocols and standard phrases, which undermines their ability to work autonomously. This scripting of work can create a pressurized environment which inhibits displays of emotion and which can create tensions between workers attempting to do the work in a meaningful manner and just doing the work to get through as many customers as possible (Korczynski, 2003). The emphasis on soft skills and new forms of work may obscure the routine and repetitive nature of much service employment (Ritzer, 1997).

Third, many governments now push the development of such skills as the basis of development, sometimes to the exclusion of more technical forms of skill formation. Such skills are seen as being important to the attitudinal restructuring of the workforce: creating a culture of work which is more flexible and adaptable. In various developing economy contexts, soft skills are viewed as a key dimension of the changes required for a more 'western', 'developed' and market-facing culture. Some MNCs such as McDonald's have been major drivers of such developments in the same way that Ford was a major pioneer of the assembly-line approach to production in the early 20th century.

The move towards soft skills can create a dimension of work where skill is more symbolic than formal and driven by new forms of control. In some developing countries, such developments may create a policy discourse of skill formation and a set of policy objectives that emphasizes soft skills with notions of social dialogue and associated institutional arrangements often excluded from the policy discourse for ideological reasons. The increasing fascination with 'gamification' at work – the use of gaming or gaming-type approaches to create a learning and developmental environment (and presumably a more motivating place to work, as Dale, 2014, discusses) – can also create a false climate of engagement which is primarily symbolic and even trivial.

Management development and soft skills

In many respects, this dimension of skills is becoming significant to the area of management development too. In quoting and building on Sparrow (1996), Mabey and Finch-Lees (2008: 192) argue that British approaches to management development are 'preoccupied with "soft" skills, especially the ability to motivate, lead and get the best from teams'. The view that management needs to think more in terms of the qualities of leadership and thus a range of interpersonal skills which allow for a more socially engaged approach in ethical, visionary and personal terms (Alldredge and Nilan, 2000) is becoming increasingly important, although that does not mean management attitudes and approaches to the rights of workers may be softer or more socially oriented. In effect, the training of management is partly being driven by an emphasis on soft and not just technical skills: this is clear from the emphasis on socialization in business schools in terms of networking, communication skills and social skills becoming almost as important as acquiring substantive knowledge.

Managing from a neoliberal and marketized perspective is an ideological development, and this is enshrined in the role of consultancies and business schools in the way they drive cultures of management (see Chapter 10 on business schools and consultancies). This raises some difficult ethical issues, as we will discuss later on.

However, there are other drivers to such developments as well, not just the process of Americanization and the nature of neoliberal management education (which takes much of its cue from the United States through accreditation bodies). The nature of work within MNCs means there are likely to be real pressures on management in terms of coping with an array of cultures and ethnicities in their workplaces and especially on international assignments (see Collings et al., 2007). By their very nature, international assignments and ongoing cross-national and cross-ethical project-based work, for example, bring together a range of individuals where communication, cultural adaptation and awareness and sensitivity to ethical differences and behaviour move increasingly to the forefront of the work of managers at all levels. It is for this reason that diversity management, for example, is seen as central to the new skills portfolios of management (see Chapter 5 on diversity and equality). The problems begin when soft and 'emotional' skills are seen as more important than having a systematic understanding of the cultures and values of the people management deals with (Sippola and Smale, 2007). The same applies to the increasing emphasis on notions of 'well-being' that have entered management discourse and practice as a way of countering the increasing pressures of work and creating a climate for reflecting on broader personal health levels: although these may create a new vision of soft skills based on coping with pressures placed on you at work in an individualized manner. To that extent, these 'skills' can be highly symbolic and individualized.

Furthermore, in an age of continuous communication and with the impact of the internet, the need to modify and control communication at a range of levels brings a new set of pressures on managers as employees. Expectations of constant accessibility and accountability mean that social interactions are increasingly scrutinized. The need to develop forms of leadership around notions of transparency and openness may clash with and slow down decision-making processes. Hence management development increasingly focuses on the modification of management work with an emphasis on the processes of communication and not just the content. However, to what extent this is more a matter of controlling risk than engendering transparent management is questionable. MNCs therefore increasingly engage with the development of soft skills in a range of work groups as an essential aspect of their expansion, and this is often reflected in the approach to skills taken by states that receive FDI (Shakir, 2009). The following short case study illustrates some of the issues that can emerge in relation to soft skills; it uses the example of changes in higher education.

Case studies: Soft skills, organizational politics and learning in higher education (the case of Malaysia)

It is argued that for a country to develop further, it is essential that potential graduates are taught a range of new skills which are central to what many perceive to be at the heart of recruitment practices within MNCs and large, organized companies in general, and which dovetail with developments in contexts such as the United States. These skills, according to Baharun et al. (2012: 8795) in the Malaysian case, for example, entail that:

> graduates must change their attitude when entering the job market as employers placed greater emphasis on the ability of graduates to fulfil their responsibility and keep appointments. On the other hand, based on experience, employers found graduates to be lacking in this positive attitude. The present findings indicate that undergraduates reported a relatively lower ability to fulfil responsibility, manage time and the inability to improve knowledge after graduation. This suggests that skills development opportunities during their study in university is a key issue that needs to be addressed.

The Ministry of Higher Education announced that the development of soft skills was a high-priority issue and objective in Malaysia in the past few years (Shakir, 2009). Key personal attributes in terms of organization, communication skills and general presentation have also been seen as essential for potential employees in various parts of the South Pacific as well (Bhanugopan and Fish, 2009).

It is therefore suggested by various experts that there is a need for formal educational processes to be supplemented with the learning of such soft skills. In India, the investment in soft skills was seen as essential if the nation was to draw in investment in such key service sectors as call centres, as this would facilitate the development of a more proactive customer-service orientation and attract overseas investors in financial services, for example (Crome, 1998). Many such developments are driven by a view of learning which is influenced by liberal market economic approaches. The focus is on 'adaptability' and not necessarily their abilities: the emphasis is on an individualized and culturalist (Americanized) view of what effective employees should be like as opposed to the obligations of the state to systematically train them and facilitate worker voice on matters related to training and development.

Questions

1. What are the key elements of soft skills and why are they important?
2. In a development context, why would soft skills be important and not just technical skills? Why would governments take such an interest in the development of soft skills as well?
3. Thinking in terms of soft skills outlined earlier, how would soft skills be the basis for a deeper development of our emotional attachments to work and our customers?
4. What are the costs of over-emphasizing soft skills and how is this agenda open to abuse as a form of control and exploitation of workers? Can it displace a commitment to harder and more technical skills?

Employment relations and learning: questions of rights and emancipation

The question of learning is a broad issue involving various organizations, institutions and movements. Within the EU, for example, including trade unions became a focus of interest in the past. In the past 20 years or so, the quality of skills and the adaptability of workers in a more fragmented and ever-changing labour market – where long-term jobs are increasingly less likely – has come an agenda to develop 'human resources'. The delivery of new forms of training in terms of basic skills and soft skills, for example, has been a major part of the EU's agenda (Greenwood and Stuart, 2006) linked to the social dimension of the EU that is meant to act as a counterweight to economic and market priorities (Mathers, 2010). Faced with these challenges, training, skills development and certification have become increasingly prominent issues for unions as they aim to ensure their members are appropriately rewarded for their skills and are able to adapt to labour market change (Cooney and Stuart, 2012). In addition, the intensification of migration has meant that there is a perceived need to engage large groups of migrants who may be excluded from accessing learning and skills development, especially at the lower-skills end (see Mustchin, 2012; Perrett et al., 2012). Although more recently the impact of the 2008 economic crisis and the policies of austerity have acted to constrain such developments due to the growing interest in worker 'flexibility' (Hastings and Heyes, 2018).

In other contexts, such as the United States, learning and the development of basic skills is an important feature of local community worker centres, which involve unions and community groups (Fine, 2006). While state funding varies across these different contexts, the new learning agenda is more expansive than some management-focused academics would have us believe, and within this, unions play a role (Heyes, 2007; Stuart, 2019).

Fusing the learning agenda into a broader development agenda for workers has been the basis of discussions within trade unions and social movements. Hence, as mentioned previously, learning and skills development is clearly a political issue (Heyes and Stuart, 1998). Many social organizations such as charities and non-governmental organizations (NGOs) view learning and training as a major vehicle for political and economic development. However, training is partly driven by the perception of some development agencies that training is a less problematic and less challenging issue for involving employers, governments and unions in capacity building and the policy process (*Polidano, 1999*) and be focused on simply adjusting workers to new forms of exploitation and acceptance of low-skilled jobs (Verger and Novelli, 2010): for some, NGOs become internalized within the economic logics of neoliberalism and minimal support services (Muhammad, 2018). Although, the role of NGOs is an important factor in extending training and development in various contexts in terms of worker rights as well as regulation.

An alternative approach which is not solely fixated with soft skills is to focus on the concept of capabilities (Sen, 2005). The argument is that we need to look across a person's ability to be autonomous, creative, socially engaged and reasoned, and their capacity for self-development and even play (Nussbaum, 2000). International Labour Organization (ILO) programmes such as Decent Work place a strong emphasis on the right of workers to be developed and trained in a more systematic and meaningful manner (ILO, 2020). These initiatives are meant to frame a global response which places worker rights at the heart of the employment and training agenda as opposed to just an array of symbolic 'soft skills'.

Conclusion

When we think in terms of training and development in relation to systems of work, it is clear that there are various dimensions to this discussion. The way skills are developed is both complex and nuanced. This chapter has pointed out how skills can be developed in a systematic manner on the one hand but also in a more ad hoc and symbolic manner on the other, with approaches often determined by institutional contexts and the role of the state. Students at universities are constantly being told that the substantive content of their degrees is only one part of their development, and that they also need communication, teamworking and emotional skills to be able to utilize their technical knowledge. However, to what extent this secondary feature begins to replace the first in terms of emphasis is a matter of conjecture. This chapter has also noted that different national contexts present varied responses to training in terms of the extent of resourcing, social participation, the focus of policy and the nature of the skills developed. However, as stated earlier, 'soft skills' have become an important feature within the arena of training and development, often with negative implications. Global organization, mobility and production bring a second tier and set of issues to the forefront in terms of cultural training and ethical awareness. These are the fundamental skills supposedly needed within global organizations and a global workforce, yet this can sometimes become an end in itself and be abused as a way of creating a more adaptable and therefore exploitable workforce and management (see Chapter 12 on lean production).

The chapter has pointed to the way MNCs have an uneven impact on the development of skills. The nature of the context in which they operate is important, and the way in which state agencies respond to and facilitate MNC investment is also significant. The nature of change within these institutional contexts – partly driven by the presence of MNCs – is another salient factor. However, the impact of MNCs does not in itself ensure any deep or lasting commitment to the development of the skills of workers and managers, especially in an age when capital moves in and out of countries and regions at ever greater speed, thus not allowing jobs and skills to be embedded (Knell, 1993).

The chapter ends with the new social and inclusive agenda for skills and learning which has emerged. The increasing engagement with learning and skills by trade unions, NGOs and the ILO presents us with a new alternative to short-term and narrow skill formation, although much will depend on the levels of resourcing and political commitment from governments in terms of broader understandings of *capabilities*.

Reflective questions

1. What are the principal differences between national approaches to training and why are they important?
2. How do governments try to ensure they are attractive to overseas investors in terms of skills?
3. What are the positive and negative impacts of MNCs in terms of skills development within countries and what do you think explains this?
4. What are soft skills and how are they linked to globalization?
5. What benefits do such developments bring for workers and managers?
6. What are the possible issues that emerge in relation to soft skills in terms of (a) work intensification, (b) the development of your skills and (c) the position and role of more technical skills formation?
7. How can learning be linked to a broader development of individuals and what role can an understanding of capability theory provide?

Recommended reading

- Busemeyer, M. R. and Schlicht-Schmälzle, R. (2014) 'Partisan power, economic coordination and variations in vocational training systems in Europe'. *European Journal of Industrial Relations*, 20(1): 55–71.
- Hughes, J. (2005) 'Bringing emotion to work: Emotional intelligence, employee resistance and the reinvention of character'. *Work, Employment and Society*, 19(3): 603–25.
- Lloyd, C. and Payne, J. (2019) 'Rethinking country effects: robotics, AI and work futures in Norway and the UK'. *New Technology, Work and Employment*, 34(3): 208–25.

References

Abdullah, W. A. W. (1994) 'Transnational corporations and human resource development'. *Personnel Review*, 23(5): 50–70.

Alldredge, M. E. and Nilan, K. J. (2000) '3M's leadership competency model: An internally developed solution'. *Human Resource Management*, 39(2–3): 133–45.

Almond, P., Gonzalez, M. C., Lavelle, J. and Murray, G. (2017) 'The local in the global: Regions, employment systems and multinationals'. *Industrial Relations Journal*, 48(2): 115–32.

Baharun, R., Suleiman, E. S. and Awang, Z. (2012) 'Changing skills required by industries: Perceptions of what makes business graduates employable'. *African Journal of Business Management*, 6(30): 8789–96.

Bain, P. and Taylor, P. (2000) 'Entrapped by the "electronic panopticon"? Worker resistance in the call centre'. *New Technology, Work and Employment*, 15(1): 2–18.

Bhanugopan, R. and Fish, A. (2009) 'Achieving graduate employability through consensus in the South Pacific island nation'. *Education + Training*, 51(2): 108–23.

Busemeyer, M. R. and Schlicht-Schmälzle, R. (2014) 'Partisan power, economic coordination and variations in vocational training systems in Europe'. *European Journal of Industrial Relations*, 20(1) 55–71.

Busemeyer, M. R. and Thelen, K. (2020) 'Institutional sources of business power'. *World Politics*, 72(3): 448–80.

Collings, D. G., Scullion, H. and Morley, M. J. (2007) 'Changing patterns of global staffing in the multinational enterprise: Challenges to the conventional expatriate assignment and emerging alternatives'. *Journal of World Business*, 42(2): 198–213.

Cooney, R. and Stuart, M. (2012) *Trade Unions and Workplace Training: Issues and International Perspectives*. Abingdon: Routledge.

Cornelius, N., Todres, M., Janjuha-Jivraj, S., Woods, A. and Wallace, J. (2008) 'The social enterprise and capacity, capabilities and quality of life'. *Journal of Business Ethics*, 81(2): 355–70.

Crome, M. (1998) 'Call centres: Battery farming or free range?' *Industrial and Commercial Training*, 30(4): 137–41.

D'Cruz, P. and Rayner, C. (2013) 'Bullying in the Indian workplace: A study of the ITES-BPO sector'. *Economic and Industrial Democracy*, 34(4): 597–619.

Dale, S. (2014) 'Gamification: Making work fun, or making fun of work?' *Business Information Review*, 31(2): 82–90.

Edward, W. (2020) 'The Uberisation of work: The challenge of regulating platform capitalism. A commentary'. *International Review of Applied Economics*, 34(4): 1–10.

Evans, P., Pucik, V. and Björkman, I. (2002) *The Global Challenge: International Human Resource Management*. Boston: McGraw-Hill Education.

Fine, J. (2006) *Workers' Centers*. Ithaca: Cornell University Press.

Greenwood, I. and Stuart, M. (2006) 'Employability and the flexible economy: Some considerations of the politics and contradictions of the European employment strategy'. In L. E. Alonso and M. Martínez Lucio (eds), *Employment Relations in a Changing Society: Assessing the Post-Fordist Paradigm*. London: Palgrave. pp 104-19

Grugulis, I. (2007) *Skills, Training and Human Resource Development: A Critical Text*. London: Routledge.

Hall, P. A. and Soskice, D. (2001) *Varieties of Capitalism and Institutional Complementarities*. Oxford: Oxford University Press, pp. 43–76.

Handy, C., Gordon, C., Gough, I. and Randlsome, C. (1988) *Making Managers*. London: Pitman.

Hastings, T. and Heyes, J. (2018) 'Farewell to flexicurity? Austerity and labour policies in the European Union'. *Economic and Industrial Democracy*, 39(3): 458–80.

Heyes, J. (2007) 'Training, social dialogue and collective bargaining in Western Europe'. *Economic and Industrial Democracy*, 28(2): 239–58.

Heyes, J. and Stuart, M. (1998) 'Bargaining for skills: Trade unions and training at the workplace'. *British Journal of Industrial Relations*, 36(3): 459–67.

Hughes, J. (2005) 'Bringing emotion to work: Emotional intelligence, employee resistance and the reinvention of character'. *Work, Employment and Society*, 19(3): 603–25.

ILO (2020) *2.0 Skills and Employability*. Geneva: ILO. Available at: www.ilo.org/global/topics/dw4sd/themes/skills/lang--en/index.htm (accessed 3 October 2020).

Jomo, K.S. (2017) '"Malaysia Incorporated": Corporatism a la Mahathir'. *Institutions and Economies*, 6(1): 73–94.

Kapstein, E. (2002) *Virtuous Circles? Human Capital Formation, Economic Development and the Multinational Enterprise*. OECD Development Centre Working Paper No. 191. OECD.

Kaufman, B. (2011) 'Comparative employment relations: Institutional and neo-institutional theories'. In M. Barry and A. Wilkinson (eds), *Research Handbook of Comparative Employment Relations*. Cheltenham: Edward Elgar, pp. 25–54.

Knell, J. (1993) 'Transnational corporations and the dynamics of human capital formation: Evidence from West Yorkshire'. *Human Resource Management Journal*, 3(4): 48–59.

Korczynski, M. (2003) 'Communities of coping: Collective emotional labour in service work'. *Organization*, 10(1): 55–79.

Lakemann, T. and Lay, J. (2019) *Digital Platforms in Africa: The 'Uberisation' of Informal Work* (GIGA Focus Afrika, 7). Hamburg: GIGA German Institute of Global and Area Studies – Leibniz-Institut für Globale und Regionale Studien, Institut für Afrika-Studien. Available at: https://nbn-resolving.org/urn:nbn:de:0168-ssoar-65910-4.

Lane, C. (1989) *Management and Labour in Europe: The Industrial Enterprise in Germany, Britain and France*. Aldershot: Edward Elgar.

Lillard, L. and Tan, H. (1992) 'Private sector training: Who gets it and what are its effects?' *Research in Labor Economics*, 13: 1–62.

Lloyd, C. and Payne, J. (2002) 'Developing a political economy of skill'. *Journal of Education and Work*, 15(4): 365–90.

Lloyd, C. and Payne, J. (2009) '"Full of sound and fury, signifying nothing": Interrogating new skill concepts in service work – the view from two UK call centres'. *Work, Employment and Society*, 23(4): 617–34.

Lloyd, C. and Payne, J. (2019) 'Rethinking country effects: Robotics, AI and work futures in Norway and the UK'. *New Technology, Work and Employment*, 34(3): 208–25.

Mabey, C. and Finch-Lees, T. F. (2008) *Management and Leadership Development*. London: Sage.

Martin, C. J. (2017) 'Skill builders and the evolution of national vocational training systems'. In C. Warhurst, K. Mayhew, D. Finegold and J. Buchanan (eds), *The Oxford Handbook of Skills and Training*. Oxford: Oxford University Press, pp. 36–53.

Martínez Lucio, M., Skule, S., Kruse, W. and Trappmann, V. (2007) 'Regulating skill formation in Europe: German, Norwegian and Spanish policies on transferable skills'. *European Journal of Industrial Relations*, 13(3): 323–40.

Martínez Lucio, M. and Stuart, M. (2011) 'The state, public policy and the renewal of HRM'. *International Journal of Human Resource Management*, 22(18): 3661–71.

Mathers, A. (2010) 'Learning across borders: A European way?' In A. Ferus-Comelo and M. Novelli (eds), *Globalisation, Knowledge and Labour*. London: Routledge.

Mohrenweiser, J., Zwick, T. and Backes-Gellner, U. (2019) 'Poaching and firm-sponsored training'. *British Journal of Industrial Relations*, 57(1): 143–81.

Muhammad, A. (2018) 'Rise of the corporate NGO in Bangladesh'. *Economic and Political Weekly*, 53(39): 45–52.

Mustchin, S. (2012) 'Unions, learning, migrant workers and union revitalization'. *Work, Employment and Society*, 26(6): 951–67.

Nickson, D., Warhurst, C. and Dutton, E. (2005) 'The importance of attitude and appearance in the service encounter in retail and hospitality'. *Managing Service Quality*, 15(2): 195–208.

Noorbakhsh, F., Paloni, A. and Youseef, A. (2001) 'Human capital and FDI inflows to developing countries: New empirical evidence'. *World Development*, 29(9): 1593–610.

Nussbaum, M. C. (2000) *Women and Human Development: The Capabilities Approach*. Cambridge: Cambridge University Press.

Payne, J. and Keep, E. (2005) 'Promoting workplace development: Lessons for UK policy from nordic approaches to job redesign and the quality of working life'. In B. Harley, J. Hyman and P. Thompson (eds), *Participation and Democracy at Work: Essays in Honour of Harvie Ramsay*. Basingstoke: Palgrave, pp. 146–66.

Perrett, R., Martinez Lucio, M., McBride, J. and Craig, S. (2012) 'Trade union learning strategies and migrant workers policies and practice in a new-liberal environment'. *Urban Studies*, 49(3): 649–67.

Pilz, M. (2009) 'Initial vocational training from a company perspective: A comparison of British and German in-house training cultures'. *Vocations and Learning*, 2(1): 57–74.

Polidano, C. (1999) *The New Public Management in Developing Countries*, Institute for Development Policy and Management Working Paper No. 13, November 1999. Manchester: Manchester University.

Ritchie, B. K. (2002) *Foreign Direct Investment and Intellectual Capital Formation in Southeast Asia*. Paris: OECD Development Centre.

Ritzer, G. (1997) *The McDonaldization Thesis: Explorations and Extensions*. London: Sage.

Sen, A. (2005) 'Human rights and capabilities'. *Journal of Human Development*, 6(2): 151–66.

Shakir, R. (2009) 'Soft skills at the Malaysian institutes of higher learning'. *Asia Pacific Education Review*, 10(3): 309–15.

Sippola, A. and Smale, A. (2007) 'The global integration of diversity management: A longitudinal case study'. *International Journal of Human Resource Management*, 18(11): 1895–916.

Sisson, K. and Storey, J. (1988) 'Developing effective managers: A review of the issues and an agenda for research. *Personnel Review*, 17(4): 3–8.

Sparrow, P. R. (1996) 'Careers and the psychological contract: Understanding the European context'. *European Journal of Work and Organizational Psychology*, 5(4): 479–500.

Stuart, M. (2007) 'Introduction: The industrial relations of learning and training: A new consensus or a new politics?' *European Journal of Industrial Relations*, 13(3): 269–80.

Stuart, M. (2019) 'Training and development–whose interests are being served?'. In G. Gall (ed.) *Handbook of the Politics of Labour, Work and Employment*. Edward Elgar Publishing.

Tasli-Karabulut, V. and Keizer, A. (2020) 'Multinational corporations as institutional entrepreneurs: The dynamic interplay between automobile firms and the Turkish vocational education and training system'. *Industrial Relations Journal*, 51(3): 153–68.

Taylor, P. and Bain, P. (2005) '"India calling to the far away towns": The call centre labour process and globalization'. *Work, Employment and Society*, 19(2): 261–82.

Verger, A. and Novelli, M. (2010) '"Education is not for sale'. Teachers unions' multi--scalar struggles against liberalizing the education sector'. In A. Ferus-Comelo and M. Novelli. (eds.) *Globalization, Knowledge and Labor*. London: Routledge.

Vidal, M. (2019) 'Contradictions of the labour process, worker-empowerment and capitalist inefficiency'. *Historical Materialism*, 28(2): 1–35.

Winterton, J. and Winterton, R. (1997) 'Does management development add value?' *British Journal of Management*, 8(1): 65–76.

10 The learning environment of managerialism: the role of business schools and consultancies in a global market

Carlos J. Fernández Rodríguez

Learning objectives

- To explain the role of business schools and consultancy for the study of globalization and multinational corporations
- To outline the importance of such organizations in the transmission of management philosophies and practices
- To conceptualize the link between neoliberalism and market-oriented policies and the nature of management education and learning
- To raise ethical and political issues in relation to the manner in which such bodies have evolved in various contexts

Introduction

This chapter will focus on institutions that traditionally have played a key role in the diffusion of management values and knowledge, in order to understand the way they frame what is commonly understood as good management as well as the socio-economic and ideological implications of such perspectives. To do so, first, the background in which that dissemination of management takes place will be analysed, highlighting the important role that business schools and consultancies play in such dissemination. The key debate about the Americanization of organizational life – usually linked to any discussion regarding management diffusion – will then be described, followed by a selected case study. Finally, the tensions, issues and future scenarios regarding these actors will be discussed in a brief conclusion.

Background: regulation, institutions and the dissemination of management

According to many authors, since the late 1970s there has been a shift in the regulation of the capitalist system (Jessop, 2019; Vidal, 2011). The post-war period of 1945–75 featured a regulated model of capitalism (Fordism) through an implicit social pact between capital, labour and the state. It relied on both Keynesian economic policies and mass production processes: these implied long-term investments and strategies, and therefore a need for stability (see Chapter 1 on globalization and employment and Chapter 14 on technology). However, since the late 1970s, a new economic scenario (post-Fordism) has emerged, characterized by a shift towards a deregulation of financial and labour markets in order to stimulate free market competition on a global scale (Alonso and Martínez Lucio, 2006; Harvey, 2005). The inability of Fordism to maintain benefits in a context of increasing competitiveness, more fragmented markets and political and social turmoil led to a shocking economic crisis and the subsequent reaction in the form of a managerial turn (Boltanski and Chiapello, 2005). New pro-market discourses became hegemonic and have highly influenced the sphere of the political, with the result that there has been a prioritization of more capital-biased approaches and a decline in social-democratic pacts in favour of neoliberal policies (Jessop, 2019; Piketty, 2014). In this context the obsession to thrive in boisterous markets has increased the interest in management, helping to develop an industry linked to management knowledge.

The new management ideologies are considered by some scholars to be what is justifying people's commitment to capitalism and rendering this commitment attractive. They represent the *new spirit of capitalism* (Boltanski and Chiapello, 2005; du Gay and Morgan 2013) since they imply certain moral and ethical values that differ from the ones that were relevant just a few decades ago. For example, in the 1950s and 1960s, long-term planning and bureaucratic organization were considered to be the core values inside an organization, while post-Fordist new management-oriented discourses and practices highlight the importance of new values such as innovation, flexibility, knowledge and entrepreneurship (Boltanski and Chiapello, 2005; Dardot and Laval, 2013). These values have spread through different organizations largely via specific institutions and channels, making management knowledge very visible in numerous ways, ranging from the production of a specialized literature (either academic or popular) to the implementation of routine organizational practices.

In fact, some scholars, such as DiMaggio and Powell (1983), have pointed out that in many current organizations there is a surprising homogeneity of forms and practices, which they described as *institutional isomorphism*. For example, it is possible to think that in almost every firm (no matter what its geographical location) with a certain number of employees, we are going to find similar departments: marketing, production, HRM and finance. In their classic paper, DiMaggio and Powell argued that organizations suffer different pressures that lead them to adapt themselves to the uncertainties of the surrounding environment. They distinguished three mechanisms through which that institutional isomorphic change would take place: a *coercive* one – pressures exerted either by other organizations on which they are dependent or by cultural expectations from society; a *mimetic* one – where other models are simply followed to provide an answer to uncertainty; and a *normative* one – whose source is professionalization, primarily in two ways: the legitimization of a cognitive framework developed by specialists and the development of professional networks which help to diffuse innovations through a specific field. In this sense, it would be possible for us to argue that the normative mechanism might be playing a very important role in the development of such an isomorphism in management knowledge inside firms, once some of their managers might have learnt specific managerial skills in a business school, or a consultant might have been hired to develop a strategy of organizational change. Therefore management ideologies would be contributing towards shaping companies in a similar way – for example, networks, e-business and so on – so that values such as flexibility or empowerment would be embraced in most of them. They provide certainties in a complex environment.

However, management knowledge is also influenced to varying degrees by social, political and economic factors, and can therefore show remarkable differences across national contexts in terms of organization and functioning (Whitley, 2008). The diversity of models of capitalism (Hall and Soskice, 2001; see Chapter 11 on varieties of capitalism) also implies that the tendency to isomorphism is limited by contextual approaches and adaptations, particularly local ones. Therefore, while most of the generation of management knowledge originates from Anglo-Saxon culture, the concrete use of the theories produced might differ in places such as Argentina, Turkey, China, Indonesia or South Africa. Besides, many scholars have indicated that while certain motifs such as commitment to work or uncritical views towards firms remain stable, these discourses are also characterized by the constant incorporation of new jargon and managerial tools, to the extent that it is possible to speak of management fads and fashions (Abrahamson, 1991; Collins, 2000). The field of management knowledge is prolific in terms of managerial solutions to common problems of organizations, which means that new concepts will emerge quite regularly, such as quality circles, excellence, business process re-engineering, emotional intelligence, balanced scorecard or knowledge management.

Research has indicated that certain institutions and actors are fundamental to the dissemination of different management theories, among them business schools and consultancies (Engwall et al., 2016; Grey 2016). If we follow the scheme of Mazza and Álvarez (2000; see also Table 10.1), the creation of management theories and practices as well as their diffusion can be conceptualized as a three-phase process: production, diffusion and legitimization. While Mazza and Álvarez's paper is focused on the third stage (the popularization of management topics via the popular press), the authors also discuss the ways in which business schools (and other educational institutions) and consultancy firms are involved in the first two stages of the process. In the production phase, they elaborate on formal managerial knowledge following the rules of academic production, creating new or recycled theories. These theories are spread during the next stage of diffusion by management education institutions and consulting firms, which combine scientific knowledge on management (providing academic validation) with a practical knowledge that engages with the more down-to-earth aspects. In this critical phase, social legitimacy and crucial linkages of both educational institutions and consulting firms with key actors in various fields (politics, organizations and so on) help to build an essential background to extend the diffusion of theories outside the business community. Therefore it is relevant to explore the role that business schools and consultancies have played in the development and transmission of managerial knowledge since their creation, as we will see in the next section.

Table 10.1 Creation and diffusion of management theories and practices

	Actors	Knowledge	Arguments	Audience
Production	Universities Business schools Consulting firms	Formal/ scientific	Management as science	Business community Management scholars
Diffusion	Business press Consulting firms Business schools	Scientific/ practical	Management as techniques and rules of thumb	Business community Professionals
Legitimation	Popular press Business press Large firms	Ideological	Narratives of management success	Business community Society at large

Source: Mazza and Álvarez (2000: 572).

Institutions and ideas: the history of business schools and consultancies and US influence through research and education

While several institutions in Europe (particularly in France) and the United States included commerce as their main programme of studies, it is widely agreed that the Wharton School of Finance and Commerce of the University of Pennsylvania (founded in 1881 by the industrialist and philanthropist Joseph Wharton, hence the name) is considered to be the oldest collegiate business school in the world (Grey, 2016). Soon other schools followed in the United States, usually as part of top universities (Chicago, Columbia, Harvard) despite some objections being raised over the status of business and commerce as scientific disciplines (Engwall, 2009). Following the footsteps of the Wharton School and others, they offered specialized courses for current and future executives on topics ranging from accounting to marketing and finance. The first Master of Business Administration (MBA) programme was offered by Harvard Business School in 1910, and some years later their case study approach revolutionized the teaching methods of this type of institution. An extensive body of publications emerged, mostly influenced by F. W. Taylor's theories of scientific management (Guillén, 1994). The field of management education expanded notably after the Second World War, once fascism had been defeated and Western Europe needed the financial aid of the US Marshall Plan to rebuild the war-damaged economies. The importance of this plan has been discussed by many scholars (Kipping, 1999; Schröter, 2005) in terms of the importance of transferring forms of managerial knowledge to the countries of Western Europe (this topic will be discussed in the next section).

From the 1950s onwards, American business schools became not only the institutions where future top executives received their specialized education and improved their business skills, but also a channel for the transmission of a certain 'American way of business', which spread all over Europe and helped to build American cultural hegemony in the capitalist bloc.

Therefore, institutions such as Chicago, Dartmouth, Columbia, Harvard, Kellogg, Stanford and MIT Sloan became pivotal, and European institutions either engaged with the new American approach to knowledge while still keeping their own identities (as in the case of the London Business School (LBS) and the Nordic business schools) or were simply spin-offs from American institutions (the main example of this is INSEAD). They also helped to develop, in many cases with direct assistance, more management schools overseas, not only in Europe but also in other countries and regions that fell under US political influence (e.g. Turkey and the Latin American countries).

Nevertheless, the most important expansion of business schools took place in the 1980s, pushed by several factors: the technological drive of an economy which helps to stimulate enormous growth in the financial markets inside the framework of a new capitalist deregulation (post-Fordism); the rise of neoliberal governance trumpeting the so-called 'enterprise culture', praising business-oriented values such as innovation, competitiveness and entrepreneurship; and economic globalization (see Chapter 11 on varieties of capitalism). Business schools have since then become extremely popular as they provide an education that meets the new requirements of largely deregulated economies: being the holder of an MBA has become the compulsory entry point to the upper echelons of business (Grey, 2016). The language of managerialism permeates these schools (Fleming, 2020). Nevertheless, the roles of these schools are by no means limited to mere transmission of education: they are also the producers and disseminators of managerial knowledge, helping to reinforce the ideological dominance of business-oriented thinking and thus crucial supporters of neoliberal capitalism. For example, some of the most important management gurus are professors in these top business schools – fine examples are Michael Porter and Rosabeth Moss Kanter at Harvard Business School and Philip Kotler at Kellogg School of Management, Northwestern University.

The consulting industry has also been a key actor in the dissemination of different waves of managerial expertise during the 20th century (Engwall et al., 2016). The origins of management consulting are Anglo-American. The founders were US pioneers in the late 19th century, whose main role was to help manufacturers to become more productive and efficient. Some authors (Kipping, 1999) claim that the first management thinkers were also the first consultants, and F. W. Taylor, Arthur D. Little, Frank and Lillian Gilbreth and Elton Mayo, for example, developed their main theoretical contributions directly from their empirical work (in the form of analysis and further assessment) in industrial firms. Nevertheless, during the 1930s, a new type of consulting firm emerged in the United States that proved to be very influential and was to shape the image of the profession. It was no longer associated with shopfloor or office improvements but rather with wider organizational issues, providing both short-term and long-term strategic business plans, specialized assessment in different departments and activities inside the corporations, and providing a certificate of 'professionalism' that helped to reduce anxiety among managers. McKinsey, founded in 1926, became the blueprint for other consulting firms, with their famous dress code, their 'up or out' promotion policy and an image that resembled that of law firms (Kipping, 2011). They also tended to hire many of their consultants from a selected number of business schools, forging a strong relationship between both types of institution. Soon, new companies developed consulting services, including some that in the beginning provided mainly auditing and tax services, such as the pioneer firm Arthur Andersen (founded in 1913).

During the 1960s, the consulting industry experienced a boom in response to a rapidly changing industrial and economic structure, and managerial fashions spread rapidly among companies. American consulting firms developed a strategy of internationalization with the beginning of overseas activities and work. During the 1980s and 1990s, there was an expansion of the consulting industry, with an unprecedented growth and visibility (Kipping and Clark, 2012). The market environment became more uncertain owing to global competition, and more managers and companies were willing to look for advice. Nowadays the structure of the consulting industry is organized around accountancy-based firms (reduced to a sort of Big Four: Ernst & Young, KPMG, Deloitte and PwC – PricewaterhouseCoopers); multinational companies whose core business is consulting, such as Accenture (a spin-off of the defunct Arthur Andersen and the largest consulting firm in the world); well-known medium-sized consultancies such as McKinsey, Boston Consulting Group, Arthur D. Little, Bain and Hay; IT companies and business-school-based consultancies focused on specific niches; and small firms and sole practitioners at the local level. The consulting industry has an important role as a channel of diffusion of managerial services and practices (Engwall et al., 2016; Kipping and Clark, 2012). These firms provide different services to help companies reorientate their strategies, activities and management. Reputation and professional image are important aspects in this business of conultancy, to the extent of being key drivers of competition in the market (Glücker and Armbrüster, 2003). Hence the consulting industry has built a social and business image of being a knowledge-intensive sector, where their employees – highly skilled experts in the latest management techniques and innovations and whose commitment to the customers is expressed by working long hours on different projects – advise managers and workers about the newest management solutions for contemporary business problems, transferring new 'philosophies of management'. Consultants are seen to exert important influence in the current business scene, acting as almost the vanguard of a new neo-bureaucratic management style (Sturdy, 2011; Sturdy et al., 2015).

The emerging role of consultants cannot be fully understood without noticing the strong connections that these companies have with business schools and even management gurus, the source of most of the innovations offered through their consulting services. For example, management gurus such as Tom Peters, Robert Waterman and Kenichi Ohmae were McKinsey employees for many years; many others were also executives or managers for other, less well-known companies. Other gurus also created their own consulting companies once their ideas became popular. Consultants from McKinsey were initially Harvard Business School (HBS) graduates, building a long-lasting relationship between consulting firms and business schools from which employees were recruited (Kipping, 2011). Given the global scope that consulting industry activities have, these networks are crucial to the dissemination of managerial practices: students from top business schools receive their education and knowledge from top management gurus; once they get their MBAs, they are hired by top consulting firms; at some point they join new companies, but their background and practices have already been modelled under the influence of these institutions; these processes help to extend the influence of managerial theories; in addition, they contribute to the expansion of a certain analysis style or attitude towards organizational problems from a specific point of view, which will be discussed in the next section.

Case study: A Spanish business school

Our selected case study is an initiative undertaken by a religious order in the 1950s in Spain that wished to create an institution to train managers, combining the most modern management knowledge with a solid Christian morality. In this case study, three issues will be dealt with: first, the importance of Americanization as a political project; second, how that project evolved over time through specific features; and, finally, how culture helps to shape Americanization, adapting it to the specific interests of the local elites.

During the development period the Spanish economy underwent in the 1960s, several business schools with links to Catholic groups were launched in the private sector. The goal was to 'modernize' management in an economy marred by inefficiencies, backwardness and a corrupt state, and modernization was associated with one significant source: the United States. The school in our case study established a link with a very prestigious American business school, adopted the case study method as a basis for teaching and launched the first MBA studies programme in the 1960s. The very strong relationship between the schools owed much to the closeness of the Spanish Franco regime and the US government during the Cold War, but also to views shared by the American business school managers and the religious order members who founded the Spanish school. In fact, both advocated technocracy in terms of economic ideologies and commitment to work, supporting *Franquismo* (the dictatorship governing Spain from 1939 to 1975) to turn to a more 'free market' approach in the late 1950s. Democracy was not imported in that move, though. Business schools like this provided an encounter between entrepreneurial ethics and particular views of Christian morality. Their contribution was aimed at shaping the values of Spanish managers. The idea was to turn these Catholic managers towards Protestant work ethics, helping to rationalize the economy while avoiding any criticism of the politics of *Franquismo*. This business school soon gained enormous prestige at the postgraduate level.

(Continued)

The transition to democracy in the 1970s in Spain did not appear to erode this prestige, and the school rapidly evolved through the different stages of the Americanization process. Heavily influenced by American models, its academic programmes have been shaped around a managerial and pro-business approach tied strongly to the relationship between the business school and Spanish firms. The expansion of the Spanish economy during the 1980s and 1990s helped not only to attract students from all over Europe and Latin America, but also to develop strong networks and many subsidiaries in the latter. In a neoliberal scenario, the school abandoned the project of Spanish 'modernization' to compete in the new European market of business higher education. The move has been successful, at least according to international rankings such as those appearing in the *Financial Times*, *The Economist* and the *Wall Street Journal*, where the school has frequently appeared in top positions. In addition, the school undertook new strategies that followed global trends in the field of higher education. To strengthen the quality of their MBA programmes (e.g. studentships in business schools abroad, visiting professors and so on), some changes have been implemented. The need to hire teaching staff with papers accepted by the Institute for Scientific Information's (ISI) journals to cope with the growing influence of a 'publish or perish' mentality in the field has led not only to changes in the profiles and backgrounds of the academics (there is a lesser role for management practitioners, for example, who were key figures in the past), but also to policies in which the school funds the doctoral studies of senior lecturers in prestigious universities. These policies have a contradictory effect: on the one hand, they strengthen the quality of the research and broaden perspectives on management studies; but, on the other hand, they reinforce their technocratic approach, particularly once most of the members have committed to publishing in top American management journals. Thus the Americanization project is maintained through different stages.

Finally, it is important to highlight the importance of the local culture when looking at business education models. In this case study, it is essential to point out the critical role that schools like this provided locally through the formation of elites. The extraordinarily high fees charged by the school have limited their catchment to the upper and upper-middle classes, who attempt to preserve their social position and wealth, in this case by holding top positions in corporations. Needless to say, the school not only provided their students with skills, but also gave them an important range of contacts and networks that were extremely useful in the context of a Southern European culture. In addition, the religious order behind the school had close links with the right-wing elites of the country. Ironically, while promoting modernization through free market policies and better management, the school's role reinforced elitism and maintained strong class divisions through the transition to democracy.

Questions

1. How does the Americanization project evolve through the story of this Spanish business school?

2. Why does it evolve in this way?
3. According to this case study, are modernization and economic liberalism associated with democracy?
4. What does the case reveal about the politics of business schools?

The emergence of Anglo-Saxonization and Americanization as models for dissemination and the role of business schools and management consultancies

The international expansion of both management consultancies and business schools has led to an interesting debate about what kinds of managerial practices are disseminated around the world. For example, in top business schools English has become the lingua franca for international business communication, pushing a certain isomorphism in the way that business analyses are developed throughout the world. Scholars such as Tietze and Dick (2013) take this argument further and claim that the spread of the English language and the increasing dominance of a management discourse have strong links with tacit assumptions and specific ideologies, encouraging the emergence of identities in line with neoliberal market economies. Moreover, other researchers (e.g. Djelic, 1998; Schröter, 2005) have argued that business schools and consultancies, among other institutions, might be conceived as vehicles for a process of Americanization of economies and societies all over the world (see also Chapter 11 on varieties of capitalism).

What does this concept of Americanization mean? According to most of the scholars who have reviewed this issue, the concept expresses the influence that American businesses and managerial ideas have enjoyed in other regions in the world, mainly Europe but also Japan and Latin America, to very different degrees (Djelic, 1998; Rodríguez Ruiz and Martínez Lucio, 2010). This process is associated mainly with the post-Second World War period and post-Marshall Plan American politics, and is deeply interconnected with the development of American capitalism. The Marshall Plan in particular set the conditions for a transfer of US management models, exporting American practices and attitudes towards business in European economic life (Kipping and Bjarnar, 1998). However, it can also be claimed that this process has extended itself far beyond the Marshall Plan. For example, Schröter (2005) indicates that Americanization has tended to occur in waves. The first wave took place in the period 1870–1945, its outcome being the widespread adoption of Taylorism and Fordism by European companies. The next period (spanning 1945–75) represents a post-war boom in which

Americanization can be basically understood as a mission. The enlarged role of the economy in society, the efforts to improve productivity, new commercialization techniques, competition as a cure-all and individualization would be the main issues that American experts were interested in transferring. Some countries were excluded from the Marshall Plan (e.g. Spain), but further assistance was provided later. Finally, the third wave of Americanization has been taking place since the 1980s, featuring deregulation, privatization as a policy to help the growth of GDP, and reinforcement by globalization. Despite these waves, however, Schröter considers that only the years 1945–55 can properly be labelled as real Americanization, since there was an explicit American project with which to take the US management models to Europe. If there has been more influence from America than elsewhere, that is because the United States is the society of reference for most of the world. Kipping (1999) concurs in pointing at scientific management as the first wave of the internationalization of American managerial ideas. Nevertheless, the influence before the Second World War would have been relatively small, at least until the Great Depression, when European companies began to seek improvements in productivity and performance, and found answers in the more technologically advanced American companies. This process was reinforced during the war, when there were widespread efforts to improve labour productivity. Kipping claims that the influence of American consultancies was not high in the immediate post-war period: the US Marshall Plan administration preferred to employ managers and executives rather than consultants. This situation changed from the late 1950s, however: with the recovery of European industry and corporations, American consulting firms were made welcome and increased their influence.

Americanization also strongly impacted on European business schools. It is important to note that some of them, particularly in the Nordic countries, had a strong German influence before the Second World War, after which there was a consolidation of American dominance (Engwall, 2009). Influence was spread by launching new business schools with American staff and learning methods (the prestigious INSEAD being the most notable example) or at least some kind of assistance (including personnel from American institutions; for example, IESE in Spain had strong ties with Harvard Business School). American business schools as well as their international branch campuses also became a magnet for aspiring elites all over the world, helping to create an almost whimsical fantasy of graduates as 'world-class operators' (Siltaoja et al., 2019). The US model has been dominant since then in the field of higher management education (Grey, 2016), leaving an indelible stamp on the way curricula, subjects, teaching methods and management problems are designed, selected and presented. Thus organizations are analysed from a perspective in tune with capitalist values, hiding intrinsic problems within these organizations, such as conflicts, exploitation, power relations, authoritarianism and gender and race discrimination. Instead, values identified with the American Dream are promoted, emphasizing individualism, self-reliance and free market ethics.

Finally, other authors have pointed out that American business schools have contributed, along with other institutional actors, to integrate native elites in developing countries into the international business world through the transmission of hegemonic neoliberal ideologies presented as scientifically validated knowledge. In this regard, and referring particularly to Latin American business schools, Ibarra-Colado (2006) defines the subordination of the latter to their North American peers (expressed by importing management knowledge from the 'centre') as a process of 'epistemic coloniality'. This process would have been assisted by the increased translation and distribution of textbooks by large American and other publishing houses from English-speaking countries. In these textbooks there could be found a well-defined project of dissemination of the principles of hegemonic managerial ideology. This process of epistemic coloniality was to help shape the views of the elites of semi-peripheral and peripheral countries, helping to connect them to the international centres of business while obscuring national peculiarities and struggles (Alcadipani, 2017). Business schools, in particular, have contributed dramatically to the cooptation of elites, proving that they have an underlying function of providing mechanisms of social selection, particularly in the Latin countries (Schröter, 2005). Moreover, they have provided and transferred management knowledge and skills to the dominant classes in certain nations while in the main ignoring social inequalities, structural economic problems or even the lack of political liberty. These cases of epistemic coloniality are not limited to Latin America and the non-west, however, as not all European countries were world financial centres during the 20th century (Fernández Rodríguez and Gantman, 2011).

Tensions, issues and futures: competing cultures and contexts, the politics of consultancy firms, networks and the political dimension

In sum, the narrative of Americanization seems to be a controversial one, but it is only one of the issues affected by polemics and criticism regarding business schools and the consulting industry, once they are subjected to the critical gaze of scholars. This section will give an account of some of the most relevant critiques.

The main source of criticism is focused on the type of management knowledge provided by these institutions. It has been claimed that management in itself cannot be labelled an exact science (Whitley, 2008) – it would have a status similar to other social sciences, where the approach to knowledge would be strongly influenced by the ideological values of the researcher. Thus it is important to point out that there is a clear relationship between how management topics are addressed and the ideological values of the different scholars. For example, schools of thought such as Critical Management Studies make their critical approach to management and organizations very explicit (Alvesson and Willmott, 1992, 2012; Parker, 2018). However, most of the so-called mainstream management thinkers have rarely expressed their values in such a clear way, highlighting their compromise with the promotion of free market economics and the support for managers as controllers of rationality inside organizations. Therefore business schools and consultancies would be responsible for exporting a specific American business model whose theoretical foundations are far from the neutrality they claim to have. Rather than an empirically tested neutral science without values, management is actually greatly influenced by pro-capitalist ideologies and rhetoric (Parker, 2002, 2018). Apart from the aforementioned Americanization, managerial ideologies emphasize a view, also noted earlier, that hides or denies salient features of organizations such as conflict, collision of interests, discrimination, power games and inner politics. Moreover, they have disregarded ethics (the economic crisis of 2008 highlighted reprehensible behaviour by those who were in charge in large corporations: see, for example, Locke and Spender, 2011), which has been substituted by calls to a morality based on a strange tension between individualization and a strong commitment to the enterprise culture. Parker (2018) actually has accused them of celebrating and extolling egoistic behaviours as being rational, and picturing capitalism as common sense, thus denying other forms of organization. They have also been accused of being biased towards white American male images (Grey, 2016), despite efforts to promote diversity.

In addition, their dual approach to knowledge brings some problems to the fore. On the one hand, a supposedly scientific body of theory is provided by experts, in some cases in the form of a magical solution to companies' struggles, while, on the other hand, cases are explained to illustrate the best decisions that managers are able to take. But where exactly is the link between the two approaches if the practices are based on the charismatic vision of successful managers when theory should be grounded in more serious methodologies and achieve an abstract dimension? It is a complex issue since management knowledge in itself is quite contextual and difficult to grasp compared with other academic disciplines. However, it becomes even more complex when economic interests pervade the whole discipline. Kieser (2002), for example, mentions the marionette theory – developed by the German sociologist Werner Sombart – to explain the role of consultancies, highlighting that the knowledge being marketed by them is intended to provide a fictitious advantage for products where a real one would not be possible. Consultancy services thus help to build illusions of safety and certainty among managers. To do so, consultants need to portray themselves through an image of being 'top performers', which ends up leading them to extreme professional anxieties (Borguain and Harvey, 2018; Mühlhaus and Bouwmeester, 2016).

In fact, it is noticeable that serious management thinkers have sometimes engaged with so-called 'pop' management. Business schools and consultancies have also been criticized because of the role they play in launching and disseminating management fads (Collins, 2000). According to Mazza and Álvarez (2000), the process of diffusion of these fads resembles the way the fashion industry disseminates its new seasonal collections. Thus the metaphors of 'haute couture' and 'prêt-à-porter' are used to explain the different approaches towards the creation of management knowledge by distinct actors in the field. According to these authors, since the beginning of the 1980s the 'haute couture' approach (which produces complex theories published in either academic books or peer-reviewed journals and aimed at promoting intellectual discussion) has gradually been turning into a 'prêt-à-porter' approach, which relies on tacit knowledge and experience-based rules and whose channels of diffusion are bestseller books and the popular press (newspapers and magazines), thus helping to increase the popularization of management issues. The eventual goal is not so much to provide an accurate theory but to sell more books and charge higher conference fees, and theorists finally decide to turn themselves into management gurus.

This also has a consequence for another issue: the professionalization of managers and consultants, which remains controversial. It is not clear what functions a manager, or a consultant, performs if we compare them with a doctor or an engineer, say. In the case of consultancies, some authors (Kipping, 2011) have claimed that there has been excessive importance attributed to 'image professionalism', in which the image of both firm and individual (the 'impression', or brand reputation) performs almost a more important role that the quality or definition of the services provided (Alvesson and Robertson, 2006; Clark and Fincham, 2002; Glücker and Armbrüster, 2003). What in fact exists is a tension between professionalism and market logic that is difficult to solve, so professionalism is defined in a very narrow way, and rhetoric eventually plays a major role. In fact, some authors have labelled consultants as agents of anxiety and sellers of security, and even esoteric experts (Alvesson and Johansson, 2002). They argue that there is a permanent tension among the profession of consultants: they claim to work according to principles of professionalism but then disregard those same principles if it is necessary for business reasons. This also leads, according to recent research, to anxiety among consultants regarding their status and performance (Gill, 2015; Sturdy et al., 2015).

Finally, there is an issue related to the influence these institutions also have on the field of education – for example, in its marketing – to the extent that it is possible to speak of 'corporate universities' (Wedlin, 2006; see also Parker, 2018). The hegemony of management and its emphasis on efficiency have meant the closing of many university humanities departments because they are not profitable, while relocating resources to faculties with a bigger role in producing revenues (such as business schools). Furthermore, business schools often offer spectacular facilities (Chang and Osborn, 2005). Education is turning into a market, and rankings become important to incorporate otherwise reluctant universities into the neoliberal project. Since the *Financial Times* published the first MBA/business schools rankings in 1998, and one year later their world rankings, the development of these rankings has been astonishing, strengthening rules such as rationalized rituals of inspection and boundary-work to set limits within the community (Wedlin, 2006). Given the fact that the main references in the field represent mainstream thinking, it is not surprising that the remainder of the institutions get their inspiration from them. Additional developments, such as the Research Assessment Exercise (RAE), which has become the Research Excellence Framework (REF) in the United Kingdom, also involve contradictory effects. It appeared that RAE/REF would pursue a fairer distribution of resources across the United Kingdom's academia, but in fact it helps to enhance two contradictory effects: on the one hand, it attempts to stimulate intellectual production, but, on the other hand, in the case of management, it promotes publishing in American journals (which are dominated by scholars from top business schools, rewarding managerial contributions over critical ones), so it promotes mainstream thinking (Mingers and Willmott, 2013). This issue is in any case very complex as RAE/REF exercises can ironically promote a tool for change. For example, they improve the chances of management scholars getting an academic position in business schools, because they highly value publications in top journals (something that many experienced 'hero managers' fail to achieve). Therefore, a new door is opened for alternative views when some of those top journals publish papers by critical scholars.

Conclusion

This chapter has provided an overview of the role that business schools and consultancies play in the dissemination of managerial ideas. A brief history of both actors has been included, pointing at their functions as creators and disseminators of management knowledge as well as their involvement with Americanization. It has been argued that both institutions are essential to shaping views among managers and practitioners that help to promote free market economics, individualism and competitiveness. These views were expressed clearly in the managerial discourses that formed the 'new spirit of capitalism', offering ideological justifications for the new organization of economy and labour under the post-Fordist regime (see Chapter 12 on lean production). The influence of these values has become so strong that pro-managerial discourses have shaped the political, social, economic and organizational agendas, leaving little room for alternative voices.

Despite this clear ideological hegemony, during this century events such as corporate scandals (the collapse of Enron being the most notable of these) and in particular the unethical practices of executives in the financial sector that erupted during the economic crisis of 2008 have helped damage the reputation of both institutions to some extent. Business schools and consultancies need to re-evaluate their current compromise with the Anglo-Saxon neoliberal agenda. They should try to adapt themselves to a new scenario in which new sensibilities are likely to transform the ways in which the business world is understood. The current volatile scenario might also stimulate changes in public opinion, where the public could express its discontent with even the concept of management itself, thus offering an opportunity to develop new and more ethical approaches to organization analysis. Some authors such as Parker (2018) have even suggested, in a very provocative way, that all business schools should be shut down, being substituted by new institutions (such as the schools of organizations), focused on teaching alternative ways to problematize both the economy and organizations. To do so, it would be essential to highlight the positive outcomes of new and alternative forms of cooperation instead of praising the the likes of Silicon Valley-type corporations. Parker's objective is to vindicate university model more in line with the free thinking institution of the 1960s.

Moreover, while drastic value changes in business schools and consultancies seem unlikely, perhaps we can still claim that the hegemony of the Anglo-Saxon model is at stake. New economic powers are emerging, and their populations and executives have been raised with different values from those of the American Dream. There are also prospects for a possible European business school ethos in the making, different from that in the United States (Wedlin, 2006). It is also interesting to notice how a critical current in organizational theory has gradually become institutionalized in some business schools, particularly in the United Kingdom, with an explicit critical and radical approach (see, for example, Parker, 2018; Rowlinson and Hassard, 2011). Therefore important challenges to the current way that business schools and consultancies are developing and disseminating their innovations seem to be quite certain in the near future. However, the scenario remains undecided, and social struggles might play an important part in the way that management knowledge will be reconfigured.

Reflective questions

1. How many types of institutional isomorphism would exist according to the theory developed by sociologists DiMaggio and Powell (1983)?
2. Which institution developed the first MBA programme?
3. List the stages that the so-called process of Americanization has followed.
4. What is controversial about the issue of the professionalization of managers and consultants?
5. Discuss the role of business schools and consultants in the development of pro-market values in society.

Recommended reading

- Abrahamson, E. (1991) 'Managerial fads and fashions: The diffusion and rejection of innovations'. *Academy of Management Review*, 16(3): 586–612.
- Rodríguez Ruiz, Ó. and Martínez Lucio, M. (2010) 'The study of HRM in Spain: The Americanization of Spanish research and the politics of denial?' *International Journal of Human Resource Management*, 21(1): 125–43.
- Rowlinson, M. and Hassard, J. (2011) 'How come the critters came to be teaching in business schools? Contradictions in the institutionalization of critical management studies'. *Organization*, 18(5): 673–89.
- Sturdy, A. (2011) 'Consultancy's consequences? A critical assessment of management consultancy's impact on management'. *British Journal of Management*, 22(3): 517–30.
- Whitley, R. (2008) 'Varieties of knowledge and their use in business and management studies: Conditions and institutions'. *Organization Studies*, 29(4): 581–609.

References

Abrahamson, E. (1991) 'Managerial fads and fashions: The diffusion and rejection of innovations'. *Academy of Management Review*, 16(3): 586–612.

Alcadipani, R. (2017) 'Reclaiming sociological reduction: Analysing the circulation of management education in the periphery'. *Management Learning*, 48(5): 535–51.

Alonso, L. E. and Martínez Lucio, M. (eds) (2006) *Employment Relations in a Changing Society: Assessing the Post-Fordist Paradigm*. Basingstoke: Palgrave Macmillan.

Alvesson, M. and Johansson, A. W. (2002) 'Professionalism and politics in management consultancy work'. In T. Clark and R. Fincham (eds), *Critical Consulting: New Perspectives on the Management Advice Industry*. Oxford: Blackwell, pp. 229–46.

Alvesson, M. and Robertson, M. (2006) 'The best and the brightest: The construction, significance and effects of elite identities in consulting firms'. *Organization*, 13(2): 195–224.

Alvesson, M. and Willmott, H. (eds) (1992) *Critical Management Studies*. London: Sage.

Alvesson, M. and Willmott, H. (2012) *Making Sense of Management: A Critical Introduction*, 2nd edn. London: Sage.

Boltanski, L. and Chiapello, È. (2005) *The New Spirit of Capitalism*. London: Verso.

Borguain, A. and Harvey, J.-F. (2018) 'Professional image under threat: Dealing with learning–credibility tension'. *Human Relations*, 71(12): 1611–39.

Chang, G. C. and Osborn, J. R. (2005) 'Spectacular colleges and spectacular rankings: The "US News" rankings of American "best" colleges'. *Journal of Consumer Culture*, 5(3): 338–64.

Clark, T. and Fincham, R. (eds) (2002) *Critical Consulting: New Perspectives on the Management Advice Industry*. Oxford: Blackwell.

Collins, D. (2000) *Management Fads and Buzzwords*. London: Routledge.

Dardot, C. and Laval C. (2013) *The New Way of the World: On Neoliberal Society*. London: Verso.

DiMaggio, P. and Powell, W. (1983) '"The iron cage revisited": Institutional isomorphism and collective rationality in organizational fields'. *American Sociological Review*, 48: 147–60.

Djelic, M.-L. (1998) *Exporting the American Model: The Postwar Transformation of European Business*. Oxford: Oxford University Press.

du Gay, P. and Morgan G. (eds) (2013) *New Spirits of Capitalism? Crises, Justifications, and Dynamics*. Oxford: Oxford University Press.

Engwall, L. (2009) *Mercury Meets Minerva*. Oxford: Pergamon Press.

Engwall, L., Kipping, M. and Üsdiken, B. (2016) *Defining Management – Business Schools, Consultants, Media*. New York: Routledge.

Fernández Rodríguez, C. J. and Gantman, E. (2011) 'Importers of management knowledge: Spain and Argentina in the 20th century (1955–2008)'. *Canadian Journal of Administrative Sciences*, 28(2): 160–73.

Fleming, P. (2020) 'Dark academia: Despair in the neoliberal business school'. *Journal of Management Studies*, 57(6): 1305–11.

Gill, M. J. (2015) 'Elite identity and status anxiety: An interpretative phenomenological analysis of management consultants'. *Organization*, 22(3): 306–25.

Glücker, J. and Armbrüster, T. (2003) 'Bridging uncertainty in management consulting: The mechanisms of trust and networked reputation'. *Organization Studies*, 24(2): 269–97.

Grey, C. (2016) *A Very Short, Fairly Interesting and Reasonably Cheap Book about Studying Organizations*. London: Sage.

Guillén, M. (1994) *Models of Management: Work, Authority and Organization in a Comparative Perspective*. Chicago: University of Chicago Press.

Hall, P. A. and Soskice, D. (2001) *Varieties of Capitalism: The Institutional Foundations of Comparative Advantage*. New York: Oxford University Press.

Harvey, D. (2005) *A Brief History of Neoliberalism*. Oxford: Oxford University Press.

Ibarra-Colado, E. (2006) 'Organization studies and epistemic coloniality in Latin America: Thinking otherness from the margins'. *Organization*, 13(4): 463–88.

Jessop, R. (2019) 'Ordoliberalism and neoliberalization: Governing through order or disorder'. *Critical Sociology*, 45(7–8): 967–81.

Kieser, A. (2002) 'Managers or marionettes: Using fashion theories to explain the success of consultancies'. In M. Kipping and L. Engwall (eds), *Management Consulting*. Oxford: Oxford University Press, pp. 167–83.

Kipping, M. (1999) 'American management consulting companies in Western Europe, 1920–1990: Products, reputation, and relationships'. *Business History Review*, 73(2): 190–221.

Kipping, M. (2011) 'Hollow from the start? Image professionalism in management consulting'. *Current Sociology*, 59(4): 530–50.

Kipping, M. and Bjarnar, O. (eds) (1998) *The Americanization of European Business: The Marshall Plan and the Transfer of US Management*. London: Routledge.

Kipping, M. and Clark, T. (2012) 'Researching management consulting: An introduction to the handbook'. In T. Clark and M. Kipping (eds) *Oxford Handbook of Management Consulting*. Oxford: Oxford University Press, pp. 1–26.

Locke, R. and Spender, J. C. (2011) *Confronting Managerialism: How the Business Elite and Their Schools Threw Our Lives Out of Balance*. New York: Zed Books

Mazza, C. and Álvarez, J. L. (2000) 'Haute couture and prêt-à-porter: The popular press and the diffusion of management practices'. *Organization Studies*, 21(3): 567–88.

Mingers, J. and Willmott, H. (2013) 'Taylorizing business school research: On the "one best way" performative effects of journal ranking lists'. *Human Relations*, 66(8): 1051–73.

Mühlhaus, J. and Bouwmeester, O. (2016) 'The paradoxical effect of self-categorization on work stress in a high-status occupation: Insights from management consulting'. *Human Relations*, 69(9): 1823–52.

Parker, M. (2002) *Against Management*. Cambridge: Polity Press.

Parker, M. (2018) *Shut Down the Business School: What's Wrong with Management Education*. London: Pluto.

Piketty, T. (2014) *Capital in the Twenty-First Century*. Cambridge, MA: Harvard University Press.

Rodríguez Ruiz, Ó. and Martínez Lucio, M. (2010) 'The study of HRM in Spain: The Americanization of Spanish research and the politics of denial?' *International Journal of Human Resource Management*, 21(1): 125–43.

Rowlinson, M. and Hassard, J. (2011) 'How come the critters came to be teaching in business schools? Contradictions in the institutionalization of critical management studies'. *Organization*, 18(5): 673–89.

Schröter, H. G. (2005) *Americanization of the European Economy: A Compact Survey of American Economic Influence in Europe since the 1880s*. Dordrecht: Springer.

Siltaoja, M., Juusola, K. and Kivijärvi, M. (2019) '"World-class" fantasies: A neocolonial analysis of international branch campuses'. *Organization*, 26(1): 75–97.

Sturdy, A. (2011) 'Consultancy's consequences? A critical assessment of management consultancy's impact on management'. *British Journal of Management*, 22(3): 517–30.

Sturdy, A., Wright, C. and Wylie, N. (2015) *Management as Consultancy: Neo-bureaucracy and the Consultant Manager*. Cambridge: Cambridge University Press.

Tietze, S. and Dick, P. (2013) 'The Victorious English Language: Hegemonic practices in the management academy'. *Journal of Management Inquiry*, 22(1): 122–34.

Vidal, M. (2011) 'Reworking Postfordism: Labor process versus employment relations'. *Sociology Compass*, 5(4): 273–86.

Wedlin, L. (2006) *Ranking Business Schools: Forming Fields, Identities and Boundaries in Management Education*. Cheltenham: Edward Elgar.

Whitley, R. (2008) 'Varieties of knowledge and their use in business and management studies: Conditions and institutions'. *Organization Studies*, 29(4): 581–609.

Section 3

The changing ideologies and practices of global production

11 Socioeconomic context and varieties of capitalism: what difference do they make to work?

Leo McCann

Learning objectives

- To discuss the broader national and international contexts into which organizations and employment relations are embedded, showing that there are important differences across the world in terms of national institutions, practices and traditions of economic governance and work and employment relations
- To explore the nature of these differences in national business context, such as the differences between so-called 'liberal market economies' (LMEs – e.g. the United States and the United Kingdom (UK)) and 'coordinated market economies' (CMEs – e.g. Germany and Japan). What are the impacts of these 'varieties of capitalism' (VoC) on employment relations in firms located in different regions?
- To explore the extent to which national differences in business context and practice might be becoming less significant as the world economy is increasingly integrated under the pressures of globalization and the growth of transnational corporations and 'global best practice'
- To provide a critical case study which explores the problems of trying to operate internationally when national traditions of business (especially when it comes to work and employment conditions) can be so distinct from, and possibly incompatible with, each other

Introduction

The concept of 'globalization' (McCann, 2018; Steger, 2020) that emerged so powerfully in the 1990s has strongly influenced the ways in which workplaces and the wider economy are characterized and understood. It is commonplace to regard the international econonomic environment as increasingly interconnected and interdependent, perhaps to the degree that the systems and practices of business, management and labour are *converging* on a common set of 'best practices' suited to a turbulent, fast-moving and volatile globalized world.

There is a rich tradition in academic work, however, that disputes the extent of globalization, pointing instead to continued *divergence* in business systems. These arguments are central to the 'varieties of capitalism' (or VoC) school of thought (see Dore, 2000; Hall and Soskice, 2001; Whitley, 1999). This literature argues that different ways of structuring, financing and staffing firms across the world remain powerful and resilient. Indeed, skepticism about globalization and 'globalism' has recently grown in intensity following tumultuous political developments often said to represent globalization in decline: authoritarian populism, the phenomenon of President Trump and Trumpism, the collapse of mega-regional free-trade agreements, Britain's exit from the European Union and the prospect of a Chinese–US trade war (King, 2017; McCann, 2018).

This chapter discusses and explains the continuing international differences between national business and employment systems. Even amid a globalized economy, the chapter describes distinct national-level entities that shape the management of work in a variety of ways. This is explained by briefly outlining the theoretical approach of VoC and the 'convergence versus divergence' debate, addressing this by exploring how and why ideas of 'global best practice' filter between nations. Particular attention will be paid to the spread of 'American-style' corporate governance from the United States to the world, and to the spread of so-called 'lean production' from Japan to the world. The chapter encourages readers to consider how ideas of global best practice are 'received' by host nations, and how they are emulated, resisted, translated and often rejected.

What is 'global best practice'?

Multinational corporations (MNCs) play a central role in debates around globalization. Many versions of the globalization story have MNCs as central characters, contributing to the increasing acceleration and integration of cross-border trade and investment. MNCs also develop ideologies of globalization that further spread the awareness of people around the world that they are increasingly being drawn into global relations (McCann, 2018; Steger, 2020). Business schools, MBA programmes, consulting and mainstream business literature develop and spread the ideology of globalization (see Chapter 10 on management education and consultancies). They describe an integrated global economy where MNCs must radically restructure themselves to become more competitive, flexible, agile and adaptable. MNCs are portrayed as genuinely global firms, operating genuinely global strategies. These strategies include hiring the best 'talent' from anywhere in the world, and undergoing culture change which is designed to obviate the need for employees to be represented by trade unions. Firms are encouraged to develop 'global talent management programmes' to identify, recruit and retain the 'best and the brightest' staff who have the requisite soft skills to cope with flux, uncertainty and change (see Chapter 9 on training and development). A 'global sourcing' model is adopted in which labour and management are recruited from all over the world and posted to all points globally.

While this extreme vision of hypermobile, globalized expert workers and genuinely footloose MNCs has some credibility, it is hard to reconcile this picture with daily realities for the vast majority of employees and companies. While mainstream business literature emphasizes a global mindset and hypermobility, VoC reminds us that the world system tolerates a wide diversity of organizational and economic forms, and that national, rather than international, forces remain very powerful, restricting the development of the truly 'global' employment practices portrayed in mainstream business sources.

The present chapter argues that many MNCs are attempting to develop 'global' HRM strategies, and there are clear signs of a globalized ideology of 'best practice' that has its roots in the United States. However, both practice and theory are problematic in several ways because national and regional institutions restrict the prospects for establishing truly universal systems. There are also competing 'models' or forms of 'best practice' emerging from nations other than the United States, such as Japan, Germany and Denmark. I suggest that, in order to fully understand the emerging internationalized economy, observers need to sensitize themselves to both local and transnational pressures, forces and institutions that replicate themselves over time. Changes are highly contingent, and care must be taken when asserting the superiority or appropriateness of one model over another, because enthusiasm for, and advocacy of, various models can wax and wane rapidly (see McCormack, 2008, and Whitley, 2009; see Chapter 2 on MNCs). The following section provides some theoretical backing to these claims, by outlining the VoC approach in more detail.

The 'varieties of capitalism' approach: an introductory background

VoC as a body of literature offers detailed and useful discussions of the wide range of diversity in business activity that undoubtedly still exists in a globalized economy. Detailed expositions of VoC have been produced by, among others, Hall and Soskice (2001), Whitley (1999), Amable (2003) and Coates (2000). Work in core VoC theory tends to focus at a 'system' or 'meso' level, usually aiming to provide overviews which can be helpful for theoretical and conceptual development. These texts provide extensive detail on the main claims made by VoC theoreticians, but the abstractness of this literature can be off-putting, and some find the lack of detail on firms and daily work practices frustrating. Findings from company-level studies often reflect what VoC theory predicts, but can just as often contradict it.

VoC's main contribution to our knowledge – and it is a powerful one – is that the world economy tolerates a wide diversity of national business systems. VoC theorists draw out the similarities and differences in capitalism across the world, pointing to the various ways in which the business environment in place across nations (in particular, nations' various *institutions*) structure what is possible for economic actors such as managers, employees, bankers, governments and trade unionists. In their analysis of business environments, VoC authors often subdivide economies into several key sectors, effectively into *clusters of institutional phenomena* that have structuring effects on economic action and actors. These clusters provide the 'rules of the game' for economic action across different societies, and they put in place enablements and constraints on economic behaviour. They frame what is possible and what is less possible for firms, unions and other actors, making certain behaviours and outcomes more likely to occur and others less likely (Whitley, 1999: 3).

VoC draws much of its influence from *institutional theory*, an approach most widely used in the disciplines of sociology, political studies and organizational studies. Institutional theory argues that economic action cannot be fully understood by the conventions of 'rational-choice' economics, which emphasizes 'universal laws' of supply and demand that apply in essentially the same form across all societies. Instead, institutionalists claim that economic action is simply one form of *social* action, and can therefore only be understood with reference to the broader social structures in which economic action takes place. The academic term often used is *embeddedness* – forms of economic and business interaction and exchange are embedded in social institutions, such as national legal frameworks or social norms of what is morally and cultural appropriate. These customs, laws and structures differ across nations and regions. VoC theory is, therefore, an important counterweight to neoliberal arguments about the inevitability of western-driven globalization. VoC thus reflects a somewhat sceptical approach to globalization.

Perhaps the most famous distinction between economic models was made by Hall and Soskice in the introductory chapter to their edited volume *Varieties of Capitalism* (2001). They lay out LMEs versus CMEs as the two fundamental types of economic model. The binary division of LMEs and CMEs has, however, been challenged by numerous authors for being somewhat simplistic and general (see Amable, 2003, and Whitley, 1999). Other authors, such as Jackson and Deeg (2007) provide comprehensive and invaluable analyses of the strengths and weaknesses of the literature on comparative capitalism. They conclude that the split between CMEs and LMEs, while somewhat crude, does make sense empirically and theoretically.

Specifically, the models refer to the features described in the next two sections.

Liberal market economies

Liberal market economies (LMEs) are national economies characterized by a high degree of openness to globalization and world trade, which have been through substantial processes of neoliberal deregulation and privatization since the 1980s (see Dore, 2000: 2–19). Fundamental to LMEs are the *processes of marketization and financialization*, routes by which ever-greater parts of national economies are opened up to competition, with 'shareholder value preached as the sole legitimate objective of corporate executives' (Dore, 2000: 5; Lazonick and O'Sullivan, 2000). In other words, LMEs are increasingly dominated by financial interests over and above those of other stakeholders (such as government or labour). An excellent overview of the growth of financialization, showing how it is increasingly spreading to CMEs, is provided by Dore (2000), who compares the United States and UK (paradigmatic examples of LMEs) with Germany and Japan (the most powerful CMEs). Institutions of LMEs have been transformed to facilitate increased marketization, such as changes to corporate and employment law, which have handed more power to fund managers and corporate management, tempting them to take ever-greater risks with the (increasingly globalized) financial markets. Time horizons for firms are shrunk as executives look to make decisions that will please investors, that is decisions that will result in a short-term uplift in share prices. Such short-term thinking makes it hard to sustain long-term investment in costly projects, especially in manufacturing sectors. LMEs are, therefore, usually characterized by large services sectors while their industrial and manufacturing sectors have been allowed to decline. In the realm of corporate governance, firms have what is known as an active 'market for corporate control', whereby companies are threatened with hostile takeovers if their share price falls. LME nations such as the United States or the UK (representative of what is often labelled 'Anglo-Saxon capitalism'), therefore, have a reputation for being ruthless, unstable, ever-changing environments where there is no long term for investors, managers or employees. Just as company ownership is vulnerable to change, working careers are also disrupted, and staff would be wise not to expect loyalty from their employer. Staff would be likely to have several employers over the course of their working life.

Change can be a good thing, of course. A more positive appraisal of LMEs would point to their dynamic and fast-moving nature, their willingness to shift into new economic sectors and undertake radical innovations, with access to financial liquidity which can flood in and out of new markets as needed. Perhaps, therefore, LME firms are best exemplified by Silicon Valley high-tech start-ups, initially funded with venture capital before becoming publicly listed giants. The United States is home to the most valuable public companies in the world, the Big Five tech giants of Amazon, Apple, Google, Meta and Microsoft. On the other hand, famous industrial giants such as Ford, General Motors, US Steel and Radio Corporation of America (RCA) have struggled with decline, uncertainty and even collapse in the last three decades.

Coordinated market economies

In terms of ideal types, coordinated market economies (CMEs) are characterized as essentially the opposite to LMEs. Typical CME nations such as Japan and Germany have a much higher role for state regulation (and even ownership) of the economy, and the processes of marketization and financialization have proceeded much more slowly. Large firms in CMEs tend to be more stable in terms of their organizational, ownership and employment conditions. Stock markets play a much-reduced role in CMEs. There is often little or no market for corporate control: companies are insulated from takeover by purchasing and maintaining mutually defensive blocks of shares in each other and by much stricter legal frameworks which limit the possibilities for leveraged buyouts.

The great advantage of this less marketized, less turbulent system is that it provides long time horizons for forward planning, often something essential for companies to be able to genuinely compete in world-class manufacturing sectors. Long-range planning also lends itself to *incremental innovation*, whereby firms make steady, continual and small improvements to existing technologies, perfecting them over many years to improve their quality, safety, efficiency and robustness. German machine tools and cars, for example, are widely regarded as the highest quality in the world, based on years of engineering experience built up over the long term. Firms from CME nations also tend to be strong in technologies which require many years to perfect, such as petrol-electric hybrid vehicles (the Toyota Prius has been a huge success, for example). The archetypal CME firm (such as Bosch or Hitachi) focuses its energies on quality and customer satisfaction, in high-end manufacturing and engineering sectors. CMEs at large (especially Germany and Japan) tend to be export-led economies. Large firms typically employ their core staff on what are effectively 'jobs-for-life' contracts, and employees enjoy generous terms and conditions in return for hard work and loyalty. In several CMEs (notably Germany), powerful laws exist stipulating that all large firms must have Works Councils and other forms of 'codetermination' whereby employees and unions are brought into company decision-making. CME firms tend to be less interested in so-called global best practice as it pertains to employment issues, and instead look internally for staff development, promoting employees gradually after years of service. Firms in CMEs such as Canon or Siemens tend to make a virtue out of employment stability, arguing that genuinely developing and defending their own traditions of corporate culture and of nurturing internal talent over years represent the most effective way of maintaining quality and competing globally (Jacoby, 2005: 168).

CME firms often have generous seniority-based pay, promotion and pension systems. Trade union density and collective bargaining coverage tend to be substantially higher in CMEs than in LMEs. Corporate life for those working inside CME firms is often quite strictly controlled, with the benefit that jobs are secure, worker participation is encouraged and there is potential for promotion and career development. There are fewer reasons for staff to wish to job-hop under CME conditions, and this also applies to managers, even to senior managers; there is a much less developed market for corporate control and therefore less demand for 'top management talent' to be recruited into senior positions. Compared to LMEs, corporate reorganizations are therefore rarer in CMEs, and there is much less emphasis on radical restructuring or dramatic new 'visions and values' coming down from senior executives.

The main weakness of CMEs is that they can be slow to get out of less well-performing sectors and markets, and shareholders' interests are neglected in favour of internal stakeholders such as employees and pensioners; shareholders often receive moderate or poor returns on their investments. The internal, lifetime employed engineers and product specialists often dominate company strategy, expending too much capital and labour on making technically highly advanced products that customers do not necessarily want, retailers struggle to sell and stock market analysts do not rate.

Using this basic ideal-type division into two models, VoC authors develop explanations for how these models can be expected to behave across numerous dimensions, typically across their financial, labour and innovation 'systems'. These are the subsectors of national economies which, according to VoC, are affected by various institutional structures that, to a large extent, define and shape their behaviours.

Financial system

The ways in which firms are able to gain access to capital under the different institutional regimes of LME or CME play a hugely important explanatory role in VoC theory. Financial systems under LMEs are described as open, 'arm's length', liquid and competitive, in which 'lenders and users remain relatively remote from one another' (Whitley, 1999: 49), and where riskier, more liquid forms of finance are tapped by firms, such as securities traded on stock markets or private equity financing. Lenders and investors expect firms to deliver returns on these investments in the short term. In CMEs, financial markets are less liquid, and the 'dominant institutions' here are either large, 'universal' banks, as in Germany, or 'a combination of commercial banks and long-term credit banks coordinated by state agencies and ministries, as in France, Japan and some other countries' (Whitley, 1999: 49). Under typical CME conditions, lending organizations are much more closely linked to corporations, locked into long-term partnerships that both parties have little incentive to break. Critically, these 'bank-based' or 'credit-based' financial systems typical in CMEs allow firms to develop much longer-term strategies than is usually possible in LMEs. VoC theory tends to suggest that this is the main reason why capital-intensive industries such as manufacturing have survived and prospered in CME nations (especially in the archetypes of Germany and Japan), and declined so drastically in LMEs such as Britain and the United States.

The financial system also lays out the 'rules of the game' for corporate governance. What are large firms for? Whose interests do they claim to serve: those of their owners (shareholders), or of insider stakeholders (such as employees, the local regional government or business allies)? The Anglo-Saxon approach has, especially since the rise of neoliberalism in the 1980s, explicitly focused on shareholder returns as the only true purpose of a major corporation. (This view is widely labelled 'shareholder value logic' (SVL)). SVL compels firms to focus intensely on 'the bottom line', scrutinizing their quarterly financial statements and constantly looking for areas where they can reduce their costs and hence boost their stock rating and share price (Lazonick and O'Sullivan, 2000). SVL is strongly associated with the decline of post-war 'managerial capitalism' and the rise of 'investor capitalism' (Useem, 1996). Firms in LMEs therefore have weak managers and strong owners; shareholders have considerable power to force a replacement of top management if stock market performance is poor. In stark contrast, CME firms tend towards strong managers and weak owners – the model is closer to the classic form of managerial capitalism where firms are controlled by insiders, often lifetime employees who have worked their way to the top and usually place the firms' interests ahead of those of shareholders.

Innovation system

As hinted at above, the ways in which firms design, launch, develop and maintain their products and services tend to differ under the institutional domains of LMEs and CMEs. Hall and Soskice (2001: 39–43) offer a particularly detailed account of these aspects, arguing that different nations develop different specializations according to the institutional structuring of their economies. They note that the kinds of sectors CMEs specialize in (mechanical engineering, consumer durables, machine tools) depend on incremental innovations, and are 'just the reverse' of those that LMEs specialize in (medical engineering, biotechnology, information technology), where radical innovations are more important.

In my own experience of research into Japanese firms (Hassard et al., 2009), I was repeatedly struck by employees' obsessive attention to detail, and the way in which Japanese middle managers in industrial corporations wore practical, engineering-style uniforms rather than suits. The entrance lobby to the corporations we visited for our research interviews were practical and humbly furnished, and they invariably featured display cases of the companies' products over time with highly detailed explanations as to how this particular part was progressively reduced in size over many years of research and incremental improvements. They were like exhibits in a museum. This is precisely the image of *kaizen*, or 'continuous improvement', that Japanese firms are renowned for. Theoretically, ideal-typical LME firms tend to specialize in much more radical forms of innovation, enabled by a financial system which embraces entrepreneurship and the risk of failure, as firms try to develop new disruptive 'killer apps' that can shift the direction of entire industries. On the other hand, CME firms tend to specialize by making incremental improvements over time to existing technology in order to build up market share by building their products to extremely exacting standards. (In practice, however, this 'radical/incremental' division can be highly artificial).

Education and labour system

VoC authors have consistently demonstrated that the ways in which states and firms develop employees' skills and how they put these skills to work (i.e. their systems of employment relations or HRM) differ considerably across national business systems. CMEs tend to have relatively strong labour unions, which have a greater say in workplace affairs than they do under the typically 'adversarial' management–labour relationship in LMEs (Hall and Soskice, 2001: 59; Thelen, 2001). In CMEs, the long-term focused financial systems and incremental innovation systems help facilitate, and are facilitated by, long-term skills development. CME labour markets have less of the 'poaching' and job-hopping so common in LMEs. CME governments, trade unions and employers traditionally have worked closely together to invest long term in workforce skills development, backed by strong levels of certification and professionalization. In LMEs, by contrast, labour markets are flexible and deregulated, where employers have more of a free hand to 'hire and fire' workers to and from any position (known as 'employment at will' in the United States), and employees, for their part, are much more willing and able to leave companies in search of better opportunities. Hall and Soskice (2001: 19) present a graph which plots stock market capitalization along the *x*-axis and the strictness of labour laws along the *y*-axis, indicating one cluster of countries that exhibits high levels of employment protection and low forms of financialization (namely, CMEs such as Germany, Italy, France, Japan, Finland and Denmark) and another cluster exhibiting low levels of employment protection and high degrees of financialization (namely, the United States, Canada, Australia and Britain). Jacoby (2005), in a powerful and detailed analysis of five Japanese and five US corporations, very usefully links forms of corporate governance with the kinds of employment relations that result. LME firms typically pay less attention to HR matters, and their HR departments are relatively weak and marginalized players in the corporate hierarchy, whereas for CME firms, HR or personnel divisions tend to play central roles in shaping company strategy.

Crucially therefore, for most VoC authors, the subsystems of finance, labour/education, innovation system and others interact and interlock, meaning that continuity of processes over time is likely, making change difficult to achieve. For example, it might be tempting for firms and governments to try to liberalize German labour markets to make them more flexible and to release cost savings. But doing so would disrupt the sophisticated and long-term focused German skills system, which would in turn threaten its incremental innovation system which underpins its leadership in world-class engineering and manufacturing. So perhaps it is best to shelve or abandon plans to introduce Anglo-Saxon-style flexible labour markets. This is the concept of *path dependence*, an important idea in institutional theory which suggests that prior history lays out the tracks for what is possible in the future. The interlocking of institutional subsystems is often described as 'complementarity'. In many ways, the concepts of embeddedness, path dependency and complementarity are the foundation stones of VoC theory. They provide the main conceptual basis for VoC's sceptical arguments about globalization and convergence. According to VoC, the rules of the game are structured in such complex ways that international pressures for transformation are unlikely to result in radical change.

While the typically more abstract core VoC theoreticians such as Hall and Soskice, Amable and Whitley tend to be agnostic about the ethical and moral value of different systems, regional specialists such as Dore (2000: 219) can be much more explicit in their defence of the traditions of CMEs such as Japan and Germany, claiming that 'the processes of marketization and financialization are a bad thing'. With questions about the moral and ethical value of different models of capitalism in mind, we turn to the next section, which discusses the ways in which models become popular and unpopular, how elements of them spread and diffuse into other nations and what this means for work and employment in large organizations.

The emergence of Anglo-Saxonization and Americanization

Having sketched out the broad ideas of VoC theory and the main competing models, we can now turn to explore the ways in which different models have increasingly been exposed to each other in an era of internationalizing economic relations, where ideas of 'best practice' rapidly move across national borders. There is strong evidence of attempted moves in CMEs towards adopting forms of corporate governance that more closely resemble LME institutions, and that these changes to corporate governance increasingly open the door for the development of LME-style employment relations (see Chapter 16 on regulatory change). However, both of these transformations are far from complete, and there is also evidence of resistance and translation as the new forms of best practice are developed.

CME nations are undergoing significant changes towards SVL- and LME-style investor capitalism (Morris et al., 2008). The shift from managerial to investor capitalism has been very pronounced in the UK and the United States since the 1980s, and is visible in parts in France, Japan, Germany and other CMEs. The pressure for change (both from external and internal actors) is certainly there, but the effects on the ground have not always travelled as far. Some companies domiciled in CMEs have always been western-focused and have long traditions of adopting LME-style features, such as Sony, which is often regarded by western financial observers as having the 'best' (i.e. the most western-looking) corporate governance and accounting standards and the clearest and most useful annual reports (Roche, 2005: 183). Dore (2000) and Jacoby (2005), however, argue that these changes in corporate governance have not necessarily resulted in significant changes to employment practice. Claims about the 'inevitable' erosion of lifetime employment in Japan have circulated for many decades, yet the trends towards flexible labour markets are modest, with many traditional Japanese employment features retained (McCann and Monteath, 2020).

It is also important to bear in mind that the flow of best practice ideas is not all one way; it is not simply a case of American ideas flowing to CMEs. Many features of CMEs have been adopted or advocated in LMEs. Perhaps the most notable example is that of 'lean manufacturing', which has spread from Japan to many parts of the world (Stewart, this volume). American, British and European car manufacturing establishments have widely adopted lean concepts, or at least used them as the inspiration for other managerial technologies such as Total Quality Control, continuous improvement and Six Sigma. Interestingly, lean concepts are not always implemented 'properly' in alien environments (see, for example, Graham 1995, and Delbridge, 1998 – see also Chapter 12 on lean production). Lean was developed through many years under CME financial and employment systems that emphasized long-term investment and genuine focus on quality improvement. Lean adoption under the short-term financial imperatives of the LME financial and employment system instead tended to mean that lean adoption was often more rhetorical than real. In recent years, lean has even been taken up as a panacea for public sector organizations such as the UK National Probation Service, HM Revenue and Customs and the National Health Service. Again, the results are questionable, demonstrating confusion, resistance and a great deal of rhetorical window-dressing about its beneficial effects (McCann et al., 2015; Waring and Bishop, 2010).

US-style corporate governance is spreading to East Asia (Dore, 2000) and has an increasingly large footprint in Europe (Goyer, 2007: 200–1). Traditional German systems for coordinating management–labour relationships are arguably crumbling (Kinderman, 2005). This is potentially hugely important because corporate governance reform can facilitate changes to employment relations (Dore, 2000; Hassard et al., 2009; Jacoby, 2005; Morris et al., 2008). Open markets for corporate control provide the legitimacy for shareholder value to be reframed as the central organizational principle for firms, opening the door to American-style employment relations (Smith and Walter, 2006: 44). This is certainly the argument of those who accept the globalization and convergence picture. However, in accordance with VoC, the adoption and spread of actual 'best practice' is slow, contingent and contradictory and faces considerable resistance. In what follows, I attempt to highlight this situation with reference to a fictional case study, in which executives in a US firm consider whether or not to go ahead with the plan to buy up the stock and eventually purchase a rather conservative Japanese firm.

Case study: A difficult phone call

In this fictional case study, a US private equity firm, Reflexus Capital, is pursuing the possibility of investing in small- and medium-sized Japanese technology firms. Mike Gifford is an executive vice president for Overseas Ventures at Reflexus. He has been working in Japan for the last three months meeting various representatives of mid-sized Japanese firms in the fields of consumer electronics, biotechnologies and renewable energy. He has been impressed by the advanced technology being developed in these companies, and by the close attention to detail showed by managers and engineers in the companies he visited. He was surprised and rather impressed to learn that senior managers in these companies – even their owners – were themselves technically very competent engineers who seemed passionate about the precise workings of their companies' projects and products.

Over the last few weeks, he had settled on one company as a possible candidate for Reflexus to invest in. The target is Ohmatsu Systems, a company developing highly specialized materials for renewable energy generation. Some at Reflexus are talking about a complete buyout, even about replacing its top management, or at least inserting some new management figures from outside. But the closer Mike got to recommending a go-ahead to senior management, the more worried he was becoming as to whether or not this whole idea was wise. That evening he was due to place a call to Ed McCulloch, global strategy leader at Reflexus. He had not been looking forward to making the call.

Ed: 'Mike, hi! How's it going?'

Mike: 'Yeah, OK, it's ah, going great.'

Ed: 'So what's up with this Ohmatsu thing? Are we going for it or what?'

Mike: 'Yeah, ah, well, you know it's a great company. The guys there, Mr Hatsumano, they are just great guys and some of their products are really exciting, you know?'

Ed: 'Sure yeah. Mike, remind me, what's the story on 'Comp and Bens' [compensation and benefits] out there? How are they all paid?'

Mike: 'It's all salary, mostly. They get a salary with a possible twice-yearly bonus. It's kind of strict, you know, a lot of it seems to be based around your length of service, your seniority. Pensions are Defined Benefit'

Ed: 'Really? Still? Well, we'd have to sort that out. And what kind of share plan do they all have – you know, the execs, guys like Katayama?'

Mike: 'There isn't one'

Ed: 'No stock options at all? How are they motivated?'

Mike: 'Its, ah, it's hard to explain. They just don't seem to know the idea or don't really value it. They sort of say, er, "we do things this way", or "it is important to have a hierarchy". They are kind of vague about it, but I sort of know what they mean.'

Ed: 'What do you mean by that, Mike?'

Mike: 'Well, I feel sometimes . . . I feel that maybe sometimes it is important to respect the structures they've already got in place. It's like Katayama-san, he's pretty impressive. They seem to respect him a lot, you know. They don't do much without consulting him on everything. He's been there, like forever, since the company started. He knows everything about the product, his whole life is invested in it.'

There is a long silence.

Mike: 'Ed? You still there?'

Ed: 'Yeah. Yeah, I'm just thinking.'

Mike: 'There's something else. This whole thing, they are real tied in with the local mayor's office here. They are all set on Ohmatsu playing a part in this urban redevelopment they're doing. They call it Super Enviro Town. It's all there in the mayor's office, they've got all these plans laid out. I hear Katayama and the mayor came through the same grad school together, they go way back.'

Ed: 'Hmm. OK. So let's see. You want to give this a couple more days? I'm getting a bit of heat back here on this. They are all kinda keyed up on this, you know, "give me an answer" sort of thing?'

(Continued)

Mike: 'Yeah, I can imagine'.

Ed: 'OK, Mike. You, ah, you put all this in an e-mail to me, right? OK? Then call me by, uh, let's say Tuesday? Tuesday same time, and then we'll work out what to do. You happy with that?'

Mike: 'Er, that should be OK, yeah.'

Ed: 'Bye, Mike.'

Mike: 'Er, yeah OK, bye. Bye.'

The line goes dead. Mike replaces the handset in an oddly slow and careful way.

Questions

1. What impression does the case study give as to the employment relations and overall working culture of Japanese companies?
2. To what extent is this traditional Japanese working culture likely to be effective in an increasingly globalized world?
3. Why was Mike becoming sceptical about the prospects for Reflexus to get involved in Ohmatsu?
4. What should Mike do here? What should he recommend to Ed? What options does he realistically have?
5. Does the case study rely on stereotypes? Or is there some accuracy to the way the US and Japanese characters are portrayed?

Conclusion: tensions, issues, alternatives, futures

The above discussion has highlighted the social and political implications of the pre-eminence of LMEs, and the rhetorical dominance of the US-driven model of investor capitalism and shareholder value, arguing that this model has been increasingly ascendant in the last three decades. But it has also widely discussed the powerful and still-existing alternative in the form of the CME model. The years 2007–9 will long be remembered for the dramatic collapse of confidence in investor capitalism as the subprime mortgage crash deeply tarnished the value (ethically and financially) of the US model (Whitley, 2009). This event is likely to reinforce scepticism among managers, workers and unions in CMEs about the motives, knowledge and competence of high-profile, globally educated 'international managers' who 'drop in', lecture the locals about globalization and best practice, then 'fly off' again. The very idea of globalization itself, for so long promoted as an inexorable force for good, is currently widely unpopular and 'in crisis' (King, 2017; McCann, 2018: 109–27; Steger, 2020: 123–8).

US ideas of best practice in corporate governance and employment relations clearly have a dominant rhetorical force in global capitalism. But these ideas are not simply or easily exported to other regions; they are adapted and translated as they diffuse, sometimes replacing, sometimes melding and sometimes clashing with existing practices and institutions. In some cases, western ideas are accepted and promoted in CME environments. Elsewhere, the German New Social Market Initiative is a home-grown movement pressuring German employers' associations to adopt more Anglo-Saxon employment relations, advocating a diminution of the traditional power of German trade unions and codetermination (Kinderman, 2005). However, it still seems clear that the differences in models of capitalism remain powerful and important, and that there are significant institutional barriers to the unproblematic adoption of LME concepts in CME nations. These barriers are unlikely to ever disappear. But it is equally clear that powerful forces of globalization and liberalization (while periodically unpopular) also show no real signs of declining in importance, and we can probably expect national models to show further erosion, blurring and scrambling in years to come. In such a complex and unpredictable scenario, it becomes more and more necessary for firms, unions and individual workers to develop effective strategies for facing up to increased levels of competition, marketization and uncertainty, to try to prepare for as many eventualities as they can, to work out a core set of ideas and principles about what forms of organization and employment are effective and just, but also the capacity to rethink their assumptions about how markets operate, what customers require and how competitors are moving. Employees need to develop and retain the right abilities, educational and professional credentials and attitudes, and to nurture an aptitude for critical thinking, to evaluate the effectiveness (or otherwise) of so-called 'global best practice', and of employers, their workplace representatives and themselves as economic actors in a turbulent and difficult era.

Reflective questions

1. To what extent does globalization require firms to radically restructure their people management and corporate governance structures?
2. Can firms genuinely be global in their outlook? Why are they so keen to project this kind of internationalized image?
3. Is there a global best practice for human resource management and the appointment and retention of 'talent'? Or will effective ways of working always be contingent on local histories and structures?
4. Globally speaking, are 'jobs for life' and internal career ladders now things of the past? Why or why not?

Recommended reading

- Campbell, J. L. and Pedersen, O. K. (2007) 'The varieties of capitalism and hybrid success: Denmark in the global economy'. *Comparative Political Studies*, 40(3): 307–32.
- McCormack, K. (2008) 'Sociologists and "the Japanese model": A passing enthusiasm?' *Work, Employment and Society*, 21(4): 751–71.
- Morris, J., Hassard, J. and McCann, L. (2008) 'The resilience of "institutionalization capitalism": Managing managers under "shareholder capitalism" and "managerial capitalism"'. *Human Relations*, 61(5): 687–710.

References

Amable, B. (2003) *The Diversity of Modern Capitalism*. Cambridge: Cambridge University Press.

Campbell, J. L. and Pedersen, O. K. (2007) 'The varieties of capitalism and hybrid success: Denmark in the global economy'. *Comparative Political Studies*, 40(3): 307–32.

Coates, D. (2000) *Models of Capitalism: Growth and Stagnation in the Modern Era*. Cambridge: Polity.

Delbridge, R. (1998) *Life on the Line in Contemporary Manufacturing: The Workplace Experience of Lean Production and the 'Japanese' Model*. Oxford: Oxford University Press.

Dore, R. (2000) *Stock Market Capitalism: Welfare Capitalism, Japan and Germany versus the Anglo-Saxons*. Oxford: Oxford University Press.

Goyer, M. (2007) 'Capital mobility, varieties of institutional investors, and the transforming stability of corporate governance in France and Germany'. In B. Hancke, M. Rhodes and M. Thatcher (eds), *Beyond Varieties of Capitalism: Conflict, Contradictions and Complementarities in the European Economy*. Oxford: Oxford University Press.

Graham, L. (1995) *On the Line at Subaru-Isuzu*. Ithaca: Cornell University Press.

Hall, P. and Soskice, D. (eds) (2001) *Varieties of Capitalism: The Institutional Foundations of Comparative Advantage*. New York: Oxford University Press.

Hassard, J., McCann, L. and Morris, J. (2009) *Managing in the Modern Corporation: The Intensification of Managerial Work in the US, UK and Japan*. Cambridge: Cambridge University Press.

Jackson, G. and Deeg, R. (2007) 'Towards a more dynamic theory of capitalist variety'. *Socio-Economic Review*, 5(1): 149–79.

Jacoby, S. (2005) *The Embedded Corporation: Corporate Governance and Employment Relations in the USA and Japan*. Princeton: Princeton University Press.

Kinderman, D. (2005) 'Pressure from without, subversion from within: The two-pronged German employer offensive'. *Comparative European Politics*, 3(4): 432–43.

King, S. D. (2017) *Grave New World: The End of Globalization and the Return of History*. New Haven: Yale University Press.

Lazonick, W. and O'Sullivan, M. (2000) 'Maximizing shareholder value: A new ideology for corporate governance', *Economy and Society*, 29(1): 13–35.

McCann, L. (2014) *International and Comparative Business: Foundations of Political Economies.* London: Sage.

McCann, L. (2018) *A Very Short, Fairly Interesting, and Reasonably Cheap Book About Globalization.* London: Sage.

McCann, L., Hassard, J., Granter, E. and Hyde, P. (2015) 'Casting the lean spell: The promotion, dilution, and erosion of lean management in the NHS'. *Human Relations,* 68(10): 1557–77.

McCann, L. and Monteath, G. (2020) 'Restoring the missing context in HRM: Habitus, capital and field in the reproduction of Japanese repatriate careers'. *Human Resource Management Journal,* 30(40): 478–93.

McCormack, K. (2008) 'Sociologists and "the Japanese model": A passing enthusiasm?' *Work, Employment and Society,* 21(4): 751–71.

Morris, J., Hassard, J. and McCann, L. (2008) 'The resilience of "institutionalization capitalism": Managing managers under "shareholder capitalism" and "managerial capitalism"'. *Human Relations,* 61(5): 687–710.

Roche, J. (2005) *Corporate Governance in Asia.* Abingdon: Routledge.

Smith, R. C. and Walter, I. (2006) *Governing the Modern Corporation: Capital Markets, Corporate Control, and Economic Performance.* Oxford: Oxford University Press.

Steger, M. B. (2020) *Globalization: A Very Short Introduction,* 5th edn. Oxford: Oxford University Press.

Thelen, K. (2001) 'Varieties of labor politics in the developed democracies'. In P. Hall and D. Soskice (eds), *Varieties of Capitalism: The Institutional Foundations of Comparative Advantage.* New York: Oxford University Press.

Useem, M. (1996) *Investor Capitalism: How Money Managers Are Changing the Face of Corporate America.* New York: Basic Books.

Waring, J. J. and Bishop, S. (2010) 'Lean healthcare: Rhetoric, ritual, and resistance'. *Social Science and Medicine,* 71(7): 1332–40.

Whitley, R. (1999) *Divergent Capitalisms: The Social Structuring and Change of Business Systems.* Oxford: Oxford University Press.

Whitley, R. (2009) 'U.S. capitalism: A tarnished model?' *Academy of Management Perspectives,* 23(2): 11–22.

12 Globalization and lean production in the remaking of labour intensification?

Paul Stewart

Learning objectives

- To engage the reader in the debate on lean production in relation to globalization
- To explain the meanings of lean production and the consequences for workers and managers
- To outline the relation between lean production and neoliberalism
- To outline the consequences of lean production in terms of health and safety

Introduction

The question of globalization of work and employment is not only about the organizational, technical and financial strategic imperatives of transnational corporations and transnational forms of regulation. This is because globalization is just as much concerned with the power of new ideas and views about how the employment relationship and work are organized. In other words, globalization is also about management ideology and the fact that ideologies have a very powerful role in defining the nature of the organization of work. That said, while management is the dominant force in the employment relationship, the actual organization of work will be mediated by the quotidian interactions between workers and employers making the idea that there can be 'one best way' or *model* of working highly implausible.

It is in this light that lean production, its technical attributes aside, can be understood as a powerful contemporary management ideology. Its origins lie in the rise to prominence of what for some were perceived to be highly successful forms of work organization and firm strategy. Lean, it is argued, originated in Toyota's production system in Japan and due to its perceived success was taken as an exemplar of a form of working that would solve the crisis in late 20th and early 21st century capitalism.

Characteristically, when describing what they take to be lean production, managers and some academics refer only to a number of associated organizational techniques and processes including just-in-time (JIT) delivery systems, a quality- and product-check inventory system known as *kanban* (assessing the quality and authenticity of upstream product delivered by your co-worker who is also to be seen as a 'business partner') and teamworking and team meetings whose main role is to encourage and deliver continuous improvement (*kaizen* is the Japanese word) and reduce waste in the system (*muda*, another Japanese word).

The chapter considers:

1. The social origins of lean production. There are three ways in which the concept of lean has been used to make sense of work, labour and the organization. Thus lean as description/lean as reinvention of already existing management practices/lean as distinctive and vital to the new political economy whose origins, supposedly, account for Japan's post-Second World War economic success. Often, managerial advocates (who sometimes seem almost evangelical in their enthusiasm) put the latter view forward seeing lean as in some sense revolutionary. Yet, for sure we can say that lean is vital in generating what Benanav (2019) describes as socioeconomic turbulence. There is another strand to this 'lean-as-wholly distinctive' view, which is critical of lean's impact on work and employment. This is a view, broadly stated, held by some critics of management and capitalism.
2. Lean – the context of the crisis of Fordism.
3. The dimensions of lean production – lean as distinctive: managerial and Marxist perspectives.
4. The meaning of the lean society – lean as ideology (the 'leanistas').
5. Case study of lean as ideology and practice – notes from a comparative study of automotive assembly plants, BMW (UK), GM (Poland) and VW-Poland.

The social origins of lean production

The advent of neoliberal economic strategies (see Chapter 11 on varieties of capitalism) has been characterized by what at first glance appears to be a paradox – less external (state) regulation of business together with tighter company-driven regulation of work by myriad forms of monitoring and surveillance. However, the significant paradox is not that of less external regulation and greater internal regulation since, after all, it stands to reason that the greater the degree of external unpredictability, the more a firm will want to tighten up its internal life, including the procedures governing how work is carried out. It could be said that the unitarist character of lean production is very well suited to such circumstances, and especially neoliberal capitalism where the external business environment has become especially febrile and in frequent crisis. Arguably, the significant paradox is that lean production was born in the more highly regulated economy of post-Second World War Japan. More highly regulated that is than the contemporary neoliberal environment where it is trumpeted as capitalism's saviour. The supposition that lean can resolve the problems of economic crisis *within* the organization (whether in manufacturing or the service economy) is really quite weak when a longer-term perspective is required before any such claims can be made. The fact that it could be considered both response to and agent of economic problems is a theme to which this chapter will return. We need to be extremely sceptical of any claims by champions of neoliberalism who see crisis resolution in the extension of lean to the wider society in respect of the way our non-work lives are organized.

While the advocates of lean will see its extension as an inherent good with any downside attributed to poor and inadequate implementation, nevertheless a number of commentators argue that it is lean that is implicitly responsible for increasing levels of stress in society and that this needs to be challenged, not by operationalizing lean more efficiently but, on the contrary, by rejecting lean in its entirety. From this perspective, lean production is taken as an indication of broader changes not just to society-in-work per se, but also to capitalist society in general. *Flux tendu* is the term introduced by the French sociologist Jean-Pierre Durand (2007, 2019) to account for the seeming encroachment of more than simply the techniques of lean production into our everyday lives and society. While his argument centres on the manner in which lean production changes the ways in which we work, together with a focus on the nature of the wider employment relationship, he is also concerned to highlight how lean impacts the wider society: the whole of our lives, and not just the time spent at work, is increasingly being affected by the imperatives (and the philosophy) of lean. Perhaps we are already in the lean capitalist society (Durand, 2007)? Developing this theme in *Creating the New Worker* (2019), Durand explores the historical genesis of what he sees as lean's 'invisible revolution' in the cultivation of individualizing employment relations. His analytical starting point combines Gramsci's Marxism and Lacanian psychoanalysis interpreting the lean society as one in which individuals are themselves constrained agents playing within the framework of a new type of social reality. The latter limits our spaces for autonomous action precisely by defining (capitalist hegemony) the contours of our activity. While workplace hierarchies appear flatter than during so-called Fordism, this perception serves all the better to obscure the constitution of new, ever more invasive, forms of subordination typical of lean working (Durand, 2019: 13–99, 311).

Furthermore, we can see the outworking of lean imperatives across myriad cultures and national boundaries and as lean hegemony spreads far and wide, it has impacted even those organizations, specifically trade unions, that workers traditionally would have looked to for defence against the erosion of their working conditions (Martínez Lucio and Stewart, 2009). As lean spread across organizational boundaries to embrace all moments in company global supply chains one feature of this has been the expansion of organizational insecurity. This is an interesting paradox. In seeking control over all activity along the commodity chain, the very organizational and technical features of lean actually build in a different kind of insecurity. In the period beginning in the late 1980s, while lean claimed to protect the organization from the insecurity of a febrile external neoliberal environment, it seemed a good idea therefore to bring as much of the production process under the control of the parent firm. However, as we know, this has left companies and whole sectors, from food production to automotive assembly to electronics, to identify three, subject to the potentially disruptive effects of global JIT production. The organizational measures originally adopted within the confines of the firm to confront one form of insecurity have led to new organizational insecurities.

Another irony is that while huge budgets are expended on developing the culture of the new worker, the actual experiences of working in the 'new' organizations of the lean society frequently undermine the rhetoric espoused by advocates of lean. While not the focus of their study of the variety of worker interpretations and opposition to lean, Alcadipani et al. (2018) nevertheless allow us to highlight at least two problematic features of the presumption made by lean advocates. The first is whether there can ever be one best form of lean, and second, relatedly, that lean can be implemented as if it were a cooking recipe. We could argue that both are based upon the fallacy that we are all the same, we all react in like manner to management imperatives and moreover that management practices are indeed more or less practically implantable as if work was somehow free of already existing relations of social power within and out the employment relationship.

Our objective then is to understand more accurately the developments and *raison d'être* of this late-20th-century and early-21st-century form of management both at the level of the workplace and society. So-called lean production is frequently seen to be the cure-all to the problems of falling profitability in the period beginning in the late 1970s and early 1980s. This was the beginning of the end of the post-Second World War consensus based on Fordist production and consumption strategies in the Keynesian era. This new dominant management paradigm of lean, vital to what is known as the *accumulation strategy* (how capital and labour interact in the creation of profit), began to shift the burden of risk onto non-core businesses (second- and other-tier suppliers) and subordinate social groups and the workforce in general. In recent decades, the rationale of reducing costs and enhancing productivity through organizational changes and the development of new forms of human resource management (HRM) have had a tendency to become universal (both nationally and globally) across all sectors, including the public sector and non-profit organizations (in health and social care, for example).

A number of interrelated questions need to be borne in mind throughout our discussion of the character of lean production. First, as regards the UK, how did the concept of lean production grow out of the debate about so-called 'Japanization'? Second, to what extent can we say that changes in work, frequently described as lean, remain unchallenged at the level of the workplace and employment relations? After all, as Martin (2017, 2018), Alcadipani et al. (2018) and Mackenzie et al. (2020) have demonstrated, it is only to be expected that attempts to introduce workplace change will be challenged by others with the inevitable consequence that the outcome will almost certainly differ from the intention (Mackenzie et al., 2020: 26–9). As Mackenzie et al. (2020: 1) argue:

> More significantly, we illustrate the exercise of a more encompassing form of power, showing how lean harnesses the inherently exploitable desire for recognition among hitherto marginalised workers, and its role as a form of 'human capital'. [They illustrate lean's] subtle, deleterious and persistent effects within the analytical frame of neoliberal governmentality.

Third, at the collective level, how have trade unions challenged lean production? Fourth, to what extent is lean production as effective as it is claimed to be by its advocates and, moreover, what are its limits and contradictions?

Specifically, we will here be concerned with what happens to those whose work is affected by what we term a 'regime of lean production'. This will be explored through a case study in the automotive sector.

The context: the crisis of Fordism and the rise of lean production

Globally, neoliberal economic and political strategies (see Chapter 1 on globalization and employment and Chapter 11 on varieties of capitalism) really took off in the period symbolized by the fall of the Berlin Wall in late 1989. Even though capital's offensive may have drawn succour from the collapse of bureaucratic socialism, the social and economic foundation of its newfound vigour was quite separate and grew out of what we generally understand to be the crisis in its own pattern of capital accumulation and economic organization, Fordism (see Chapter 1 on globalization and employment and Chapter 14 on technology and work).

By Fordism, we are referring to the social and economic context in which the pursuit of profit by means of employment and wider state and social strategies was based upon the incorporation of labour and trade unions (see also Hirst and Zeitlin, 1991). Typically, in post-Second World War Europe, this necessitated a welfare state supported by general taxation sustained in turn by strong, autonomous trade unions committed to negotiations with management at the company and sectoral level (in some European countries, these amounted to pacts): it was a coming together of mass production and mass consumption (see Chapter 1 on globalization and employment). This was a period in which management too was seen to gain, and principally owing to the strength of national trade unions, capable of maintaining workplace peace (see Chapter 3 on trade unions and employment relations).

Seen to have been undermined by the crisis in profitability and commodity production in the early 1970s, Fordism came to be associated with inflexible labour relations, inflexible commodity production techniques and an over-regulated economic system (especially by those on the right of the political system though this presumption eventually included those on the social democratic left). The fact that this perception was based on an overgeneralization of the origins of the capitalist crisis in the late 20th century had no bearing on the attractiveness of this view, and it usefully provided the backdrop for a series of attempted prognoses and remedies. If Fordism was seemingly unable to resolve the economic crisis that began in the 1970s, how would the crisis be resolved? Often, the concept of neoliberalism is used to sum up the attack by capital on state regulation and good labour standards, and what some commentators termed lean production arguably became central to the supposedly new phenomenon of globalization.

Yet the specific intellectual origins of 'lean production', though framed in this period, came from an apparently distinctive source seemingly disinterested, at least initially, with state regulation focusing simply upon the drivers of business success. In the mid to late 1980s, a number of management consultants, policy analysts and a cadre of academics argued that Japan, seemingly protected to some degree from the 1970s crisis, could be held up as a beacon of hope for western capitalism. More especially, some argued that the explanation for Japan's post-war economic success lay not only with the structure of its business organization and employment relations, but more decidedly in its internal workplace and labour process relationships. As we shall see below, it is here that the origins of the so-called Japanization debate lay. This debate is important in understanding the nature of the origins of the concept of lean production.

The dimensions of lean production: origins of the lean production agenda

i)   Lean as distinctive: a managerialist perspective from an Anglo-Saxon context

The debate in the United Kingdom (UK) about the character and significance of lean production first gained prominence with Oliver and Wilkinson's *The Japanisation of British Industry* ([1988] 1992). It was here that the so-called Japanization school which developed the concept of Japanization from Peter Turnbull (1986) began. The term *lean production* was subordinated to a broader concern with the theme of transfer of what were interpreted as Japanese management practices. The main thesis was that the significant and transformative management practices in Britain for the foreseeable future would be essentially Japanese. (See Ackroyd et al. (1988) for an alternative reading of the notion of Japanization. For Oliver and Wilkinson, if the perceived practices were not identifiably Japanese, then they would act as such, by proxy (in the form of what were termed 'functional equivalents' – a yardstick vital to the lean production school). So-called Japanese management practices would become the benchmark against which the effectiveness of new management techniques would be judged. (See also Elger and Smith's introduction to their *Global Japanisation* (1994), in which they spell out the range of interpretations and significance of the term.)

While a greater sophistication subsequently infused the Japanization position in a special issue of the *Journal of Management Studies* (1995) (*JMS*) in 1995, in many respects the outcome merely reinforced existing weaknesses in the approach, because here too the specialness of Japan was retained. The debate on so-called Japanization was revisited in a special issue of *Employee Relations* in 1998 and, again, at the 2012 British Universities Industrial Relations Association in a conference paper on Japanese inward investment in Poland. Maciej Bancarzewski subsequently developed the theme of the question of Japanization in Poland in his doctoral thesis at the University of Hertfordshire in 2015.

However, the difficulty with the Japanization frame of reference was that an obsession with the Japanese origins of lean production techniques effectively led to a certain inability to think of the techniques as transferable from one place (culture) to another. After all, if something is culture-bound then transferability is an evident problem and of limited help to managers. Nevertheless, one certainly positive development came out of the *JMS* papers: a rejection of an explicit genuflection to the work of the International Motor Vehicle Program (IMVP) group (Oliver and Wilkinson, 1992: 5–9, 15). (The IMVP was coordinated by the Massachusetts Institute of Technology and comprised academics and managerial consultants.) As a consequence, greater emphasis was placed upon the theme of employee domination, as this now seemed to be inscribed in the very idea of Japanese management practices according to critics. On one level, this could be viewed as having led to a more positive emphasis on the independent role of labour because in the 1988 and 1992 Japanization texts, the problem of employee domination tended to be subsumed within a framework emphasizing the creative tension involved in the management of 'high dependency' relationships (Oliver and Wilkinson, 1992: 82–7). Here, organizational and technical features of the new workplace such as JIT placed employees in a potentially very powerful position – as the system of production became more prone to disruption due to JIT – despite the fact that they rarely sought to realize this power. The answer given by managerialist writers on Japanization as to why workers effectively acquiesced was that the management regime allowed for some element of employee benefit in welfare and involvement programmes in Japan (e.g. stable employment). Yet, the import of extra-work institutions was typically ignored when writing about the nature of worker 'commitment' beyond Japan. One important problem with the Oliver and Wilkinson thesis was that it had little direct empirical grounding in terms of workplace research based upon employee responses. The major advance of the research reported in the 1995 *JMS* special issue (1995) was that this absence of field research into employee responses was addressed by several of the contributors such that the 'dark side' of this management was stressed – 'the iron fist in the velvet glove', to quote the conclusion's epithet on Japanese management (*JMS*, Wilkinson et al., 1995). A fatalistic view of labour control was expounded: collective, autonomous labour could not establish an independent agenda.

With the advance of the lean production paradigm at the end of 1980s, all of these discomforting problems associated with the difficulty of the transfer of what were arguably culturally specific management practices could be laid to rest (so the managerial evangelists hoped). For the first time, the key reference points in the theme of Japanization would be stripped to their technical essentials. Lean production might well have been invented in Japan, but the conundrum ends there. This was not to say that social, cultural and organizational matters did not figure in the account, either in its original version in Womack et al. (1990) *The Machine that Changed the World* or in the work of British counterparts, and notably in the writing of Dan Jones, one of the authors of the *Machine...* and his colleagues working with the Andersen Consulting group, merely that they were seen to be secondary to the overriding technical imperatives of lean production. In a notable exception to the usual technological determinism underlying the assumptions of the lean production school, Oliver et al. (1993) gave some credence to the role of leadership in the implementation of lean strategies. However, even in this instance, social relations were perceived to be significant only in so far as they conformed to the imperatives of 'lean' management behaviour. Technology and its proper implementation (in the right institutional context that included teamworking and *kaizen*) was the key to the 'one best way' of achieving manufacturing success (see, *inter alia*, Jones, 1992; Oliver, 1991; Oliver et al., 1994).

The solution to economic failure, according to *The Machine that Changed the World* (Womack et al., 1990) and later Andersen Consulting (Oliver et al., 1994), was to be found by introducing the organizational and technical truths of lean production. The main social and employee relations argument put forward by the IMVP team was that trade unions had to help the firm and adapt to the requirements of international competition. It must, in other words, give up on what was seen as the old-fashioned nostrums of independent trade unionism – a by-word for confrontation – and the existence of trade unions as institutions set up to protect workers from the consequences of working in a capitalist economy (see Chapter 17 on trade unions internationally). The hope for advocates of lean production was that lean might oversee the creation of a new form of 'industrial citizenship' (Womack et al., 1990: 103 see Jones, 1992) whereby worker participation would be linked to production requirements. In the UK, some vitality was restored to the lean prognosis through an internal critique. This emphasized the way in which the earlier enthusiasts underestimated the obstacles to bringing employees on-board the great new 'enterprise' of lean transformation. The early work of Seddon and Caulkin (2007) (see also Vanguard Consulting, 2014) in particular has been taken up by a range of public sector organizations seeking to apply the methods drawn from manufacturing to public services. Seddon argued that the interpretation and application of much of the IMVP research, and especially in its popularized versions such as the one purveyed in Womack et al., (1990), derived from a limited understanding of the origins *and meaning* of lean, following Ohno's insights (Toyota's key figure in this regard) into the Toyota production system. The long-term project of the international network GERPISA (1993) demonstrated how narrow the IMVP view of technical and socio-economic change was (Boyer and Freyssenet, 2002; Charron and Stewart, 2004; Durand, 2007). For these researchers, the variety of practices that could be described as lean and the myriad contexts in which so-called lean was present merely served to illustrate that there that could be no 'one best way' (see Jurgens et al., 1993, for the classic empirical rebuttal, and more recently, Jurgens and Krzywdzinski, 2016).

ii)   Lean as something distinctive: a Marxist and political economy perspective

While there is a second strand to the view of lean production as distinctive, considering it to be in many respects a break from the past and notably Fordism, the conclusions drawn about its origins, purposes and trajectory are entirely different from those advanced by lean 'evangelists'. Arising from a Marxist political economy perspective, one strand in this approach sees lean as a capitalist strategy, or following Miliband (1989) a form of 'class struggle from above' response to the problems that enveloped Fordism. The view is that because lean was developed in response to the crisis of Fordism it is a managerialist (qua consultant, academic-consultant) capitalist, agenda for restoring profitability in a post-Fordist context. That said, perhaps inevitably, not all Marxist critics focus upon the same concerns. For example, Tony Smith (2000) considered what exactly the lean response to the crisis of Fordism comprised.

For Smith (2000: 6–8), the rise of lean production should be traced to the crisis of the Fordist pattern of capital accumulation in the last decades of the 20th century expressed in terms of six problematic features of the economy, work and organization of the Fordist era of accumulation:

1. 'Constant capital'. This includes problems with the high costs of raw materials, inventory costs, and the 'inflexibility of machinery'.
2. 'Circulation time', by which he is referring to the rising costs associated with the delivery of stock, retooling, bureaucracy and quality.
3. Problems associated with the link 'between science and capital form'. This refers to 'the separation of research and development departments from other divisions in the Fordist corporate structure'.
4. Relations between capital and labour in work. This refers to perceived increasing costs of a separate cadre of managers. Also, worker struggles against work and for higher wages are seen to be out of sync with productivity. Relatedly, perceived problems with quality are specifically linked to the separation of quality control from the actual process of production.
5. The relations between the consumer and capital. Problems here are associated with Fordism in general, that is, massification and standardization of products and services leading to the neglect of consumer desires and interests.
6. The institutional separation of the various units of capital along the supply chain leading to increased expense and unnecessary (in the workplace) investment in planning, tracking and implementation processes.

The question considered by Smith was the extent to which lean could be understood as leading to the development of new patterns of capital accumulation in both private and public sector organizations. Moreover, he saw lean as advancing the dispersal and integration of new and information technologies around the system that was a highly defining feature of lean, namely the 'second age of information technology' (Smith, 2000: 13). Thus lean could deliver considerably higher levels of productivity, quality and product innovation (Smith, 2000: 22–3) than was possible under Fordism.

Furthermore, however we define 'skill', Smith confidently cited evidence in favour of new skills for certain categories of worker. If commodity production is carried out in divided labour markets (skilled–less skilled work), lean reinforces this characteristic by considerably *reducing the condition of labour for many* while also *creating a core of more highly skilled workers* experiencing better labour conditions. What is more, whatever may be the socioeconomic differences between skilled and less skilled workers, the myriad negative outcomes associated with lean management processes *generally speaking* reinforce the conflict at the heart of workplace relations between managers and workers. Specifically, for Smith, lean recreates and sustains three inherent, antagonistic features of the capital–labour relationship: structural coercion, exploitation and the real subsumption of labour.

Nonetheless, while Smith's assessment and critique offers a radical view by taking lean to be a distinctive feature of the political economy with very specific effects on labour and employment, others dispute the very notion that lean represents a break with the past. Some have argued that frequently our assessment of lean relies too heavily on what its advocates claim. The result is that researchers may overestimate its actual uniqueness and thus scope for solving organizational and economic crises.

Thus in the late 1980s when debates began over the meaning of what on occasion are still referred as new management techniques, some researchers argued that lean production was too limited as a way to account for the nature and provenance of the social and technical tools being introduced. (Usually these were seen to comprise JIT, *kaizen, muda* and teamworking. Among the most prominent researchers we can include Berggren (1993, 1995), Kenney and Florida (1991) and Milkman (1991).) This was argued by Williams et al. in the UK 1992a, b, c, 1993). Their argument, derived from a radical tradition in accounting and economics, was that the very term lean production provided an implausible understanding of the nature of new production and management practices, and they challenged the advocates' claims to originality, especially those proffered by Womack et al (1990). For Williams et al., it was Ford's, as opposed to Toyota's, 'lean production' model that was truly revolutionary. The first and major innovation established by Ford, initially at Highland Park between 1909 and 1916, was the ability to strip labour out of the labour process (Williams et al., 1992c: 522). The significant advance was not in the extension of the principles of mass production; rather, innovation was evident in the creation of what Williams et al. described as a 'proto-Japanese' (ibid.: 519) factory. It was with this factory regime that Ford really established the foundations of new production arrangements, the lessons of which were lost over the next 40 or so years, only to be rediscovered by Toyota in the 1950s (ibid.: 546).

The meaning of 'lean': society and ideology

While the above two sections outline the debate about lean production with respect to key advocates and critics, there is another set of issues concerning the politics and consequences of what is termed lean production for society more broadly. From this perspective, it is necessary to recognize the extent to which lean production can be understood as an ideology promoting claims to workplace innovation whether or not these are wrapped in the cloak of a 'lean enthusiast'. The most significant of lean's current evangelists in the UK is Radnor (see Radnor et al., 2012; Radnor and Boaden, 2008; Radnor and Johnston, 2013) who, together with a range of associates affiliated to universities and management consultancies, promote the verities of lean essentially as a set of *soi-disant* change practices designed to save organizations time and money. A combination of technical change is allied to not always defined, let alone proven, management practices that squeeze out pluralism and independent actor-trade union actions that are not linked to the rhythm and tempo of the organization's needs. While not an old form of unitarism the objectives are socially quite similar, relying heavily upon a specific form of ideological hegemony typically described as something like 'continual culture change'. The sectors offered advice extend from the currently moribund UK university sector through to local government, the National Health Service and the Scottish government (Radnor et al., 2006). Evidence of change is hard to define and usually described as ongoing where the positive views of expert witnesses are frequently drawn from those within determinate hierarchies committed to the pre-existing ideology of 'lean-as-good'.

What we might describe as the 'lean ideology' promotes the belief that there is 'one best way' to improve performance, productivity and work organization: this will of necessity depend principally upon JIT, *kaizen*, teamworking and a form of employee involvement that negates independent worker representation such as trade unions in a variety of ways (Stephenson, 1995). For example, management may neutralize a trade union's workplace agenda by tying it up in workplace practices – such as agreeing to sanction the election of team leaders; by excluding them entirely from the company; or, where unions are accepted, by tying them into the company belief system as happened in high-profile cases such as Nissan UK in the 1980s and the American UAW in NUMMI in Fremont, California. There have been, it is important to note, a range of interesting examples where trade unions, while being unable to block the introduction of lean practices, were able to continually challenge management and its lean imperatives. Arguably the most powerful trade union response to lean production can be witnessed in the celebrated example of CAMI (a joint venture between Suzuki and GM in Canada) where the Canadian Auto Workers (CAW) successfully intervened in the implementation of lean production strategies (CAW, 1990; Rinehart et al., 1997, see also Stephenson, 1995 and Stewart et al., 2019).

In other words, while management and management consultants approach workplace change in an ideological fashion, what they are describing, advocating and implementing has very particular consequences even if the account they provide of what it is they are introducing is open to question. The ideology reflects while reinforcing material changes. Many of these changes can be seen to be central to the operation of what has come to be termed lean production.

However, this is where the question about the nature of lean production becomes even more interesting: the advocates of lean miss the point about what it is that lean represents in their account of workplace and management change. How might we better explain the evident changes highlighted in a range of studies which point to the negative features of lean production? A second closely related question the advocates ignore is, 'Who are the main beneficiaries of these changes to work?' Finally, they also ignore the question, 'What is the link between lean production and neoliberalism today?' We can take these three questions together.

Smith's argument is important since he links together structural coercion, exploitation and the real subordination of employees. This trio of factors belies the rhetorical win–win world of lean production. Also, one of the questions we should explore more fully is his view that lean is a more advanced capitalist management approach. We can say that for many in management it is an undoubted advance to be able to micro-manage the production process, and this of course includes the ability to tie labour into the companies' nostrums about work and organization: the company man or woman following the 'one best way' and 'working smarter not harder'. However, we also now understand much more about the wider social, economic and ecological inefficiencies attendant on the introduction of lean. Lean production may be more efficient for one or other company, but we also know that it is not only at the expense of workers who carry the cost in terms of the squeeze on their own personal and family time (let us not forget too that many managers also suffer from the pressure to perform lean's sometimes punishing work schedules). Specifically, as argued by Smith, structural coercion, exploitation and the real subordination of labour are at the root of lean production across the political economy within and beyond the realm of commodity production (see below Martin, 2017; 2018).

The importance of lean for neoliberals and 'lean capitalists' cannot be overstated: for them it has achieved iconic status. It is taken to represent everything that is the opposite of what they see as the downside of so-called Fordism. For advocates of lean, capital (the employer) in the old system of Fordism bears disproportionate costs in what the employer takes to be high wage rates encompassing good pay and conditions, including pension provision. Under Fordism, the immediate costs of injury and early exit are in the main borne by the employer, the state and the worker by means of the social wage (welfare state provision including a sound deferred wage-pension). However, with early exit increasingly a feature of ever more pressurized work under lean production, the state, as opposed to the employer, bears more of the burden of health and social care and notably where the worker permanently exits employment. In the society dominated by lean production, the employer and advocates of lean within governments committed to commodification of ever increasing spaces of social welfare, argue that it is insufficient to assume that this burden will continue to be met through the social wage and especially since from their perspective it is certainly not up to the employer to pay. 'We', the workers, must pay not only financially but physically and emotionally as well. Pay with our physical and emotional health. This is a crucial point of principle for those committed (lean evangelists) to the view that others (not the immediate employer) should bear the cost of the new world of lean production. Yet with a rise in early retirement in many sectors and the acceleration in the concentration of private as against social wealth characterizing the political economy of the contemporary neoliberal society, it has to be asked whether this is fair. In other words, the discussion about the nature of lean-in-the-workplace very quickly becomes a discussion about the relationships between work, employment and the wider social context. Thus, does 'lean working' presuppose the 'lean society'? We leave this question for discussion since it is one thing to argue that lean management strategies are being implemented across society and quite another large step to argue we live in a 'lean society' à la Durand (2019). If we are living in the lean society, is this an even more intensive variant of capitalism? If this is so, could one argue that it is in fact a new type of capitalism?

A new type of society or not, nevertheless we can recognize the invasion of lean working methods (we might even refer to it as 'lean politics') throughout society. Consider for a moment that the costs of reproduction in the lean political economy are carried largely by workers when they are in work (see the case study and the impact on health and welfare). Employers' additional costs can be eliminated with early job exits. After employment, early retirement costs owing to injury or an inability to cope with the pressure of lean working routines means that costs are increasingly carried by the state and its agencies – costs, moreover, which lean neoliberal capital and its supporters in government seek to reduce with ever more stringent regulations for unemployment and disability benefit. Martin (2018), a critical labour studies scholar and a critical Marxist, is concerned with the lean character of work and labour relations for state employees who are amongst the latest to be hit by lean's long march through the various sectors of the economy. These employees work in local government and health and social care, and they are also now finding that lean management practices are being introduced into their workplaces either as part of the process of commodification or as vital in the drive to introduce proxy forms of commodification aimed at reducing labour and technical costs. Correspondingly lean will for sure always accompany, usually implicitly, an attack upon workplace pluralism. Martin (2017, 2018) places his examination in the intersection between the politics and ideology of the neoliberal state and lean production *within* the state, and this is important. State employees who themselves are being made to work under lean management regimes are increasingly 'working', as part of their labour process, with those workers who are the inevitable casualties of the paradigm of lean production, or 'management by stress' (Parker and Slaughter, 1988). Being pushed out of employment too early is certainly not a problem for a system designed to seek and eliminate weakness in production. It is, of course, a problem for those workers forced out (too soon) and for those other workers who have themselves to cope with the consequences of this aspect of economic exclusion in their role as state employees. As Mackenzie et al. (2020) point out, the governmentality of lean subordination does not go unchallenged by employees in myriad ways.

So, what kinds of working conditions can lead to circumstances which employees may find increasingly intolerable?

Excerpts from a study of automotive assembly plants in Poland and the UK made by a team of shopfloor workers and academics using a research technique known as Participatory Action Research (PAR) can be used to shed light on questions of the impact of lean on workers. The study comprised four facilities; however, due to constraints of space the excerpt references three: BMW-UK, General Motors-Poland and VW Poland. The study describes what may be termed a 'New Regime of Subordination'. Another feature of this landmark study is that unlike much pro-lean production research, the study is based upon long-term engagement with shopfloor workers, taking into account the views and experiences workers have of lean over a 20-year period mostly in the UK.

Case study: Ideology and practice of lean production in automotive assembly in Poland and the UK

This is an excerpt taken from Stewart et al. (2016) UK. The article reports on research carried out by a network of academic researchers and shopfloor workers. The UK team in the network used a version of PAR over a period of nearly two decades exploring the impact of lean production on assembly workers.

Bullying at work

In all four plants, stress and ill-health patterns were subject to a vicious circle in a context of work-place cultures of managerial discipline and in some cases bullying. Various interviewees provided their own anecdotal experiences of bullying and harassment by managers more often than not related to failure to keep up with the work pace, or with defects or machine downtime problems. While such incidents, normally involving public reprimand, could be demeaning and humiliating the climate of fear was underpinned by the constant threat of disciplinary procedures. For example:

> People do jobs where they shouldn't do but they do it because they want an easy life, they don't want to get into trouble, they don't want to be troublemakers but they do things over and above the minimum. [. . .] Eduardo a friend of ours [. . .] must fit 40 or 50 grommets on each car each hour a day. So he's doing 40 grommets times 54 times ten hours a day. He missed one grommet and they wanted to discipline him. (Assembly operator, BMW-UK)

[and]

> [A] couple of years back I injured my shoulder in the plant. I was off for months [. . .]. I had a really intimidating sort of like term of absence review. I was called in to face two managers – normally it's just the one manager. Basically it was a case of bullying. (Body plant, production operator, BMW-UK)

These experiences were echoed in the survey results. Analysis of questions related to company sickness and absence procedure showed that overall, 73 per cent of an aggregate of workers in the four plants felt pressurized into coming to work when unwell, 80 per cent felt pressurized into returning to work soon after illness and 86 per cent felt managers were more interested in productivity than the reasons given for sickness.

Management bullying was reported by GM-Poland workers: 47 per cent of GM-Poland workers (26.2 per cent of the VW-Poland workers) said that they experienced some form of bullying. They linked this to the specificity of the production system which for the sake of meeting production targets compromised physical and psychological well-being:

> I can say for sure that this plant is oriented to the highest profits. Managers don't even care about quality [. . .]. I mean that a worker in this plant is humiliated by low salary, large workload (maximum exploitation) and it would be best if he doesn't speak and works for a bowl of rice. (GM-Poland, general assembly, R76)

Although interviews at VW-Poland did not reveal a high degree of management pressure and bullying, a different picture emerged from an open question in the questionnaire in which

(Continued)

workers could anonymously raise their concerns about various forms of bullying. [. . .] Here are some examples:

> Unjustified criticism, frequent suggestions that 'if you don't like it, leave the job', spreading gossip, sarcasm, unclear orders, lack of equal treatment (pay raise, bonus). (VW-Poland, assembly, R41)

Questions

1. What would you see as the major problems emerging from this new regime of production?
2. Why do you think these problems are likely to emerge?
3. What changes does lean impose in terms of management–worker relations as outlined by the discussion on bullying?
4. In what ways can the experiences recorded in the case study be related to management ideology?

Conclusion

This chapter has considered the three main approaches to understanding the concept of lean production. In the first approach, we examined the claims by those who see lean as in some sense representing a revolutionary break, beginning in the late 1980s, from previous approaches to work often described as Fordist. The advocates here include managers, management consultants and a range of pro-management academics. The ideological nature of this view was examined. However, there is also a much more critical current within this approach of lean-as-revolutionary that, while arguing for its innovation and greater efficiency, sees it as having a downside for many workers. In this second approach, a range of critics argue that lean production is to all intents and purposes not in the least revolutionary: more a case of old wine in new bottles. The third approach argues that while there is something useful to be had in the use of the term lean production, the term itself does not allow for an adequate account of the origins of what is termed lean production nor of what 'lean production' does especially to people at work. To understand what 'lean' is, the protagonists of the third approach argue that the best way to interpret lean is to hold up the claims of its advocates to the light of empirical enquiry. Our case study illustrates an attempt to do just this. The essential claims of the proponents of lean – the 'leanistas' – are: lean is more efficient for everyone; it is more democratic and participatory; in allowing people to work 'smarter not harder' it reduces workplace stress and pressure while increasing empowerment. However, to what extent might the empirical evidence of studies of worker experiences from different sectors suggest that far from the benign workplace regime delivering the empowerment its advocates claim, lean is in fact a new form of 'class struggle from above' assisting, and thereby extending, existing workplace regimes of subordination. Perhaps lean is the new means by which the employer seeks to take control of the shopfloor and workplace more broadly. Does this mean that, in response, greater employee control of society should be a necessary next step? Although the case study does not seek to answer this question, it is certainly a reasonable one to contemplate.

It is possible to argue that lean represents an evolution of existing means by which the workplace and other forms of social organization are coordinated. Moreover, related to its origins in capitalist production techniques, its principal role is to reduce costs, principally those involving human labour. Lean firms and lean work strategies as confirmed by management-academic consultants are therefore concerned with taking labour out of production, reducing management defined labour (and other) inefficiencies. Thus, despite the rhetoric from advocates of lean that it represents a win–win strategy, in fact management and capital are the ultimate beneficiaries. Consequently, cost is displaced onto others and the wider society, which bear the burden in terms of unemployment, employee injury and social and material waste.

This is the backdrop to a febrile environment: continual change, continual uncertainty where lean is a critical ingredient. Lean, as we have argued elsewhere, is a response to and a generator of socioeconomic turbulence. (See our argument in Stewart et al. (2019) which draws from Benanav's (2019) argument on contemporary changes to global capitalism.) The elephant in the room? Consultants are well aware of turbulence – they promote it with the mantra that constant change is desirable. While one world, the world of actually existing humans, promotes global summits to address the socioeconomic and environmental problems of over-consumption, in the parallel world of lean propagandists the issue should not be defined as *over*-consumption per se. Rather *plus*-consumption is how we should better understand development and change.

Thus, by overlooking the fact of lean's broader social inefficiencies, its advocates ignore the wider costs to our world of ever-faster conception-to-execution rates as firms chase the next exciting product. JIT and *kanban* stock control make it possible to enact swift changes that develop and market another product line almost before the previous one has been amortized (costs realized). Never mind the terrifying environmental costs of the mountain of waste created by the seemingly endless drive to find the next new product winner. In other words, while lean has achieved much for the owners of successful companies, the often-great cost to others must be added to the social and economic balance sheet.

It is important that we recognize the social, economic (and political) factors driving lean. These are organizational, workplace and economic changes and they lie at the heart of the political economy of contemporary capitalism. To describe lean production simply as a system of organizational and technical variables is unsustainable. Moreover, we know, following the critical perspectives of researchers such as Alcadipani et al. (2018) and Mackenzie et al. (2020) that the governmentality of the repressive social technology known as lean is not simply accepted by people, that – appearances notwithstanding – employees everywhere themselves challenge the taken-for-granted verities of lean production, if not collectively, then for sure individually.

Reflective questions

1. Outline the three main ways in which lean production can be understood. You should also distinguish the variations within approaches one and three.
2. Is lean production an ideology of work put forward by management or is it actually a new form of work? Or is it both? What is meant by the term 'leanistas' – who are they? Another way to look at the question is to consider whether lean is just a new way of describing the ongoing intensification of existing management practices.
3. Referring to the case study, consider how the authors address at least two assumptions of those who advocate the supposed benefits of lean production: lean work is good for you and lean leads to better workplaces.
4. What are the differences in perspective between those who see lean production as being just concerned with new forms of work unconnected with wider society, and those who see in lean the basis of a new type of society embracing our lives beyond the world of work?

Recommended reading

- Kenney, M. and Florida, R. (1991) 'Transplanted organisations: The transfer of Japanese industrial organization to the US'. *American Sociological Review*, 56: 381–98.
- Mackenzie, E., McGovern, T., Small, A., Hicks, C. and Scurry, T. (2020) '"Are they out to get us?" Power and the "recognition" of the subject through a "lean" work regime'. *Organization Studies*, 42(11): 1721–40.
- Martin, D. (2017) 'Making tax and social security decisions: lean and deskilling in the UK Civil Service'. *New Technology, Work and Employment*, 32(2): 146–59.
- Stewart, P., Mrozowicki, A., Danford, D. and Murphy, K. (2016) 'Lean as ideology and practice: A comparative study of the impact of lean production on working life in automotive manufacturing in the United Kingdom and Poland'. *Competition and Change*, 20(3): 147–65.
- Stewart, P., Richardson, M., Danford, A., Murphy, K., Richardson, T. and Wass, V. (2009) *We Sell Our Time No More. Workers' Struggles Against Lean Production in the British Car Industry.* London: Pluto Press.

References

Ackroyd, S., Burrell, G., Hughes, H. and Whitaker, A. (1988) 'The Japanisation of British industry?' *Industrial Relations Journal*, 19(1): 11–23.

Alcadipani, A., Hassard, J. and Islam, G. (2018) '"I shot the Sheriff": Irony, sarcasm and the changing nature of workplace resistance'. *Journal of Management Studies*, 55(8): 1452–487.

Bancarzewski, M. (2015) *Japanese Foreign Direct Investment: varieties of capitalism, employment practices and worker resistance in Poland*. Phd University of Hertfordshire.

Benanav, A. (2019) 'Automation and the future of work'. *New Left Review*, 119: 5–38.

Berggren, C. (1993) 'The end of history?' *Work Employment and Society*, 7(2): 163–88.

Berggren, C. (1995) 'Japan as number two: Competitive problems and the future of alliance capitalism after the burst of the bubble economy'. *Work, Employment and Society*, 9(1): 53–95.

Boyer, R. and Freyssenet, M. (2000) *The Productive Models: The Conditions of Profitability*. Basingstoke: Palgrave-Macmillan.

Brenner, M., Fairris, D. and Ruser, J. (2004) '"Flexible" work practices and occupational safety and health: exploring the relationship between cumulative trauma disorders and workplace transformation'. *Industrial Relations*, 43: 242–66.

CAW (1990) *Workplace Issues, Work Reorganisation: Responding to Lean Producton*. Willowfield: CAW Research and Communications Departments.

Charron, E. and Stewart, P. (eds) (2004) *Work and Employment Relations in the Automobile Industry*. Basingstoke: Palgrave Macmillan.

Coffey, D. (2006) *The Myth of Japanese Efficiency: The World Car Industry in a Globalizing Age*. Cheltenham: Edward Elgar.

Durand, J.-P. (2007) *The Invisible Chain: Constraints and Opportunities in the New World of Employment*. Basingstoke: Palgrave Macmillan.

Durand, J.-P. (2019) *Creating the New Worker: Work, Consumption and Subordination*. Basingstoke: Palgrave Macmillan.

Elger, T. and Smith, C. (1994) *Global Japanization: The Transformation of the Labour Process*. London: Routledge.

Employee Relations (1998) Special issue. *Employee Relations*, 20(3).

Fucini, J. and Fucini, S. (1990) *Working for the Japanese*. New York: Free Press.

Garrahan, P. and Stewart, P. (1992) *The Nissan Enigma: Flexibility and Work in a Local Economy*. London: Mansell.

GERPISA (1993) 'Trajectories of automobile firms'. *In Proceedings of the Group for the Study of the Auto Industry and its Employees*. Paris: University d'Evry-Val d'Essone.

Graham, L. (1995) *On the line at Subaru-Isuzu: The Japanese model and the American Worker*. Ithaca, NY: ILR/Cornell University Press.

Hirst, P. and Zeitlin, J. (1991) 'Flexible specialisation versus post-Fordism: Theory, evidence and policy implications'. *Economy and Society*, 20(1): 1–56.

Humphrey, J. (1995) 'The adoption of Japanese management techniques in Brazilian industry'. *Journal of Management Studies*, 32(6): 767–87.

Jones, D. (1992) *Lean Production (An Update)*. Paper presented to the Lean Production and European Trade Union Co-operation, TGWU Centre, 6–11 December, Eastbourne, UK.

JMS (1995) Special issue. *Journal of Management Studies*, 32(6).

Jurgens, U. and Krzywdzinski, M. (2016) *New Worlds of Work. Varieties of Work in Car Factories in the BRIC Countries*. Oxford: Oxford University Press.

Jurgens, U., Malsch, T. and Dohse, K. (1993) *Breaking from Taylorism: Changing Forms of Work in the Automobile Industry*. Cambridge: Cambridge University Press.

Kenney, M. and Florida, R. (1991) 'Transplanted organisations: The transfer of Japanese industrial organization to the US'. *American Sociological Review*, 56: 381–98.

Kenney, M. and Florida, R. (1993) *Beyond Mass Production: The Japanese System and Its Transfer to the US*. Oxford: Oxford University Press.

Mackenzie, E., McGovern, T., Small, A., Hicks, C. and Scurry, T. (2020) '"Are they out to get us?" Power and the "recognition" of the subject through a "lean" work regime'. *Organization Studies*, 42(11): 1721–40.

Martin, D. (2017) 'Making tax and social security decisions: Lean and deskilling in the UK Civil Service. *New Technology, Work and Employment*, 32(2): 146–59.

Martin, D. (2018) 'Lean in a cold fiscal climate: The public sector in an age of reduced resources'. *Public Money and Management*, 38(1): 29–36.

Milkman, R. (1991) *Japan's Californian Factories – Labour Relations and Economic Globalisation*. Los Angeles: Institute of Industrial Relations, University of California.

Miliband, R. (1989) *Divided Societies: Class Struggle in Contemporary Capitalism*. Oxford: Oxford University Press.

Oliver, N. (1991) 'The dynamics of just-in-time'. *New Technology, Work and Employment*, 6(1): 19–27.

Oliver, N. and Wilkinson, B. [1988] 1992) *The Japanization of British Industry: New Developments in the 1990s*, 2nd edn. London: Blackwell.

Oliver, N., Delbridge, R., Jones, D. and Lowe, J. (1993) *World Class Manufacturing: Further Evidence in the Lean Production Debate*. Paper presented to the British Academy of Management Conference, September, Milton Keynes, UK.

Oliver, N., Jones, D., Delbridge, R. and Lowe, J. (1994) *Worldwide Manufacturing Competitiveness Study: The Second Lean Enterprise Report*. Andersen Consulting.

Parker, M. and Slaughter, J. (1988) *Choosing Sides: Unions and the Team Concept*. Boston: South End Press.

Radnor, Z. J. and Boaden, R. (2008) 'Editorial: Lean in the public services: Panacea or paradox?' *Public Money and Management*, 28(1): 3–7.

Radnor, Z. and Johnston, R. (2013) 'Lean in UK Government: internal efficiency or customer service?'. *Production Planning & Control*, 24(10–11): 903–15.

Radnor, Z. J., Walley, P., Stephens, A. and Bucci, G. (2006) 'Evaluation of the lean approach to business management and its use in the public sector'. *Scottish Executive Social Research*. Available at: http://www.scotland.gov.uk/Publications/2006/06/13162106/0

Radnor, Z., Holweg, M. and Waring, J. (2012) 'Lean healthcare: the unfilled promise?' *Social Science and Medicine*, 74(3): 364–71.

Rinehart, J., Huxley, C. and Robertson, D. (1997) *Just Another Car Factory: Lean Production and Its Discontents*. Ithaca: ILR Press.

Seddon, J. and Caulkin, S. (2007) 'Systems thinking, lean production and action learning'. *Action Learning: Research and Practice*, 4(1): 9–24.

Smith, T. (2000) *Technology and Capital in the Age of Lean Production: A Marxian Critique of the 'New Economy'*. New York: SUNY Press.

Stephenson, C. (1995) 'The different experience of trade unionism in two Japanese transplants'. In P. Acker, C., Smith and P. Smith (eds), *The New Workplace and Trade Unionism*. London: Routledge.

Stewart, P. and Garrahan, P. (1995) 'Employee responses to new management techniques in the auto industry'. *Work, Employment and Society*, 9(3): 517–36.

Stewart, P., Lewchuk, W., Yates, C., Saruta, M. and Danford, A. (2004) 'Patterns of labour control and the erosion of labour standards: Towards an international study of the quality of working life in the automobile industry (Canada, Japan and the UK)'. In E. Charron and P. Stewart (eds), *Work and Employment Relations in the Automobile Industry*. Basingstoke: Palgrave Macmillan.

Stewart, P., Mrozowicki, A., Danford, D. and Murphy, K. (2016) 'Lean as ideology and practice: A comparative study of the impact of lean production on working life in automotive manufacturing in the United Kingdom and Poland'. *Competition and Change*, 20(3): 147–65.

Stewart, P., Pulignano, V. and Mrozowicki, A. (2019) '"Lean production is dead, long live lean production": Lean, neo-liberal crisis, turbulence and the consolidation of regimes of subordination'. *Warsaw Forum of Economic Sociology*, 10(1): 19.

Stewart, P., Richardson, M., Danford, A., Murphy, K., Richardson, T. and Wass, V. (2009) *We Sell Our Time No More. Workers' Struggles Against Lean Production in the British Car Industry*. London: Pluto Press.

Turnbull, P. J. (1986) 'The "Japanisation" of production and industrial relations at Lucas electrical'. *Industrial Relations Journal*, 17(3): 193–206.

Vanguard Consulting (2014) Available at: www.thesystemsthinkingreview.co.uk.

Wilkinson, B., Morris, J. and Mundy, M. (1995) 'The iron fist in the velvet glove: Management and organisation in Japanese manufacturing transplants in Wales'. *Journal of Management Studies*, 32(6): 819–30.

Williams, K., Haslam, C., Williams, J., Cutler, T., Adcroft, A. and Johal, S. (1992a) 'Against lean production'. *Economy and Society*, 21(3): 321–54.

Williams, K., Haslam, C., Adcroft, A. and Johal, S. (1992b) 'Factories or warehouses'. Mimeo.

Williams, K., Haslam, C. and Williams, J. (1992c) '"Ford versus Fordism": The beginning of mass production?' *Work, Employment and Society*, 6(4): 517–55.

Williams, K., Haslam, C., Adcroft, A. and Johal, S. (1993) 'The myth of the line: Ford's production of the Model T at Highland Park, 1909–16'. *Business History*, 35(3): 66–87.

Womack, J. P., Roos, D. and Jones, D. T. (1990) *The Machine that Changed the World*. New York: Rawson Associates.

13 Restructuring, policy and practice: an international comparison of approaches

Christopher J. McLachlan, Robert MacKenzie,
Alexis Rydell, Roland Ahlstrand, Jennifer Hobbins,
Martin O'Brien and Betty Frino

Learning objectives

- To understand the causes and consequences of restructuring on an international level
- To explore the practices, processes and policies adopted to mitigate the effects of restructuring on individuals
- To understand the contextual factors that shape the implementation of restructuring
- To understand the varied national approaches to the regulation of restructuring
- To critically compare government responses to economic crises

Introduction

Organizational restructuring is a persistent feature of modern political economy, with profound implications for employment. Dealing with the employment effects of organizational restructuring is thus a prevalent issue within contemporary international human resource management (IHRM). Restructuring can involve events such as mergers and acquisitions, outsourcing, downsizing and plant closures. Regardless of the form of restructuring, the consequences are often changes in the employment status of individual workers, including layoffs, wage reduction, reduced working hours and termination of employment.

Restructuring often results in redundancies, with serious social, economic, psychological and physiological effects. Research highlights consequences such as poor physical health, emotional and psychological distress, financial hardship, with negative effects on home and family life, and a weakened labour market position including the risk of finding lower-quality employment (Dobbins et al., 2014; Jahoda, 1982). Redundancies have profound social and economic effects on individuals and families, with knock-on effects to local communities (Brand, 2015; de Vries and Balazs, 1997; Donnelly and Scholarios, 1997). Organizational restructuring is therefore a policy issue that must be viewed in the broader context of economic restructuring. Individual incidents of organizational restructuring take on a cumulative effect during times of economic crises, such as the 2008–9 global financial crisis and the 2020 Covid-19 crisis, putting increased pressure on different forms of policy response and support provision for displaced workers. Therefore addressing the effects of restructuring is a critical issue for organizations, stakeholders and policy-makers as reflected in regulatory interventions at various levels and growing interest within broader corporate social responsibility (CSR) agendas.

This chapter addresses the multifaceted aspects of restructuring, reviewing the causes, organisational level perspectives, national and supranational institutional contexts and debates around 'restructuring regimes'. The chapter then builds on the analytical framework of restructuring regimes with reference to three countries: Sweden, the United Kingdom (UK) and Australia. Some critical reflections on comparative national approaches follow, including discussion of the implications of the Covid-19 crisis for national policy responses.

Restructuring: causes and consequences

There are many causes of restructuring with several factors often interacting. Pressure for change has been associated with globalization, shorthand for the increased internationalization of capital, transnational business structures and the expansion of global markets. The investment and divestment decisions of MNCs can have far-reaching consequences, making restructuring a key aspect of contemporary IHRM (see Chapter 1 on globalization and Chapter 2 on multinational corporations (MNCs)). At any level, 'planned changes in organizational structure that affect[s] the use of people' (Cascio, 2012: 336) are typically implemented by management professing to improve the efficiency, productivity and competitiveness of the company, in an effort to achieve greater overall organizational performance. Whether termed 'layoffs', 'downsizing' or 'redundancies', a common characteristic of such restructuring is making employees' jobs redundant. The basic economic rationale for employers is that it is easier to control future costs than future revenues (Wilkinson, 2005), with employment costs viewed as the primary means to achieve this. As a result, employees and their associated costs – wages, pensions, overtime or bonuses – are typically the first to be cut when costs need reducing. Critics have argued that the notion restructuring improves organizational performance is generally accepted among managers as the dominant normative schema for tackling cost reduction (McKinley et al., 2000): restructurings are legitimized as part of organizational life and viewed as the primary response to poor economic climates and recessionary pressures (McKinley et al., 2000). Furthermore, the deregulation of global capital markets and internationalization of accounting rules facilitating global private equity buyouts are driving management more than ever to prioritize maximising shareholder value by cost-cutting through lay-offs and outsourcing (Cushen and Thompson, 2016).

There is no empirical consensus as to whether restructuring achieves its desired goals of efficiency, productivity and competitiveness. Restructuring has been associated with jumps in share prices, based on assumptions of cost-cutting and efficiencies generating productivity improvements and profitability. However, gains tend to be short-lived as stock prices stabilize over time (Hallock, 2009) and firms that intended to appear 'lean and mean' could end up 'lean and lame' through the loss of skilled personnel necessary to grasp new business opportunities (Guthrie and Datta, 2008). Restructuring has therefore been found to have an equivocal impact on subsequent organizational performance (Guthrie and Datta, 2008). Moreover, restructuring can harm firms if implementation lacks a strategic focus on humanizing motivational practices for employees that remain (Cregan et al., 2020).

People made redundant through restructuring have been characterized as 'victims', in contrast to 'survivors' who retain their jobs (Brockner, 1988; de Vries and Balazs, 1997) or 'endurers', who face job displacement and internal redeployment (McLachlan et al., 2021). Brockner (1988) highlights the dangers of 'survivors' syndrome', referring to negative work-related attitudes leading to lower employee morale and productivity due to fears over job insecurity, distrust towards management and work intensification. In turn, for endurers, the experience of redeployment heightens their reliance on the efficacy of the management of restructuring: and both survivors and endurers may perceive restructuring as a violation of the psychological contract (McLachlan et al., 2021).

For 'victims', the stigmatization of redundant workers can be an obstacle to finding new employment, with some firms being wary of hiring 'labour market lemons' unwanted by their previous employers (Turnbull and Wass, 1997). Displaced workers may also suffer career 'scarring', meaning that even those returning to full-time employment carry long-term effects in terms of disruption to career advancement and overall lifetime earnings (Fervers, 2019). Research suggests older workers and women are disproportionately disadvantaged when it comes to labour market transition following redundancy, in terms of access to new jobs or the threat of occupational downgrading (Gonäs and Tyrkkö, 2015; Jolkkonen et al., 2018; Oesch and Baumann, 2015). Such experiences have led to growing interest in some policy circles, notably Sweden, in the issue of developing 'sustainable working lives' for individuals affected by redundancy.

Contextual factors that shape restructuring

Recognition of the effects of restructuring on displaced workers has generated a concern for understanding the support available. The processes and practices organizations implement to ameliorate the effects of redundancy are central to the burgeoning debates around 'socially responsible restructuring' (SRR) (Ahlstrand, 2010; Bergström and Diedrich, 2011; Cascio, 2002; Rydell and Wigblad, 2012). In restructuring involving mass layoffs, it is common that stakeholders such as employees, unions, local authorities and politicians pressurize companies to assume social responsibility when dealing with the impact of restructuring. SRR may therefore reflect broader commitments to a CSR agenda, in which firms engage in 'actions that appear to further some social good, beyond the interest of the firm and that which is required by law' (McWilliams and Siegel, 2001: 117; see also Chapter 18 on sustainability and IHRM).

Why would companies voluntarily act in ways that may be considered 'socially responsible'? The evident negative effects job losses have on individuals and communities should provide an ethical case compelling management to mitigate the adverse effects of restructuring. However, mass lay-offs typically attract media and government attention, creating an external pressure on management to act in the public interest and limit potential reputational damage. For instance, the approach taken by multinational telecom company Ericsson's to its plant closure in Norrköping, Sweden, at the beginning of the 2000s (Ahlstrand, 2010) was based on its desire to maintain its reputation by taking into consideration prevailing societal expectations regarding the company's behaviour. Similarly, such external pressures compelled a change in approach in the MNC Chrysler's plant closing in Kenosha, Wisconsin, in 1987 (McMahon, 1999). An initial judgement of 'irresponsibility' from local government officials was reversed after the company changed its downsizing strategy to enact due process, which facilitated a plan to improve local labour market opportunities for those affected. Therefore external pressure, including negative media coverage, may harm the company brand, which in turn can lead to market share losses and decreased profits. Acting 'morally correct' to ease the pain caused by restructuring is not the only factor shaping being 'socially responsible'.

SRR is manifest in going beyond statutory requirements in areas including the advance notice and consultation with employees and other stakeholders, the employment transition support for affected individuals (such as retraining, possibilities for redeployment within the organization, generous packages for voluntary redundancy and early retirement), plus, potentially, compensation for local communities.

In common with CSR, what is considered as SRR is shaped by national and institutional settings (Bergström and Diedrich, 2011). Therefore, 'minimum compliance' in terms of going just beyond statutory requirements remains a key critique of socially responsible approaches to restructuring. Compliance issues become even more problematic where compulsion relies on soft regulation such as codes of conduct. The European Commission and International Labour Organisation have outlined explicit goals aimed at protecting displaced workers from downturns and economic crises. However, as noted, without the backing of regulatory mechanisms with the 'bite' to compel compliance, adherence to such codes remain voluntaristic (see Chapter 16 on regulation).

At a national level, the basic obligations for organizations in cases of restructuring are regulated by combinations of law and collective agreements. Approaches to restructuring therefore vary by institutional contexts, creating different options and constraints that shape decision-making (see Chapter 3 on industrial relations systems). There are key differences in collective bargaining practices, constraints on industrial action, information and consultation processes, advance notice periods, severance pay and employment protection regulation. For instance, the United States regulates advance notice through the Worker Adjustment and Retraining Notification (WARN) Act of 1988, which states that companies must notify employees at least 60 days in advance if the restructuring event involves more than 100 job losses. Notably, the United States is a country where managerial prerogative usually is unchallenged and, with some statutory exemptions, 'contract at will' employment allows employers to dismiss employees without warning or justification. A similar restructuring event involving more than 100 job losses in Sweden would legally require at least six months' advance notice to the public employment service office. Similar variation can be found in short-time working (STW) schemes, where firms experiencing economic difficulties temporarily reduce the hours worked while their employees receive income support for the hours not worked. In Germany and Sweden STW is underpinned by law and collective agreement, while in the UK STW is traditionally left to ad hoc arrangements at the company level.

Variations in institutional context are also reflected in the nature of support offered to displaced workers and, crucially, the actors involved in supplying such support. Although support for job searching historically tended to be the role of state employment services, there has been a notable trend towards the privatization of support in many countries and the increased involvement of private sector providers. Combinations of statutory regulation and collective agreements underpin a variety of approaches to support for displaced workers in terms of basic job searching, career counselling and retraining. The level and availability of support thus also varies. As seen below, Sweden is characterized by a more extensive availability of advanced transition support mechanisms, underpinned by collective agreements covering the majority of the workforce. The UK by contrast reflects a more ad hoc approach, with advanced transition support mechanisms being available on a less extensive basis, often underpinned by joint regulation but reflecting the lower levels of union density and coverage of collective agreements compared to Sweden.

Trade unions can therefore play a crucial role in shaping restructuring processes and employee outcomes. The degree of union influence and crucially the balance between consultation and negotiation varies by context, both national and sectoral. Unions adopt a range of strategies towards restructuring, from attempts to resist restructuring to engaging with management to mitigate effects on employees through employment transition support (Pulignano and Stewart, 2013). The picture is more complex in the case of MNCs: restructuring decisions may be made by top management in another country, limiting the influence of national-based unions in host-country subsidiaries. In cases of 'regime shopping', when MNCs move facilities to countries with less restrictive institutional arrangements and cheaper labour costs, the solidarity between unions is particularly imperative (see Chapter 2 on MNCs and Chapter 17 on international employee representation).

The internationalization of capital reflected in the investment and divestment activities of MNCs poses similar challenges for national-level regulation. Therefore, in addition to national regulatory contexts, supranational bodies have taken an increasing interest in the regulation of restructuring. Ensuring continued employment for employees affected by restructuring has been an explicit goal of, for instance, the International Labour Organization (ILO), the European Commission and the European Union (EU; see Chapter 16 on regulation). In 2009, the ILO, with the participation of government, employers' and workers' delegates from member states, adopted the 'Global Jobs Pact', a policy instrument to reduce the time lag between economic recovery and decent work opportunities following the global financial crisis of 2008–9. At a European level, the EU set up the European Globalisation Adjustment Fund (EGF) in 2006, to offer funding to support people losing their jobs in cases of major structural changes in world trade patterns due to globalization (Stuart et al., 2007). The longer-standing European Social Fund (ESF) was created via the Treaty of Rome (1957) to mitigate the consequences of economic crises, and create a more inclusive society and fairer life opportunities. The ESF not only provides support with job searching but also careers advice, education, training, mentoring, and coaching for entrepreneurship and business creations.

Restructuring regimes

Despite the role of supranational bodies, the key locus of regulation remains at the national level. One way of conceptualizing national variations in approaches to restructuring and support for displaced workers is through the 'regimes of restructuring' framework (Gazier, 2008), understood 'as the combination of adjustment mechanisms and measures controlled or adopted by a particular group of actors' (Bergström, 2019: 97). Regimes are based on governance mechanisms related to labour market regulation and expenditure, leading to the identification of three ideal types: *market-oriented* approaches, in which employers and employees are the key actors; *negotiated* approaches, which involve employers' associations and trade unions; and *state-administered* approaches, based on government agencies and authorities. Through these actors different forms of adjustment measures are implemented: 'wage and labour cost adjustments', which avoid or limit redundancies by reducing wages or postponing wage increases; 'quantitative adjustments', which limit or reduce the supply of labour through redundancies, early retirement and STW; and 'qualitative adjustments', which rely on the provision of training and education for displaced workers (Bergström, 2019).

National regimes are categorized according to their dominant approach to restructurings, although this does not preclude the possibility of the coexistence of adjustment mechanisms within national regimes (Bergström, 2019). For instance, countries such as Sweden and the Netherlands have been categorized as *negotiated* regimes, focused on qualitative adjustments, and skills development to promote job-to-job transitions. However, this does not exclude the possibility of support from the state or using quantitative adjustment mechanisms such as STW schemes. The UK, the Czech Republic, Bulgaria and Slovenia are considered *market-oriented* regimes, focused on reductions in labour costs, mainly by wage cuts and wage freezes. There are, however, overlaps between quantitative mechanisms. Some UK companies have agreed working-time reductions (effectively STW without wage compensation). In Bulgaria, the Czech Republic and Slovenia governments have introduced publicly funded STW schemes. In Sweden, STW schemes are coordinated and funded by the social partners (with provision for state funding at times of economic crisis).

Below, the restructuring regimes of Sweden, the UK and Australia are explored in detail. The section examines the role of the state and other key actors, the varying quantitative and qualitative adjustment mechanisms utilized and contrasts the overall characteristics of the respective regimes (see Chapter 11 on varieties of capitalism).

Sweden

The Swedish restructuring regime is characterized as negotiation-oriented, anchored in the law on collective agreements from 1928 and the 'Saltsjöbaden Agreement' from 1938, when the social partners agreed that labour relations should be carried out through collaboration and agreed rules of industrial action.

The state usually plays a passive role in company restructuring, leaving its coordination up to regions, local community, unions and management.

Following the 2008–9 financial crisis, there was evidence of company-level STW schemes that were based on collective agreements and funded by the social partners. In 2013, legislation set out a more interventionist approach from the state, directly funding STW schemes when 'particularly deep downturns' are imminent, due to broader economic crisis. The state pays a part of employees' wages to compensate for reduced working hours, in order to save jobs, avoid bankruptcies and to sustain viable companies during and after economic crises. These changes in state support reflect a proactive approach based on lessons learned from the 2008–9 financial crisis, but also indicate a slide towards more quantitative adjustments.

Collective bargaining is central to the regulation of dismissals in restructuring processes and implementing adjustment mechanisms, mainly qualitative adjustment mechanisms. Transition Agreements by which employees get support to find new jobs cover the majority of the Swedish labour market. For instance, employers and unions in the manufacturing industry can apply for grants from *Trygghetsfonden TSL*, an insurance organization founded and financed by the social partners, to receive support in dealing with redundancies. In turn, *Trygghetsfonden TSL*, have agreements with companies offering transition programmes providing job-search training, counselling, competence development and other activities to support the transfer of redundant workers to other jobs. Criteria for participation in collective transitions support varies but typically only cover permanent workers, pointing to a distinction often apparent in terms of the support provided to permanent and temporary workers during and after restructuring processes.

Although collective agreements underpin the process of restructuring, three labour laws also supplement the Swedish regime. For instance, in 1974 the Employment Protection Act (Lagen om anställningsskydd) (LAS) was introduced, which specified, among other things, that in redundancy situations a period of notice must be given of between one and six months, depending on tenure of employment. LAS also prohibits summary dismissal and contains rules on selection criteria, which are semi-compulsory; the main rule is 'last-in-first-out'. Some companies have concluded collective agreements with the unions that extended terms of notice beyond that specified by LAS, up to 12 months for permanent employees with ten years' tenure. The extension highlights the division between the core and peripheral workforce: LAS provides relatively high levels of protection for permanent workers compared to temporary workers. Employers' organizations have been critical of LAS because they claim that it unduly fetters numerical flexibility by narrowing the possibility of quantitative adjustment of workforces due to fluctuations in demand. Currently, the Swedish government is considering increasing flexibility within LAS by, for instance, loosening the 'last-in-first-out' rule to allow companies more freedom in restructuring decisions. Unions have nonetheless contested these proposals, arguing they disproportionately impact older workers and increase job insecurity. In addition, unions have emphasized the role of the social partners and collective agreements in resolving 'last-in-first-out' dilemmas, reflecting a commitment to the traditional negotiated regime.

Emerging from ideas of industrial democracy in the 1970s, The Codetermination Act (Medbestämmandelagen) (MBL) underpins collective agreements that oblige employers to inform and consult trade unions on any important change in the company that can impact employees. MBL also allows unions to influence choice and content of the adjustment mechanisms in restructuring situations. Prior to taking action, employers are required to inform unions of the reasons for the projected redundancies and the number of employees affected. The employer must also provide local unions with the opportunity to examine the financial records, accounts and other documents relating to the business operations. In some cases, unions appoint a wage earner consultant that helps them evaluate management's arguments for the restructuring decision and sometimes provide alternative evaluations or restructuring plans (Olsson, 2004). Hence, MBL opens up a possibility for the unions to have a say with regard to adjustment mechanisms, but no right of veto; management retain the decisive power, resulting in the law being scornfully referred to as a 'honk and drive' regulation.

The Employment Promotion Act of 1974 (Främjandelagen) (FL) stipulates that management have to inform the public employment service in advance in order to enable them to prepare for handling the effects of restructurings including notifications and possible layoffs. The time range of the advance notice varies, from two months up to six months if more than 100 employees are affected. The combined effect of the MBL, LAS and FL regulations means that larger restructuring events involving redundancies seldom take less than six months and not seldom approximately one year or longer, from the public announcement until the final day of operation. This time period is important, not only because of the implications for different kinds of transition programmes for employees, or applications to get state-funded support to STW schemes, but also because it gives local stakeholders the opportunity to plan for attracting replacement industries in order to mitigate adverse effects of the job losses (Rydell and Wigblad, 2012).

UK

The restructuring regime in the UK can be characterized as market-oriented. Adjustment mechanisms have predominantly focused on reductions in labour costs by employers, typically involving wage cuts or freezes for employees. The aftermath of the 2008–9 financial crisis illustrated that large-scale redundancies are also a prevalent feature of the UK's market-oriented regime. Nonetheless there was some investment by social actors (government, trade unions) in qualitative adjustments such as retraining and job search programmes for redundant workers. Other quantitative adjustment mechanisms such as widespread early retirement or STW schemes have not historically been common in the UK, though some firm-level examples do exist.

There are three main pieces of legislation related to restructuring and redundancy. Historically, the *Redundancy Payments Act 1965* was the first piece of legislation that addressed the 'problem' of redundancy, and codified in law the market-oriented focus on restructuring being a private 'problem' between employers and employees. The Act obliged employers to give greater consideration to the implementation of redundancies, and passed some of the costs of redundancy onto employers by setting minimum levels of severance payments. The rationale for this Act has changed little since, and its provisions have been subsumed in the *Employment Rights Act 1996*. The 1996 Act also set criteria for making redundancies, including the employment status of affected individuals eligible for statutory redundancy pay, setting the qualifying period for statutory redundancy pay at two years tenure and the level of redundancy payments dependent on tenure and age. Nonetheless, it is common for severance payments to go beyond the statutory minimum.

The *Trade Union and Labour Relations (Consolidation) Act 1992 (Amendment) Order 2013* establishes the length of consultation periods with potentially affected employees (often through employee representatives such as trade unions or works councils), which again sanctioned restructuring as a private issue to be resolved through a market-oriented approach. The consultation period for employers proposing 100 or more redundancies is 45 days, and 30 days for 20–100 redundancies. The 2013 Amendment Order reduced the consultation period from 90 days and 60 days respectively, following lobbying from employers groups. That said, employers must make prior notification of proposed redundancies to the relevant Secretary of State.

Employers can request assistance with restructuring procedures from the Advisory, Conciliation and Arbitration Service (ACAS), an arm's length state institution that provides advice on employment issues. ACAS Codes of practice on redundancy emphasize legal compliance, the exhaustion of alternatives to redundancy prior to dismissals and consideration of available skills and training provision. Basic procedural information is also provided on consulting with employee representatives, ways to avoid compulsory redundancies and redundancy selection criteria. However, employers' engagement with ACAS when conducting restructuring is voluntary, indicative of the lack of a state-administered approach to the management and anticipation of restructuring.

Despite the largely market-oriented regime, certain institutions within the UK also function as qualitative adjustment mechanisms that assist affected employees. Institutions such as the *Citizens' Advice Bureau* and *Jobcentre Plus* provide support to the unemployed, including workers displaced by restructuring. The *Rapid Response Service (RRS)* represents a restructuring-specific adjustment mechanism and is typically coordinated through Jobcentres. The extent of RRS varies between Scotland, Wales, Northern Ireland and regions of England, and depends on the level of funding from associated agencies and institutions, and was formerly coordinated through *Regional Development Agencies*. The *Education and Skills Funding Agency* also provides government funding to help employees retrain and reskill following redundancy. The latter relies on local partnerships between employers and Higher Education/Further Education institutions for the provision of training, and depends on access to available funding, as the UK's market-oriented regime means there is no codified obligation for employers to engage in such partnerships.

Devolved government in Scotland, Wales and Northern Ireland has facilitated the creation of additional support, much of which reflects more qualitative adjustment mechanisms based on negotiated, stakeholder partnerships between state bodies, trade unions and support agencies. The Welsh Assembly established the *Welsh Government Redundancy Action Scheme (ReAct)*, which offers recruitment and training support for redundant employees and discretionary awards for vocational training. Similarly, the *ProAct* scheme offers funding to employers to provide upskilling for employees during downturns in the business cycle as a type of anticipatory measure. Both *ReAct* and *ProAct* also work in close partnership with *Careers Wales* to deliver this provision.

The engagement of trade unions in this partnership approach has also been key and has reflected elements of a more negotiated approach to the management of restructuring in the UK. For example, *Communitas* (formerly *Steel Partnership Training*), a training provider established by the *Community* union (formerly the *Iron and Steel Trades Confederation*) played a key role in coordinating the 'Team Wales' multi-agency response to restructuring in the Welsh steel industry. In Scotland, the *Partnership Action for Continued Employment (PACE)* is an additional scheme coordinated by Skills Development Scotland, providing counselling on career development and directing redundant workers to access to training. In Northern Ireland, additional partnerships to support redundant workers can be coordinated through the *Labour Relations Agency, Careers Service* and *Citizens' Advice Northern Ireland*. While negotiated approaches between employers, employees and trade unions are not characteristic of the UK's restructuring regime, more decentralized collective bargaining since the 1980s has meant that more quantitative and qualitative adjustments in the management of restructuring can be found at the firm-level.

A more negotiated approach to restructuring based on collective bargaining processes tends to be common in large organizations with a strong union presence or public sector heritage in such sectors as steel, automobile and telecoms. Nonetheless, the role of the state in such a negotiated approach has been largely absent in the UK.

Australia

The restructuring regime in Australia can also be characterized as market-oriented. The freedom and interests of private enterprise is central to restructuring, with the state role largely accommodating employers to shed jobs in times of need, and incentivising other third-party private sector actors to assist the unemployed and create jobs, leaving unions with a minimal role which is diminishing further over time. The issue of restructuring is notionally covered by the *Corporations Act 2001 (Commonwealth)*. However, this legislation is focused more on the administration of bankruptcy and related issues such as receivership, voluntary administration and liquidation. Pertinent issues relating to affected workers are covered within the national employment relations system, consisting of the *Fair Work Act 2009 (Commonwealth)* legislation and rulings of the Fair Work Commission regulator.

The Fair Work Act describes a consultation process that requires employers to notify employees who may be affected by proposed changes, including providing information about the changes and expected effects, discussing steps taken to avoid and minimize negative effects on the employees, and considering employees' suggestions about the changes (Fair Work Ombudsman, 2020). Ultimately, the interests of the employer are paramount and the emphasis within the legislation then shifts to quantitative adjustment and redundancy.

National Employment Standards (NES) within the Fair Work Act define minimum redundancy pay, from four to 16 weeks' wages, and notice periods ranging between one and four weeks, both based on tenure. Some exclusions apply for small businesses, casual workers, independent contractors, apprentices and trainees. As the NES only define the minimal safety net in the national industrial relations system, in practice there are inconsistencies in the application of the consultation process, minimal notice and redundancy pay as many Australian workers are covered by more generous employment agreements negotiated at the industry or enterprise level.

On a voluntary basis, some large employers have assisted redundant employees with sponsoring job fairs, or financial contributions to government employment initiatives. However, as long as employers comply with legislation the responsibility for employees is largely handed over to the state for employment assistance. Public employment assistance services were privatized in the mid 1990s. Potential providers compete for contracts from the state via a tender process and are awarded a percentage of referrals from the public sector social security provider; subsequently, job service providers are paid for defined short- and long-term employment outcomes (Jobs Australia, 2016). However, until 2019, the financial generosity of the redundancy payment affected workers' eligibility for social security, meaning they may have to wait to qualify for referral into the employment assistance system.

In most cases, the role of unions in restructuring is limited. Since the mid-1970s union density in Australia fell from over 50 per cent to less than 15 per cent. However, unions continue to negotiate industry and enterprise level employment agreements. Their role in the restructuring process largely depends on what has been concluded in the agreement. Subsequent strategies they may take on an ad hoc basis include negotiating early retirement and voluntary redundancy options, increasing redundancy payments, negotiating temporary adjustments to pay and conditions to minimize job losses. Negotiating power is shaped by union density in the industry or firm. Apart from potential threats of industrial action, unions are mostly passive in the restructuring process and at the whim of employer actions.

While the majority of restructuring is left to market forces, Australian governments have intervened on an ad hoc basis involving large-scale plant closures or mass redundancies (Beer, 2015). Previous governments have offered financial restructuring packages assisting particular industries to adjust to emerging economic conditions or enterprise assistance ensuring the survival of particular firms. More recently, government reaction has been to allow firms to downsize or exit, with labour market programmes providing additional assistance to the private sector job service provider network, in addition to investment attraction schemes to encourage private sector job creation. These reactive policies tend to be reserved for high-profile cases concentrated in provincial areas and declining industries, such as Mitsubishi in Adelaide (2004) and BlueScope Steel in Wollongong (2011). Tens of millions of dollars of additional assistance to the private sector job service providers have supplied displaced workers with support. In addition, investment attraction schemes provide matched funding to encourage private sector firms to expand or relocate in affected regions and create jobs in diversified industries. The outcomes of these measures in terms of assisting redundant workers, and creating new jobs in local labour markets, have been weak (Anaf et al., 2014; O'Brien and Burrows, 2019). While often announced with much fanfare and pitched by politicians as proactive and worker friendly, in practice these policies have generally been short-sighted, inflexible and lacking in key stakeholder engagement.

Case study: Automotive restructuring in Sweden, the UK and Australia

The Swedish truck manufacturer Scania, owned by German Volkswagen AG, carried out a restructuring programme involving skills development and education for about 5,000 blue-collar workers over 18 months, as a response to the financial crisis in 2008–9. The programme ran concurrently with production, with the workforce rotating between the two on a fortnightly basis. Education was provided in collaboration with municipal adult education and involved core subjects of mathematics, Swedish and English. The programme was combined with several other components. The *Crisis* agreement underpinned a STW scheme based on a four-day workweek at 90 per cent of the original wages. A second agreement, when the crisis agreement expired, involved fewer working hours but without wage reductions. A third component was the decision not to lay off permanent workers, due to the strong job protection written into the pre-existing *Flexibility* agreement. In addition to the 'normal' notice periods of six months, permanent workers had extended notice periods up to a maximum of twelve months. Importantly, the *Flexibility* agreement allowed temporary workers to make up 30 per cent of the workforce, for individual periods of six months. Thus, to make fast cost reductions, Scania did not extend contracts for 1,000 temporary workers. The contracts ended, in some cases, within a couple of weeks.

Japanese multinational car manufacturer Nissan announced in January 2009 that it would be making 1,200 redundancies from its 5,000 strong workforce at its Sunderland plant in the North East of England, UK. Following a slump in global demand, the plant experienced an increasing amount of non-production days along with a plan for fewer shifts in order to reduce oversupply. The trade union, Unite, used the 90-day consultation period to try and minimize the amount of compulsory redundancies through voluntary redundancy and early retirement programmes, while emphasizing the importance of not losing key skills in the region. The Business Secretary Peter Mandelson (Labour Party) said that the government would do everything it could to help the affected workforce. In particular, the Regional Development Agency 'One NorthEast' would assist affected workers in finding alternative employment in the region. One NorthEast coordinated the response by setting up a task force with representatives from Nissan, JobCentre Plus, the Learning and Skills Council, Sunderland Council, Business and Enterprise North East, the Confederation of British Industry and the North East Chamber of Commerce. The task force worked to support affected employees by providing advice on job search, establishing job fairs, careers support, retraining opportunities, updating CVs and interview skills. The job losses at Nissan UK had a heightened political sensitivity given it is one of

(Continued)

the largest employers in the region and was built in the 1980s as a way of addressing one of the areas of the UK worst hit by unemployment.

The US car manufacturer Ford announced a three-year closure programme with 1,200 redundancies at its Australian plants in Geelong and Broadmeadows in 2013, with production ceasing in October 2016. In response to the announcement, Prime Minister Julia Gillard promised AU$39 million of federal and state government support funding (later increasing to AU$67 million). The support was intended to focus on creating new regional employment opportunities via the Geelong Region Innovation and Investment Fund, providing assistance to businesses in the automotive supply chain and helping affected workers via the Geelong Skills and Jobs Centre and private sector job service providers. At the company level, in 2013 the Australian Manufacturing Workers' Union (AMWU), Ford and Auto Skills Australia developed the Ford Transition Project offering one-on-one career counselling to help the hundreds of remaining employees move into the next phase of their working lives. Redundant workers were offered literacy and numeracy classes, transport to job fairs and connection to training opportunities in the industry of their choice. Despite promises from the Labor government at the point of the announcement, the change of federal government in September 2013 to a coalition between Liberals and Nationals undermined commitment to the wider economic adjustment programme. Although AMWU National Official, Dave Smith, described the handling of the closure as a good example of managing redundancy, he was critical of government support: 'Ford and the union have been working together to assist workers in transitioning to new employment but the federal government has done nothing to assist the process.'

Questions

1. Who are the key actors in each of the cases and how do their roles differ?
2. How do the cases illustrate the differing combinations of quantitative and qualitative adjustments?
3. In what ways are the different approaches to restructuring in Sweden, the UK and Australia evident in these cases?

Critical reflections: comparing national restructuring regimes

Understanding the role of actors, regulation, institutional support and forms of adjustment in each of the countries illustrates the varied approaches to restructuring. Nonetheless, as Bergström (2019) acknowledges, there remains considerable variability *within* national regimes. While there is utility in the regimes framework it is important to recognize its limitations in capturing the full range of restructuring processes and practices that may exist. This section offers some critical reflections on features of the above national cases that may not be fully acknowledged by the regimes framework.

For instance, there is a tendency within the work and employment literature to paint Sweden as an ideal case; however, the picture may not be so rosy. Industrial 'peace clauses' in collective agreements mean unions are not permitted to take industrial action in response to restructuring (or for any other workplace dispute). Furthermore, collective agreements underpinning transition support do not always extend to temporary workers, which means they have less protection and access to support in restructuring situations. The Australian regime also entails a disproportionate burden carried by temporary/casual workers.

In the UK and Australia, despite being primarily market-oriented regimes, governments occasionally intervene in high-profile cases of restructuring, perhaps involving politically sensitive regions or to save sectors of the economy from failing. As noted, the UK government has sometimes responded by bringing together key stakeholders in 'task forces' to support affected workers and communities. Similar approaches have been observed in Australia. However, despite considerable political fanfare around government interventions in the automotive and steel industries, state-funded job creation schemes were undersubscribed and ultimately produced disappointing outcomes.

Similarly, pockets of joint regulation reflecting a negotiated-type regime exist in the UK and Australia (Johnstone, 2019; McLachlan et al., 2021; Snell and Gekara, 2020). However, these have not been widespread and governments in both countries justify minimal state intervention on the basis that restructuring is a 'private' matter between employers and employees. The UK employment system in particular has been largely characterized as voluntarist, with comparatively weak regulation of restructuring in terms of employment protection and support. The stark difference between widespread union involvement in restructuring in Sweden and the pepper-pot distribution of union involvement in Australia and the UK reflects broader institutional differences. Australia and the UK have witnessed several decades of successive government hostility towards unions and an absence of state legitimation of their role, particularly as an actor in a broader political sphere beyond the workplace. In 2018, union membership density for Australia and the UK was 14 per cent and 23 per cent respectively. In the same year union membership in Sweden stood at 68 per cent, with over 90 per cent of the workforce covered by collective agreements, and notwithstanding periodic attempts to reduce their influence during periods of right-wing government, unions enjoy greater state legitimization and embeddedness in Swedish society as a social and political actor.

The willingness of governments to engage unions in policy discussions often change at times of major crisis; such was the Covid-19 outbreak in 2020. As a consequence of extensive lockdowns of economies many organizations have undergone some form of restructuring, which has caused hardship for millions of workers, families and communities. The respective responses to the global pandemic were illustrative of the institutional differences between the restructuring regimes of Sweden, the UK and Australia.

Sweden's proactive, coordinated approach to restructuring was demonstrated by the use of pre-existing measures around STW, reinforced by crisis state funding, which allowed firms to manage their labour costs with reduced recourse to redundancies. Many people lost their jobs but it would have been worse without state support. Lessons were learned from the 2008–9 global financial crisis, and Sweden was thus arguably prepared for future economic downturns.

In contrast, the UK and Australia represent more ad hoc, reactive cases as the lack of a pre-emptive intervention, such as STW, resulted in hastily developed job retention schemes. Furthermore, although the measures taken represented unprecedented peace-time state intervention in the labour market they were arguably motivated by a need to support the respective national economies via stimulus programmes rather than the well-being of affected workers. In Australia, the JobKeeper Payment scheme initially provided firms with a fortnightly AU$1,500 (£850) wage subsidy per employee, covering approximately 3.6 million workers at its peak before being gradually wound down (Australian Government Treasury, 2020). However, Covid-19 was also used as a catalyst for industrial relations reform and changes to the Fair Work Act, with the government and employers arguing for more flexibility and less complexity in order to maximize job creation in the post-Covid recovery. While unions were involved in initial industrial relations reform discussions, ultimately the government imposed their own recommendations, which were largely in favour of employers when no consensus emerged. In the UK, companies could apply for state funding through the Coronavirus Job Retention Scheme to furlough staff. The scheme subsidized 80 per cent of monthly wages up to a maximum of £2,500 per employee and 8.9 million jobs were furloughed at its peak in 2020 (ONS, 2021). Interestingly, the UK government's involvement of unions echoes a state-led negotiated process, a departure from regime type but indicative of an overall ad hoc approach. Furthermore, the furlough scheme was to be replaced after six months by another temporary measure, the Job Support Scheme, a quantitative adjustment mechanism that would have effectively represented the UK's first state-led coordination of STW. That this policy change was abandoned in one of several government U-turns in this area again speaks to the overall ad hoc approach.

The Covid-19 crisis provides a lens through which to view the broader themes outlined in this chapter. Although restructuring may be ubiquitous, the ways these play out are shaped by institutional context; similarly, the implications for employment and the support put in place to mitigate the consequences of restructuring for individuals and communities vary considerably. As noted, such national-level regulation may inform the investment and divestment decisions of MNCs. Restructuring regimes offer one way to understanding the varying approaches taken by national governments in terms of market, state-administered or negotiated governance and adjustment mechanisms. Building on the concept of regimes, the comparison of Swedish, UK and Australian approaches to restructuring highlights the divergence between proactive, pre-emptive interventions and more ad hoc, reactive responses and crucially the differing roles played by key actors in the process.

Reflective questions

1. What factors might influence the restructuring decisions of MNCs?
2. In what ways can firms, governments and other actors intervene to mitigate the effects of restructuring on individuals?
3. What are the key differences between market, state and negotiated regimes of restructuring?
4. What do the respective responses to the Covid-19 crisis illustrate about proactive and ad hoc policy approaches to restructuring?

Recommended readings

- Ahlstrand, R. (2015) 'Integrative strategy, competitiveness and employment: A case study of the transition at the Swedish truck manufacturing company Scania during the economic downturn in 2008–2010)'. *Economic and Industrial Democracy*, 36(3): 457–77.
- Bergström, O. (2019) 'Changing restructuring regimes in 11 European countries during and after the financial crisis'. *European Journal of Industrial Relations*, 25(2): 95–111.
- Dobbins, T., Plows, A. and Lloyd-Williams, H. (2014) '"Make do and mend" after redundancy at Anglesey Aluminium: Critiquing human capital approaches to unemployment'. *Work, Employment and Society*, 28(4): 515–32.

References

Ahlstrand, R. (2010) 'Social responsibility in connection with business closures: A study of the close-down of Ericsson Telecom facilities in Norrkoping and Linkoping'. *Economic and Industrial Democracy*, 31(4): 537–55.

Anaf, J., Newman, L., Baum, F., Ziersch, A. and Jolley, G. (2014) 'Policy environments and job loss: Lived experience of retrenched Australian automotive workers'. *Critical Social Policy*, 33(2): 325–47.

Australian Government Treasury (2020) *Job Keeper Update*. Available at: https://ministers. treasury.gov.au/ministers/josh-frydenberg-2018/media-releases/jobkeeper-update-0

Beer, A. (2015) 'Structural adjustment programmes and regional development in Australia'. *Local Economy*, 30(1): 21–40.

Bergström, O. (2019) 'Changing restructuring regimes in 11 European countries during and after the financial crisis'. *European Journal of Industrial Relations*, 25(2): 95–111.

Bergström, O. and Diedrich, A. (2011) 'Exercising social responsibility in downsizing: Enrolling and mobilizing actors at a Swedish high-tech company'. *Organization Studies*, 32(7): 897–919.

Brand, J. E. (2015) 'The far-reaching impact of job loss and unemployment'. *Annual Review of Sociology*, 41: 359–75.

Brockner, J. (1988) 'The effects of work layoffs on survivors: Research, theory, and practice', in B. M. Staw, and L. L. Cumming (eds), *Research in Organizational Behavior*. Greenwich: JAI Press, pp. 213–55.

Cascio, W. F. (2002) 'Strategies for responsible restructuring'. *Academy of Management Perspectives*, 16(3): 80–91.

Cascio, W. (2012) 'Downsizing and redundancy', in A. Wilkinson, N. Bacon, T. Redman and S. Snell (eds), *The Sage Handbook of Human Resource Management*. London: Sage.

Cregan, C., Kulik, C. T., Johnston, S. and Bartram, T. (2020) 'The influence of calculative ("hard") and collaborative ("soft") HRM on the layoff-performance relationship in high performance workplaces'. *Human Resource Management Journal*, 31(1): 1–23.

Cushen, J. and Thompson, P. (2016) 'Financialization and value: Why labour and the labour process still matter'. *Work, Employment and Society*, 30(2): 352–65.

De Vries, M. F. K. and Balazs, K. (1997) 'The downside of downsizing'. *Human Relations*, 50(1): 11–50.

Dobbins, T., Plows, A. and Lloyd-Williams, H. (2014) '"Make do and mend" after redundancy at Anglesey Aluminium: Critiquing human capital approaches to unemployment'. *Work, Employment and Society*, 28(4): 515–32.

Donnelly, M. and Scholarios, D. (1998) 'Workers' experiences of redundancy: Evidence from Scottish defence-dependent companies'. *Personnel Review*, 27(4): 325–42.

Fair Work Ombudsman (2020) Available at: www.fairwork.gov.au/how-we-will-help/ templates-and-guides/fact-sheets/minimum-workplace-entitlements/notice-of- termination-and-redundancy-pay (accessed 2nd May 2020).

Fervers, L. (2019) 'Healing or deepening the scars of unemployment? The impact of activation policies on unemployed workers'. *Work, Employment and Society*, 35(1): 320.

Gandolfi, F. and Hansson, M. (2011) 'Causes and consequences of downsizing: Towards an integrative framework'. *Journal of Management and Organization*, 17(4): 498–521.

Gardiner, J., Stuart, M., MacKenzie, R., Forde, C., Greenwood, I. and Perrett, R. (2009) 'Redundancy as a critical life event: Moving on from the Welsh steel industry through career change'. *Work, Employment and Society*, 23(4): 727–45.

Gazier, B. (2008) 'Comparing processes across Europe'. In B. Gazier and F. Brüggeman (eds), *Restructuring Work and Employment in Europe*. Cheltenham: Edward Elgar, pp. 11–31.

Gonäs, L. and Tyrkkö, A. (2015) 'Changing structures and women's role as labor force'. *Nordic Journal of Working Life Studies*, 5(2): 89–108.

Guthrie, J. P. and Datta, D. K. (2008) 'Dumb and dumber: The impact of downsizing on firm performance as moderated by industry conditions'. *Organization Science*, 19(1): 108–23.

Hallock, K. F. (2009) 'Job loss and the fraying of the implicit employment contract'. *Journal of Economic Perspectives*, 23(4): 69–93.

Jahoda, M. (1982) *Employment and Unemployment: A Social-Psychological Analysis*, Vol. 1. Cambridge: Cambridge University Press.

Jobs Australia (2016) *Submission: Productivity Commission Inquiry into Human Services – Identifying Sectors for Reform*. Available at: www.pc.gov.au/__data/assets/pdf_file/0019/205129/sub268-human-services-identifying-reform.pdf

Johnstone, S. (2019) 'Employment practices, labour flexibility and the Great Recession: An automotive case study'. *Economic and Industrial Democracy*, 40(3): 537–59.

Jolkkonen, A., Koistinen, P., Kurvinen, A., Lipiäinen, L., Nummi, T. and Virtanen, P. (2018) 'Labour market attachment following major workforce downsizings: A comparison of displaced and retained workers'. *Work, Employment and Society*, 32(6): 992–1010.

McKinley, W., Zhao, J. and Rust, K. G. (2000) 'A sociocognitive interpretation of organizational downsizing'. *Academy of Management Review*, 25(1): 227–43.

McLachlan, C. J., MacKenzie, R. and Greenwood, I. (2021) 'Victims, survivors and the emergence of "endurers" as a reflection of shifting goals in the management of redeployment'. *Human Resource Management Journal*, 31(2): 438–53.

McMahon, T. F. (1999) 'From social irresponsibility to social responsiveness: The Chrysler/Kenosha plant closing'. *Journal of Business Ethics*, 20(2): 101–12.

McWilliams, A. and Siegel, D. (2001) 'Corporate social responsibility: A theory of the firm perspective'. *Academy of Management Review*, 26(1): 117–27.

O'Brien, M. J. and Burrows, S. (2019) 'Assessing the effectiveness of regional policy responses to mass redundancies: The case of the Illawarra Region, Australia'. *Economic Papers*, 37: 270–6.

Oesch, D. and Baumann, I. (2015) 'Smooth transition or permanent exit? Evidence on job prospects of displaced industrial workers'. *Socio-Economic Review*, 13(1): 101–23.

Olsson, B. (2004) Att organisera förändring: designperspektiv på organisationsförändringar i tillverkningsindustrin [Organizing Change: Design Perspective on Organizational Changes in the Manufacturing Industry]. Gothenburg: Chalmers Tekniska Högskola.

ONS (2020) CJRS Statistics, October 2020. *HMRC*. Available at: www.gov.uk/government/publications/coronavirus-job-retention-scheme-statistics-october-2020/coronavirus-job-retention-scheme-statistics-october-2020

ONS (2021) Coronavirus and the latest indicators for the UK economy and society: 15th April 2021. Available at: ons.gov.uk.

Pulignano, V. and Stewart, P. (2013) 'Firm-level restructuring and union strategies in Europe: Local union responses in Ireland, Italy and the Netherlands'. *Work, Employment and Society*, 27(5): 842–59.

Rydell, A. and Wigblad, R. (2012) 'The quest for CSR in closedowns'. *Nordic Journal of Working Life Studies*, 2(3): 143–60.

Snell, D. and Gekara, V. (2020) 'Unions and corporate social responsibility in a liberal market context: The case of Ford's shutdown in Australia'. *Journal of Industrial Relations*, 62(5): 713–34.

Stuart, M., Forde, C., MacKenzie, R. and Wallis, E. (2007) 'An impact study on relocation, restructuring and the viability of the European Globalisation Adjustment Fund: The impact on employment, working conditions and regional development'.

Turnbull, P. and Wass, V. (1997) 'Job insecurity and labour market lemons: The (mis) management of redundancy in steel making, coal mining and port transport'. *Journal of Management Studies*, 34(1): 27–51.

Wilkinson, A. (2005) 'Downsizing, rightsizing or dumbsizing? Quality, human resources and the management of sustainability'. *Total Quality Management and Business Excellence*, 16(8–9): 1079–88.

14 Technology and the organization of work

Kendra Briken and Robert MacKenzie

Learning objectives

- To outline stages of technological development and how these affected the organization of work
- To understand the role of technology in relation to the human contribution to production
- To recognize the factors that shape the introduction of new technologies in the workplace
- To appreciate how international variations in the use of technology reflect management decisions shaped by different institutional contexts

Introduction

The purpose of this chapter is to understand the relationship between technology and the organization of work. The decisions made by management over the introduction and use of new technologies clearly hold implications for the way work is organized and the way people are managed, which in turn reflect strategic differences in the role of labour within production. Central to this chapter is the relationship between technology and the role of human labour within the production process: the extent to which technology enhances the role of human labour, acts as a control over labour to ensure the contribution of workers and may ultimately serve to supplant human labour. The relationship between technology and human labour is dynamic and contingent: it is prone to change and outcomes differ by context. These themes are explored through examining some key developments in the history of technologies of production, from early mechanization to Industrie 4.0, and what they have meant in terms of the management of the employment relationship. The chapter demonstrates that the relationship between technology and the organization of work is not deterministic, but rather is socially mediated, and can lead to different outcomes across time and place, shaped by institutional context, worker resistance and gender regimes. A case study of Amazon.com's fulfilment centres provides an opportunity to explore issues relating to changes in the organization of work, the use of technology, the role of labour and the influence of the broader institutional and economic context.

Technology and the role of labour

New technologies may lead to very different approaches to the organization of production and the management of people, reflecting variations in institutional context and national management systems. In turn, over time new technologies have created imperatives for convergence in management approaches, around the sharing of what is seen as the latest best practice by consultancy firms or influential international business schools. Equally, technologies foster divergence, for example in facilitating multinational corporations' (MNCs) strategic investment based on an international division of production, global value chains and regime shopping. Without technologies such as networked communications or information and communication technologies (ICTs), MNCs as we know them today would not operate the way they do. New technologies allow for the division of labour between different company sites, and they inform strategic orientation and investment decisions of MNCs. In an organizational context, technologies open up opportunities for approaches to the management of people, but they do not prescribe the outcome. Decisions over the technologies of production and the introduction of new technologies are made by management, with varying degrees of prerogative. Technologies present management with opportunities for strategic choice over their adoption and which management system to implement, albeit this is often a path-dependent choice, operating within the influence of social processes and institutional context, as we will see in the following sections.

This chapter will focus on management's strategic use of human labour power and the role human resource management (HRM) perspectives assign to the human factor in the production process. Differing approaches to HRM reflect alternative ways of reconciling the imperatives of ensuring the desired level of effort or contribution of labour to the production process, while harnessing the inherent creativity of labour and the advantages this may bring to production. Technology and its reflection in the organization of production has played a role in both, from the limiting of worker discretion and the assertion of technical control to underscore the extraction of effort through to management techniques aimed at 'digging the gold from workers' brains'.

The history of technologies at work can be told in many ways. We investigate the complex interconnections between technology and how the role of labour as a resource used for value creation and extraction is framed. Our point of departure is the assumption that the logic of capitalism is to continuously increase accumulation, based on the surplus derived from labour within the production process. One way to do this is to increase the amount of surplus that can be derived by increasing working hours, for example by lengthening the working day. Alternatively, management may seek ways of improving the productivity of labour, here again technology plays an important role. Technology is often associated with ways of increasing the efficiency of labour, enhancing or augmenting the human input into the production process through the implementation of new or improved tools and machinery. This logic is repeated from the artisan workshops of early manufacture, through the mechanization of the factory system and into the digital age. However, the contribution of labour to production can also be increased through the intensification of work, and again technology plays a role, from the speeding up of assembly lines to the use of monitoring and surveillance to discipline workers into a faster pace of work.

As our definition suggests, technology is more than a simple technique but rather is a holistic term including work organization. Technology can be defined as the techniques, skills, methods and processes to produce goods and services. Technology is to be separated from inventions. Inventions such as the steam engine or the internet are important for changes in technology. They allow for the introduction of new processes, and they enable the use of different skills, methods and techniques. Understanding technology as a process allows us to shine a light on the interconnectedness between techniques, work organization and human labour.

Technologies of production increase the productivity of human labour by supporting human tasks, a logic that dates back to the use of simple tools such as a hammer. Here, we focus on the related changes in skill utilization, management control and power. To showcase the connection between the role of people in the production process and the impact technologies have, we take four different processes as points of departure: mechanization, automation, computerization, digitalization. *Mechanization* includes connecting different tools, as seen for example in the mechanical loom. Another example is the assembly line where pieces are moved mechanically towards the worker. Mechanization represents the movement from the use of simple tools to more complex machinery, which in turn became powered by external forces but crucially was controlled by the worker as a means of enhancing the contribution of their labour. *Automation* reflects the process of replacing the human input with machinery designed substitute for the role of the worker (Benanav 2020). The difference to mechanization would be that a work piece would be treated by machines only. Often production relies on semi-automated processes and human labour is used still to do tasks during assembly. Only when no human would be directly involved in the assembling process anymore, would we argue to have reached fully automated production (or services, such as handling data). *Computerization* refers to the introduction of technology capable of processing large amounts of data; crucially, this provided the basis for integrating previously discrete operations – for example, linking stages of production with stores and logistics to facilitate Just in Time (JIT) management (Noble, 1984). Technological advances led to the ability to collect and process data in real time, facilitating contemporaneous feedback into the production system. Whereas computerization relied on the processing of data and decision-making external to the production process, *digitalization* facilitates the exercise of these processes within production. Here technology is interacting directly with the worker, learning from the human user, processing and feeding back corrective directions. Digitalization has been associated with the decoupling of some work from physical space, for example facilitating more mobile approaches to previously office-bound work, or work mediated through the cloud rather than gathering workers in a specific location. Cloud work, although relying on very material computing space, server farms and energy, can be organized independently from physical spaces and, as we will show with the case of Industrie 4.0, even allows production processes to move not only control and surveillance, but also planning and maintenance work into the virtual space (Huws, 2003).

Often the stages outlined above are connected to changes framed as Industrial Revolutions. In this perspective, each of the so far four 'Revolutions' reflects core inventions that offered new strategic choices to organize work with regard to techniques, skills, methods and processes or to manage people differently. It needs to be acknowledged here that each of the revolutionary steps is also dependant on broader changes in society. The 18th-century inventions of the steam engine and the first steps in mechanization would not have made the same impact if they had not been accompanied by the colonial extraction of raw materials, done by slave labour; as much as the theory of the firm suggests management might have its foundations in the building of the railway systems, the supervisory systems used in the colonial plantations have been crucial to informing approaches to controlling human labour at work (Braverman, 1998; Cooke, 2003). The division of labour plays an important part in management systems, as does the access to cheap and available labour. Such employment strategies have been enabled by a variety of state policies, such as 'welfare to work' or 'guest worker' programmes, through which specific groups of potential workers have been made more susceptible to low-paid work. Child labour was a feature of the early factories of advanced economies and continues in the supply chains of some MNCs; women's work has persistently been devalued on the basis of it being seen as less skilled; from cross-border seasonal workers to targeted recruitment in sending economies by firms and labour market intermediaries, migrant labour has similarly been associated with low-paid work (MacKenzie and Forde, 2009). Management's access to easy-to-replace labour makes investment in fixed capital technologies less attractive in some sectors. Technology can make human tasks obsolete or create new ones, they can change or shift. Often, the introduction of new technologies is related to job losses (Frey and Osborne, 2017). It is also the case, as we will see, that the introduction of technologies might lead to the need for more skilled labour and hence better job quality, but often only temporarily. Technologies may provide opportunities for the expression of technical skills, but changes in technology and the organization of work may also take this away (MacKenzie et al., 2017). Even at the stage of earliest mechanization, company owners and, later on, planners and engineers faced choices over the organization of production and the use of human labour. The stages outlined above reflect historical progression, but also existing parameters for decision-making in the contemporary economy. Today, craft brewery owners might deliberately decide to use pre-automated bottling processes to succeed in a small niche market. Online retailers might choose to use human labour in their warehouses instead of robots since workers are cheaper to replace (see case study). Technology is in flux, and so is the workplace.

Technology and the organization of work across time

Our starting point in analysing the connection between new technologies and the organization of work is to understand the role of human labour. Technology in this respect has a triple function: it is facilitating the contribution of human labour power to the production process; management uses technology to control the contribution of human labour to value creation; last but not least, technology is used to supersede human labour.

Historically, the term the First Industrial Revolution has been used to describe the early introduction of technologies connected to mechanization and the amplification of power needed in production facilitated by the invention of the steam engine. Instead of hydraulic, human or animal power, tools could be run based on this new technique, increasing the productivity of labour by supporting the tasks performed by workers in production. Beginning in simple manufacture and continuing into the mechanization of production, the important point for this stage of technological development is that the tools and machinery based on mechanical systems augment human labour without replacing it. In order to comprehend the role of technology, it is important to understand the organization of production. In 1832, the English mathematician Charles Babbage wrote on the principle of the division of labour:

> That the master manufacturer, by dividing the work to be executed into different processes, each requiring different degrees of skill or force, can purchase exactly that precise quantity of both which is necessary for each process; whereas, if the whole work were executed by one workman, that person must possess sufficient skill to perform the most difficult, and sufficient strength to execute the most laborious, of the operations into which the art is divided. ([1832] 1982: 175–6).

As noted by the Scottish economist and philosopher Adam Smith in *The Wealth of Nations* (1776), one of the attributes of such a division of labour was that organizing production on the basis of the repetition of simplified tasks allowed for the development of 'machines' to aid in their performance.

In understanding changes in the organization of production associated with mechanization it is important to be wary of technological determinism. Technologies of production are not manna from heaven applied neutrallly in pursuit of technical efficiencies. Take the early days of advances in mechanization in England. Technologies of production grew in size, which led to increased centralization in larger units of production, factories, to accommodate bigger machinery and provide the external power they needed, initially from water and then from steam engines. At the same time, there were strong continuities between the levels of technology used in the early factories and those used in dispersed, home-based manufacturing and with regard to the actual work done by the workers. The key difference was in asserting control over the working hours of labour, removing the uncertainty inherent in the home-based, dispersed manufacture in which workers had greater discretion over the time they chose to expend their labour power (Marglin, 1974). Also, even though developments in mechanization ultimately meant centralized organization overcame the cost advantages of dispersed manufacture, the adoption of such technology did not happen overnight, nor was it universal – indeed small-scale production continued to coexist on the basis of squeezing costs on labour and materials (Landes, 1986).

What we can learn from the early accounts of the use of new technologies and what holds still today is that *the relationship between technology and the organization of production is not deterministic but contested*. The introduction of technologies of production is socially mediated, reflecting the power relationship between the owners of capital and the sellers of labour power: employers and employees. The existence of a technology of production does not guarantee its adoption; rather, this provides management with choices over the organization of production, which again reflect the power relations between employers and employees and may be constrained by institutional context. The decision to adopt particular technologies can also lead to a specific path dependency, but it does not necessarily mean it is the only solution. Such choices can also include wrong decisions, as investment in technology is always based on bounded rationality (Fleming, 2019).

Mechanization, division of labour and the assembly line

The principles of the division of labour outlined by Smith and Babbage became guiding lights for the growing caste of management. As mechanization developed, new systematic approaches to management theory emerged. In 1911, Frederick W. Taylor published *The Principles of Scientific Management*, capturing the zeitgeist of contemporary industrial capitalism and the so-called efficiency movement (Noble, 1984; Taylor, 2003). Core to scientific management was the separation of *conception* and *execution* of work, removing discretion from the worker over the performance of their work. Every skill could be reduced to a set of tasks independently of the skills of the person. Crucially, the planning of each and every task would lie exclusively with management, in the form of efficiency experts and engineers framed as specialists for workplace planning. Echoing the observations of Smith and Babbage, the division of labour based on the fragmentation of work into simplified tasks and the separation of conception and execution reduced the skills needed to perform work: the skills needed by previous generations of workers to perform work could be embedded in the design of the technologies of production (Braverman, 1998) (see also Chapter 1 on globalization for a discussion of Fordism). *Taylorism* created a model for production and the management of people that would be emulated across mass production industries and services, albeit to varying extents and in numerous guises.

A telling example of how this school of thought shaped the forms of production in its technological innovation approach is the association of assembly-line production and Taylorism. Ford's introduction of the assembly line was based on the assumption that the parts moving towards the worker would increase productivity by increasing the assembly rates. Developed in the meat processing industry before being applied to mechanized car manufacturing, the emergence of the assembly line reflected a particular attitude to the role of labour within the production process. Rather than being designed to harness the creative potential of labour, the organization of production was designed to limit the discretion of the worker, to reduce the need for the application of skill. The separation of *conception* and *performance* was not determined by the introduction of new production technology but rather reflected the basis on which the technology had been designed: this was not an evolutionary process but pursued on the basis of systematic observation of workers performing their tasks, which informed the design of technology that reduced the opportunity for decision-making and application of skill. The close monitoring of workers' performance continued with the introduction of assembly-line technologies: time and motion studies allowed specialists to calcu-late the rate at which tasks should be performed, which then informed the setup of the assembly line. The speed of the assembly line thus determined the pace of work, thereby ensuring the contribution of labour by countering the assumed propensity of workers for 'soldiering' or withholding effort (see Chapter 1 on globalization and Chapter 12 on lean production).

Redefining workspaces

It was with the next step, the automation of specific parts of production, that the connection between skills and knowledge needed by previous generations of workers became embedded in and replaced by new technologies of produc-tion. It is telling how during the heyday of the first wave of automation in the 1950s and 1960s the public discourse was concerned with what they predicted as technological unemployment. At the same time, focusing through the lens of empirical studies, researchers showed the increasing emergence of non-manual skills in production. As a perhaps non-intended side effect, instead of deskill-ing and job destruction, new, specialized tasks such as surveillance and regula-tion were needed to keep the new and mostly semi-automated systems running. Studies in industrial sociology at that time often hinted at a binary development in respect to the future of work, suggesting a polarization thesis as an outcome of rising automation. Jobs would require a smaller proportion of workers being upskilled but with the majority being downgraded. It is against this background that Harry Braverman's (1998) *Labour and Monopoly Capitalism* was written, point-ing to a general trend towards deskilling in modern production methods. The described shift to automation is a good example of how new technologies impact production and reproduction, and thus shows how technological innovations are deeply connected with social relations. To make full use of the productivity gains of (semi-) automated production, machines could run for 24 hours a day, seven days a week. Human labour was organized around machine times, and shiftwork saw a come-back. Though often remunerated better than day shifts, the detrimen-tal effects to workers' health have been documented ever since.

It is in this light we can see the second phase of automation and how the focus on specialist-driven workplace planning led to at least three emerging develop-ments. First, workers' collective action put pressure on employers to improve working conditions. Second, the organization of the production process in itself questioned the idea of the separation of planning and execution on the level of human–machine relations. Last but not least, on a global level, supply-and-demand relationships changed in what is often called the 'global shift'. Starting in the 1970s, the redistribution of added value changed. The global division of labour followed a 'Taylorist' pattern in that industrial workforces were shrinking in the 'core' developed economies, specifically with regard to highly deskilled parts of industry; a process offset by the integration of workers in developing economies in the periphery into global production chains. These workers often were left with the dangerous, dull and dirty tasks that, given extant levels of technology, could be automated were there the imperative for such capital investment. It shows how management decisions regarding technology need to be understood with regard to surrounding labour markets and wage levels. With access to low-wage economies, it made sense from a value creation point of view to make use of the much more flexible and expandable human labour than invest in technology. The textiles industry represents a prime example of such an international division of labour. Since the latter decades of the 20th century, textiles production has been in decline in developed economies, with companies closing factories in their home countries in favour of outsourcing to supply chains in developing economies (see Chapter 1 on globalization). Pre- and post-production functions like research and development or marketing often remained in the headquarters location, but production itself was moved to lower-wage economies. The modern textiles industry is also an example of various levels of technology of production coexisting in different parts of the sector, again often reflecting an international division of labour. Computer-generated bespoke manufacturing operates at one end of the range of possibilities, while traditional large-scale factory production and even the continuation of 'putting-out' to home-based manufacture can be found in developing economies such as Pakistan and Bangladesh (Donaghey and Reinecke, 2018). The coexistence of approaches represent choices made over the organizing of production that were not determined by the availability of the most advanced technology, but rather strategies informed by the availability of low-cost labour within supply chains, reflecting a division of labour between advanced and developing economies.

Computerization: merging automation, information and communication technologies

The history of computerization can be dated back to the designs for the first mechanical calculation machines drawn in the 19th century by the English mathematicians Charles Babbage (quoted earlier on the principle of the division of labour) and Ada Lovelace (who composed the first algorithm). Although it would be a century before a working machine was built, their ideas and designs were antecedents to modern computers, artificial intelligence and machine learning. Computing offered the solution to two problems emerging with the growth of administrative and office work: the handling and storing of information.

Mechanical computing devices developed through the first half of the 20th century were clunky machines, mainly used for accounting tasks. It was the switch to electronic computing in the 1950s, and crucially the development of the microchip, that allowed for the exponential rise of both the capacity for storing data and the miniaturization of computing hardware (Castells, 2009: 28–76). The electrification of computing set in motion the diffusion of computer-based technologies across workplaces. Computerization marks a twofold process: firstly the use of newly available hardware – the computer – as a tool for the automation of production processes, and secondly, the use of the hardware to create a new space, or platform, for collaboration and communication between functions within the organization. In manufacturing production processes, it led to advanced automation framed as computer-integrated manufacturing (CIM), but crucially, the computer also changed white-collar work. Beyond the shopfloor, devices such as the desktop computer became affordable; the typewriter, used since the end of the 19th century, was replaced by the word processor, or the first stand-alone desktop computing devices. Clerical work began to change just as manual work had. The world of office work that expanded with the rise of the big companies was also targeted for costs and efficiency gains, and the electrification of computing supported the agenda for the rationalization of the ever expanding clerical workforce.

In production, computerization allowed for decision-making to be further centralized and controlled by management, and, crucially, displaced from the actual workplace. New computer technology displaced labour and enabled deskilling, as machines controlled by programming further removed decision-making and judgement from the shop floor.

Whereas computerization could be employed to enhance the application of Taylorist principles, as has been stressed throughout the chapter, technology provides options rather than determines the organization of production. As has also been stressed, management choices over the organization of production and the use of technology are embedded in social relations and shaped by institutional context. The augmenting of Taylorist control and further separation of planning and execution offered by computerization was, as noted previously with regard to automation, met with resistance by workers. Similarly, the opportunities presented by computerization, such as the integration of operational processes, led to different outcomes in other institutional contexts. In Japan, the ability to link production processes to logistics and accounting systems based on the capacity to retrieve and process data through ICT underpinned the development of just-in-time (JIT) techniques. JIT was one aspect of a Japanese management system, the attempted emulation of which through its reinterpretation as lean production would challenge the path-dependent prominence of Taylorism in the United States and elsewhere. Again, of importance here is the underlying perspective on the role of labour in production. By contrast these approaches eschewed Taylorist management practices in search of harnessing the creative capacity in what remained of human labour in computerized production processes. In principle, low-skilled labour was – if not replaced by technology or outsourced – considerably reoriented through job rotation, teamworking and continuous improvement processes.

The origins of lean production can be traced back to the 1980s when companies specifically in the western industrialized parts of the global economy started adopting and adjusting their production model in line with Japanese Toyotism (see Chapter 12 on lean production). The shift towards what was branded lean production in the English-speaking context, and the roll-out throughout industries and services, was heavily influenced by a five-year study published by the Massachusetts Institute for Technology (MIT). After benchmarking the automotive sector globally, the authors draw the conclusion Toyotism should be seen as the most efficient and hence the new 'one best way' for production. Toyotism in itself was not a new idea and not directly related to changes in technology; however, the emergence and availability of ICT were crucial to the shift in managerial systems. Another key principle, continuous improvement, reflected an inversion of the logic of separation of planning and execution by harnessing the expertise of those performing the tasks, the workers, rather than relying on the intervention of specialists, engineers and work-planners. The normalization of incremental innovation from exception and expert tasks to daily routine on the assembly line was closely connected to the widespread integration of information technology (IT) and new control software tools.

Where Taylorist technologies compromise creativity, for the workforce in lean production the pendulum swings back to making workers' knowledge part of their task. Trying to 'dig in the gold of worker's brains' was a common phrase when group- or teamwork inspired by Toyotism was introduced under lean production. Part of this knowledge capture involved switching from (individual) company suggestion schemes to (collective) continuous improvement processes, which made workers or teams responsible for improving their work environments. Over time, improvements delivered by the semi-autonomous work groups became part of performance management schemes, which put an even stronger pressure on groups and single workers to disclose their situated knowledge. The mainstream debates around teamwork in the 1990s and the connection to semi-autonomous work have been criticized in this regard: workers delivering their own rationalization.

From the mid 1990s onwards, there was an increasing potential to get a real-time insight into all processes, making it easy to compare each and every work unit. The software allowed companies to coordinate all resources, information and activities needed to complete their processes, from order fulfilment, billing and HRM to production planning, in real time. Although framed by manufacturers as an increase in visualization and transparency to allow workers to integrate their knowledge and to continuously improve their workspaces, the real-time data also became a proper self-control tool for labour. This was a crucial point for the development of machine learning and the connection to work. Via the use of performance data to monitor and control the labour process, human labour can thereby in turn facilitate ongoing and future contribution in a continuous loop which has tightened over time, from time and motion studies to IT capable of contemporaneous assessment and feedback.

New production regimes, like lean management or high-performance work systems, integrated workers and aimed at extracting the tacit aspects of workers' knowledge. The separation between execution and planning was ostensibly superseded. Employee empowerment, voice or 'employee engagement' were put on the agenda, but they came at a price, including the displacement of more traditional forms of independent collective representation based on recognition of more adversarial relations (see Chapter 12 on lean production).

'Gonna get myself connected': human–machine relations and the Fourth Industrial Revolution

The term Industrie 4.0 was coined in 2011, at the Hannover Messe industry fair in Germany. Starting as a national industrial strategy, over time the label was adapted throughout European countries, with equally impactful initiatives driven globally – for example in China (2015, 中国制造2025 [Made in China 2025]), or in the United States (2013, Manufacturing USA) – focusing on production at first, and on what was called the smart factory. Just as the smartphone allows connecting with all data flows continuously, the vision of Industry 4.0 suggests that companies already widely served with IT systems, such as economic resource planning (ERP) or, more recently, people analytics in human resources (HR), will now be able to combine the data flows in real time. These systems were designed to support the day-to-day transactions of the business rather than enable data analytics. In the smart factory, the once heterogeneous data that is typically siloed throughout the organization can be brought together and used for predictive analytics. The focus is on an attempt to build so-called intelligence into the operating system, with agents and collections of computational entities producing an 'intelligent' dynamic control system. Crucially, the digital circuits generated will be based on extracted real-time human data. The extraction of data can be achieved through distributing devices such as tablets to employees, or more advanced technology summed up under the heading of wearables, such as wristbands, data gloves or data glasses. All these different devices can track and trace data from finger moves, eye blinks, heart beats and steps walked. In essence, what once seemed rather dystopian now is feasible – the in-depth corporeal control of the individual worker. In other words, it is not even the breaking down of work tasks, but it is the fragmentation of the working body in functional fits and fixes (see Chapter 15 on platform work).

The new quality of this wave of digitalized automation lies precisely in the merging of control, data extraction and prediction. New technologies enhance the capacity to increase the flexibility of capital by extracting knowledge through recording and capturing workers moves, both failures and, more importantly, their successful problem-solving action. Wearables and sensors are capable of monitoring each and every (inter-)action at every given moment without the worker knowing what happens to their data (Upchurch and Moore, 2018). The important point in regard to knowledge capture is neither the control nor the information-gathering aspect. It is the workers' very own interactions with the system they are connected to that are recorded, fed back and processed while they are working. Under 4.0, instead of consciously serving the machine, workers now unconsciously deliver their tacit knowledge. Herein lies the twofold character of new technologies: they incorporate science but at the same time are used as machines to record expert knowledge that is then incorporated into the system (Briken, 2020).

From a labour process perspective, the integration of control and knowledge extraction at the same point in production represents the important qualitative potentiality of new technologies. Instead of ubiquitous technological control delivering real-time data to engineering or other departments, as associated with lean production, control and information collection are levelled down to direct interaction with the worker, materializing in different digitally led assistive systems, including decision-making 'advice', but more importantly the continuous loop of feedback and correction for the worker (Butollo et al., 2019).

The human–machine relation is thus central to 4.0 in the attempt to close the still existing bottleneck between planning and execution. Previous applications of Taylorist principles of the division of planning and execution never reached the level of fully automated production and still required human surveillance and unplanned maintenance intervention. Under Industrie 4.0, the analysis of big masses of data makes such operations 'predictable'. As framed from an engineering perspective, 'Current machines can only passively listen to the operators' commands and react... A smarter machine system, on the other hand, should be able to actively suggest task arrangements and adjust operational parameters to maximize productivity and product quality' (Lee et al., 2014: 3).

Situated knowledge has been harnessed by capital for years to create an ever more exchangeable workforce. Under lean production, the workers are enticed to collaborate, complementing the bounded rationality of the technological system. Today, engineers and IT developers claim to have overcome the bounded rationalities inherent in humans with all-encompassing machine rationality reflected in digital decision-making systems that predict the problem-solving once done by the worker. The reality of the so called 'smart working' or 'agile' concepts of work is less one where the worker has agency, but rather one where they have become an agent of and led by the big data streams of which they are part (Briken, 2020; Butollo et al., 2019). How far the latest iteration of digitalization might be able to dismiss the creative capacity of human labour remains questionable (Pfeiffer, 2014), but as before it will again be contested by workers' struggles (Moore and Woodcock, 2021; Mueller, 2021).

Case study: Warehouse work – too tricky to automate?

The last decades have seen the rapid expansion of online retailing, regarded by many as emblematic of the rise of the 'platform economy', enabled by new technologies: internet access, miniaturization of devices such as handheld scanners, GPS-led navigation and tracking systems and data services capacities. A defining characteristic of companies entering the retail market is that networked ICTs and innovative platforms are underpinned still by the very materiality of warehousing, distribution and logistics: the food ordered needs to be delivered, so do clothes, kitchenware and books. In countries imposing partial lockdown to avoid the spread of the Covid-19 virus, platformed services were seen as key to supplying the population with essential goods. Items would come straight to the doorstep – but none of the steps in this process would be fully automated. Pickers in warehouses would run through the long aisles to chase the items and to fulfil the individual orders, with each customer rarely ordering the same goods twice.

From a labour market perspective, new technologies here facilitated what is sometimes called job shift. Job losses in bricks and mortar retail have been accompanied by job creation in warehousing. Though neutral on the labour market balance sheets, the socio-structural changes this job shift includes are far reaching. Retail jobs tend to be filled by women, the option for part-time work allowing them to juggle the combination of care challenges and work. Retail stores are to be found in the inner cities and accessible with public transport. Warehouses are often in more remote areas. Access is scarce and more time-consuming. Working hours tend to be less flexible and the work demands different skills sets: retail work is based on communication and emotional labour, and warehouse work on physical fitness and stamina – the signatures of a job that still is seen in a gendered way: as men's work.

From a logistics perspective, the move from large rather static to individualized constant flow retailing challenged the traditional business operations and labour process within warehousing. Instead of pallets sitting in the warehouse waiting for bulk deliveries to bigger department stores, thousands of single orders digitally assembled by the customers at home in front of their screens, click by click, had to be organized and dispatched in the material world. Warehouses became distribution centres. In the 1990s, conveyor belts would bring a batch of goods to shelves, where workers led by handheld scanners would pick what their electronic list suggested. Engineering and production planning literature calculated that order-picking was the most time-consuming operation, accounting for 55–75 per cent of warehousing cost. In line with lean management ideas, they also suggested that continuous improvement processes should have a high priority in organizing warehousing.

From a technological innovation perspective, it was Amazon.com that challenged batch production in distribution. In the early 2000s, they started to change the inner logics of their warehouse logistics. Today, Amazon.com's fulfilment centres reflect lean management in the purest sense: planning and execution are separated to the extent that all strategic decisions are made in the US headquarters only (Briken and Taylor, 2019). The data Amazon.com gathers through in-house artificial intelligence (AI) development allows for data streams mirroring the real-time motions of every single commodity ordered. In other words: Amazon.com know where their goods are to a very high reliability. The density of time and motion measurement of both goods and human resources is consequential for the labour process. For decades, warehouse work was physically demanding, but included space for workers' discretion. In a fulfilment centre, these pores of the working day are closed with the use of constant monitoring and comparing of real-time data with predicted picking and packing times. None of the stages in the fulfilment process requires specific qualifications. Training is done on the job, with a half-day introduction to the system. On the one hand, the basic challenge for workers is reduced to the physical: hitting the targets means running many miles, while being navigated from one shelving section to another by a handheld device. On the other hand, sanctions are notorious. Amazon applies a 'three strikes out' policy: calling in sick is already one strike while not meeting the hourly targets can lead to another. Despite the well documented bad working conditions in their facilities around the world, Amazon.com never seems to struggle to hire the workers needed.

The case of the United Kingdom (UK) is insightful. In 1998, Amazon.com opened their first UK-based warehouse in Milton Keynes. In 2021, their number had risen to 17, with an estimated 27,000 employees. Over the festive season, or during other peak times, this number can easily double. Then Amazon.com would hire thousands of seasonal workers across the country. Situated in de-industrialized areas with higher unemployment rates, job centres and temporary employment agencies are never short of supplying human labourers. Amazon.com also praises itself with paying above average compared to competing logistics and delivery companies. While actively organizing against trade union representation, the company set up so called employee associations, engaging workers by incentivizing their participation with bonuses or supervisory functions within the fulfilment centres.

(Continued)

With cheap labour under its control, automation seems unlikely for the moment, but soon we might see the handheld device replaced by a wristband (as announced by Amazon.com's CEO Jeff Bezos in 2021) or data gloves to collect ever more data (Delfanti and Frey, 2021). While it might be useful and even fun to monitor your health during your workout at the gym, what if your employer can monitor your blood pressure and then makes assumptions on your stress levels? From a health and safety perspective, it is sometimes argued this could be to the benefit of the workers, by decreasing stress induced by anxiety over making mistakes and avoiding skeletomuscular side effects of carrying handheld devices. Of course, with less of a focus on targets and outcomes, these issues might also be solvable without new technologies.

Questions

1. How does the technology and organization of work enhance management's control and surveillance over the workforce?
2. What options does the onsite HR management have to enhance job quality in fulfilment centres?
3. Regularly, Amazon.com suggests that the next generation of warehouses might be fully automated. What are the factors that will influence the outcome?
4. Internationally, more and more trade unions are campaigning against Amazon.com, some using the slogan 'Workers not Robots'. What concerns might trade unions have regarding the employment practices of Amazon.com?

Insurrections, interruptions, institutions

In focusing on grand narratives of technological change and associated management systems or approaches to the organization of work, from scientific management to lean production and more recently Industry 4.0, there is the danger of overemphasizing their homogeneity and ubiquity, or the smooth linear progression from one to the next. In some ways, this reflects the exaggerated influence of their fetishizing into management fads promoted by consultants and business schools (see Chapter 10 on the role of business schools and consultants). The introduction and dissemination of new technologies tend to be incremental and experimental, socially mediated processes, but more importantly, new technologies do not come without friction. Technologies of production reflect historical negotiations, compromises, victories and defeats over the changes in the mode of extracting value in the labour process. Such changes have been met with and shaped by collective resistance, from the Luddites of early-19th-century England resisting the changes to labour practices threatened by new technologies of textiles factories, to the car workers of early-20th-century Detroit resisting Ford's imposition of the assembly line and associated disciplining of labour.

The influence of labour over shaping the introduction of technologies of work may also be a reflection of the broader institutional context. As stressed throughout the chapter, the institutional context in which firms operate shapes the choices available to management over the technology and organization of production. Institutional complementarities, such as education and training systems, may encourage investment in advanced technologies of production; similarly the degree to which access to lower-cost labour may be closed off by trade unions and labour market regulation may promote capital investment. In some contexts, unions may also have more direct influence over the use or introduction of new technology. In Sweden, for example, changes in the organization of production due to new technology are often subject to mediation by collective agreements (Ahlstrand, 2015). Inspired by Toyotism, the implementation of 'integrated' production systems in Sweden in the 1990s, for example, illustrates the importance of institutional context. Work in Sweden is characterized by strong traditions of regulation by the social partners, unions and employers' associations, manifest in the importance of collective agreements over the introduction of change (see Chapter 12 on lean production). Although the social partners represented the competing interests of capital and labour, there was a negotiated collaborative approach to the adaptation of Japanese production systems associated with Toyotism to the Swedish context. The management agenda for emulating Japanese production systems was driven by the promise of productivity gains, with which the unions made pragmatic accommodation based on integrating the 'good work' aspects in terms of worker involvement (Ahlstrand, 2015). Local collective agreements regulated the introduction of JIT principles and new wage models linked to skill development, flexibility in work organization and commitment to continuous improvement. In time, the traditional negotiation system became supplemented by an informal workplace joint consultation over decision-making within the production process. As interest in lean production grew internationally, management and unions again worked to adapt it to the Swedish context in the form of effective production systems. The institutional constraints ensured the engagement with lean production would not be based on management prerogative, but rather reflected Swedish traditions of collaborative working between the unions and employers (Ahlstrand, 2015).

Gender matters: social shaping of the technology perspective

The relation between technology and the organization of work is also mediated by the broader gender relations and connected gender regimes. As socialist feminists have argued, 'The current sexual division of labour and associated gender relations of technology are therefore historically specific, but a central feature of modern work; conversely the organization of wage labour in general is central to the positioning of women themselves' (Webster, 1996: 23). This is reflected in gendered hierarchies, with women under-represented in senior management roles, and gendered labour markets, with women over-represented in low-paid, precarious work. Women are in the majority when it comes to part-time work due to the ongoing unequal distribution of housework and the lack of support for caring responsibilities (both for children and adults). The most telling example might be the care sector, with a workforce dominated by women but managed usually by men. Sectors including caring, cleaning and cooking tend to have lower pay and are often framed as 'low skilled', and skills are 'naturalized' as reflections of normative female characteristics (Cockburn, 1983). Work is often physically demanding and remains labour intensive; the availability of (relatively) cheap labour in these sectors has led to far less investment in technology to improve working conditions. Instead, technologies in these sectors are used to increase control and further fragment the labour process, and are often linked to lean production (Moore and Hayes, 2017). Following the start of the Covid-19 crisis in 2020, the UK care sector saw an unexpected uptake in the use of new technologies to increase job quality for paid carers (MacLeavy, 2021). This response was in large part due to labour shortages in the care sector due to new immigration restrictions associated with Brexit. Extending the framing to intersectional approaches, gender, race and class are all impactful on how technological systems are implemented (MacKenzie and Wajcman 1985), how much deskilling is acknowledged as problematic and how collective struggles are recognized.

Conclusion

This chapter has focused on some of the grand narratives of change in the technologies of production and the organization of work. It is important to recognize that technological advancements did not unfold in a linear progression. Stages of development ran concurrently, either overlapping as incremental processes of dissemination led to new technologies of production becoming dominant or coexisting and thereby offering management strategic options regarding the organization of production and work. The former process may be seen in the historical shift to the dominance of assembly-line production within the automotive industry; even here, high-skill techniques persist in the 21st century for small batch production of luxury cars. The longer running concurrence of technologies of production may be seen in the textiles sector, where the opportunities presented by digitalization have been embraced to allow online customers to upload bespoke designs for manufacture by digitally controlled machinery, while simultaneously previous generations of loom technology continue to be widely employed in the mass production of garments for low-cost high-street outlets. These variations demonstrate that change in the use of technology is not simply about converging to some 'best practice' or 'universal' management approach – it depends a range of interventions (see Chapter 2 on MNCs, Chapter 8 on developing economies, Chapter 11 on varieties of capitalism and Chapter 16 on regulation). The sharing of management practices associated with new technologies of production may reflect processes of emulation or isomorphism (DiMaggio and Powell, 1983); however, we must also recognize the role of consultants and business schools in promoting notions of best practice and management fads (see Chapter 10 on business schools and consultants).

Empirically, it can be shown how the use of technology is socially mediated, reflecting the balance of power between capital and labour both at the point of production, the workplace, and in terms of the broader societal balance of power shaped by the intersectionality of class, race and gender. The choices made by management over technologies of production are not just shaped by the ability of labour to resist or influence changes in the workplace, but also by broader factors informing the basis for such choices. That some sectors, such as care or cleaning, remain labour-intensive despite the availability of suitable technological alternatives reflects the gender composition of the workforce, and in turn a broader gender regime that facilitates the devaluing of associated skills and diminution of labour market power.

The ability of labour to shape the use of technologies of production may also be a reflection of the broader institutional context. In some contexts, collective bargaining may mediate the introduction of new technologies of production, but beyond this the influence of institutional context may be reflected in education and training regimes or state labour market regulation, by turn shaping the availability skills and employers access to lower cost labour. Just as management have always had different options in their choices over the use of technology and the organization of production, variations in institutional context and the availability of access to varying sources of labour power have informed the investment decisions of MNCs. The exploitation of lower costs for even skilled labour has seen the exacerbation of an international division of labour in sectors as diverse as textiles and IT, the former taking advantage of cheaper labour to maintain the profitability of older technologies, the latter using advances in ICT to access cheaper labour by offshoring and outsourcing more routine and labour intensive programming tasks. This latter point also reminds us of the ongoing role of labour in the story of advances in the technology of production. Despite proclamations dating back to the mid 20th century, and highly contemporary examples of fetishizing the possibilities of AI and robotics, fully automated production, devoid of human labour, remains an unfulfilled vision. As most users of everyday technology know, even so-called plug-and-play gizmos need a human to follow, adjust and rearrange infrastructure, or to interact to allow the technology to work smoothly. The introduction of new technologies is a contingent and socially mediated process. We might see loops and repetition, trial and error, and more importantly different phases of incremental introduction. What we can learn from early waves of automation is that the transformation of production systems moves slowly (Howcroft and Taylor, 2014). However, the attempts by management to replace, reorganize or reskill human labour are constantly bound to the rationale of value generation, extraction and exploitation within a growth-oriented economic system. The implementation of new technologies is a socially mediated process from which workers' voices tend to be structurally excluded, and so remains a contested terrain for workers' individual and collective struggles.

Reflective questions

1. In what ways do variations in the technology and organization of work reflect differing views on the role of labour in production?
2. How can technology be used to enhance the contribution of workers?
3. What factors influence the introduction of new technologies of work?
4. Why do different levels of technological development often coexist?

Recommended readings

- Briken, K. (2020) 'Welcome in the machine: Human–machine relations and knowledge capture'. *Capital and Class*, 44(2): 159–71.
- Geissler, H. (2018) *Seasonal Associate*. South Pasadena: Semiotexte. (A novel based on autoethnographic experiences.)
- Howcroft, D. and Taylor, P. (2014) 'Plus ça change, plus la même chose? – researching and theorising the "new" new technologies'. *New Technology, Work and Employment*, 29(1): 1–8.

References

Ahlstrand, R. (2015) 'Integrative strategy, competitiveness and employment: A case study of the transition at the Swedish truck manufacturing company Scania during the economic downturn in 2008–2010'. *Economic and Industrial Democracy*, 36(3): 457–77.

Babbage, C. ([1832] 1982) *On the Economy of Machinery and Manufactures*, 4th edn. New York: Augustus M. Kelley.

Benanav, A. (2020) *Automation and the Future of Work*. London and New York: Verso Press.

Braverman, H. (1998) *Labour and Monopoly Capital: The Degradation of Work in the Twentieth Century* (25th-anniversary edn). New York: Monthly Review Press.

Briken, K. (2020) 'Welcome in the machine: Human–machine relations and knowledge capture'. *Capital and Class*, 44(2): 159–71.

Briken, K. and Taylor, P. (2019) 'Beyond constrained choice – labour market coercion and oppressive work in Amazon fulfilment centres'. *Industrial Relations Journal*, 49(5–6): 438–58.

Briken , K., Chillas, S., Krzywdzinski, M. and Marks, A. (2017) (eds), *The New Digital Workplace: How New Technologies Revolutionise Work*, 1st edn (Critical Perspectives on Work and Employment series). Palgrave Macmillan.

Butollo, F., Jürgens, U. and Krzywdzinski, M. (2019) 'From lean production to Industrie 4.0: More autonomy for employees?' In U. Meyer, S. Schaupp and D. Seibt (eds), *Digitalization in Industry*. Cham: Palgrave Macmillan.

Castells, M, (2009) 'The information technology revolution'. In *The Rise of the Network Society*, Vol. 1, 2nd edn. pp. 28–76.

Cockburn, C. (1983) *Brothers: Male Dominance and Technological Change*. Pluto Press.

Cooke, B. (2003) 'The denial of slavery in management studies'. *Journal of Management Studies*, 40(8): 1895–916.

Delfanti, A. and Frey, B. (2021) 'Humanly extended automation or the future of work seen through Amazon patents'. *Science, Technology, and Human Values*, 46(3): 655–82.

DiMaggio, P. J. and Powell, W. (1983) 'The iron cage revisited: Institutional isomorphism and collective rationality in organizational fields'. *American Sociological Review*, 48: 147–60.

Donaghey, J. and Reinecke, J. (2018) 'When industrial democracy meets corporate social responsibility – a comparison of the Bangladesh Accord and Alliance as responses to the Rana Plaza disaster'. *British Journal of Industrial Relations*, 56(1): 14–42.

Fleming, P. (2019) 'Robots and organization studies: Why robots might not want to steal your job'. *Organization Studies*, 40(1): 23–38.

Frey, C. B. and Osborne, M. A. (2017) The future of employment: How susceptible are jobs to computerisation?, *Technological Forecasting and Social Change*, 114(C): 254–280.

Howcroft, D. and Taylor, P. (2014) 'Plus ça change, plus la même chose? Researching and theorising the "new" new technologies'. *New Technology, Work and Employment*, 29(1): 1–8.

Huws, U. (2003) *The Making of a Cybertariat: Virtual Work in a Real World*. New York: Monthly Review Press.

Kristal, T. (2019) 'Computerization and the decline of American unions: Is computerization class-biased?' *Work and Occupations*, 46(4): 371–410.

Landes, D. (1986) 'What do bosses really do?' *Journal of Economic History*, 46(3): 585–623.

Lee, J., Hung-An, K. and Shanhu, Y. (2014) 'Service innovation and smart analytics for Industry 4.0 and big data environment'. *Procedia CIRP*, 16: 3–8.

MacKenzie, D. and Wajcman, J. (eds) (1985) *The Social Shaping of Technology*. Philadelphia: Open University Press.

MacKenzie, R. and Forde, C. (2009) 'The rhetoric of the good worker versus the realities of employers' use and the experiences of migrant workers'. *Work, Employment and Society*, 23(1): 142–59.

MacKenzie, R., Marks, A. and Morgan, K. (2017) 'Technology, affordances and occupational identity amongst older telecommunications engineers: From living machines to black-boxes'. *Sociology*, 51(4): 732–48.

MacLeavy, J. (2021) 'Care work, gender inequality and technological advancement in the age of COVID-19'. *Gender, Work and Organisation*, 28(1): 138–54.

Marglin, S. A. (1974) 'What do bosses do? The origins and functions of hierarchy in capitalist production'. *Review of Radical Political Economics*, 6(2): 60–112.

Moore, P. V. and Woodcock, J. (eds) (2021) *Augmented Exploitation: Artificial Intelligence, Automation and Work* (Wildcat: Workers' Movements and Global Capitalism series). London: Pluto Press.

Moore, S. and Hayes, L. J. B. (2017) 'Taking worker productivity to a new level? Electronic monitoring in homecare – the (re)production of unpaid labour'. *New Technology, Work and Employment*, 32(2): 101–14.

Mueller, G. (2021) *Breaking Things at Work. The Luddites Were Right About Why You Hate Your Job*. New York and London: Verso.

Noble, D. (1984) *Forces of Production: A Social History of Industrial Automation*. New Brunswick: Transaction Publishers.

Pfeiffer, S. (2014) 'Digital labour and the use-value of human work. On the importance of labouring capacity for understanding digital capitalism'. *Triple C*, 12(2): 599–619.

Shestakofsky, B. (2017) 'Working algorithms: Software automation and the future of work'. *Work and Occupations*, 44(4): 1–49.

Taylor, F. W. (2003) *Scientific Management*. London: Routledge.

Upchurch, M. and Moore, P. V. (2018) 'Deep automation and the world of work'. In P. Moore, M. Upchurch and X. Whittaker (eds), *Humans and Machines at Work: Dynamics of Virtual Work*. Cham: Palgrave Macmillan.

Webster, J. (1996) *Shaping Women's Work: Gender, Employment and Information Technology*, 1st edn. London: Routledge.

Zuboff, S. (1988) *In the Age of the Smart Machine: The Future of Work and Power*. New York: Basic Books.

15 New technology and International Human Resource Management: platforms and platform work

Debra Howcroft

Learning objectives

- To explain the role of platforms and platform business models
- To outline the key elements that characterize platform work
- To conceptualize the link between venture capital and the nature of platform firms
- To highlight the fragility and future viability of platform modes of organizing, illustrated by the case study of Uber

Introduction

In the international human resource management (IHRM) literature, the topic of new technology and its role in shaping working practices and experiences has largely taken a back seat in debates and discussions (see Chapter 14 on an outline of new technology and work more generally). The last few years have witnessed a significant shift as growing attention has been paid to what has been termed the 'gig economy' among media and policy circles. This has led to an intensification of interest among academics, with conferences and journal special issues devoted to researching what many claim represents a distinct challenge to our understanding of employment relations. As a variant of non-standard employment, this type of work has come to be associated with insecurity, precarity, poor levels of remuneration and limited scope for collective bargaining. Critical to our comprehension of the gig economy is the platform, which is technically defined as a digital environment which facilitates the running of software. Platforms take multifarious forms and offer a range of products and services, such as online retailing (e.g. Amazon, eBay), transportation services (e.g. Didi Chuxing, Lyft) and social networking (e.g. Instagram, TikTok). The aim of this chapter is to examine externally facing labour platforms and hone in on one of the most contentious examples: Uber.

If we consider the brief history of platform work we can see how the area has developed over time and the ways in which the evolving terminology reflects shifts in public perception. There are different terms, often referring to the same phenomena, as well as debates as to what should be included/excluded when discussing platform work. These origins matter since aspects of the different foundations filter through to our contemporary understanding of platform work. In 2006, Howe (2006) coined the term crowdsourcing to refer to how internet infrastructure is used to leverage the crowd to contribute to tasks that could alternatively be performed by employees or contractors, categorically relating crowdsourcing to outsourcing. The focus on crowdsourcing was later eclipsed, particularly in the United States, as the concept of the sharing economy gained traction. This was based on the principles of collaborative consumption and commons-based peer production (Benkler and Nissenbaum, 2006) which involves groups of people who share the use of a good or service, leading to more cooperative and less hierarchical connections and interactions. Examples typically include open software projects such as Wikipedia, but this extended to face-to-face exchanges such as couchsurfing and car sharing. Recently, the term gig economy has become more widely used and this refers to the capital-labour relationship that mediates workers' supply and consumer or professional demand for the completion of small tasks or 'gigs' (Gandini, 2019: 1040). The gig economy is often illustrated with reference to transportation and delivery services, using platforms such as Uber, Lyft, Didi, Deliveroo and Foodora, but in reality platform work is far more heterogeneous and covers a broad range of services and products.

Research on platforms originates from various disciplinary areas such as computer science, business and management, law and sociology, which leads to a different focus and orientation in the object of study. The business and management literature is more inclined to adopt the perspective of how the use of labour platforms deliver 'business benefits'. It is presented as an opportunity to create and capture value with the sourcing of cheap labour or expertise (Zhao and Zhu, 2014). For online work, accessing labour via a platform which is independent of location enables numerical scaling of work execution without any significant transaction costs or logistical hurdles. At the heart of platform work is the assumption that transaction costs will be reduced as the technological architecture seamlessly reduces the expense associated with searching, matching and communicating with workers. These transaction costs do not disappear – they are simply shouldered by workers instead (Howcroft and Bergvall-Kåreborn, 2019).

Another body of literature has been concerned with the social and cultural value of platforms, particularly with regard to the concept of the sharing economy. Built on a narrative of collaboration and community, the sharing economy has been variously described as a social movement and an egalitarian vision, enabling people to connect directly rather than relying on large corporations, thereby appealing to the ideals of equality and sustainability. Enthusiasts claim it represents a form of disruptive innovation that is capable of reallocating wealth across the value chain, away from corporations and towards small producers and consumers, serving as an alternative to more traditional forms of market and hierarchy (see Benkler and Nissenbaum, 2006, and Shirky, 2010). However, the very concept of the sharing economy has been questioned, since its core is centred on monetary transaction (McCann, 2015), forming an uneasy partnership between markets and the social good (Slee, 2015). This led Scholz (2017) to declare that 'no-one could have believed that the ideological bubble of the sharing economy would deflate so quickly' as various platform companies became associated with some of the worst features of global capitalism (Schor, 2020), including exploitative transactions. At this juncture, a more critical literature has emerged, along with a proliferation of empirical research examining worker experiences, much of which has clustered around a few platforms, notably transportation network services and Mechanical Turk (MTurk). Within this body of critically-oriented research, a great deal of attention has focused on algorithmic management and employment misclassification in the form of 'bogus' self-employment.

The aim of this chapter is to contribute to the more critical debates on platform work. While there is a rich literature documenting workers' experiences, there is generally less attention paid to the platforms themselves, which is the focus of the next section. This follows with an overview of the characteristics of platform work, which considers the labour pool, the employment contract and control and coordination. This sets the scene for the case study which examines the oft-cited example of Uber. Finally, conclusions are drawn.

What are platforms and platform business models?

Platforms are presented as a success of technological innovation, centred upon predominantly influential young companies that are seen to pose a serious threat to established industry incumbents and are thus deeply disruptive. They function as digital environments that are characterized by near-zero marginal cost of access, reproduction and distribution (McAfee and Brynjolfsson, 2017). In contrast with the binary relationship that typifies employer–employee relations, platform work is largely portrayed as consisting of a three-sided relationship: the platform, the requester of work and the worker. This allows platforms to self-identify as neutral parties, suggesting that they serve as intermediaries in managing what economists describe as a two-sided market. Platform intermediation has a distinct logic based on network connections and the curating of digital connectivity, extracting rent from workers. As Joyce (2020: 543) points out, this triadic relationship is far from equal and 'turns out on closer inspection to be a big capitalist company, its workforce and some customers – hardly a novel configuration'.

There is ambiguity surrounding what exactly constitutes a platform and the term 'suggests a lot while saying very little' (Gillespie, 2010: 351). This opaqueness benefits the owners of platforms as their multifarious configurations enables them to appeal to various interests such as consumers, advertizers and venture capitalists. Platform firms may not necessarily experience the highest levels of revenues or profitability, yet they do have the highest market value; this is led by Microsoft, Amazon, Apple, Alphabet-Google and Facebook in the United States and Alibaba and Tencent in China (Cusumano et al., 2020). While Thompson (2019) makes the point that we should focus on 'actual existing capital' given that only two out of the top 50 companies by revenue are tech giants (Amazon and Apple); nevertheless, there is a longstanding belief in the future value of tech firms and the likelihood that they will deliver big payouts (Langley and Leyshon, 2017). Consequently, we are witnessing a goldrush mentality, whereby financial interests supporting platform firms focus on the longer-term pursuit of winner-takes-all returns (Sundararajan, 2016) and the hope of a future payoff.

The viability of many start-ups is dependent upon investor expectations that a firm will generate value at some later point. Compared with the 1990s dot-com boom, this represents a more patient form of capital investment (Rahman and Thelen, 2019), which has been concentrated in a smaller number of firms, with individual investors seeking a larger stake in potential jackpot monopolies. This enables platforms to maintain an asset-light balance sheet and remain loss-making for longer. This is one of the reasons why venture capital is tolerant of an unprofitable present since it assumes potential market domination in the future.

Positioning themselves as a digital intermediary or 'conduit' that facilitates exchange enables platforms to claim they are tech firms, in the hope of attracting speculative capital to sustain growth. Given that so many platforms are start-ups, finance is critical to their ability to invest in the technical infrastructure that enables activities to be globally distributed at low marginal cost. Once the infrastructure has been developed, platforms can open up their technology to external parties who then provide an extensive range of applications and services as they extract a surplus from each transaction. Generating network effects, whereby value increases geometrically as more people use it, is critical to expanding market share. These firms are prioritizing rapid up-scaling and extracting revenues from circulations and associated data trails (Langley and Leyshon, 2017). Benefits accrue as those that make it beyond a tipping point become hard to dislodge (Gawer, 2014), leading to extreme dominance by a few large corporations, usually Silicon Valley technology companies (Srnicek, 2017).

The belief in platforms extends to the belief in platform business models, which tend to be viewed as something essentialist based on concepts such as the value proposition, the revenue model, the market opportunity and the competitive environment. This has been heavily researched within the business and management literature with celebratory articles focusing on technology, architecture and value creation (Zott et al., 2011). Following on from what is arguably the failure of dotcom companies in the 2000s, when the concept of the business model took hold, the reformulated version of the platform business model continues to influence investors, with platforms valued at two to four times higher than companies with more traditional business models (Libert et al., 2016). Of the approximately 200 unicorns (a privately owned start-up whose value is believed to be in excess of $1 billion), between 60 and 70 per cent claim that they are based on platform business models (Cusumano et al., 2020). For new ventures such as platforms, which lack the traditional symbols of reliability, the role of the business model is to present a compelling vision of future potential, which is critical to raising capital and sustaining growth. Those business model narratives can be especially shaky when new firms set out to dislodge incumbents, and thus need to emphasize distinctiveness while not appearing to be too radical as to lack credibility (Rahman and Thelen, 2019). Here, the concept of the sharing economy has served as a useful rhetorical device, enabling start-up companies to latch onto its widespread popularity, thus strengthening the integrity of emergent platforms.

While reports differ widely on the extent of the growth of platform work, there is overall consensus that this is on the increase, particularly in certain areas of economic activity such as ride-hailing. There are three key reasons for the expansion of platform work. First, technological innovation has seen the creation of a vast global network which facilitates connectivity and enables scalability at speed (Gawer, 2014). This has enabled platform firms to gain a foothold in a number of international markets. Second, as the business literature informs us, platforms provide access to a variety of skills and expertise that can expand and contract on demand, with significantly lower labour costs and an absence of employment regulation. This is seen to benefit firms who are seeking novel forms of profit maximization. Finally, the cumulative impact of work-related changes (such as increasing precarity, insecurity and the desire of employers to offload risk) within a context of crisis and austerity means that platform work can provide either a supplementary or primary source of income, particularly for those who may be underpaid, underemployed or have limited access to traditional labour markets (for a discussion on management practices and work intensification see Chapter 12).

Characteristics of platform work

In this section, some of the basic characteristics of platform work will be outlined. These elements are shaped by the pivotal role played by the platform, as discussed above. While it is important to recognize the heterogeneity of platforms and platform work, nevertheless there are a number of fairly common characteristics that will be outlined: the labour pool, employment contracts and control and coordination.

The labour pool

In order to recruit labour that is willing to offer products and services via the platform, the concept of flexibility is utilized, tapping into the notion of the digital nomad (Aroles et al., 2020) with the promise of being able to select when and how often you work and using straplines such as 'live your work dream'. This has led a number of optimists to suggest that this type of work presents new job opportunities, providing alternatives for those weakly attached to the labour market, as well as offering flexibility that can accommodate care obligations (OECD, 2017). Ostensibly, platform work offers a number of benefits: by lowering barriers to entry and enabling access to a global labour market, it provides a meritocratic space that enables self-sufficiency and income generation; it provides spatial and temporal flexibility enabling self-determination for those with familial responsibilities who struggle to 'fit' corporate structures; and the absence of the supervisory function enables levels of autonomy that are distinct from organizational hierarchical control. Platform work is also seen to present a means whereby people who are marginalized by traditional employment structures can become self-employed and generate income in uncertain times. The concept of 'micro-entrepreneurship' (Botsman, 2015) is utilized to imply that anyone can monetize their underused skills and assets, enabling inclusive growth for those ordinarily excluded from conventional labour markets.

For labour, the majority of tasks tend to be tightly bounded as digitization facilitates fragmentation as larger work activities and projects are divided into fairly menial one-off activities (De Stefano, 2016). Consequently, encounters are largely transactional rather than relational, suggesting an extreme form of commodification. The bounded nature of the work means that there can be a significant amount of unpaid labour time spent waiting, searching or bidding for one-off tasks (Berg, 2016) in what is effectively a piecework system. Labour arbitrage determines levels of pay. This refers to the practice of utilizing workers from lower cost geographies and paying them local wages. This practice is not unique to platforms and is at the core of outsourcing processes that have fragmented the labour process (Taylor, 2015). In the absence of a formal employer with practices of wage-setting by job category, there is wide variation in earnings levels among individuals who are carrying out comparative work.

Given the nature of the working conditions, platform work is essentially stripped down to a financial transaction based on the sale and purchase of labour and so the issue of payment is critical (Joyce, 2020). There is an important difference between those platform workers who use the platform for supplementary income (to augment earnings, usually from another job) and those whose livelihoods are dependent on their income from the platform (Forde et al., 2017). Schor (2020) argues that this distinction is crucial for understanding the variety of work experiences. She argues that supplemental earners are more likely to have 'outside options' and therefore enjoy greater levels of autonomy and control when it comes to accepting and rejecting work, leading to higher levels of satisfaction and improved earnings. By contrast, dependent earners are placed in a weaker bargaining position and face greater insecurity. This is especially the case where platforms exhibit near-monopoly space, reducing alternatives and thus heightening dependency.

Employment contracts

Key to the generation of network effects is the platform's ability to attract a substantial number of workers. Platform work draws on the narrative of 'being your own boss'. This taps into the sharing economy rhetoric, which suggests that workers can become 'micro-entrepreneurs': 'People who are empowered to make or save money by offering their existing assets or services to other people' (Botsman, 2015). Identifying as a tech firm rather than, say, a taxi firm or retailer boosts platforms self-identification as a digital matching service – hence, workers are predominantly classified as 'independent contactors' (Berg, 2016). This relieves platforms of the costs and responsibilities associated with being a 'real' employer, enabling platforms to undercut wage-paying competitors as they pursue expansion. The process of 'legal engineering' shifts responsibility to workers who are personally liable for collecting, reporting and paying taxes (Felstiner, 2011). At the same time, the absence of legal protection alleviates the regulatory requirements and costs associated with paying the minimum wage that ordinarily applies to employers. Self-employment classification sees a shifting of the burden of risk from capital to labour and workers live that tension, resulting in a growing 'crisis of attachment' (McCann, 2014). Reliance on voluntary initiative (in the form of self-employment) is usually advantageous to capital (Burawoy, 1979) as poor performance equates with limited access to further work (for discussions on the changing nature of work and its fragmentation see Chapter 1).

Platform labour marketplaces have grown in the shadow of the law (Cherry, 2016) and openly challenge or avoid regulation to enable growth, often investing heavily in lobbyists (McNeill, 2016). The resistance of platforms to existing employment regulation is not that unique and it mirrors many of the facets of non-standard employment and the shift of employment-related risk to workers. If it is the case that platforms operate as mere middlemen, then the classification of workers as independent contractors would not even be brought into question. Yet there are numerous ongoing lawsuits regarding employment misclassification as litigation is revealing platform work for what it is: 'labour without overhead' (Shapiro, 2020). Taking advantage of gaps in employment law, while scaling quickly, helps platforms become 'too big to ban' (Pollman and Barry, 2017), even though operating in legal grey areas risks being associated with ethical breaches which can create reputational damage and influence investor enthusiasm.

Control and coordination

For platforms to be credible providers of services and/or products, trust between workers and requesters is deemed critical (Kornberger et al., 2017). It is assumed that trust can be captured and measured in the form of online customer ratings, creating a digitalized history of performance evaluations, which serve as a basis of evidential access for future work. However, given that performance evaluation is effectively outsourced to individual requesters/consumers, there is an absence of standardization of what is ultimately an output based on variable and subjective opinions. Accountability for the entire digitalized process is offloaded onto workers because there are no options to rate the platform separately. Many online ratings are problematic, with negative reviews being associated with race, gender and age discrimination (Cherry, 2019; Ge et al., 2016). Questions have been raised concerning the extent to which customers are qualified to provide a fair and objective evaluation, given that platforms lever negative reviews as disciplinary instruments, resulting in workers being deactivated from the platform.

There is a proliferation of literature around algorithms and the perceived ability of technology to exert control over work. It is worth noting that technical control is not new and there is a long history of research examining this, with examples such as Taylor and Bain's (1999) classic article on 'an assembly line in the head' which studied the application of computer telephony in call centres (see also Chapter 12 on lean production). With platforms, algorithmic management allows companies to internally oversee myriads of workers in an optimized manner over a large scale (Lee et al., 2015). Given that many base their success on access to a substantial labour supply, direct assessment of the quality of the labour process can be both time-consuming and costly, and so, in this respect, algorithms serve as a proxy for management. In the absence of direct control, algorithms provide a semblance of quality assurance as they present behavioural nudges in the form of automated messages to incentivize, homogenize and generally control how workers function within the system, ensuring service delivery aligns with their interests (Shapiro, 2020). Replacing the role of an actual line manager or supervisor with algorithms enables minimal intervention from the platform which helps sustain the notion of workers as independent contractors, thus relieving some of the pressure on platforms to pay wages and associated costs.

With platform work, there is generally less concern with explicit control at the point of production since this represents one element in the wider circuit of capital. Platforms are creating a networked mode of market dominance, based primarily on direct ownership of the technological infrastructure as opposed to control of labour, but control of labour becomes an outcome of emergent systems. Surplus is generated from circulation and the process of exchange, so coordinating that process efficiently is critical. Hence investment is placed in technological infrastructure (as opposed to labour) that enables the curation of each and every transaction and also provides the coordination mechanisms to foster up-scaling. The model is based on building critical mass, reaping economies of scale, value-skimming transactions, expanding market share, wiping out competitors and aiming for a jackpot initial public offering (IPO), referring to a stock market launch.

Schor (2020) describes platform work as a 'retreat from control' and argues that this is the lynchpin to understanding what is unique about platform work. She describes this as a 'new labour regime' as platform workers have greater autonomy over scheduling and how their work is executed. This position contrasts with some of the more critical writings which emphasize enhanced control, usually focusing on algorithmic control in particular (see Wood et al., 2019). Rather than the locus of control centring predominantly on algorithms, the overall combination of nudges, metrics, online ratings, independent contractor status and a fragmented labour process is woven together to create a more subtle form of control, but one which is no less powerful.

Case study: Uber

Uber presents an interesting case study since it is one of the fastest growing start-ups in Silicon Valley (Kavadias et al., 2016) which quickly attracted significant levels of venture capture investment. Originally seen to epitomize the sharing economy, Uber drew on the values and practices associated with peer-to-peer collaboration, deploying the inclusive language of 'ridesharing' with taxi drivers defined as 'partners' (Uber, 2019). Over time, its questionable practices have polarized opinion, to the extent that 'few inventions have caused more controversy' (Berger et al., 2017). Founded in 2009, Uber's growth was rapid and within just a few years there were around half as many Uber and Lyft drivers as there are taxi drivers in the United States (Cramer and Krueger, 2016), transforming personal transportation services in a short space of time. By 2019, Uber claimed it had 91 million monthly active customers (Uber, 2019) as the platform achieved a 'taken-for-granted' status and dominance became self-perpetuating.

Uber's pursuit of rapid scalability entails the recruitment of a vast off-the-books labour force and research from the United States shows that Uber's introduction into the labour market led to a proliferation of self-employment among taxi drivers (Berger et al., 2017). This initially involved leveraging the principles of the sharing economy to entice non-taxi drivers to the platform at the same time as attracting experienced drivers. Drivers wishing to sign-up encounter very low entry requirements, which includes the licensing, plate fees or commercial insurance fees that traditional taxi drivers face (Peticca-Harris et al., 2020). Research on app-based transportation companies in New York City found that the expanding workforce draws principally on migrant workers who are confronted with restricted labour markets and are the primary financial providers for their families (Parrott and Reich, 2018). Uber attracts potential drivers by comparing average earnings across various driving jobs, indicating that they offer the most lucrative earnings. This is supplemented with other financial incentives such as subsidizing fares so that drivers receive a higher share and offering 'referral' bonuses for recommendations (Uber, 2019). In reality, there have been accusations of inflationary claims (Calo and Rosenblat, 2017) with one study showing that 85 per cent of app-based transportation workers are earning below the minimum wage and that the vast majority (80 per cent) had to purchase a vehicle, with many resorting to subprime loans (Parrott and Reich, 2018).

In the initial stages, the sharing economy rhetoric seemed sufficiently convincing to attract workers who were looking to earn extra income to supplement their regular employment. In a highly-cited US survey by Hall and Krueger (2015), the findings show that the number of new drivers more than doubles every six months. Yet ongoing recruitment is essential since 30 per cent of drivers are no longer actively using the system after the first six months, signalling problems with turnover and retention. Over time, as various loss-leading enticements attracted experienced drivers from other taxi firms, creating the necessary network effects, incumbents were pushed out of the market (Waheed et al., 2015). Consequently, the labour pool increased its proportion of experienced taxi drivers, who are more likely to rely on the platform to earn a living. The lack of alternatives creates dependence, which then enables Uber to increase commission levels, taking a larger proportion of each fare at a later date. A study in Los Angeles confirms the negative impact of Uber on the taxi industry as the number of rides significantly dropped when Uber and Lyft entered the market, resulting in widespread job loss (Waheed et al., 2015).

Tensions between scale and reputation arise when basic operations are based on a contingent labour force and so Uber seeks various mechanisms for controlling labour. Drivers are regularly forced to agree to new terms and conditions whenever they log in to the platform (Calo and Rosenblat, 2017). They have no individual price-setting capacity and so pay varies according to labour supply and demand within each specific location. Pay rates are subject to unilateral change by Uber and are often announced with no prior warning (Zwick, 2017). Drivers' queries and concerns are directed to call centres, many of which are outsourced to the Philippines, thereby nullifying drivers' ability to challenge their terms and conditions, raising questions about fairness (Fiesler et al., 2017).

As with many platforms, creating layers of direct managerial control to oversee the workforce would negate the benefits of low cost and also dispute their position as a digital intermediary. Uber's technological infrastructure includes complex algorithms, which play a prime role in the provision of micro-level evaluation of interactions with minimal direct intervention. For example, performance metrics are displayed on an assemblage of digital devices on the dashboard and include number of trips, number of hours online, fares per hour, acceptance rate and driver overall rating, all of which are compared with 'top drivers' (Rosenblat and Stark, 2016). Internal algorithms are augmented with customer evaluations of job performance which also feed into workforce management. Uber mediates each interaction which facilitates the extraction of vast amounts of data, the analysis of which provides fertile ground for digital market manipulation (Calo and Rosenblat, 2017). Uber seeks to gain advantage by restricting the amount of information available to drivers, as in the case of accepting a trip without prior knowledge of location or destination (known as blind ride acceptance). On other occasions, Uber are vague when presenting information, such as with surge pricing, where heat maps indicate areas of high demand in order to attract drivers to a particular locale.

Uber's strategy is to rapidly up-scale, lock in consumers and displace competition in order to achieve monopolization of territory. At the outset, Uber set out to challenge or avoid regulation and took on the role of a consumer champion, hampered by regulation in its quest to counter the established 'taxi monopoly'. Uber provoked various regulatory 'flashpoints' in different spatial contexts, including (unfair) competition, employment and

(Continued)

labour issues, social policy and social benefit concerns, taxation avoidance and consumer safety (Thelen, 2018). Subsequent scale helps to ensure challenges to legal grey areas become publicly salient as Uber became an indispensable amenity in many urban geographies. This bolsters the 'too-big-to-ban' strategy as the unpopularity of licence withdrawal creates an unwillingness of authorities to intervene when consumer alternatives are either costlier or absent (see, for example, the 2017 'Save your Uber in London' petition with almost one million signatures).

Uber's 'go-it-alone' (Cohen and Kietzmann, 2014: 291) approach has resulted in numerous rolling and costly lawsuits, initiated by governments, drivers, passengers and competitors. Although the majority of legal challenges have taken place in the United States, the global reach of Uber means that in 2017 it was embroiled in more than 73 major cases in 25 different markets (Radu and Borg-Psaila, 2017). Having the financial clout to employ lobbyists and stall the legal process using appeals enables Uber to trade while buying time in anticipation of monopolization. For example, in 2020 voters in California were balloted on Proposition 22, which would allow firms like Uber and Lyft to continue classifying drivers as contractors rather than employees and would exempt them from Californian labour law. While drivers and advocates of labour rights opposed Proposition 22 because it enabled companies to sidestep their obligations, the proposition was passed. The victory was helped by the combined financial campaigning efforts of Silicon Valley tech companies (including Uber, Lyft, Instacart and DoorDash), which amounted to around $200 million. The success or failure of these measures were seen to symbolize the future of the gig economy, since fulfilment of employer obligations would destabilize financial viability and the ability of platforms to undercut competitors. Proposition 22 is just one of many examples that illustrate how Uber is positioned in a high-stakes game: if it is to expand quickly, it must operate in legal grey areas; but operating in those grey areas exposes it to reputational damage and sanction which could undermine its capacity to grow, potentially affecting company valuations. This precarious balance between the pursuit of growth while engaging in regulatory arbitrage has recently come to a head with the ruling from the United Kingdom (UK) Supreme Court in February 2021 that drivers are to be classified as workers rather than self-employed, because they are in a position of subordination and dependency to Uber (Venkataramakrishnan and Croft, 2021). This landmark judgement sets a precedent for the treatment of gig economy workers in both the UK and elsewhere, because foreign courts pay attention to legal decisions in other jurisdictions. There are significant implications for Uber and the likelihood of a steep rise in operating costs, which will seriously challenge its potential future profitability.

Although taxi driving has long been economically precarious, drivers have been able to exercise a degree of autonomy with control over their schedule, including where to pick up passengers, how best to interact with them and how to navigate geographically (Occhiuto, 2017). Working as an Uber driver appears to negate the positive aspects of taxi-driving and so drivers may well switch to an alternative platform with better working conditions, creating mobility power (Smith, 2006). Organizing collectively could also offer a route to improved conditions and there is increasing evidence of resistance and worker mobilization, particularly among transportation and food delivery platforms, with examples such as Gig Workers Rising and Rideshare Drivers United in the United States. In the UK, the first organic and bottom-up trade union in over a century was set up: the Independent Workers of Great Britain, whose recent campaign is fighting to end unfair key worker termination by Deliveroo and UberEats. Much of the focus is on litigation, with less attention paid to collective voice and recognition of the right to collective bargaining (Aliosi, 2019). Nonetheless, there are increasing numbers of workers building active solidarity, which is emerging in various forms to foster collective agency and challenge workplace conditions (Tassinari and Maccarrone, 2020). For example, the 2017 #DeleteUber social media campaign, which emerged in response to what was perceived as an attempt by Uber to break the strike by taxi drivers at JFK Airport in the wake of Trump's travel ban on Muslim-majority countries (Cresci, 2017). Widespread online condemnation served as a focal point around which other negative stories started to accumulate, indicating public dissatisfaction with Uber's treatment of drivers and disregard for regulation. This troubled investors and left Uber with difficulties in November of that year in raising equity funding at a price that would continue its valuation trajectory.

While Uber's brisk impact on the traditional taxi industry has led many to surmise that platforms are an unstoppable force that cannot be curtailed, an initially positive perception of Uber as an innovative platform is being eroded as the extent of its questionable operational practices emerge. From its initial representation as one of the pioneers of the sharing economy, Uber quickly morphed into the company that symbolized the much-maligned gig economy. Actions have consequences and the shift in public perception has led to a disastrous IPO on the stock market in 2019 that was far lower than expected (Bond et al., 2019). This has led some to question the very foundations of Uber's 'transformative business model' (Kavadias et al., 2016) and raise concerns about its future viability. This is especially pertinent given the UK Supreme Court ruling which may have devastating consequences for its business model (Venkataramakrishnan and Croft, 2021).

Case study questions

1. Why is Uber, with zero levels of profitability, able to attract significant amounts of venture capital?
2. What are the consequences of the increasingly global dominance of Uber on traditional taxi firms and transportation labour markets?
3. What is the impact of the 2021 UK Supreme Court ruling on Uber's competitiveness?
4. What are the longer-term implications of the 2021 UK Supreme Court ruling for Uber and platform work more widely?

Conclusion

This chapter has examined platforms and platform work in order to reflect the growing interest in what many perceive to be a fundamentally distinctive form of work. However, it is important not to overstate the significance of platform work given that the vast majority of employment, certainly in the Global North, is based on full-time, permanent contracts with an identifiable employer. This is not intended to deny the importance of the growth of platform work, particularly as firms look to capitalize on new opportunities. In the context of a global pandemic and the associated economic and social fallout, firms may well seek new forms of exploitation and cost-reduction, making it more likely that outsourcing tasks and activities on a piecework basis via platforms will continue to expand both numerically and into novel areas of employment.

Reflective questions

1. Why are people attracted to working on platforms?
2. How does control manifest in platforms?
3. What are the consequences of the comparatively low pay rates on the employment relationship?
4. Should labour platforms be classified as employers and provide the associated social and economic obligations to workers?
5. Should platform firms be subjected to national and international regulation? What are the problems associated with this?

Recommended reading

- Gandini, A. (2019) 'Labour process theory and the gig economy'. *Human Relations*, 72(6): 1039–56.
- Howcroft, D. and Bergvall-Kåreborn, B. (2019) 'A typology of crowdwork platforms'. *Work, Employment and Society*, 33(1): 21–38.
- Tassinari, A. and Maccarrone, V. (2020) 'Riders on the storm: Workplace solidarity among gig economy couriers in Italy and the UK'. *Work, Employment and Society*, 34(1): 35–54.

References

Aliosi, A. (2019) *Negotiating the Digital Transformation of Work: Non-Standard Workers' Voice, Collective Rights and Mobilisation Practices in the Platform Economy*. EUI Working Paper MWP 2019/03.

Aroles, J., Granter, E. and de Vaujany, F.-X. (2020) '"Becoming mainstream": The professionalisation and corporatisation of digital nomadism'. *New Technology, Work and Employment*, 35(1): 114–29.

Benkler, Y. and Nissenbaum, H. (2006) 'Commons-based peer production and virtue'. *Journal of Political Philosophy*, 14(4): 394–419.

Berg, J. (2016) 'Income security in the on-demand economy: Findings and policy lessons from a survey of crowdworkers'. *Comparative Labor Law and Policy Journal*, 37(3): 2016.

Berger, T., Chen, C. and Frey, C. B. (2018) 'Drivers of disruption: estimating the Uber effect'. *European Economic Review*, 110: 197–210.

Bond, S., Bullock, N. and Bradshaw, T. (2019) 'Uber seeks $91.5bn valuation in this year's largest IPO'. *Financial Times*, 25 April.

Botsman, R. (2015) 'The changing rules of trust in the digital age'. *Harvard Business Review*, 20 October.

Burawoy, M. (1979) *Manufacturing Consent*. Chicago: University of Chicago Press.

Calo, R. and Rosenblat, A. (2017) 'The taking economy: Uber, information, and power'. *Columbia Law Review*, 117(6): 1623–90.

Cherry, M. A. (2016) 'Beyond misclassification: the digital transformation of work'. *Comparative Labor Law and Policy Journal*. Available at: http://ssrn.com/abstract=2734288.

Cherry, M. A. (2019) 'Age discrimination in the on-demand economy and crowdwork'. *Berkeley Journal of Employment and Labor Law*, 40(1): 29–60.

Cohen, B. and Kietzmann, J. (2014) 'Ride on! Mobility business models for the sharing economy'. *Organization and Environment*, 27(3): 279–296.

Cramer, J. and Krueger, A. B. (2016) 'Disruptive change in the taxi business: The case of Uber'. *American Economic Review*, 106(5): 177–82.

Cresci, E. (2017) '#DeleteUber: How social media turned on Uber'. *The Guardian*, 30 January. Available at: www.theguardian.com/technology/2017/jan/30/deleteuber-how-social-media-turned-on-uber.

Cusumano, M. A., Yoffie, D. B. and Gawer, A. (2020) 'The future of platforms'. *MIT Sloan Management Review*, 61: 46–54.

De Stefano, V. (2016) *The Rise of the 'Just-in-Time Workforce': On-demand Work, Crowdwork and Labour Protection in the 'Gig Economy'*. Research paper, ILO, Geneva, Conditions of Work and Employment Series, No. 71.

Felstiner, A. (2011) 'Working the crowd: employment and labor law in the crowdsourcing industry'. *Berkeley Journal of Employment and Labor Law*, 32: 143–203.

Fiesler, C., Bucher, E. and Hoffman, C. P. (2017) 'Unfairness by design? The perceived fairness of digital labor on crowdworking platforms'. *Journal of Business Ethics*, 156: 987–1005.

Forde, C., Stuart, M. and Joyce, S. (2017) *The Social Protection of Workers in the Platform Economy*. Report PE 614.184. European Parliament, Brussels. Available at: www.europarl.europa.eu/RegData/etudes/STUD/2017/614184/IPOL_STU(2017)614184_EN.pdf.

Gandini, A. (2019) 'Labour process theory and the gig economy'. *Human Relations*, 72(6): 1039–56.

Gawer, A. (2014) 'Bridging differing perspectives on technological platforms: Toward an integrative framework'. *Research Policy*, 43(7): 1239–49.

Ge, Y., Knittel, C. R., MacKenzie, D. and Zoepf, S. (2016) *Racial and Gender Discrimination in Transportation Network Companies*. National Bureau of Economic Research Working Paper 22776. Available at: www.nber.org/papers/w22776.

Gillespie, T. (2010) 'The politics of "platforms"'. *New Media & Society*, 12(3): 347–64.

Hall, J. and Krueger, A. (2015) *An Analysis of the Labour Market for Uber's Driver-Partners in the United States*. Princeton University, Industrial Relations Section, Working Paper 587.

Howcroft, D. and Bergvall-Kåreborn, B. (2019) 'A typology of crowdwork platforms'. *Work, Employment and Society*, 33(1): 21–38.

Howe, J. (2006) 'The rise of crowdsourcing'. *Wired*, Issue 14.06. Available at: www.wired.com/wired/archive/14.06/crowds_pr.html

Joyce, S. (2020) 'Rediscovering the cash nexus, again: Subsumption and the labour-capital relation in platform work'. *Capital and Class*, 44(4): 541–52.

Kavadias, S., Ladas, K. and Loch, C. (2016) 'The transformative business model'. *Harvard Business Review*, 94: 90–8.

Kornberger, M. Pflueger, D. and Mouritsen, J. (2017) 'Evaluative infrastructures: Accounting for platform organization'. *Accounting, Organizations and Society*, 60: 79–95.

Langley, P. and Leyshon, A. (2017) 'Platform capitalism: The intermediation and capitalisation of digital economic circulation'. *Finance and Society*, 3(1): 11–31.

Lee, M. K., Kusbit, D., Metsky, E. and Dabbish, L. (2015) 'Working with machines: The impact of algorithmic and data-driven management on human workers'. *In Proceedings of the 33rd Annual ACM Conference on Human Factors in Computing Systems*, Seoul. Available at: https://dl.acm.org/doi/10.1145/2702123.2702548

Libert, B., Beck, M. and Wind, J. (2016) *The Network Imperative: How to Survive and Grow in the Age of Digital Business Models*. Cambridge: Harvard Business Review Press.

McAfee, A. and Brynjolfsson, E. (2017) 'Machine, Platform, Crowd: Harnessing our Digital Future. New York: W. W. Norton & Company

McCann, D. (2015) *The Sharing Economy: The Good, the Bad, and the Real*. Available at: www.neweconomics.org/blog/entry/the-sharing-economy-the-good-the-bad-and-the-real (accessed 10 December 2015).

McCann, L. (2014) 'Disconnected amid the networks and chains: Employee detachment from company and union after offshoring'. *British Journal of Industrial Relations*, 52(2): 237–60.

McNeill, D. (2016) 'Governing a city of unicorns: technology capital and the urban politics of San Francisco'. *Urban Geography*, 37: 494–513.

Occhiuto, N. (2017) 'Investing in independent contract work: The significance of schedule control for taxi driver's. *Work and Occupations*, 44(3): 268–95.

OECD (2017) *Going Digital: The Future of Work for Women*. Policy brief on the Future of Work. Available at: www.oecd.org/employment/Going-Digital-the-Future-of-Work-for-Women.pdf.

Parrott, J. A. and Reich, M. (2018) *An Earnings Standard for New York City's App-Based Drivers*. Report, Centre for New York City Affairs, New York. Available at: https://static1.squarespace.com/static/53ee4f0be4b015b9c3690d84/t/5b3a3aaa0e2e72ca74079142/1530542764109/Parrott-Reich+NYC+App+Drivers+TLC+Jul+2018jul1.pdf.

Peticca-Harris, A., deGama, N. and Ravishankar, M. N. (2020) 'Postcapitalist precarious work and those in the "driver's" seat: Exploring the motivations and lived experiences of Uber drivers in Canada'. *Organization*, 27(1): 36–59.

Pollman, E. and Barry, J. (2017) 'Regulatory entrepreneurship'. *California Law Review*, 90(3): 383–448.

Radu, R. and Borg-Psaila, S. (2017) *Uberisation Demystified: Examining Legal and Regulatory Responses Worldwide*. Paper presented to 5th International Labour Office Conference of the Regulating for Decent Work Network, Geneva, Switzerland, 3–5 July.

Rahman, K. S. and Thelen, K. (2019) 'The rise of the platform business model and the transformation of twenty-first-century capitalism'. *Politics and Society*, 47(2): 177–204.

Rosenblat, A. and Stark, L. (2016) 'Algorithmic labor and information asymmetries: A case study of Uber's drivers'. *International Journal of Communication*, 10: 3758–84.

Scholz, T. (2017) *Uberworked and Underpaid*. Cambridge: Polity Press.

Schor, J. (2020) *After the Gig*. University of California Press.

Shapiro, A. (2020) 'Dynamic exploits: Calculative asymmetries in the on-demand economy'. *New Technology, Work and Employment*, 35(2): 162–77.

Shirky, C. (2010) *Cognitive Surplus: Creativity and Generosity in a Connected Age*. Penguin Press.

Slee, T. (2015) *What's Yours is Mine: Against the Sharing Economy*. New York: OR Books.

Smith, C. (2006) 'The double indeterminacy of labour power: Labour effort and labour mobility'. *Work, Employment and Society*, 20(2): 389–402.

Srnicek, N. (2017) *Platform Capitalism*. London: Polity Press.

Sundararajan, A. (2016) *The Sharing Economy: The End of Employment and the Rise of Crowd-based Capitalism*. Cambridge: MIT Press.

Tassinari, A. and Maccarrone, V. (2020) 'Riders on the storm: workplace solidarity among gig economy couriers in Italy and the UK'. *Work, Employment and Society*, 34(1): 35–54.

Taylor, P. (2015) 'Labour and the changing landscapes of the call centre'. In K. Newsome, P. Taylor, J. Bair and A. Rainnie (eds), *Putting Labour in Its Place: Labour Process Analysis and Global Value Chains*. Basingstoke: Palgrave Macmillan, pp. 266–86.

Taylor, P. and Bain, P. (1999) '"An assembly line in the head": Work and employee relations in the call centre'. *Industrial Relations Journal*, 30(2): 101–17.

Thelen, K. (2018) 'Regulating Uber: The politics of the platform economy in Europe and the United States'. *Perspectives on Politics*, 16(4): 938–53.

Thompson, P. (2019) 'Capitalism technology and work: Interrogating the tipping point thesis'. *Political Quarterly*, 91(2): 299–309.

Uber (2019) *Form S-1 Registration Statement*. Available at: www.sec.gov/Archives/edgar/data/1543151/000119312519103850/d647752ds1.htm.

Venkataramakrishnan, S. and Croft, J. (2021) Uber Loses Landmark UK Battle as Supreme Court Rules Drivers are Workers. Available at: www.ft.com/content/9ef3a1c5-328c-460d-9261-33ea991cae62

Waheed, S., Herrera, L. and Ritoper, S. (2015) *Ridesharing or Ridestealing? Changes in Taxi Ridership and Revenue in Los Angeles 2009–2014*. UCLA Labor Centre. Available at: www.labor.ucla.edu/taxi-brief/.

Wood, A. J., Graham, M., Lehdonvirta, V. and Hjorth, I. (2019) 'Good gig, bad gig: autonomy and algorithmic control in the global gig economy'. *Work, Employment and Society*, 33(1): 56–75.

Zhao, Y. and Zhu, Q. (2014) 'Evaluation on crowdsourcing research: Current status and future direction'. *Information Systems Frontiers*, 16(3): 417–34.

Zott, C., Amit, R. and Massa, L. (2011) 'The business model: Recent developments and future research'. *Journal of Management*, 37: 1019–42.

Zwick, A. (2017) 'Welcome to the gig economy: Neoliberal industrial relations and the case of Uber'. *GeoJournal*, 83: 679–91.

Section 4

Regulation and the agenda for decent work

16 Regulating work and employment internationally: a complex tapestry

Robert MacKenzie and Miguel Martínez Lucio

Learning objectives

- To explain the meaning and development of regulation
- To identify the range of actors involved in the regulation of work and employment
- To understand the different ways that work and employment issues are regulated internationally
- To outline the dilemmas related to regulation in the transnational context

Introduction

This chapter addresses the regulation of the employment relationship and its transformation in relation to the increased internationalization of economic activity and the management of work. We explore how we should conceptualize regulation and why it is important for our understanding of the management of employment internationally. Regulation is often taken as being synonymous with the role of law and its enactment through institutions of the state; however, regulation is not solely about the government or the state but incorporates a range of actors who shape the rules and processes influencing the firm and its decision-making, and the regulatory spaces in which it operates. The chapter will examine how regulatory actors frame the rules and rights with regard to the employment relationship. We will look beyond the state and government to consider the various public, voluntary and private sector groups that influence employment systems and their management in national and, increasingly, international contexts. In addition to the traditional role played by trade unions, there is a widening array of actors shaping the economic context of management, from fair-trade organizations to social lobbies and transnational governmental institutions such as the World Trade Organization (WTO). This broadening of the notion of regulation is essential if we are to understand the different actors who shape the relations and rules of work, and the emergence of new actors and new regulatory spaces in which management operate (MacKenzie and Martínez Lucio, 2005).

This chapter also explores the role of new actors such as international consultancies, accountancy firms and think tanks in propagating the agenda for regulatory change. Rising to view in the late 1970s, such bodies provided the intellectual imperative for the emerging neoliberal political agenda in the United Kingdom (UK) and the United States. Soon established as the new hegemonic project, the neoliberal agenda represented not just a critique of the role of regulatory actors but a challenge to the idea of regulation itself, albeit often narrowly defined in terms of 'hard' legalistic state intervention. In their own terms, these actors have been successful in changing the nature of the debate, and undermining the political appetite for 'hard' regulation. The catch-all vindication, globalization, fuelled the notion that, in addition to being illegitimate, national-level intervention was increasingly outmoded: hard regulation was bad for business, but also bad for the national interests of countries wishing to attract crucial investment from multinational corporations (MNCs). Yet the imperative for regulation cannot be removed; the political appetite for hard regulation may have diminished under ongoing ideological onslaught, but this has been transposed with a growing interest in new and alternative forms of 'soft' regulation. Current modes of thinking favour some re-regulation of MNCs and their employment practices across national boundaries, through establishing codes of practice and ethical agendas in reflection of a greater interest in worker rights and social responsibility. Throughout the chapter, we will show how ideas and values that frame the economic and political context of MNCs are developed and often contested. We also address the continued and changing role of trade unions, a theme developed elsewhere in the book (see Chapter 17 for an in-depth discussion of international employee representation).

Regulation and work

The purpose of regulation is to facilitate social and economic reproduction. The logic of reproduction is based on the establishment of order and regularity, in terms of establishing shared rules and sustaining consistent decision-making processes. Regulation offers some predictability regarding the conduct of agents operating within a given environment. While the development of standard expectations regarding the behaviour of others provides the basis for social and economic interaction and reproduction (MacKenzie and Martínez Lucio, 2005), it does not imply that regulation is always effective in establishing a basis for economic activity (Jessop, 1990; Peck, 1996). Our understanding of regulation should go beyond viewing it as merely legal enactment (see MacKenzie and Martínez Lucio, 2005, 2014, and Martínez Lucio and Mackenzie, 2004). Baldwin et al. (1998) argue that three key strands of thought on regulation can be detected. The first views regulation in terms of 'targeted rules', 'accompanied by some mechanism, typically a public agency, for monitoring and promoting compliance' (Baldwin et al., 1998: 3). A second view is to be found in the area of political economy, which conceptualizes regulation as the state and its attempt to manage the economy. However, a third view adopts a broader perspective, defining regulation to include 'all mechanisms of social control – including unintentional and non-state processes . . .' (ibid.: 4).

Regulation, therefore, involves a variety of actors such as state institutions, trade unions, management networks, international state agencies and even social bodies such as international charities, to name some key examples (MacKenzie and Martínez Lucio, 2005; Martínez Lucio and MacKenzie, 2004; Regini, 2000). Regulation also encompasses a variety of levels and relations between them. The regulatory roles of organized labour and organized capital, for instance, inter-relate at various levels: from national level apex organizations of employer federations and trade union confederations, to regional or sectoral mechanisms and down to the level of company and workplace relations between management and trade unions – which may also include less institutionalized, informal practices. The actual regulatory actors and the roles they play in the regulation of social and economic relationships vary according to the context. It is important to recognize, therefore, that the panoply of actors and levels reflects the coexistence of different types of regulation. Indeed, regulation has formal and informal qualities, reflected in the increasing array of actors involved (Picciotto, 1999). Individuals and organizations may simultaneously be subject to a multiplicity of regulatory actors such as the state, employers and mechanisms of joint regulation, in addition to a range of social agencies and institutions. This tapestry of regulation is explored below, beginning with the crucial role played by the state.

The changing context of regulation

The political context of change

From the mid 1940s until the late 1970s, most developed economies – especially those European countries with a social and welfare orientation – favoured an interventionist role for the state and, whether effective or otherwise, encouraged systems of regulation through legislation or other institutionalized means (Esping Anderson, 2000). Often associated with Keynesian models of state intervention in the management of the economy and the associated redistributive mechanisms of the Welfare State, this 'Golden Age' began to falter in the European context during the mid to late 1970s (see Jessop, 2002: 55–79).

The critique presented was that the combination of extensive state intervention in the economy, increasing rigidity of labour market regulations in terms of hiring and firing workers and the steadily increasing power of trade unions had created an untenable inflationary situation. While much of this critique is disputed, the belief in structured and nationally based systems of regulation as a central feature of economic and social progress became tarnished (see Hall, 1988, and Jessop, 2002: 95–139). What began to emerge in the political mainstream from the mid to late 1970s was a political view of regulation per se as being prohibitive and costly, both for the firm and for society in general (Friedman, 1968). At an organizational level, this new agenda meant questioning a range of institutional obstacles perceived to be impeding the imperative of market forces, including mechanisms of joint regulation and even long-term employment contracts. For some, this marketization represented an 'Americanization' of employment strategies (Brewster, 2004; Guest, 1990), where the role of regulation through the state and collective organization becomes secondary to management prerogative (Whitley et al., 2005): a model that can be juxtaposed against European traditions where the state is more interventionist, and worker rights and collective representation are more influential in terms of human resource management (HRM) practices and decision-making (Brewster, 2004).

The politics of work and ideational contests

With regard to firm level HRM, the transmission of any new 'best practice' approach ultimately relies upon the agency of management and other firm-based actors such as trade unions. The implementation of 'best practice', therefore, is essentially a political process – that is to say, it is based on struggles between actors, which are shaped by the power resources available to them. Competing views and divergent values pertaining to the market and the individual exist within the same firm, not only between management and the representatives of labour but also between different cohorts of management. For example, stemming from developments associated with the Japanization debate, lean production and associated new techniques at work have been an important feature of change over recent decades, in UK workplaces and beyond (see Chapter 12 on lean production). As Stewart (1996) argues, the associated organizational and employment changes were not the inevitable outcomes of objectively superior efficiencies associated with new management systems but rather were shaped by political debates and struggles between unions, employers and even academics. Furthermore, the practices of teamworking and quality management were to a significant degree crafted not just by overseas MNCs in the early 1990s but also by consultancy firms. The contribution of other actors was also highly significant, with a facilitating political context being shaped by the role of right-wing think tanks in the United States (Heritage Foundation, founded in 1973) and the UK (Centre for Policy Studies, founded by right-wing politicians Keith Joseph and Margaret Thatcher in 1974). These institutions, unaccountable to any electorate, were central to opposing, de-legitimizing and undermining state-led regulation (see Heller, 2002; Klein, 2007: 50–1; Legge, 2002; Morgan and Hauptmeier, 2021).

There was also the expansive growth of business schools, which have in many although not all cases propagated an increasingly neoliberal view of organizations and their purpose, supported by direct intervention from consultancy firms that research, motivate and legitimate organizational change (O'Shea and Madigan, 1997; Parker, 2018). These interventions provided new regulatory actors, be they state agencies or particular consultancy firms, with the knowledge resources, technical competences and degree of legitimacy necessary for influencing the terminology and practices of new forms of management strategy (see Chapter 9 on training in the context of globalization). Yet these educational and knowledge-based spaces are changing and becoming the objects of greater internal debate and challenge: the realities of what business schools 'do' can vary, especially in light of emergent albeit fragmented ethical agendas (Martínez Lucio, 2007; see Chapter 10 on the role of consultancies and business schools and Chapter 18 on sustainability and international (IHRM)).

Even at the macro level of the global political scene, ideas of harder, management-led, HRM are propagated, both directly and indirectly. The World Bank and the IMF, as transnational and inter-state publicly funded bodies, have been crucial in extending the idea of free markets, greater competition and the virtues of continuous labour market and organizational restructuring (Klein, 2007: 267–71; Stiglitz, 2006: 211–44). These agendas find workplace expression in the harder and more performance-driven aspects of HRM.

Such agendas are therefore forged through agency and political processes, and are not simply the natural or 'best' outcome in the light of the needs of the new global market: they are not inevitable. The political project of the new right in the UK and United States in the late 1970s and 1980s defined hegemonic views towards regulation for governments on either side of the Atlantic for the next three decades. Successive governments elected from either side of the respective political divides did not demur, whether owing to ideological commitment or political expediency. It was not until the international economic crisis that emerged around 2008 that the need for government intervention returned to the mainstream political agenda. Yet, regardless of levels of state intervention in the economy in support of key sections of the banking industry that were unprecedented in the neoliberal era, the agenda did not change. Despite being tarnished by the post-2008 economic crisis, neoliberalism still held sway and ideational challenges to neoliberalism within mainstream politics were successfully resisted on both sides of the Atlantic. Consequently, even as the emergence of the Covid-19 pandemic in 2020 induced UK government intervention in the labour market unprecedented in peacetime (see Chapter 13 on restructuring), this paradoxically coexisted with a continued commitment to classic neoliberal prescription of state withdrawal.

The tapestry of transnational regulation

Frameworks and soft law

National level states, and the various bodies within them, continue to play a vital regulatory role but this role has changed overtime, notably as neoliberal agendas have coincided with increasing internationalization of economic activity. Yet even as globalization has called into question the efficacy of nationally based systems of regulation, a new tapestry of international regulation has emerged, involving a variety of actors and new forms of 'soft regulation'. As MNCs develop their own specific forms of internal governance that are neither influenced by national systems of origin nor the contexts in which they operate, it is becoming clear that there is an urgent need for new forms of global regulation. MNCs can create their own idiosyncratic management systems, but there are limits to the extent to which they can internalize their strategies to minimize external regulatory influences (see Chapter 2 on the role of MNCs).

Extending beyond the nation-state, there has been a longstanding tradition of international regulatory bodies, which took on increased importance during the new wave of economic internationalization in the 1980s and the growing concern with setting minimum benchmarks for the treatment of workers. It is too early to talk of reregulation of employment, given the weak and uneven nature of transnational regulatory bodies and the fact that the ideas underpinning them are not universally shared. However, the interaction of formal and informal regulatory processes around legal forms and codes of conduct is increasingly a part of modern business environments (Picciotto, 1999).

Codes of conduct or recommendations and resolutions over labour standards emerging from public and state related bodies are often grouped together under the heading of 'soft law' (Regent, 2003). Soft law may be seen as an approach to regulation that relies on influencing behaviour without being formally binding or backed by sanctions, and rather is traditionally reliant on peer review and monitoring by organizations such as the International Labour Organization (ILO) and the Organization for Economic Development and Cooperation (OECD) and even institutions of the Europoean Union (EU; Borras and Jacobson, 2004) for asserting any regulatory influence. The increased use of social clauses in trade agreements and contracts is another key example of how agendas for change can be promoted by international bodies. Whether setting the terms of trade between nations or between companies and their supply chains, social clauses are increasingly being used to police labour standards by ensuring the observance of internationally agreed benchmarks. The ILO has promoted the use of social clauses and has played an active part in ratifying and monitoring compliance; however, this may be seen as a privatizing or weakening of labour rights by pushing the emphasis towards a more voluntary approach (Royle, 2010). The ILO therefore plays a prominent role in promoting international codes of conduct and social clauses, which reflects an increasing interest in labour standards and the behaviour of employers from a range of bodies that are concerned with issues of malpractice, corruption and 'bad' employment practices.

International bodies

The ILO, the United Nations (UN) labour and work-related agency, was actually established as part of the UN's predecessor, the League of Nations, after the First World War (1919). The ILO historically outlined a basic body of labour codes and rights, which while often ignored were formally part of the system of inter-governmental relations. Over time, it has established more explicit sets of conventions and rules, and a vast array of research and educational activities that map and outline 'good' practices in relation to employment issues. The ILO sets the benchmarks against which firms and governments are measured in this area. Political sensitivities around issues such as child labour are directly informed by compliance with ILO standards. In addition, the key staff of the ILO attempt to create ongoing relations with key stakeholders in global supply chains – for example, in order to sustain the implementation of recommendations (Thomas and Turnbull, 2018). The ILO also provides standards across the range of everyday employment issues, which attract less media attention. Whether these standards are systematically developed or adhered to by member states is another issue and whether they represent a substantive move to establishing a strong or cohesive body of worker rights is for some questionable (Royle, 2010); however, these standards constitute a part of the international dialogue on employment and HRM.

Although the ILO has been the main vehicle for UN intervention in the field, work and employment issues also resonate throughout the UN 2030 Agenda for Sustainable Development. Several of the 17 Sustainable Development Goals involve fields of intervention relating to the role of employment in reducing poverty and inequality, or to broader economic activity, within which the role of MNCs plays a key part. These goals include: Goal 1, no poverty; Goal 5, gender equality and empowerment of all women; Goal 8, productive employment and decent work and economic growth; Goal 10, reduced inequalities; Goal 9, industry, innovation and infrastructure; Goal 11, sustainable cities and communities; and Goal 12, responsible consumption and production. As noted in Chapter 18 (Sustainability and IHRM), companies and other stakeholders are seen as key to the achievement of these goals (see https://www.un.org/sustainable development/).

The OECD has 30 members – mainly developed economies – which broadly share a free market and liberal democratic philosophy. The OECD has developed a range of economic and social agendas. For example, in relation to MNCs, the OECD has produced a set of guidelines establishing a series of principles on the approach of member states to MNCs and the behaviour of MNCs themselves. They cover a range of areas related to employment issues, through to corruption and investment matters. In addition to regulatory actors with a direct interest in employment-related issues, bodies such as the World Bank and the WTO also address the question of labour standards and the basic rights of labour organizations – although interpretation and implementation remain an issue. While such bodies are mainly focused on the economic and developmental aspects of their affiliate nations – and questions of trade – they have increasingly addressed employment and work-related issues, although their prescriptions have in the main tended to reflect a particular neoliberal orientation and vary in their social impact. Furthermore, engagement and negotiation with trade unions internationally has been uneven and remains constrained (Rueckert, 2018).

These international institutions provide a backdrop of minimum standards and benchmarks that do influence the way that firms behave in relation to their workforce. How much and how often such international standards influence the body of worker rights and working conditions may depend on the industrial sector and its national, or in some cases transnational, traditions of labour organization (see Chapter 17 on international employee representation). However, the main point is that there exists an array of international bodies addressing work issues and cross-national labour standards, which impact upon employment relations and management at the transnational level. They have not possessed a strong regulatory and sanctioning role in many cases, but that does not detract from the fact that there is a growing tapestry of international labour bodies and human resource (HR) influencing agencies that to some extent challenge the vogue for panegyrizing globalization.

The EU: soft law with a harder edge

International employment regulation is not always 'soft' or voluntary and may have the potential for sanctions and more stringent regulatory processes. In some regions of the world, countries are beginning to form more permanent systems of supranational economic and social governance. The most developed manifestation of this is the EU, a political structure of 27 European nation-states, which has a range of social and employment related rules and laws. This has included systematic frameworks of employee-HR-related regulations on issues such as mass redundancy, health and safety, working hours, discrimination and the conditions of posted workers (see Chapter 7 on international labour mobility). Furthermore, the European Works Councils Directive provides legislation on worker participation in MNCs (see Chapter 17 on international employee representation) and signifies a key *supranational* aspect of employment regulation within the EU.

Although hard regulation continues to play an important part in the influence the EU has over employment, political expediency in the post-Maastricht era has come to see an increasing emphasis being placed on soft regulation and the pursuit of policy agendas through soft law (Borras and Jacobson, 2004). With a long tradition within the EU (Borras and Jacobsson, 2004), soft regulation may not be legally binding but nonetheless can be seen as having an actual impact – or regulatory bite – in terms of social and labour market policy through the provision of normative frameworks that shape the conduct of political and social actors (Snyder, 1994; Trubek and Trubek, 2005). Since the impasse of the mid 1980s in the area of social and labour market policy, the EU has increasingly moved away from a top-down approach to regulation, driven by hard legislation and backed up by sanctions (Jepsen and Pascual, 2005). Recognizing the need for a more participative approach, the European Commission developed its key mechanism for the application of soft regulation in the 'Open Method of Coordination'. Originally developed in the late 1990s and unveiled at the Lisbon Summit of 2000 as a policy mechanism for implementing the European Employment Strategy, the Open Method of Coordination was subsequently rolled out to other policy areas, such as social exclusion and pensions. This represented a more participative approach to regulation, engaging stakeholders from both community and national levels in the development of guidelines for achieving policy goals and benchmarks for measuring success (Regent, 2003; Scharpf, 2002; Watt, 2004; Tholoniat, 2010). Crucially, *plans* and *programmes* for policy responses to these EU-level guidelines would be left to national actors to develop. Success would be assessed by benchmarking against other national cases (Arrowsmith et al., 2004).

Failure to meet targets would not be met with sanctions; rather, any improvement would be encouraged through the sharing of good practice. Although soft law proponents suggest that 'shaming' through peer reviews also offers some form of sanction (Trubek and Trubek, 2005).

The increased emphasis given to soft law is seen as politically expedient and presents the most binding approach to regulation possible in the post-Maastricht era (Watt, 2004), offering sufficient ambiguity to facilitate interpretation into a wide range of policy outcomes and thus accommodate an increasingly diverse range of employment systems within an expanded EU. Alternatively, the increased emphasis given to soft law has been cited as contributing to the fragmentation of the regulatory influence of the EU in the area of social and labour market regulation, promoting an inconsistency of application and exacerbating a downward pressure on standards (Gold, 2009). The efficacy of soft law depends on politicians and social actors representing the interests of employers and labour operating at the supranational, national and local level: actively engaging in social dialogue; providing guidelines and benchmarks for the development of policy; and asserting peer pressure to influence behaviour and promote compliance. As noted by Regent (2003), the soft law of the 'Open Method of Coordination' is not targeted towards individuals but rather towards member states, which may choose to implement their policy response through hard law. The combination of 'hard' and 'soft' law, and the mechanisms that enforce or promote them, contribute to the panoply of multi-level governance within the EU, which in turn provides a unique supranational regulatory space within the broader picture of international regulation.

When will governments listen?

The developing tapestry of supranational, international and national bodies is creating a framework of regulation affecting firms and their HR practices. It is part of an evolving international dialogue on labour rights that has emerged since the end of the Second World War and is underpinned by the Universal Declaration of Human Rights (see Cassese, 1992). There remains a great degree of cynicism regarding the development of such rights owing to the highly variable responses of national governments and multinational employers. There is also concern that the assertion of such rights favours the production regimes of developed economies and disadvantages developing ones, where competitive advantage based on low labour costs have become common government strategies for economic development (see Chapter 8 on developing economies).

Another school of thought in the form of the 'boomerang theory' is more optimistic and argues that governments which ignore the increasing establishment of international rights systems may be shamed and compelled in the longer term to subscribe to them (Risse et al., 1999). Even if this is symbolic in the first instance, over time the presence of even soft and minimal regulations establishes expectations within countries and their social actors. Trade unions, political bodies, ethically based consumer groups and even other nation-states (Norway, for example, has been highly active on these issues) can reference such standards as a way to coax reticent governments and employers.

Cooperation, competition and new agendas

The developments described above dovetail with an increasing interest in social responsibility and ethics within HRM (Pinnington et al., 2007; see Chapter 18 on sustainability). In relation to major issues such as child labour there are emergent external pressures on both employers and national governments from non-governmental organizations (NGOs) such as Oxfam or War on Want. Movements such as 'Fairtrade', which campaigns for a decent wage for workers in the global agricultural sector – notably coffee – and in the textiles industry, have provided a new reference point for ethically based regulation that is of growing importance. However, there is also the question of the extent to which adherence to soft regulation based on externally derived codes of conduct or pressure from NGOs is also dependent on 'self-regulation' by companies, notably MNCs. Commitments to corporate social responsibility (CSR) or sustainability agendas may be buttressed by such external soft regulation but equally adherence to soft regulation may be highly variable and prone to shifts in corporate agendas (see Chapters 13 on restructuring and 18 on sustainability). Moreover, there is the danger that greater engagement between NGOs and corporate sustainable development or CSR agendas may lead to co-option of the former by the business community (Burchell and Cook, 2013).

The relationship between trade unions and NGOs highlights another important feature of the tapestry of regulation: the extent to which mechanisms of regulation are complementary or competing. There are positive examples of cooperation between NGOs and trade unions, sharing information, drawing the attention of consumers to the working conditions under which goods are produced or even raising awareness of the benefits of unionization among hard-to-reach workers in MNC supply chains (Donaghey and Reinecke, 2018). The cooperative activities of trade unions and NGOs have been crucial in persuading organizations to sign up to voluntary codes of practice over their employment policies and have played an important role in policing adherence to such codes. More broadly, soft regulation or the implementation of soft law may often rely on the capacity of trade unions to influence the process, not necessarily through collective agreements – although these may play an important role – but also through the ongoing interaction between actors in the regulatory space they occupy at the level of the workplace or beyond. Even statutory interventions, such as Health and Safety regulations, can be seen to benefit in terms of their efficacy from the support of other mechanisms of regulation, in this case trade union health and safety representatives. In short, within the tapestry of regulation, different forms of regulation and a diverse range of regulatory actors may complement one another, or be seen to have complementarities in their regulatory impact. However, this may not always be the case, and regulatory actors may indeed compete or conflict with one another (see Chapter 8 on developing countries and Chapter 17 on international employee representation). In extreme cases, competition may result in more hostile developments where one actor seeks to displace or replace another, in effect colonizing the regulatory space in which they operate (MacKenzie and Martínez Lucio, 2005, 2014). In terms of relations between trade unions and NGOs, the many examples of cooperation and complementarities of practice must be tempered by less frequent but important cautionary tales of actors set in competition. There are cases where employers promote a positive corporate image through endorsement by the fair trade movement while simultaneously engaging in anti-union activities in their production sites (Frundt, 2007), and many of these 'ethical' agendas in global supply chains ignore issues of women's rights and experiences (Prieto-Carrón, 2008).

Returning to more positive collaborations, coordinating international cooperation on social issues and the rights to participation at work in MNCs has emerged as a renewed role for international trade union organizations (see Chapter 17 on international employee representation). While these bodies have less resources than national states (Smith et al., 1998) and, indeed, compete with each other for scarce resources (Claude and Weston, 1992), they do form part of the global set of institutions that contribute to the tapestry of regulation shaping the political and economic context in which IHRM exists (Lillie and Martínez Lucio, 2004). Such bodies play a regulatory role in terms of diffusing expert knowledge, informing and educating public agencies and national states (Baehr, 1999); they therefore constitute a counterpoint to the private and market-driven networks of consultancies and think tanks. These developments echo the interest in stakeholder theories of ethics in employment-related matters, which espouse a more pluralist understanding of voice and the role of different actors (Greenwood and De Cieri, 2007). What is more, a growing number of informal and work-activist-based union networks have emerged, aimed at exchanging information on campaigns and coordinating across a range of disputes and mobilizations (see Wills, 1998, for an early discussion of these developments). The politics of such networks has given rise to broad coalitions, combining trade unions with a diverse range of peace campaigners, environmentalist and anti-capitalist groups into movements that are both innovative and increasingly entrenched (Thomas, 2007). These networked movements have engaged with and used the internet and social media as a key part of their communication and coordination strategies (Panagiotopoulos and Barnett, 2015). The internet and social media have, therefore, provided a forum for discussion and a conduit for the transmission of critiques of MNCs. Ethically oriented consumer groups are utilizing this medium to bring pressure to bear on the activities of MNCs and the ethicality of their approaches to such issues as employment and sustainable resourcing. While there may be a more individualist and consumerist orientation to contemporary capitalism (Alonso, 2006), a new politics of consumption is emerging that places social and employment issues on the agenda through the use of alternative information platforms and networks.

Even business schools have begun to engage with new agendas around ethics and a growing interest in CSR, although how extensive this is remains a question for debate (see Steyaert et al., 2016). In the UK context at least, control over the content and direction in which these agendas develop is becoming another politically contested terrain, counterposing mainstream managerial approaches and the more critical and progressive traditions that coexist in many business schools. Although interest in CSR tends to be dominated by concerns over environmental impact, which remain prone to the usual problems with self-regulation and suspicions of 'green-washing', there have been attempts to broaden the CSR agenda to include work and employment issues. Debates around socially responsible restructuring, for example, have promulgated the need for employers to recognize their responsibilities towards employees made redundant through corporate restructuring and provide support and training to improve their chances of transition into employment elsewhere (Forde et al., 2009; see Chapter 13 on restructuring). This is a classic case where regulatory complementarities lead to more positive outcomes. Employers' self-regulation of socially responsible restructuring can be made more effective by the presence of joint regulation by trade unions, and the involvement of the state through the statutory requirement of support for displaced workers in finding or preparing for new employment, or through the commitment to broader active labour market policies.

These new dimensions of transnational regulation are a vital part of the environment that MNCs inhabit. Indeed, they encourage MNCs to internalize regulatory roles themselves, as they increasingly need to ethically police their organizations and create sustainable and legitimate operations.

Case study: Regulating labour standards – types of social clause

International employment regulation often suffers from a lack of enforceability and there are also concerns in various countries that such regulation can hamper economic development, and hence social development, in the long term. One way of creating a framework for a greater commitment to dignity and fairness at work is through the development of social clauses in trade agreements. According to Lim:

> In the context of international trade, a social clause essentially refers to a legal provision in a trade agreement aimed at removing the most extreme forms of labour exploitation in exporting countries by allowing importing countries to take trade measures against exporting countries which fail to observe a set of internationally agreed minimum labour standards . . . While the focus is presently on trade measures, social clause provisions have been linked to non-trade arrangements. For instance, the US Overseas Private Investment Corporation (OPIC), a government agency which offers insurance to US companies operating in developing countries, will withdraw its services from projects in countries not taking steps to adopt and implement laws that extend a set of internationally recognised labour standards. It has also been suggested that social clauses should also be added to development aid and loan programmes. At present, while the ILO actively promotes the ratification and supervision of Clauses, it cannot force compliance or impose financial, commercial or other sanctions; rather, it relies on persuasion and peer pressure to encourage States to meet their obligations. Nevertheless, despite not having a punitive enforcement mechanism, the ILO has in practice attained an influence that goes beyond legal formality.
>
> (Lim, http://actrav.itcilo.org/actrav-english/telearn/global/ilo/guide/hoelim.htm)

However, most social clauses are voluntary rather than being tied into trade agreements. Therefore, even one of the more direct or interventionist of transnational regulatory levers relies on 'persuasion' and 'peer pressure' and is largely voluntarist in nature. What this means is that both campaigning and communication are vital for the develop- ment of a robust system of regulation. In relation to peer pressure, it also means establishing benchmarks and mechanisms which highlight practices and literally shame those who do not abide by higher standards of employment rights and are not improving working conditions. According to Howard-Hassmann (2005: 35–6):

Human rights social movements have benefited from the ease of travel and communications of the last thirty years . . . Nevertheless, as global communication erodes geographical remoteness, the universal principle of human rights becomes one upon which local actors can base their demands for justice. If the capitalist-owned mass media ignore a particular human right, the technology of global communications nevertheless allows its pursuit through the formation of independent media groups, chat rooms and websites. Global consumer campaigns against abusive labour practices such as employment of child labour have been particularly successful. The Rugmark campaign, for example, tells consumers whether rugs they have purchased from Asia are made without child labour, exerting pressure for improved labour standards in producing countries such as Pakistan and Iran (Forsythe, 2000; Pangalangan, 2002). Retail companies are also susceptible to consumer pressure on human rights grounds, such as in the case of the Swiss grocery chain, Migros. Migros inserted a 'social clause' in its contract with Del Monte to ensure that working conditions on Del Monte's pineapple farms in the Philippines were above average (Pangalangan, 2002).

Questions

1. In what ways can social clauses be used strategically to improve labour standards?
2. What are the problems with relying on social clauses to improve labour standards?
3. Why do some use the term *soft regulation* and how can it be most effective?
4. What other ways are there for raising issues of dignity and rights at work in the context of globalization?

Conclusion

This chapter has argued that the concept of regulation should be central to any discussion of employment relations and HRM at the transnational level. Regulation involves various spaces and actors, and in any given context these will vary. There has also been a shift in the way regulation is viewed and who is involved in it. Where once stood the apparatus of the state and direct forms of intervention there is now an even more complex scenario. While there has been a move towards more marketized economies where the remit of regulation is limited, this is only part of the story. Such a shift towards a marketized and more individualistic perspective is itself the political product of a range of actors and knowledge networks, which can in turn be prone to shifting economic and political contingencies. The clamour for regulatory responses to the economic crises of the Great Recession following 2008–9 and the Covid-19 pandemic beginning in 2020 has highlighted the inadequacies of the marketized mantra. Sustaining the hegemony of marketized perspectives has always been a contested process, and there is again increasing concern with the need to rebuild regulation and create a more effective platform for regulating international employment issues. It would be unwise to assume that the kinds of regulations we discuss in this chapter in relation to employment relations and HRM at the transnational level will be easily marginalized. The imperative for regulation will remain. The manner in which the social consequences and political outcomes of crises develop require ever more strategic and innovative forms of state response (Rubery, 2011), as can be seen in the case of the Covid-19 pandemic.

The illusion that the emergence of market-oriented strategies would deliver a new world of autonomous managerial decision-making has been shown to be questionable and surpassed by processes of re-regulation. There are competing views on how firms should conduct their HR strategies, and in the case of MNCs this has now become a question at the centre of a range of policy and social debates (see Klein, 2007). The once-dominant view of the reassertion of the prerogative of management as a new and invigorated actor that can assimilate many of the requirements of regulation and unilaterally regulate in relation to the internal context of the firm is highly problematic and contested.

Pressures remain in terms of national governments, transnational public bodies, NGOs, social movements, consumer organizations and international trade unions structures and networks. The transnational system of regulation requires a strategic and network-based approach, creating links with civil society organizations through public debates, popular boycotts and consumer actions. This necessitates a more democratic and participative view of regulation, which brings stakeholders closer to the centre of activity. Regulation, far from disappearing or being terminally weakened by the marginalization of national states, has become a significant and ever more complex reality. There are undoubtedly issues related to the content of social clauses or the implementation of codes of practice, and the need for a stronger presence of worker organizations to back up voluntary arragements (Cooke et al., 2019; Royle, 2010). It would also be easy to dismiss this tapestry of often soft regulation, voluntary codes of practice and pressure groups as not being sufficiently coordinated or backed by meaningful sanctions to provide an international equivalence to the regulatory role historically played by national states. Yet, given the obvious disparities in the geopolitical context, such direct comparisons become essentially meaningless. Regulation in the current global context involves a move towards combinations of actors at different levels: from national states to transnational bodies (both institutionalized and voluntary in character) and even social and private associations that lobby and highlight employment issues. Thus both hard and soft forms of regulation coexist to form the basis of a more complex international tapestry, in which the efficacy of the latter is notably improved by the presence of the former.

Reflective questions

1. What is regulation and what are its different components?
2. How has regulation changed and what have been the pressures on more direct forms of regulation?
3. What do we mean by soft regulation and how have various organizations contributed to its development?
4. What are the challenges facing the implementation of soft regulation on a range of employment-related issues and rights?

Recommended reading

- Donaghey, J. and Reinecke, J. (2018) 'When industrial democracy meets corporate social responsibility – A comparison of the Bangladesh Accord and Alliance as responses to the Rana Plaza disaster'. *British Journal of Industrial Relations*, 56(1): 14–42.
- MacKenzie, R. and Martínez Lucio, M. (2005) 'The realities of regulatory change: Beyond the fetish of deregulation'. *Sociology*, 39(3): 499–517.
- Royle, T. (2010) 'The ILO's shift to promotional principles and the "privatization"of labour rights: An analysis of labour standards, voluntary self-regulation and social clauses'. *International Journal of Comparative Labour Law and Industrial Relations*, 26(3): 249–71.

References

Alonso, L. (2006) 'The Fordist cycle and the genesis of the post-Fordist society'. In L. E. Alonso and M. Martínez Lucio (eds), *Employment Relations in a Changing Society*. London: Palgrave.

Arrowsmith, J., Sisson, K. and Marginson, P. (2004) 'What can "benchmarking" offer the open method of co-ordination?' *Journal of European Public Policy*, 11(2): 311–28.

Baehr, P. R. (1999) *Human Rights: Universality in Practice*. Basingstoke: Macmillan.

Baldwin, R., Scott, C. and Hood, C. (1998) 'Introduction'. In R. Baldwin, C. Scott and C. Hood (eds), *A Reader on Regulation*. Oxford: Oxford University Press.

Borras, S. and Jacobsson, K. (2004) 'The open method of co-ordination and new governance patterns in the EU'. *Journal of European Public Policy*, 11(2): 185–208.

Brewster, C. (2004) 'European perspectives on human resource management'. *Human Resource Management Review*, 14(4): 365–82.

Burchell, J. and Cook, J. (2013) 'CSR, co-optation and resistance: The emergence of new agonistic relations between business and civil society'. *Journal of Business Ethics*, 115(4): 741–54.

Cassese, D. (1992) 'The general assembly: Historical perspective 1945–1989'. In P. Ashton (ed.) *The United Nations and Human Rights: A Critical Appraisal*. New York: Cambridge University Press.

Claude, R. P. and Weston, B. H. (1992) 'International human rights: Overviews'. In R. P. Claude and B. H. Weston (eds), *Human Rights in the World Community: Issues and Action*, 2nd edn. Philadelphia: University of Pennsylvania Press.

Cooke, F. L., Xu, J. and Bian, H. (2019) 'The prospect of decent work, decent industrial relations and decent social relations in China: Towards a multi-level and multi-disciplinary approach'. *International Journal of Human Resource Management*, 30(1): 122–55.

Donaghey, J. and Reinecke, J. (2018) 'When industrial democracy meets corporate social responsibility – A comparison of the Bangladesh Accord and Alliance as responses to the Rana Plaza disaster'. *British Journal of Industrial Relations*, 56(1): 14–42.

Esping Anderson, G. (2000) 'Who is harmed by labour market de-regulation?'. In G. Esping Anderson and M. Regini (eds.), *Why Deregulate Labour Markets*. Oxford: Oxford University Press.

Forde, C., Stuart, M., Gardiner, J., Greenwood, I., MacKenzie, R. and Perrett, R. (2009) *Socially Responsible Restructuring in an Era of Mass Redundancy*. Working Paper 5, Centre for Employment Relations Innovation and Change, Leeds University Business School.

Forsythe, D. (2000) *Human Rights in International Relations*. New York: Cambridge University Press.

Friedman, M. (1968) 'The role of monetary policy'. *American Economic Review*, 58 (March): 1–17.

Frundt, H. (2007) 'Organizing in the banana sector'. In K. Bronfenbrenner (ed.), *Global Unions: Challenging Transnational Capital Through Cross-Border Campaigns*. Ithaca: Cornell University Press.

Gold, M. (2009) 'Overview of EU employment policy'. In M. Gold (ed.), *Employment Policy in the European Union: Origins Themes and Prospects*. Basingstoke: Palgrave Macmillan.

Greenwood, M. and De Cieri, H. (2007) 'Stakeholder theory and the ethicality of human resource management'. In A. H. Pinnington, R. E. Macklin and T. Campbell (eds), *Human Resource Management: Ethics and Employment*. Oxford: Oxford University Press.

Guest, D. (1990) 'Human resource management and the American dream', *Journal of Management Studies*, 27(4): 377–97.

Hall, S. (1988) *The Hard Road to Renewal*. London: Verso.

Heller, F. (2002) 'What next? More critique of consultants, gurus and managers'. In T. Clark and R. Fincham (eds), *Critical Consulting: New Perspectives on the Management Advice Industry*. Oxford: Blackwell.

Howard-Hassmann, R. E. (2005) 'The second great transformation: Human rights leap-frogging in the era of globalization'. *Human Rights Quarterly*, 27(1): 1–40.

Jepsen, M. and Pascual, A. S. (2005) 'The European Social Model: an exercise in deconstruction'. *Journal of European Social Policy*, 15(3): 231–45.

Jessop, B. (1990) *State Theory*. Oxford: Polity.

Jessop, B. (2002) *The Future of the Capitalist State*. Cambridge: Polity.

Klein, N. (2007) *The Shock Doctrine*. London: Penguin.

Legge, K. (2002) 'On knowledge, business consultants and the selling of total quality management'. In T. Clark and R. Fincham (eds), *Critical Consulting: New Perspectives on the Management Advice Industry*. Oxford: Blackwell.

Lillie, N. and Martínez Lucio, M. (2004) 'International trade union revitalization: The role of national union approaches'. In C. Frege and J. Kelly (eds), *Labour Movement Revitalization in Comparative Perspective*. Oxford: Oxford University Press.

Lim, H. *The Social Clause: Issues and Challenges*. Available at: http://actrav.itcilo.org/actrav-english/telearn/global/ilo/guide/hoelim.htm (accessed 20 May 2013).

MacKenzie, R. and Martínez Lucio, M. (2005) 'The realities of regulatory change: Beyond the fetish of deregulation'. *Sociology*, 39(3): 499–517.

MacKenzie, R. and Martínez Lucio, M. (2014) 'The colonisation of employment regulation and industrial relations? Dynamics and developments over five decades of change'. *Labor History*, 55(2): 189–207.

Martínez Lucio, M. (2007) 'Neoliberalismo y neoconservadurismo interrumpido? El porqué de la existencia de una tradición crítica en las escuelas de dirección de empresas británicas'. In C. Fernandez (ed.), *Estudios Sociales de la Organización: El Giro PostModerno*. Madrid: Siglo VeintiUno.

Martínez Lucio, M. and MacKenzie, R. (2004) 'Unstable boundaries? Evaluating the "new regulation" within employment relations'. *Economy and Society*, 33(1): 77–97.

Morgan, G., & Hauptmeier, M. (2021) 'The social organization of ideas in employment relations'. *ILR Review*, 74(3): 773–797.

O'Shea, J. and Madigan, C. (1997) *Dangerous Company: The Consulting Powerhouses and Businesses They Save and Ruin*. New York: Times Business.

Panagiotopoulos, P. and Barnett, J. (2015) 'Social media in Union communications: An international study with UNI Global Union Affiliates'. *British Journal of Industrial Relations*, 53(3): 508–32.

Pangalangan, R. C. (2002) 'Sweatshops and international labor standards: Globalizing markets, localizing norms'. In A. Brysk (ed.), *Globalization and Human Rights*. Berkeley: University of California Press, pp. 98–114.

Parker, M. (2018) *Shut Down the Business School. University of Chicago Press Economics Books*.

Peck, J. (1996) *Workplace: The Social Regulation of Labour Markets*. New York: Guildford.

Picciotto, S. (1999) 'Introduction: What rules for the world economy?' In S. Picciotto and R. Mayne (eds), *Regulating International Business: Beyond Liberalisation*. Basingstoke: Macmillan and Oxfam.

Pinnington, A. H., Mackin, R. E. and Campbell, T. (2007) 'Introduction'. In A. Pinnington, R. E. Macklin and T. Campbell, T. (eds), *Human Resource Management: Ethics and Employment*. Oxford: Oxford University Press.

Prieto-Carrón, M. (2008). 'Women workers, industrialization, global supply chains and corporate codes of conduct'. *Journal of Business Ethics*, 83(1): 5–17.

Regent, S. (2003) 'The open method of coordination: A new supranational form of governance?' *European Law Journal*, 9(2): 190–214.

Regini, M. (2000) 'The dilemmas of labour market regulation'. In G. Esping-Andersen and M. Regini (eds), *Why Deregulate Labour Markets?* Oxford: Oxford University Press.

Risse, T., Ropp, S. C. and Sikkink, K. (eds) (1999) *The Power of Human Rights: International Norms and Domestic Change*. Cambridge: Cambridge University Press.

Royle, T. (2005) 'Realism or idealism? Corporate social responsibility and the employee stakeholder in the global fastfood Industry'. *Business Ethics: A European Review*, 14(1): 42–55.

Royle, T. (2010) 'The ILO's shift to promotional principles and the "privatization" of labour rights: An analysis of labour standards, voluntary self-regulation and social clauses'. *International Journal of Comparative Labour Law and Industrial Relations*, 26(3): 249–71

Rubery, J. (2011) 'Reconstruction amid deconstruction: Or why we need more of the social in European social models'. *Work, Employment and Society,* 25(4): 658–74.

Rueckert, Y. (2018) 'The Global unions and global governance: Analysing the dialogue between the international trade union organizations and the international financial institutions'. *Economic and Industrial Democracy,* 42(3): 766–84.

Scharpf, F. (2002) 'The European social model: Coping with the challenges of legitimate diversity'. *Journal of Common Market Studies,* 40(4): 645–70.

Smith, J., Pagnuncco, T. and Lopez, G. A. (1998) 'Globalising human rights: The work of transnational human rights NGOs in the 1990s'. *Human Rights Quarterly,* 20(2): 379–412.

Snyder, F. (1994) *Soft Law and Institutional Practice in the European Community.* Netherlands: Springer.

Stewart, P. (1996) *Beyond Japanese Management.* London: Taylor & Francis.

Steyaert, C., Beyes, T. and Parker, M. (eds) (2016). *The Routledge Companion to Reinventing Management Education.* London: Routledge.

Stiglitz, J. (2006) *Making Globalization Work.* London: Penguin.

Tholoniat, L. (2010) 'The career of the Open Method of Coordination: Lessons from a "soft" EU instrument'. *West European Politics,* 33(1): 93–117.

Thomas, H. and Turnbull, P. (2018) 'From horizontal to vertical labour governance: The International Labour Organization (ILO) and decent work in global supply chains'. *Human Relations,* 71(4): 536–59.

Thomas, N. H. (2007) 'Global capitalism, the anti-globalisation movement and the Third World'. *Capital and Class,* 92 (Summer): 45–80.

Trubek, D. M. and Trubek, L. G. (2005) 'Hard and soft law in the construction of social Europe: The role of the open method of co-ordination'. *European Law Journal,* 11(3): 343–64.

Watt, A. (2004) 'Reform of the European employment strategy after five years: A change of course or merely of presentation?' *European Journal of Industrial Relations,* 10(2): 117–37.

Whitley, R., Morgan, E. and Moen, E. (2005) Changing Capitalisms? *In Internationalisation, Institutional Change and Systems of Economic Organization.* Oxford: Oxford University Press.

Wills, J. (1998) 'Taking on the CosmoCorps: Experiments in transnational labor organization'. *Economic Geography,* 74: 111–30.

17 International employee representation, organization, multinational companies and International Human Resource Management

Stephen Mustchin and Nathaniel Tetteh

Learning objectives

- To understand the different ways in which workers and employees organize representation internationally
- To appreciate the context and the institutions through which employees are represented within multinational companies (MNCs)
- To understand the regulatory context underpinning different forms of international employee representation
- To understand why some MNCs engage with international worker representation (and why some do not)
- To understand the contrasting nature and utility of transnational agreements within different national and institutional contexts
- To appreciate the challenges faced by established international labour and alternative, networked forms of international labour organizing and representation

Introduction

The increasingly globalized nature of the international economy since the early 1970s, and the subsequent proliferation and increasing power of MNCs, has posed wide-ranging challenges to the position of workers and trade unions. Worker organization is typically built from the level of the workplace, with unions in most industrialized countries organized at the level of the nation-state. This is an evident limitation in a context of highly mobile capital and MNCs with operations across multiple countries and regions of the world, creating challenges for workers seeking to organize and negotiate meaningfully with power-holders within the central or headquarters management of their employers. One means by which organized labour has attempted to establish forms of countervailing power in the face of globalization and increasingly powerful MNCs is through various forms of international worker and employee representation (Levinson, 1972). This chapter explores the nature and form of such international representation, including global union federations (GUFs) (e.g. Croucher and Cotton, 2011), Transnational Collective Agreements (TCAs) (e.g. Mustchin and Martínez Lucio, 2017), European Works Councils (EWCs) (e.g. Hann et al., 2017; Kotthoff and Whittall, 2014; Waddington, 2011) and networked, less formalized worker organization outside of these more established structures (e.g. Munck, 2018; Waterman and Wills, 2001). These are explored in the context of international human resource management policy, practice and strategy within MNCs, exploring the outcomes for workers of these forms of representation and their relevance to and impact on MNCs and their behaviour.

As seen in earlier chapters (Chapter 16 on transnational regulation), the question of how MNCs are regulated, particularly in the area of labour standards and working conditions, is complex and contested. MNCs have been found to engage in 'regime shopping', or making investment decisions on the basis of regulatory, taxation and labour-law systems and their weaknesses. Public transnational regulation such as European Union (EU) law and International Labour Organization (ILO) standards (Fichter, 2020; Marginson, 2020), forms of private regulation including corporate social responsibility standards, corporate codes of conduct, accreditation through standard-setting bodies (Anner, 2018; Bourguignon et al., 2020; Donaghey and Reinecke, 2018) and transnational agreements between MNCs and GUFs (Helfen et al., 2018) represent a range of methods seeking to improve labour standards and ensure MNCs do not use their power and mobility as a means of avoiding them. The efficacy of such public and private regulation is dependent on effective means of enforcing them. While participative, democratizing logics to an extent inform the engagement of labour and civil society organizations within forms of transnational regulation, links with such local actors are crucial to both the legitimacy and effectiveness of regulation as these are the means by which regulation might be enacted and made real within workplaces and communities. The extent to which MNCs engage with transnational regulation at all, let alone with representative bodies or stakeholders, is highly variable and context-dependent. This chapter explores the nature of international worker and employee representation, research findings from the wider literature focusing on transnational regulation, representation and participation, and the effectiveness and outcomes of such institutional configurations from the perspective of the different actors within the employment relationship (for a discussion on employment relations generally see Chapter 3).

Forms of international employee and worker representation

There is a wide range of different forms of international worker representation, manifested at a number of different levels in terms of their institutional position, organizational form and the extent of their reach and influence. This section maps these different institutional arrangements and forms the basis of the discussion to follow, which draws on research on the outcomes of international worker representation in practice.

The ILO is a specialist agency of the United Nations (UN). Founded in 1919 as part of the League of Nations and then relaunched after 1945, the ILO sets international labour standards through the International Labour Code – this includes Conventions (190 to date) and numerous recommendations that it expects to be ratified by the UN's 187 member states. These standards cover issues including freedom of association and union rights, the use of child and forced labour, discrimination at work, working time, health and safety and many other, often highly technical, issues relating to working conditions and the nature of employment. Full ratification of ILO standards among member states has been patchy and inconsistent. In 1998 the ILO's Declaration on Fundamental Principles and Rights at Work streamlined this approach. Four Core Labour Standards were established as basic obligations of all member states: freedom of association and the effective recognition of the right to collective bargaining; the elimination of all forced or compulsory labour; the abolition of child labour; and the elimination of discrimination in respect of employment and occupation (Fichter, 2020: 264–5). These labour standards form the basis for many of the private forms of regulation concerning work and employment that have been established at the levels of firms, industries and some regions. Half of the ILO's governing body consists of representatives of government, with the other half equally split between employer and employee representatives. While indirect, this constitutes the peak level of involvement of employee representation within international regulatory structures (see Chapter 16 on regulation more broadly).

Regional forms of governance are also significant with regard to transnational forms of employment regulation and employee representation. Many EU regulations concern employment-related issues which member states are obliged to transpose into national law. These concern individual rights, including discrimination, parental leave and contractual issues; working conditions, including health and safety, working time and the status of part-time, fixed-term and temporary employees; and collective employment rights, including rights to information and consultation over redundancies and restructuring, and EWCs (Marginson, 2020: 244). Following the 1992 Maastricht Treaty, forms of 'social dialogue' over issues relating to social, industrial, employment and economic policies have been established, involving the consultation of social partners (European-level union bodies, including the European Trades Union Confederation (ETUC), the European sections of GUFs and employer representatives) (Streeck, 1994). The 1994 and 2009 European Works Councils Directives give workers in MNCs with operations employing at least 150 people in at least two member states the right to establish an EWC, a cross-national employee representative body with rights to be informed and consulted over business decisions, restructuring and similar (Waddington, 2011). The EU and the ILO constitute the most developed forms of 'public' or state-oriented international employment regulation, within which a range of forms of worker representation feature. These have a strong influence on the plethora of more 'private', typically firm- or industry-level forms of regulation, within multinational companies which in some cases have worker representation as a significant feature.

Firm-level employee representative councils were proposed as a form of countervailing power to increasingly powerful multinational companies from the late 1960s onwards, despite the firm opposition of multinational employers to engaging in any form of cross-national collective bargaining (Levinson, 1972). Volkswagen has had a World Works Council since the late 1960s (Croucher and Cotton, 2011), coordinating representatives of workers from across most of their global operations, engaging with GUFs, and establishing transnational agreements on union recognition, temporary agency work and other key labour standards (Bolsmann, 2007; Whittall et al., 2017). More formalized means of building links between nationally oriented trade union movements include the International Trade Union Confederation (ITUC), a coordinating body for national peak-level union confederations. The ITUC was founded in 2006 following a long period of Cold War division in which the World Federation of Trade Unions purported to represent workers in communist countries while the International Confederation of Free Trade Unions sought to represent union federations elsewhere (Carew, 2018). GUFs also have a long history, deriving from International Trade Secretariats established in the 1890s, seeking to link unions within certain industries across national borders; and they now have new significance given the extent of globalization and the increasing prominence of multinational companies. Since the late 1980s, GUFs have been instrumental in signing International Framework Agreements (IFAs) (sometimes referred to as Global Framework Agreements, or TCAs) within MNCs. Such agreements involve international employee representative bodies securing commitments from headquarters management in numerous high-profile firms to adhere to labour standards such as freedom of association and union rights, combating discrimination and eliminating the use of child and forced labour. Such firm-level agreements and how they intersect with international human resource management policy and practice are discussed further in the section that follows.

The forms of employee representation and examples of workers and their representative organizations coordinating across national borders discussed so far largely constitute more formal, established forms of representation, organization and institutional configuration. There is a long history of international solidarity among workers from different countries, generally concerned with specific disputes, wider human rights and political issues, and this has often been driven by particular union activists, groups of organized workers and left-wing political networks. A critique of official or established international labour institutions has concerned their relative distance from the workers they seek to represent, constituting 'labor bureaucracy three times removed' (Moody, 1997: 229). Tainted by Cold War politics (Scipes, 2010) and the behaviour of established international labour organizations around particular disputes, some alternative forms of worker organization have arisen in partial opposition to more formalized, institutionalized international labour. For example, the International Dockworkers Council was established by groups of organized workers in different countries as a reaction to widespread restructuring in their industry and discontent with the International Transport Workers' Federation (ITF) GUF around particular disputes such as the 1995–8 Liverpool dockers' campaign. International solidarity campaigning in protest against the mass dismissal of 500 dockworkers was felt to have been undermined by the withdrawal of support from their union (the TGWU) and by extension, that of the ITF, to which it was affiliated (Brookes, 2019: 41; Fox-Hodess, 2020).

With the growth of independent unions such as the Independent Workers Union of Great Britain (IWGB) in the UK, new forms of international coordination among workers organizing in the gig economy and other precarious sectors of employment have arisen in order to bring together drivers working for Uber or similar online platforms and attempt to organize across national boundaries. More networked, informal approaches have been made more practicable with the rise of internet communications and social media: 'Actors within and beyond the traditional labour movement have used networked technologies and organizational forms in responding to the changing structure of corporate organization and both governmental and nongovernmental forms of work regulation' (Walker, 2014: 278). More informal networking and organizing is evident outside of the established institutional structures involving international labour: in 2018, thousands of Google employees across the firm's global operations in protest over allegations of sexual harassment against some of the firm's senior executives (Hershenberg and O'Casey, 2019). International employee representation and cross-national worker organizing is manifested in a range of formal and more informal ways. The section that follows explores more specific examples of such representation and organizing, demonstrating how the interface between formal and informal structures and processes impacts on international human resource management (HRM) policy and practice, the behaviour of MNCs and ultimately the nature of working conditions within a globalized political economy.

Transnational agreements within MNCs and their implementation

While international employee representation is manifested in a number of institutional and less formal ways, it is important to evaluate the outcomes of such forms of organization in terms of how they impact on collective agreements within MNCs and secure improvements in employment and working conditions – and ultimately how such agreements affect the international HRM practices of MNCs.

Collective agreements between national and international representatives of workers and the headquarters of MNCs are a significant example of the 'outcomes' of such international representation. These include European-level agreements signed between MNC management, EWCs and in some cases European-level union federations and national representative bodies (Rüb et al., 2013). International framework agreements (IFAs) do not have the EU regulatory underpinnings of European agreements, but numerous examples exist where GUFs, sometimes in conjunction with national and regional representative bodies, including unions and EWCs, have secured such agreements with the central headquarters management of MNCs on the understanding that the agreements would be relevant across the firm's global operations (and in some cases supply chains as well). Some accounts group these European-level agreements and more expansive international agreements together under the heading of TCAs (Mustchin and Martínez Lucio, 2017). Such agreements typically commit organizations to adhere to ILO Core Labour Standards and other conventions, such as commitments to freedom of association and to union recognition, to inform and consult over restructuring decisions, to not use child or forced labour and to address discrimination and other forms of rights which can be utilized by worker representative bodies, with monitoring and conflict resolution mechanisms included to ensure their meaningful application. While such agreements typically confer rights rather than the foundation for employee–employer bargaining (Hammer, 2005), they have been a significant means by which international labour has sought to enforce labour standards given failed political attempts to commit transnational institutions such as the World Trade Organization to playing a role in regulating employment and working conditions (van Roozendaal, 2003).

All firms with EWCs obviously have substantial operations in Europe, and most MNCs with IFAs are headquartered in Europe. Only seven US-headquartered firms have signed an IFA to date, and typically such agreements feature in cases where unions and their institutional supports are comparatively strong within the national context in which they are based. Most IFAs feature in five main sectors: metal, construction, chemicals, food and services (Schomann et al., 2008), and typically where unions are relatively influential within a tradition of 'social dialogue' in the MNC's home/headquartered country. There has been a significant proliferation of such agreements since 2000, linked to the corporate social responsibility (CSR) policies of MNCs, institutional factors in home and host countries, including regulatory change, investor pressure in some cases, interventions from unions at the level of MNC headquarters and attempts to minimize disruption from industrial action within increasingly complex and vulnerable supply chains. Compared to other forms of corporate, voluntary self-regulation, including CSR or accreditation schemes, IFAs are more participative and more closely related to conceptions of industrial relations concerned with negotiation, informing and consulting than more unilateral private regulation (Papadakis, 2011: 3).

However, IFAs may be weakly understood by national or local unions, let alone national, local and supply chain management, who often lack awareness of IFAs or are reluctant to promote or acknowledge them. The Spanish clothing MNC Inditex is a signatory to an IFA, committing it to support freedom of association within its supply chains, but analysis of cases in Cambodia, where attempts by workers to unionize had been violently suppressed and union activists victimized, highlights the complexity and difficulties involved in ensuring IFAs are enforced. Local activists made links with a state labour inspector who had links to the ILO, which led to contact with the MNC headquarters referencing the terms of the IFA and the eventual reinstatement of activists and improvements in working conditions. However, it was evident that IFA terms were by no means automatically applied, and considerable worker organizing, struggle and engagement with other actors was necessary for the freedom of association stipulations in the agreement to become a reality (Gregoratti and Miller, 2011). Research on the IFA within the Accor hotel company MNC highlights the difficulties of enforcing the provisions of such agreements in sectors where unions are relatively weak and management adopt strategies of union exclusion (Wills, 2002). Local and national unions are not always affiliated to GUFs, and the non-binding nature of IFAs makes them difficult to enforce (Niforou, 2012).

Tensions exist within CSR in MNCs, as both HR management and employee representation are often separate from the CSR function despite the emphasis on labour standards in the UN Global Compact, a corporate sustainability initiative. This militates against the effectiveness and level of stakeholder involvement in such policies, and is a particular problem in countries such as some of those in the EU where there are established cooperative relationships between employer and employees and CSR involvement may be viewed as diluting such arrangements (Preuss et al., 2009: 958). IFAs suffer from a degree of fragility in that they are vulnerable to inconsistent application in more local subsidiaries and workplaces. They are also vulnerable to organizational change in terms of shifts in owner-ship of an MNC, takeovers and changes in management personnel, meaning that agreements can wither away or simply be ignored in certain circumstances if key supporters within an MNC move elsewhere or less sympathetic owners and investors gain power (for a review of regulation and social responsibility see Chapters 16 and 18).

The ILO and European Commission database on transnational company agreements provides a full list of European and international agreements within MNCs concerning work and employment (European Commission, 2021). The list covers 321 agreements overall, with 216 of these agreements 'in force'. A num-ber of MNCs have multiple transnational agreements and 152 firms are listed as currently having such agreements in place. From this it can be seen that there is a certain amount of attrition, with agreements having been signed and in some cases concluded or rescinded. These data give an indication as to where MNCs who have signed up to such agreements are headquartered – 65 TCAs have been signed by French MNCs (including Veolia, Total, Thales, Suez, Renault, Safran, France Telecom, Danone and BNP Paribas), 37 by German MNCs (including Volkswagen, Thyssenkrupp, Siemens, Rheinmetall, BMW, Bosch and Allianz) and 13 by Spanish MNCs (including Santander and Inditex). Other countries with a significant presence of headquartered MNCs with TCAs include Italy (16), Sweden (15), Belgium (14), Norway (six) and Denmark (three). It can be seen from this that, in general, MNCs are more likely to have signed TCAs in countries where unions maintain a relatively strong culture of social dialogue and institu-tional influence among senior headquarters MNC management, as in Germany, France, Sweden, Belgium and Italy. MNCs headquartered in liberal market econ-omies with a stronger culture of union exclusion, such as the United States and United Kingdom (UK), are less likely to have such agreements, and MNCs head-quartered in emerging or developing countries also show limited engagement.

Only seven US firms, four UK firms, three Japanese firms and 1 Australian firm have TCAs; there are no Chinese-headquartered firms and only one Russian, two Brazilian and three South African firms are party to such agreements.

The contents of transnational agreements, the scope of their application, means of enforcement and provisions for conflict resolution vary quite widely, but typically include reference to ILO's Core Labour Standards and in some cases cover information and consultation procedures over restructuring and similar. The G4S agreement, the 'Ethical Employment Partnership', applies to all firms owned or controlled by the security firm G4S, committing the firm to the ILO's Core Labour Standards, including support for freedom of association, union membership and representation rights, and committing them to discipline managers who breach the agreement (Brookes, 2019: 82; Fichter and McCallum, 2015; McCallum, 2013; Mustchin and Martínez Lucio, 2017). In Volkswagen, five TCAs have been agreed, including a general Social Charter (2002) covering ILO conventions on freedom of association, minimum wages, limits to working time and the prohibition of child labour; health and safety (2004); sustainability and supplier relations (2006); labour relations, (2009), including employee co-determination structures; and temporary agency work (2012), minimizing the use of agency workers and giving them rights equal to salaried employees (2012). These agreements were led by the Global Works Council and are supported and ratified by the IndustriALL GUF (Mustchin et al., 2020; Whittall et al., 2017). Such agreements are an innovative means by which workers and their international representative institutions have sought to maintain labour standards within MNCs, but there is a need to explore the dynamics and complexities surrounding how such agreements are reached and their practical impact on work and employment.

While it is evident from this overview of MNCs that have signed TCAs that there has been a significant amount of activity in this area, some caution is needed when focusing simply on the quantity of agreements, their contents, the claims they make and similar. This 'focus on form rarely acknowledges social relations of production and hardly penetrates down to how conditions of employment could actually improve' as a consequence of TCAs (Tsogas, 2018: 519). There is evidently some inconsistency in terms of how TCAs are implemented – there are numerous examples of their abuse and lack of application, notably in the United States, where legal, employer and political mobilization in opposition to union recognition and transnational agreements has been prominent (Logan, 2020). The IFA signed in IKEA was breached in the United States, where local management opposed union recognition and victimized union activists (Ramsey, 2011). In January 2019, the IndustriALL GUF suspended support for the Declaration on Social Rights and Industrial Relations at the Volkswagen global agreement due to ongoing management and political opposition to union-organizing efforts at their subsidiary in Chattanooga, Tennessee (IndustriALL, 2019). Agreements are fragile and vulnerable to ownership and management change; their application may be weak in developing countries where the institutional capacity to enforce agreements may be lacking, and some countries, notably China, are often explicitly or more informally excluded from the scope of TCAs. The section that follows explores in more detail what TCAs mean for workers, unions and the international HRM policies of MNCs, including their potential, limitations and alternative forms of organizing international employee representation.

The outcomes of international employee representation and transnational agreements

Having outlined different forms of international employee representation in terms of the institutions involved, and given an overview of agreements between such institutions and MNCs which aim to address various international labour standards, this section focuses on the outcomes of international worker organization in terms of campaigning, securing agreements with MNCs, the position of such organizations and agreements within MNCs and their international HRM practices within different national and regional contexts.

The strategies adopted by unions in terms of international activity are determined by two main factors: first, the possibility of coordination among workers and unions in different countries given the often highly competitive relationships fostered within multinational employers and sectors and the divisions these create among workers; and, second, the nature of 'pre-existing traditions and practices of transnational regulation' (Anner et al., 2006: 7). For transnational alliances of labour organizations to be successful in terms of the outcomes of their campaigning, Brookes (2019: 22–34) argues that three conditions need to be met. These are intra-union coordination, or different groups within a particular union and its leadership working together on international campaigns; inter-union coordination and reciprocal work between the different labour organizations involved; and 'context-appropriate power', where the actions of such international alliances of unions and labour 'directly threaten the core material interests of the employer with whom it is in conflict' (ibid.: 4). Drawing on examples in the docks, the service sector and hospitality, international campaigns that were less successful – for example, the 1990s Liverpool dockworkers dispute – were undermined by a lack of support for campaigning workers from national union leaders (ibid.: 60–1). In the case of US retail unions seeking to secure global agreements within Tesco in 2008–10, a lack of coordination between the US union and those elsewhere, including USDAW in the UK, undermined the wider campaign (ibid.: 86–92). Conversely, in examples where intra-union coordination was stronger, as in the campaign within Raffles hotels in South East Asia in 2004, or where coordination between unions was relatively more developed, as with the campaign that ultimately secured an international framework agreement in G4S, such campaigning is viewed as having more positive outcomes (ibid.).

In G4S, a global campaign led by the Service Employees International Union (SEIU) in the United States, in conjunction with the Uni-Global GUF and the GMB union in the UK, where G4S is headquartered, resulted, in large part due to relatively strong inter-union coordination, in the conclusion of an IFA. This agreement commits the firm to supporting freedom of association and union recognition within its global subsidiaries, along with other labour standards (Fichter and McCallum, 2015; McCallum, 2013). 'Context-appropriate power' in this case relates to G4S seeking to improve its public image, including with regard to its treatment of employees, which had the potential to affect its ability to gain and maintain contracts with public and private organizations. Additionally, G4S could potentially benefit from the wider promotion of basic employment standards in the security industry, with competitors less able to win business through undercutting them by offering worse terms and conditions of employment. The fact that the firm faced some risks from not signing such an agreement and could identify benefits they would derive from it contributed towards its relative success. While bargaining gains and union strength in G4S subsidiaries covered by this agreement have been relatively modest (Mustchin and Martínez Lucio, 2017), it serves as one of the more developed examples of an IFA signed within a historically anti-union firm headquartered in a liberal market economy.

However, not all forms of international employee representation derive from such forms of campaigning. While international worker representation and transnational agreements are often a result of campaigning and the coordination of unions and representative institutions across national borders, some MNCs evidently identify benefits from having such structures in place. MNCs that value trusting relationships with unions and adopt a stakeholder approach to management are argued to be more likely to engage with IFAs, constituting a more stable, discreet and sustained relationship with employee representative bodies than that emphasized within analysis focused more on transnational union campaigning and more conflictual approaches (Egels-Zandén, 2009). Regional examples of cross-national collaboration among representative bodies in the EU are premised more on the existence of established, cross-national regional regulation concerning information and consultation, EWCs and sectoral social dialogue (Marginson, 2020). There is also a need to look beyond the formal structures of transnational employee representation in order to understand the impact of such agreements and systems of representation on work and employment within organizations and workplaces (Niforou, 2015). Examining case studies of particular transnational agreements, their potential impact is especially evident where European regulation and associated institutions such as EWCs are present, and where union representation is relatively strong at the level of the workplace (Rüb et al., 2013: 295). For example, in Volkswagen Europe, transnational agreements concerning representation and capping the proportion of workers employed through agencies have been used effectively by unions within auto manufacturing plants in EU member states (Whittall et al., 2017). Where local unions and representative bodies are aware of, value and engage with the standards set out in such international agreements, there is significant potential both for workers to reference them and utilize them in local organizing and bargaining practice, as well as for MNCs to use such agreements to facilitate regulatory alignment among their subsidiaries (Williams et al., 2015).

Difficulties in transferring such forms of regulation and representation from the European context to less regulated national environments are evident (see Chapter 8 on developing economies). Comparing German and Swedish MNCs, it was found that the monistic, single-channel representation that features in Sweden was a stronger basis for unions to ensure that labour standards were addressed in US subsidiaries than the dual channel form of representation (involving both works councils and trade unions) that features in Germany (for a discussion on restructuring and different national contexts see Chapter 13). The formal separation of representation in the German case militates against attempts to use GUFs and IFAs as a 'tool' for transnational organizing and bargaining (Helfen et al., 2016). Cross-national coordination of unions typically focuses on relationships within sub-regions of Europe (e.g. Nordic, Southern or Central regions) and within particular sectors. German and other Central European unions are typically the most engaged with this agenda, meaning the wider regional or global scope of agreements and associated organizing may sometimes be limited, or at least concentrated in particular areas (Larsson and Törnberg, 2021). Significantly, there is a risk to wider transnational solidarity within MNC operations where headquarters management and the home country union appear too dominant within such structures, posing a further threat to the geographical coverage and cohesiveness of EWCs and associated agreements (Kotthoff and Whittall, 2014).

IFAs have typically been judged to be more effective where local worker organization and unions are relatively strong (Bourque et al., 2018). The scale of the informal economy and its intersections with the supply chains of international business, and the weakness of established unions in this sector of the global economy, has been argued to necessitate a greater engagement between established unions, GUFs and similar with social movements concerned with informally employed, non-unionized workers (Munck, 2018: 211). Given the comparative weakness of unions in so much of the global economy and labour market, there is a need to look more closely at examples of international employee representation in contexts where such local organization is not present or functioning in the same way.

Global supply chains evidently place downward pressures on working conditions for those employed in supplier workplaces. The weaknesses of private forms of regulation in many national and sectoral contexts has received significant attention from the ILO, both in terms of engaging with stakeholders in particular countries and industries and in seeking to establish alternative forms of representation and strengthened stakeholder presence in supply chains marked by breaches of labour standards and poor working conditions (Thomas and Turnbull, 2018). In countries where unions lack independence and freedom of association is limited, an alternative means of permitting worker representation has been employee representative participation in CSR committees, as with the Better Work initiative in the textiles sector in Vietnam, where some form of worker representation was required in order to meet the labour standards required by lead firms in global supply chains. Notably, this was undermined by the lack of independent union presence and wider product market dynamics, including a squeeze on production prices and production times (Anner, 2018). In the aftermath of the 2013 Rana Plaza disaster in Bangladesh, where over 1,100 textile workers were killed after the building where they worked collapsed, textile manufacturers, civil society organizations and unions agreed to new CSR-oriented governance arrangements, including the Accord for Fire and Building Safety in Bangladesh (which provides some mechanisms for worker involvement and participation) and the Alliance for Bangladesh Worker Safety (which provides less scope for formal worker involvement). The short-term impact of these forms of CSR demonstrates some immediate improvements to working conditions and adherence to labour standards, while questioning the long-term impact in a context where industrial democracy and worker involvement is so limited (Donaghey and Reinecke, 2018).

Within MNCs, research on the auto industry highlights the importance of 'political entrepreneurs' within unions, who 'develop forms of leverage independent from their relationship with management' by organizing within their home countries and establishing networks and contacts with colleagues in subsidiaries in other countries (Greer and Hauptmeier, 2008). The basis for international employee representation and associated bargaining is premised in large part on the capacity of union actors to organize transnationally, and the absence of such organization is likely to render agreements relatively weak, symbolic and difficult to enforce. The example of dockworkers, who have organized transnationally since the late nineteenth century, and the International Transport Workers' Federation GUF (Turnbull, 2006) is significant – dissatisfaction among some workers with the GUF's lack of responsiveness around key disputes had led to the formation of a rival rank-and-file international network, the International Dockworkers' Council. While effective in building networks and solidarity among workers without the bureaucratic inertia associated with the established GUF, such networks face considerable challenges in terms of the pressure placed on activists due to their weakly resourced forms of institutional support (Fox-Hodess, 2020).

The limitations of more established forms of international employee representation and institutional networks, and the emergence of new technology, communications and social media, have led to some innovative approaches to developing international networks among workers. The Union Solidarity International (USI) initiative, supported by some of the major unions in the UK, has sought to provide resources and a platform for the development of networks via social media to bring together unions, workers and related actors internationally, with some degree of success (albeit relatively limited to actors in English-speaking countries), despite pressures stemming from limited resources and some challenges in terms of membership participation and internal democracy (Geelan and Hodder, 2017). International coordination among workers in the gig or platform economy is emerging in (as yet) relatively informal campaigning and information-sharing networks. The grassroots Independent Workers Union of Great Britain hosted the founding convention of the International Alliance of App-Based Transport Workers (IAATW) in January 2020, bringing together workers 'employed' by the app-based transport services Uber, Bolt, Grab and Lyft from 23 countries in order to challenge the exploitative, precarious nature of work fostered by these relatively new technology MNCs (IWGB, 2020; Vandaele, 2021). Similarly, the Transnational Federation of Couriers was founded in late 2018 to formalize networks and campaigning developed among couriers engaged by platforms in 12 countries (Cant and Mogno, 2020). While this is indicative of some innovative activity within emerging areas of the labour market, the limited and precarious resources and institutional power of such new actors raises questions about their sustainability and long-term efficacy.

Case study: G4S, international employee representation and TCAs, and its local implementation in Ghana

Global context

G4S, a product of the merger of UK-based Securicor and Danish-owned Group 4 Falk in 2004, is the world's largest private security employer, with over 500,000 employees in over 110 countries providing security services to a diverse range of private and public sector customers.

For example, it instals and runs security systems in prisons and executes contracts for military and police services across the globe. It has been the focus of damaging coverage over the years, centred on the treatment of people within its custody, controversial collaboration with authoritarian regimes and many other examples of unethical behaviour (see www.business-humanrights.org/en/companies/g4s/). In response to union campaigning and reputational concerns, G4S is a signatory to the 'Ethical Employment Partnership', an IFA co-signed in December 2008 by Uni-Global, GMB and G4S, affirming commitments to respecting fundamental human rights, including freedom of association and union recognition, within the wider community and among those at work.

Prior to the 2008 IFA, G4S was the subject of a five-year campaign by the SEIU, which initially focused on organizing security guards in the United States. The globalization of that effort, through Uni-Global and a complex web of unions and civil society actors, utilized negative publicity to place pressure on G4S investors, ultimately resulting in the IFA being agreed (McCallum, 2013). Among the tactics used included a website of anti-G4S propaganda, protests at its annual general meetings and the publication of highly critical reports and campaign materials. These measures, in addition to a complaint submitted to the UK OECD contact point, highlighting unethical employment practices, placed the company under intense investor scrutiny and pressures arising from disinvestment (McCallum, 2013). The signing of the IFA, a formalized institutional framework for transnational worker representation, constituted a substantial shift in public position by G4S. Applicable to all entities controlled by G4S, managers were ordered to allow unionization by unions affiliated to Uni-Global, with reporting and enforcement mechanisms, including annual review meetings and joint union–employer investigations of breaches, set up to ensure compliance. By 2017 G4S had agreements with 72 different unions globally, albeit with varied membership levels across its operations and significant tranches of employees without such representation.

Local realities: G4S Ghana, the local impact of transnational agreements and employment outcomes

G4S entered the Ghanaian market in 2006 through the takeover of a large domestic security company. It employs over 6,000 people, 98 per cent of whom are security guards, and has substantial competitors, including other security MNCs such as the US-headquartered Inter-Con Security and Ghanaian-headquartered Epsilon Security and Westec Security. Nonetheless, it enjoys significant market share through its strategic acquisitions and pan-regional security-based deals with MNCs in the lucrative mining and offshore oil and gas sectors. On entry, the firm engaged in derecognizing unions, although in the years ahead, the Union of Private Security Personnel (UPSP), a local union affiliated to Uni-Global, was recognized as a consequence of the IFA. The UPSP concluded a landmark collective bargaining agreement (CBA) in 2009, the first involving a major MNC in the security sector in Ghana.

(Continued)

Prior to negotiating the CBA with UPSP, G4S was repeatedly taken to the National Labour Commission (an employment tribunal) by employees citing unfair dismissal practices, among other unethical conduct, on mass redundancies, and to the Labour Department (the state registrar of unions) on their use of anti-union strategies of harassment, threats and dismissal of workers. Following the 2008 IFA, the spirit of 'partnership' in the agreement seemed to have cascaded down to the Ghanaian subsidiary in spite of the absence of formal communication of it from the headquarters: a common failing (Niforou, 2012). This was because local management encouraged 'informal partnership relationships' (Oxenbridge and Brown, 2002: 264), which resulted in union recognition, albeit with the employer-friendly UPSP, the signing of a CBA and permission to grow through support for union recruitment. Subsequently, worker complaints markedly fell, and the CBA proved useful to UPSP and its members as they benefitted from the inception of a provident fund (a voluntary employer contribution paid out on dismissal, redundancy or retirement) (Africa Pay, 2020), significant growth of the union within G4S and consequently a raised profile for the union more generally within this hard-to-unionize sector. For example, in affiliation with Uni-Global, a partner to the IFA, outreach activities such as its 'organizing blitz' helped the UPSP recruit over 1,853 new members (UNI Global, 2014).

Despite these comparative successes, employees reported significant contractual and regulatory breaches in relation to working time, pay, occupational health and safety and union repression. For example, in terms of working time, the majority of guards are subject to 12-hour shifts six days a week and receive only their legally mandated paid holidays. This is in part due to a local cost-minimization strategy of maintaining a minimal 'core' staff and encouraging overtime, including paying guards to forfeit leave days. Workers who opted out of mandatory overtime would receive wages below the legal minimum wage, and problems with occupational health and safety protections were evident in the under-provision of personal protective equipment and in the inadequate maintenance of company vehicles and staff facilities.

Finally, in the area of unionization and worker representation, the rhetorical promise of effective collaboration with unions across all levels of the firm within the IFA of 2008 was incongruent with managerial anti-union predispositions. Local management deployed a spectrum of measures that undermined local worker representation; for example, they granted unionization to guards by recognizing only the UPSP (an employer-friendly union), and sought to co-opt or 'capture' local union officials through the provision of benefits and 'sensitization' through extensive company-sponsored training programmes. Simultaneously, tactics of union suppression through intimidation and dismissals were adopted in response to the 'threat' of unionization among office workers. Thus at the local level the conditions attached to union entry were contingent on the 'business friendliness' of the union and the continued capability of management to influence their agenda within the union and at the level of the workplace, raising considerable questions about the nature of freedom of association in this case and the realities of worker representation, in comparison to the claims made in high-profile transnational agreements with employee representative bodies.

Case questions

1. Why do some MNCs engage with international employee representation while others do not?
2. What influence does the national context in which the MNC is headquartered have on man-agement approaches to international employee representation?
3. What are the likely outcomes of international employee representation and transnational agreements in contexts of deep-rooted managerial apathy towards workers and their representatives?
4. What are the complexities of delivering on the promises of an IFA in scenarios where the labour actor adopts a business unionism approach at the subsidiary level?

Conclusion

As can be seen from this discussion, there is a diverse range of forms of representative organizations for employees that seek to organize across national borders, including EWCs, GUFs and less formal, more networked attempts to develop solidarity and coordination. The outcomes of these forms of representation include formal information, consultation and (in some cases) negotiating procedures at the European level, TCAs with EWCs, GUFs and national unions as signatories, and new networks and forms of coordination arising from particular disputes in specific sectors involving workers from multiple countries. Such representative institutions and associated agreements constitute a significant, albeit constrained and relatively modest, attempt to overcome the limitations of unions, which have historically been organized on the basis of workplaces, industries and at the national level. MNCs increasingly make a high rhetorical commitment to corporate social responsibility, typically covering themes of sustainability, environmental standards and in some cases labour standards. A common criticism of such employer-led policies is that they are weakly enforced by actors often lacking in neutrality. From the perspective of MNCs, engaging meaningfully with stakeholders representing those working in their global operations can reinforce and legitimize their CSR activity through meaningful monitoring and enforcement at the local level.

However, the impact of such developments should not be overstated. Many MNCs remain hostile or at best indifferent towards stakeholder approaches to management and engaging meaningfully with the representatives of workers. In cases where TCAs have been established within MNCs, future challenges can emerge in cases where outsourcing and offshoring make supply chains increasingly complex and fragmented, where key figures within MNC management functions move on and where commitment to stakeholder engagement is lost. Ownership change brings in new organizational actors, interests and personnel who may be less amenable to such engagement, especially where a corporate takeover is led by an entity from a country with less established traditions of social dialogue and working with employee representative bodies. TCAs can collapse or fall into obscurity when MNCs fail to ensure that the labour standards underpinning such agreements are consistently and meaningfully applied across the entirety of their global operations. Coordinating workers in different countries with different languages and with different, sometimes competing, interests is complex and challenging within individual MNCs, let alone at the sectoral or cross-sectoral level. The relative distance of formalized transnational employee representation in the form of EWCs or GUFs also presents challenges due to the highly variable levels of coordination between workplaces, unions and the international institutions they are affiliated to. In cases where such coordination has fragmented because of a perceived lack of efficacy on the part of international representative bodies, more independent, grassroots-focused forms of transnational solidarity and coordination have arisen, but these themselves face challenges due to limited resources and institutional embeddedness within the firms and sectors in which they operate.

Despite these numerous challenges and given the significant constraints on the capacity of individual countries to meaningfully uphold labour standards deriving from economic globalization and a political climate that in many cases is increasingly hostile towards employee representative bodies and transnational regulation involving stakeholders and notions of social dialogue, there is an important role for GUFs, EWCs and more informal networks of workers and employees in MNCs and internationalized sectors in holding employers to account. Diverse forms of international employee representation can strengthen the adherence of MNCs to labour standards, compelling them to prioritize employment conditions more than they otherwise would, and ensuring that the conditions established through the ILO and other international institutions that seek to promote 'decent work' and prevent employer abuses of labour standards are actually manifested within the reality of workplaces in an interlinked, globalized political economy.

Reflective questions

1. How are different forms of employee representation internationalizing?
2. Why have unions become more concerned with their international strategies?
3. What may be the consequences of this for the management of work within MNCs?
4. What is the role of international employee representation in relation to wider systems of private regulation within MNCs?

References

Africa Pay (2020) *Collective Agreements Database*. Amsterdam: Wage Indicator Foundation. Available at: https://bit.ly/2zHwfj9 (accessed 17 September 20).

Anner, M. (2018) 'CSR participation committees, wildcat strikes and the sourcing squeeze in global supply chains'. *British Journal of Industrial Relations*, 56(1): 75–98.

Anner, M., Greer, I., Hauptmeier, M., Lillie, N. and Winchester, N. (2006) 'The industrial determinants of transnational solidarity: Global interunion politics in three sectors'. *European Journal of Industrial Relations*, 12(1): 7–27.

Bolsmann, C. (2007) 'Trade-union internationalism and solidarity in the struggle against apartheid: A case study of Volkswagen'. *Historical Studies in Industrial Relations*, 23–4(1): 103–24.

Bourguignon, R., Garaudel, P. and Porcher, S. (2020) 'Global framework agreements and trade unions as monitoring agents in transnational corporations'. *Journal of Business Ethics*, 165: 517–33.

Bourque, R., Hennebert, M. A., Lévesque, C. and Murray, G. (2018) 'Do international union alliances contribute to the effectiveness of international framework agreements? A comparative study of Telefonica and Portugal Telecom'. *Economic and Industrial Democracy*, 42(3): 450–72.

Brookes, M. (2019) *The New Politics of Transnational Labor: Why Some Alliances Succeed*. Ithaca: Cornell University Press.

Cant, C. and Mogno, C. (2020) 'Platform workers of the world, unite! The emergence of the Transnational Federation of Couriers'. *South Atlantic Quarterly*, 119(2): 401–11.

Carew, A. (2018) *American Labour's Cold War Abroad: From Deep Freeze to Détente, 1945–1970*. Athabasca: Athabasca University Press.

Croucher, R. and Cotton, E. (2011) *Global Unions, Global Business: Global Union Federations and International Business*. London: Libri Publishing.

Donaghey, J. and Reinecke, J. (2018) 'When industrial democracy meets corporate social responsibility – a comparison of the Bangladesh accord and alliance as responses to the Rana Plaza disaster'. *British Journal of Industrial Relations*, 56(1): 14–42.

Egels-Zandén, N. (2009) 'TNC motives for signing international framework agreements: A continuous bargaining model of stakeholder pressure'. *Journal of Business Ethics*, 84(4): 529–47.

European Commission (2021) *Database on Transnational Company Agreements*. EC Directorate-General for Employment, Social Affairs & Inclusion. Available at: https://ec.europa.eu/social/main.jsp?catId=978&langId=en (accessed 11 January 2021).

Fichter, M. (2020) International regulation: Standards and voluntary practices'. In C. Frege and J. Kelly (eds), *Comparative Employment Relations in the Global Economy*. Abingdon: Routledge, pp. 239–59.

Fichter, M. and McCallum, J. K. (2015) 'Implementing global framework agreements: The limits of social partnership'. *Global Networks*, 15(s1): S65–S85.

Fox-Hodess, K. (2020) 'Building labour internationalism "from below": Lessons from the International Dockworkers' Council's European Working Group'. *Work, Employment and Society*, 34(1): 91–108.

Geelan, T. and Hodder, A. (2017) 'Enhancing transnational labour solidarity: The unfulfilled promise of the internet and social media'. *Industrial Relations Journal*, 48(4): 345–64.

Greer, I. and Hauptmeier, M. (2008) 'Political entrepreneurs and co-managers: Labour transnationalism at four multinational auto companies'. *British Journal of Industrial Relations*, 46(1): 76–97.

Gregoratti, C. and Miller, D. (2011) 'International framework agreements for Workers' Rights? Insights from River Rich Cambodia'. *Global Labour Journal*, 2(2): 84–105.

Hann, D., Hauptmeier, M. and Waddington, J. (2017) 'European works councils after two decades'. *European Journal of Industrial Relations*, 23(3): 209–24.

Helfen, M. O., Schüßler, E. and Stevis, D. (2016) 'Translating European labor relations practices to the United States through global framework agreements? German and Swedish multinationals compared'. *ILR Review*, 69(3): 631–55.

Helfen, M., Schüßler, E. and Sydow, J. (2018) 'How can employment relations in global value networks be managed towards social responsibility?' *Human Relations*, 71(12): 1640–65.

Hershenberg, A. M. and O'Casey, M. (2019) 'When the techies go marching in: An industry updates its sexual harassment dispute resolution policy'. *Alternatives to the High Cost of Litigation*, 37(2): 18–27.

IndustriALL (2019) 'IndustriALL suspends global agreement with Volkswagen'. Available at: www.industriall-union.org/industriall-suspends-global-agreement-with-volkswagen (accessed 25 September 2020).

IWGB (2020) 'First-ever international meeting of app-based transport workers to develop global strategy to challenge platform companies'. Available at: https://iwgb.org.uk/post/first-ever-international-meeting-of-app-based-transport-workers-to-develop-global-strategy-to-challenge-platform-companies (accessed 11 January 2021).

Kotthoff, H. and Whittall, M. (2014) *Paths to Transnational Solidarity: Identity-Building Processes in European Works Councils*. Oxford: Peter Lang.

Larsson, B. and Törnberg, A. (2021) 'Sectoral networks of transnational trade union cooperation in Europe'. *Economic and Industrial Democracy*, 42(4): 1189–1209.

Levinson, C. (1972) *International Trade Unionism*. London: Allen & Unwin.

Logan, J. (2020) 'The US union avoidance industry goes global'. *New Labor Forum*, 29(1): 76–81.

McCallum, J. K. (2013) *Global Unions, Local Power: The New Spirit of Transnational Labor Organizing*. Ithaca: Cornell University Press.

Marginson, P. (2020) 'Regional regulation: The European Union'. In C. Frege and J. Kelly (eds), *Comparative Employment Relations in the Global Economy*. Abingdon: Routledge, pp. 239–59.

Moody, K. (1997) *Workers in a Lean World: Unions in the International Economy*. London and New York: Verso.

Munck, R. (2018) *Rethinking Global Labour*. Newcastle: Agenda Publishing.

Mustchin, S. and Martínez Lucio, M. M. (2017) 'Transnational collective agreements and the development of new spaces for union action: The formal and informal uses of international and European framework agreements in the UK'. *British Journal of Industrial Relations*, 55(3): 577–601.

Mustchin, S., Martínez Lucio, M., Whittall, M., Rocha, F. and Telljohann, V. (2020) 'Framing workers' rights internationally: The case of Volkswagen and transnational collective agreements'. In T. Dundon and A. Wilkinson (eds), *Case Studies in Work, Employment and Human Resource Management*. Cheltenham: Edward Elgar.

Niforou, C. (2012) 'International framework agreements and industrial relations governance: Global rhetoric versus local realities'. *British Journal of Industrial Relations*, 50(2): 352–73.

Niforou, C. (2015) 'Labour leverage in global value chains: The role of interdependencies and multi-level dynamics'. *Journal of Business Ethics*, 130(2): 301–11.

Oxenbridge, S. and Brown, W. (2002) 'The two faces of partnership? An assessment of partnership and co-operative employer/trade union relationships'. *Employee Relations*, 24(3): 262–76.

Papadakis, K. (2011) 'Introduction and overview'. In K. Papadakis (ed.), *Shaping Global Industrial Relations: The Impact of International Framework Agreements*. Basingstoke: Palgrave Macmillan.

Preuss, L., Haunschild, A. and Matten, D. (2009) 'The rise of CSR: Implications for HRM and employee representation'. *International Journal of Human Resource Management*, 20(4): 953–73.

Ramsey, B. (2011) 'Global agreement with IKEA: Dialogue for deaf ears?' *International Union Rights*, 18(2): 18–19.

Rüb, S., Platzer, H. W. and Müller, T. (2013) *Transnational Company Bargaining and the Europeanization of Industrial Relations: Prospects for a Negotiated Order*. Oxford: Peter Lang.

Schomann, I., Sobczak, A., Voss, E. and Wilke, P. (2008) 'International framework agreements: New paths to workers' participation in multinationals' governance?' *Transfer*, 14(1): 111–26.

Scipes, K. (2010) *AFL-CIO's Secret War against Developing Country Workers: Solidarity or Sabotage?* Lanham: Lexington Books.

Streeck, W. (1994) 'European social policy after Maastricht: The "social dialogue" and "subsidiarity"'. *Economic and Industrial Democracy*, 15(2): 151–77.

Thomas, H. and Turnbull, P. (2018) 'From horizontal to vertical labour governance: The International Labour Organization (ILO) and decent work in global supply chains'. *Human Relations*, 71(4): 536–59.

Tsogas, G. (2018) 'Transnational labor regulation, reification, and commodification: A critical review'. *Journal of Labor and Society*, 21(4): 517–32.

Turnbull, P. (2006) 'The war on Europe's waterfront – repertoires of power in the port transport industry'. *British Journal of Industrial Relations*, 44(2): 305–26.

UNI Global (2014) *Guarding Wealth: Living in Poverty*. Nyon: UNI Global Union. Available at: https://bit.ly/2W6uO5q (accessed 17 September 2020).

van Roozendaal, G. (2003) *Trade Unions and Global Governance: The Debate on a Social Clause.* London: Routledge.

Vandaele, K. (2021) 'Collective resistance and organizational creativity amongst Europe's platform workers: A new power in the labour movement?' In J. Haidar and M. Keune (eds), *Work and Labour Relations in Global Platform Capitalism.* Geneva and Cheltenham: ILO and Edward Elgar, pp. 206–35.

Waddington, J. (2011) 'European Works Councils: The challenge for labour'. *Industrial Relations Journal,* 42(6): 508–29.

Walker, S. (2014) 'Media, new union strategies and non-government organizations as global players: The struggle over representation and work'. In M. Martínez Lucio (ed.), *International Human Resource Management: An Employment Relations Perspective.* London: Sage, pp. 277–92.

Waterman, P. and Wills, J. (2001) 'Space, place and the new labour internationalisms: Beyond the fragments?' *Antipode,* 33(3): 305–11.

Whittall, M., Martínez Lucio, M., Mustchin, S., Telljohann, V. and Sánchez, F. R. (2017) 'Workplace trade union engagement with European Works Councils and transnational agreements: The case of Volkswagen Europe'. *European Journal of Industrial Relations,* 23(4): 397–414.

Williams, G., Davies, S. and Chinguno, C. (2015) 'Subcontracting and labour standards: Reassessing the potential of international framework agreements'. *British Journal of Industrial Relations,* 53(2): 181–203.

Wills, J. (2002) 'Bargaining for the space to organize in the global economy: A review of the Accor-IUF trade union rights agreement'. *Review of International Political Economy,* 9(4): 675–700.

18 Sustainability and International Human Resource Management

Josef Ringqvist, David Öborn Regin, Lena Lid-Falkman and Lars Ivarsson

Learning objectives

- To understand the concept of sustainability and how it informs International Human Resource Management (IHRM) debates
- To distinguish between different dimensions of sustainability and problematize the degree to which they potentially do and do not complement each other
- To gain insight regarding the potential role of the human resources (HR) function in the pursuit of sustainability, while familiarizing readers with some critical arguments pertaining to its limits in a broader context
- To apply a stakeholder perspective to Sustainable HRM and understand some its implications in an international and comparative perspective

Introduction

During the past 30 years, sustainability has emerged as an issue of principal political and societal concern. Many of the topics involved are deeply connected with the world of work and employment. However, it was not until recently that this was recognized in HRM debates (Ehnert and Harry, 2012: 223). This chapter critically reviews some of the most prominent themes involved in debates on HRM and sustainability. We show that sustainability is becoming an increasingly important concept within IHRM for understanding the evolving role of the HR function, as heightened global awareness puts pressure, not least on large media-exposed multinational companies (MNCs), to address sustainability issues (Ehnert et al., 2016).

We start by mapping some of the general themes commonly appearing in the literature on sustainability and HRM, distinguishing between the three dimensions of economic, social and ecological sustainability. Readers are introduced to the stakeholder approach to sustainability and the issue of contextual variation with regards to stakeholder involvement (Kaufman, 2014) – reoccurring subjects throughout this chapter. We then proceed to discuss each sustainability dimension separately, beginning with what remains at the bottom line of any organization: its ability to reproduce itself economically. After that, some key HRM issues relating to social sustainability are reviewed, also conceptualized on a more general level with reference to the economic historian Karl Polanyi ([1944] 2001) and the notion of 'decommodification'. Next, we turn to the growing literature on ecological sustainability, showing that the HR function has many tools which contribute to the ecological performance of organizations. Some critical arguments questioning the possibilities of business-led ecological sustainability are also presented. As we show, the sustainability dimensions often overlap, sometimes being complementary, but sometimes also appearing to be mutually exclusive, a complex issue to which we return in the concluding discussion.

Sustainability and HRM

This chapter takes a broad approach to the association between sustainability and HRM but with a certain emphasis on the concept of Sustainable HRM (SHRM). In a review, Macke and Genari (2019: 809) identify the following terminologies linking sustainability and HRM: Sustainable HRM, sustainable work system, HR sustainability, sustainable management of HR and sustainable leadership. The authors conclude that while the literature is diverse and fragmented, the concepts cohere by recognizing '[. . .] implicitly or explicitly, the human and social perspectives of organisations and the impact that human resources have on the success and survival of companies' (Macke and Genari, 2019: 807). This in turn relates to the varying and not always explicit motivations for linking HRM and sustainability; some frame it as an issue of moral responsibility, regardless of financial effects, whereas others stress the need to couple sustainability with matters of efficiency and organizational survival (Ehnert, 2009: 62–7). Most literature tends to go beyond a purely moral approach, instead seeking to draw a connection between economic performance and sustainability; for example, Ehnert et al. (2016: 90) define SHRM as: '[. . .] the adoption of HRM strategies and practices that enable the achievement of financial, social and ecological goals, with an impact inside and outside of the organisation and over a long-term time horizon while controlling for unintended side effects and negative feedback'.

The above definition covers three commonly delineated dimensions – or bottom lines – of sustainability: economic, social and ecological. At its core, the notion of sustainability challenges us to consider each dimension in a longer time perspective, an issue of increasing concern for international regulatory actors such as the United Nations (UN) (see Chapter 16 on transnational regulation). In an influential and often cited report, the United Nations Brundtland Commission (WCED, 1987) defines sustainability as '[. . .] meeting the needs of the present without compromising the ability of future generations to meet their own needs'. From the point of view of HR, or individual companies, a longer time perspective often implies that *economic* sustainability becomes intertwined with *social* sustainability, as it relates to efforts to facilitate productive and engaged employees who are willing and able to remain in employment. Beyond individual organizations, the implications of a broader social perspective on sustainability and work are illustrated in the ongoing debate in many regions about raising the retirement age: an ageing workforce raises questions about the long-term sustainability of current working conditions and, importantly, how these vary between occupational groups.

Debates on the broader association between HRM and sustainability, pertaining particularly to the increasingly pressing *ecological* dimension, also raise fundamental questions about how corporations relate to their wider social and environmental settings. In the parlance of economic theory, many social and ecological issues tend to possess the qualities of 'negative externalities' (Kapp, 1950), referring to costs that are shifted from business to third parties such as individual employees or broader society. Responding to the often boundaryless nature of these issues, the UN has formulated 17 global sustainability goals, several of which have implications for and are related to work and employment, such as (3) health and wellbeing, (5) gender equality and (8) decent work and economic growth (www.un.org/sustainabledevelopment) (see Chapters 5 on diversity, 16 on transnational regulation and 17 on international employee representation). In order to reach these goals, the UN also highlights business and industry as *key* stakeholders, within which we suggest that the HR function can and does play a significant role.

Many recent HRM debates incorporate the notion of sustainability, often by applying a *stakeholder* perspective, which provides a framework within which to conceptualize the broader implications of organizational activities. Stakeholder approaches to HRM can be traced back to the classic distinction between the early models of HRM associated with the Harvard and Michigan schools, in which the 'soft HRM' approach of the Harvard model is based on a stakeholder perspective. A stakeholder is defined as '[. . .] any individual or group who can affect or is affected by actions, decisions, policies, practices or goals of an organization' (Freeman, 1984: 25). As is evident from such a broad definition, stakeholders include many groups – such as NGOs, trade unions, or consumers – the influence of and importance attributed to which vary substantially. When it comes to stakeholder involvement, context also plays a significant role. Some apply the varieties of capitalism (VoC) approach (see Chapters 11 on varieties of capitalism and Chapter 3 on employment relations) which classifies countries according to modes of corporate governance and industrial relations (Hall and Soskice, 2001). While it has been expanded subsequently, the original distinction was between liberal market economies (LMEs) such as the Anglo-Saxon countries, and coordinated market economies (CMEs) such as Japan and the continental European and Scandinavian countries. LMEs tend to be less stakeholder-oriented, for example having less government regulation and trade union influence (Ehnert et al., 2016: 93). Conversely, coordinated market economies (CMEs) tend to attribute more weight to stakeholders; employees have more influence via unions or works councils and regulations are more encompassing. The role of stakeholders has implications for sustainability, as argued by Kaufman: 'In stakeholder countries, governments also take a more activist role in ensuring that companies' HRM policies take into account social preferences and costs, such as for a clean environment, stable employment, and equal opportunities for women and minorities' (2014: 12). Ongoing debates concern the degree to which country-level differences persist or, conversely, whether we are witnessing a trend towards increasing convergence; Ehnert et al. (2016), for example, show that when it comes to sustainability reporting among the world's largest companies, there are no major differences depending upon whether these are headquartered in LMEs or CMEs.

Another important issue has to do with potential discrepancies between rhetoric and practice. As an example relating to the environment, there is much concern over the use of *greenwashing*, that is: '[. . .] communication that misleads people into adopting overly positive beliefs about an organization's environmental performance, practices, or products' (Lyon and Montgomery, 2015: 226). Heightened global awareness and media interest prompt companies, particularly large MNCs, to report on sustainability issues. However, as argued by Ehnert et al., '[. . .] in the absence of standardized and mandatory audit of such information, companies can report irrelevant information in order to project a desirable and transparent image [. . .]' (2016: 91). Corporations are eager to present themselves as environmentally concerned actors, and while this may often represent their true motivations, little progress appears to being made on a global scale; for example, in spite of the appearance of increasing efforts, CO_2 emissions continue to increase (Crippa et al., 2020).

Also, it often appears in rhetoric as if the three dimensions of sustainability are in 'natural harmony' with each other, and that there is little or even no contradiction between them. In reality, this often proves much more complex; there is no such thing as a natural equilibrium or state of 'balance' between the different dimensions.

This is where the above-mentioned stakeholder perspective provides one framework for understanding the relative weight attributed to each dimension. Contemplating the relationship between the three dimensions also provides an opportunity to conceptualize and rethink some of the potential contributions provided by the HR function, an ongoing debate to which we now turn.

HRM and economic sustainability

Debates on the association between HRM and economic sustainability highlight some persistent tensions regarding the conflicting loyalties of the HR function in organizations. One may distinguish between the role of HR as strategic business partner, focusing chiefly on contributing to economic performance, and a broader role, advocating sustainability issues and emphasizing the importance of a long-term perspective which also includes a wider set of stakeholders.

Historically, the traditional personnel management function is often characterized as constituting an intermediary or buffer between management and workers (Gonäs and Larsson, 2014; Marchington 2015: 178). However, attempts to increase the legitimacy and influence of HR subsequently implied moving closer to and adapting practices to management's objectives. The rise to prominence in the 1980s of the concept of strategic HRM was a step in this direction by linking HR practice more explicitly with organizational performance, 'particularly financial and market outcomes' (Kramar, 2014: 1069). As argued by Lengnick-Hall et al., 'This shift signalled a dramatic change in the role and influences of human resource professionals [. . .]' (2009: 69). The focus of strategic HRM on coupling HR with economic performance was '[. . .] an opportunity for the profession to cement its standing at board level, and contribute as a full and equal member of the senior management team' (Marchington, 2015: 176, 180). This was achieved by aligning with the overall aim of maximizing value for shareholders – for example by favouring incentive pay and outsourcing above skill upgrading and job security (Kaufman, 2014: 12).

However, critics argue that a one-sided focus on financial outcomes often conflicts with long-term organizational performance or even survival (Dundon and Rafferty, 2018; Wright and Snell, 2005). The HR function hence has, at least in rhetoric, changed and become increasingly complex; what is economically advantageous in a shorter time-period may not be sustainable in the long run. This is illustrated particularly when it comes to managing the sustainability of key resources, both human and material (Ehnert et al., 2014: 5). The extent to which such an extended time perspective actually reaches beyond rhetoric is contested; calls for more sustainable, long-term management of HR can be criticized for being overly optimistic or even naïve, overlooking constraints imposed on management by factors relating to the wider political economy such as competitive pressures in increasingly deregulated, globalized and financialized markets (Dundon and Rafferty, 2018; Thompson 2003). Variations in forms of ownership and corporate governance may play a role here, as organizations less exposed to the need to satisfy the short-term interests of shareholders may be more able to adopt longer-term perspectives. For example, it has been shown that family-owned firms with an explicit long-time orientation are more likely to opt for sustainability practices – although interestingly, without such an orientation, family ownership is negatively associated with sustainability practices, as these tend to involve the partial forfeit of family control, among other things by being subjected to external regulations (Memili et al., 2018). Nevertheless, regardless of its prospects, SHRM tends to challenge some of the premises of strategic HRM and its exclusive focus on shareholders and financial outcomes, widening the scope to include a broader set of stakeholders (Kramar, 2014: 1075). This may, for example, lead to an increasing awareness of the implications of organizational activities on current and future employees (related to the employer brand), members of the broader society or even future generations (App et al., 2012; Kramar, 2014: 1071). To be clear, the main point of SHRM is not that factors such as return to investment should be seen as irrelevant to HR (Kramar, 2014: 1085) but that a seemingly straightforward definition of economic performance is made increasingly complex when framed in a longer time perspective, in which economic resources tend to interlink with social and environmental ones.

Social sustainability

The central aspect of social sustainability as it relates to HRM pertains to employees and quality of working life (Zink, 2014; see Chapter 16 on transnational regulation), particularly in the extent to which this also contributes to economic sustainability through factors such as long-term well-being, motivation and firm loyalty, as well as the avoidance of costs related to sick leave and burnout. This section shows that many key aspects of social sustainability predate SHRM, again highlighting tensions regarding the loyalties of the HR function. Contextual differences pertaining to stakeholder involvement and working conditions, as well as some particular challenges presented by MNCs relating to regulation, are also discussed.

While we have emphasized that sustainability involves several dimensions, Richards (2020) specifically formulates an employee-centred approach to SHRM, as '[. . .] a way and a means by which HRM practice develops and oversees attempts to make sure employees are willing and able to stay in employment now and for as long as reasonably possible'. In a broader political and societal perspective, many of the issues involved are illustrated in problems posed by an ageing workforce in many regions (Eurofound, 2012; Zink, 2014: 39). In Sweden for example, the former prime minister Fredrik Reinfeldt has argued repeatedly that in order to carry the costs of the pension system, many Swedes will have to work until the age of 75. If people are expected, or even forced, to work an additional 10 years, SHRM appears vital. Consequently, recent research has responded to a previous lack of studies on HR practices and how they can help bring about sustainability for older workers (Ybema et al., 2020). In a broader perspective, Eurofound, in a report on sustainable work and the ageing workforce, concludes that there are clear differences between occupational groups when it comes to current work sustainability, and that gender also is a key aspect: 'The study highlights factors relating to unsustainability not only for low-skilled occupations and mid-skilled manual occupations, but also for high-skilled occupations, particularly women among managers and professionals [. . .]' (Eurofound, 2012: 82). Adding to this, we should emphasize issues relating to low-skilled migrant workers, who are often 'target earners' with a more instrumental work orientation, lacking motivation to organize in order to improve working conditions; partly for these reasons – not disregarding other factors related to discrimination or racism – migrant workers tend particularly to be treated as substitutable and disposable, and thus subject to more exploitative working conditions (see Chapter 7 on migration). The Swedish debate illustrates the central issue of work–life inequality in managing an ageing workforce; the public sector trade union Kommunal, for example, has called any attempt to raise the retirement age that is not coupled with measures accounting for those who are physically unable to do so a 'betrayal of worn-out bodies' (Lag and Avtal, 2020). Two key problems related to a sustainable working life are burnout and strain, the latter for example being associated with higher risk of cardiovascular disease. Beyond ageing, many solutions here relate to HRM and the design of jobs; importantly, employee decision-making latitude and reduced psychological demands (such as reduced time pressure) both help to reduce stress-related health risks. A socially sustainable working life also involves aspects related to employee voice, which tends to reduce job turnover (Freeman and Medoff, 1984).

It should be emphasized that the social dimension of HR and personnel work is far from new. As discussed above, the original HR function often was to buffer the effects on employees of the short-term pursuit of economic profit, while the shift into becoming a strategic partner may have come with a transfer of loyalties more towards employers at the cost of providing this buffering function (Marchington, 2015). The challenge remains to balance efficiency and competitiveness with the long-term well-being of employees (social sustainability). These are historical tensions which were also at the heart of the emergence of the labour movement. A classic exposition of this problematic is provided by the economic historian Karl Polanyi ([1944] 2001), who describes labour as a 'fictitious commodity' (see also Fraser, 2014) – that is, something which is treated as a commodity while not initially 'created' for the market; in contrast to other commodities, labour cannot simply be used indiscriminately without this having an effect on the human individual performing it. Markets left to self-regulate, according to Polanyi, are not equipped to deal with this problem. He therefore stresses the importance of countervailing tendencies protecting society against pure market forces – what is commonly labelled 'decommodification' – and argues that '[. . .] to allow the market mechanism to be sole director of the fate of human beings [. . .] would result in the demolition of society' ([1944] 2001, 73). Trade unions are often conceived as a countervailing force in this regard (see Chapters 3 on employment relations and 17 on trade unions internationally). This links with the discussion above about contextual variation and the weight of stakeholders; unions are one of the principal stakeholders when it comes to social sustainability (Richards, 2020). Research also shows that working conditions tend to be more favourable at workplaces with union influence and in countries with stronger unions. During recent decades, unions have lost members in most Western nations, which may provide cause for concern regarding the long-term development of work sustainability and job quality. However, unions do remain important actors in many contexts and are emerging in others.

The social dimension of sustainability can also be expanded beyond an employee-centred approach. One such broader perspective is provided by Elkington (2013), who includes human and societal values connected to wealth creation and distribution. Historically, in terms of the relation between broader social sustainability and the corporate world, the publication in 1953 of Howard Bowen's seminal book *Social Responsibilities of the Businessman* is an important contribution. Addressing business ethics and corporate social responsibility (CSR), Bowen advocated a more or less voluntary responsibility of companies for the surrounding society through self-regulation.

Issues of regulation in turn relate to another central issue of social sustainability concerning MNCs, which present particular challenges as they operate in varying regional contexts and often manage large value chains including a 'core' workforce and numerous subcontract suppliers (Marchington, 2015: 182–3; see Chapters 2 on multinational corporations and 8 on developing economies). Debates here revolve around efforts to establish common standards, such as fair labour standards, in order to counteract 'race to the bottom'-type outcomes of 'regime shopping' (see Chapter 2 on multinational corporations). Some argue that certain key MNCs in particular have grown so powerful that they have at their disposal the means to dominate political systems and nation-states, plundering scarce resources and undermining local development (see Chapters 1 on globalization and employment and Chapter 2 on multinational corporations). Consequently, one way to conceptualize a sustainable approach to managing subcontractors is the notion of sustainable supply chain management (SSCM) (Touboulic and Walker, 2015). This is defined by Pagell and Wu as follows: 'To be *truly* sustainable a supply chain would at worst do no net harm to natural or social systems while still producing a profit over an extended period of time [...]' (2009: 38). As elsewhere, it is useful to consider the importance of pressure from various groups in making sure that standards are agreed upon and upheld; the literature on SSCM conforms with other SHRM approaches by often drawing on stakeholder theory. Key stakeholders include customers, regulators (such as the ILO and the UN), industry peers and media. Others stress the primary importance of organized labour – particularly in the absence of strong governmental regulatory institutions. Drawing partly on Polanyi, Silver (2003) shows that as companies relocate geographically in search of 'cheap and controllable labour', such relocations tend to be followed by conflicts and emerging labour movements strengthening workers' rights and wages, in turn resulting in the further geographical relocation of capital.

Environmental sustainability

There is no doubt that environmental issues have increasingly taken centre stage in sustainability debates, as manifested in the enormous impact of the mass movement set in motion by Greta Thunberg. The interest in environmental sustainability is reflected in the HRM and to a lesser extent the industrial-relations literature. The field of environmental labour studies has also attracted increasing attention by exploring the complex relation between labour and the environment (Räthzel and Uzzell, 2011, 2013). In terms of HRM, environmental debates often play out under the topic of CSR or the emerging field of 'green HRM' (GHRM), which has grown steadily during the past 10–15 years (Bombiak, 2019: 1648). GHRM denotes the alignment of traditional HRM practices with the broader concept of Environmental Management, the aim being to increase environmental performance – for example by reducing toxic (or other) emissions (Kassinis and Vafeas, 2006). The HR function here is argued to offer key tools in matching employees' capabilities, commitment and involvement in support of firm-level sustainability requirements. Before elaborating on some of these tools, we start with a brief discussion about the sustainability requirements themselves: who are the actors and institutions formulating them? And (why) do firms respond?

While many advocate a proactive approach towards ecological sustainability going beyond compliance with current regulations and requirements, others emphasize the importance of *pressure* from various groups. As in the broader SHRM literature, these often draw on stakeholder theory, pointing to the wider context in which companies operate and the broad range of stakeholders presenting them with different claims (Bombiak, 2019: 1648; Guerci, Longoni et al., 2016: 263;

Kassinis and Vafeas, 2006). The underlying assumption is that organizations are more likely to opt for ecologically sustainable practices when pressured by outside actors. Locating stakeholders with interests in ecological sustainability, conceptualizing their capacity to exert pressure and influence, and identifying how firms in turn respond to such pressure are central tasks. Customers, regulators (governments and legislators) and community groups are often identified as key stakeholders, and it is shown that pressure from these groups does tend to have an effect on the ecological performance of organizations (e.g. Guerci, Longoni et al., 2016; Kassinis and Vafeas, 2006). Importantly, the HR function is often shown to have a central role in translating such pressure into actual environmental performance. This links back to debates referred to above about the legitimacy and influence of the HR function; the concrete contributions of HR practice to environmental performance arguably provide legitimate grounds for HR practitioners seeking a leading role in organizations, at least those claiming to strive towards sustainability. The growing literature on GHRM explores the effect on ecological performance of a number of HR practices, including green recruitment, training and performance management.

In terms of *recruitment*, the ecological profile and reputation of a firm is presented as an increasingly important aspect of its attractiveness among potential job applicants (Guerci, Montanari et al., 2016). One study has shown that even compared to factors such as pay, promotion and lay-off policy, a firm's ecological rating was the factor that most strongly predicted its attractiveness among potential jobseekers (Aiman-Smith et al., 2001). Research also shows that individuals are more willing to pursue employment and accept job offers from pro-environmental companies (Gully et al., 2013). The process of selection, i.e. the identification of applicants with environmental knowledge and motivation, often referred to as 'green hiring', however, does not always seem to result in higher ecological performance (Guerci, Longoni et al., 2016). Conversely, another key HR function which is shown to have a positive effect on environmental performance is green *training*, which can help create an environmentally responsible organizational culture and implement changes needed for environmental sustainability (Guerci, Longoni et al., 2016; Vidal-Salazar et al., 2012: 922; see also Chapter 9 for a more general discussion on training). Next, green *performance management* involves the '[a]ppraisal and register of employees' environmental performance [. . .]' and provision of '[. . .] feedback about their performance in order to prevent undesirable attitudes or reinforce exemplary behaviour' (Jabbour et al., 2010: 1057). Maley (2014) argues that there has been too much of a one-sided focus on short-term financial goals in performance management practices, and that both social and ecological goals should be increasingly considered. This would also be likely to have effects on sustainability, as the presence of green performance management does tend to increase environmental performance (Guerci, Longoni et al., 2016; Jabbour et al., 2010).

Having pointed to a number of HR practices with concrete implications when it comes to enhancing the environmental performance of organizations, the preceding presentation may run the risk of providing an overly one-sided assessment of the actual possibilities of profit-oriented organizations at achieving *true* long-term ecological sustainability. As we noted earlier, there are fears that CO_2 emissions may continue to increase. As suggested by Malm (2012: 147), extrapolating from the current trajectory '[. . .] we are warranted in speaking of an ongoing, 21st-century *emissions explosion*'. The question thus appears not to be simply one of increasing the speed with which current adaptions to the growing insights of environmental research are being made, but of *reversing* the current trajectory. Ultimately, in such a situation, any business-led approach to sustainability is susceptible to varying forms of critique. At the least, as argued by Bombiak (2019: 1657): 'Environmental protection presents a considerable challenge for contemporary enterprises facing the need to find a balance between the economic expansion and environment-friendly actions'. Such a 'balance', however, is no natural end product of business as usual, which is why this chapter has highlighted the crucial role played by stakeholders in influencing the behaviour of organizations.

On a more general level, this links back to the discussion about Polanyi, who aside from labour also lists nature ('land') as a 'fictitious commodity', the protection of which is argued to be equally dependent upon decommodification. Gerber and Gerber (2017) provide an example by referring to Swiss forest management, in which massive deforestations during the 19th century led to growing problems with landslides and erosion. This in turn prompted a move towards decommodification through legislation prohibiting forest clearance, making it illegal to convert forests to other uses. The point of the Polanyian perspective is that regulation provides a correction to market mechanisms, which left to their own devices are not expected to yield a state of balance between economic expansion and environmental sustainability.

Another difficult 'balancing act' pertains to some problematic aspects of reconciling social and environmental sustainability, illustrated in the complicated role of organized labour in environmental debates. This is, for example, manifested in the much debated 'jobs vs environment' dilemma facing unions (Räthzel and Uzzell, 2011; but see Ringqvist, 2021). While we pointed above to a tension between economic efficiency and social sustainability related to employee wellbeing, workers at the same time benefit from the financial competitiveness and survival of their employers. This in turn can conflict with environmental sustainability, as, for example, when the Polish coal miners' union opposed EU climate policies in order to defend the jobs of their members (Thomas and Doerflinger, 2020: 389). Some here point to the importance of socially mitigating factors facilitating a 'just transition' (Tomassetti, 2020), balancing environmental protection with the needs of workers, such as adequate retraining and protection (see Chapter 13 on restructuring and employment). However, also on a societal level, labour has an interest in productivity and economic growth as the basis for resource redistribution, full employment and welfare state consumption. This coupling of growth with 'social progress' becomes particularly problematic in light of critiques which question the very notion of a 'balance' between economic expansion and environmental sustainability, arguing that the roots of environmental degradation and climate change are located ultimately in economic growth itself (Foster and Clark, 2020).

From a growth-critical perspective, the role of the HR function in the pursuit of true ecological sustainability is indeed also limited: profit-oriented organizations, and within them the HR function, do have a role to play when it comes to the pursuit of ecological sustainability, particularly when there is a business case for such a policy. But within the logic of a critique which links ecological degradation with growth itself, there is a fundamental and hitherto unbridgeable conflict between a generalized profit-motive and true ecological sustainability: by definition, no business can afford to sacrifice the former for the sake of the latter. The stakeholder approach does not always acknowledge the arguably problematic aspects of incorporating the perspectives of multiple constituents and hence objectives in an economic system designed to recognize and reward value maximization above all else.

Case study: Sustainable coffee made by long-term investments and long-time co-workers

The passion for good coffee has been with us for more than 100 years. To take responsibility for people and environment has been natural for us just as long.

Kathrine Löfberg, chairman of Löfbergs

Löfbergs Lila is a fully family-owned international coffee-roasting company, founded in Sweden in 1906. The company has 340 employees in seven different countries, producing some 10 million cups of coffee per day, consumed in the Nordic countries and some other European countries, including the UK.

The following case description is based on interviews carried out during spring 2020 with Chairman Kathrine Löfberg, CFO (Chief Financial Officer) Fredrik Nilsson, HR Director Helena

Eriksson and Sustainability Director Eva Eriksson, as well as analysis of Löfbergs' Sustainability Reports from 18/19 and 19/20 (available at https://lofbergsgroup.com/).

Löfbergs works with renewable recyclable packaging and aims to use 100 per cent certified beans. They source their coffee from around 40,000 farmers. Together with the farmers, the company runs development projects focusing on improving living conditions and capabilities for dealing with the impacts of climate change. Löfbergs aims to contribute to a sustainable development in line with the UN Agenda 2030.

It is quite common for people to work at Löfbergs for a long time. The director of quality and sustainability, Eva Eriksson, has worked at Löfbergs for long enough to have seen some of the currently active board members grow up. However, the sustainability work extends beyond her domain. The family representatives, such as the fourth-generation owner and chairman of the board, Kathrine Löfberg, are engaged actively in international networks, such as the International Coffee Partners (ICP). The ICP is an NGO in which Löfbergs works together with seven other family-owned coffee companies in order to improve the development opportunities for small-scale coffee farmers.

Both Eva Eriksson and Kathrine Löfberg stress the historical importance of sustainability for Löfbergs, going back generations. Eva is convinced that the focus on sustainability is due to Löfbergs being a family business. Kathrine describes how the family, and hence the company, has always applied a societal dimension to their work, with engagement in the community, in people and in the environment. CFO Fredrik Nilsson argues in a similar fashion that since the family as majority shareholders take a long perspective, expensive investments aiming for long-term payback can be made.

HR Director Helena Eriksson, also a long-time employee, says that HR takes a proactive approach to well-being and actively works on inclusion and equality initiatives. Although the sustainability aspects of Löfbergs' brand or story mainly relate to sustainable production and packing, the employees are also considered an important asset. Löfbergs is affiliated to three different unions, one of which has a local union branch at the company.

Is it possible to work on sustainability in several areas at the same time? Can interests collide? Sustainability Director Eva Eriksson draws a connection between efficiency and sustainability, exemplifying with how efforts to make the production process more efficient also lead to lower energy usage and less waste produced. Kathrine Löfberg does acknowledge, however, that different types of sustainability can clash. She says that one must simultaneously look at and value the different dimensions. Focus on the here and now must be balanced with economical sustainability in the long term. Also, what is socially sustainable might not be the best for economical sustainability. One must constantly take the different sustainability dimensions into consideration.

For Löfbergs, sustainability is a part of the history as well as a continual engagement for the future of the company. It is also a reason for pride in the company. As much as a good cup of coffee.

(Continued)

Questions

1. The Löfbergs managers interviewed stress the fact that the company is family-owned with a long-term view of the future. What role does the ownership play in sustainability work? Can you see any ownership type where sustainability would not be favoured?
2. Löfbergs is a Swedish company, thus headquartered in a coordinated market economy. Does this make a difference, and if so, how?
3. The representatives of Löfbergs argue that the company is strongly committed to sustainability. Can you think of ways to evaluate such claims empirically?

Conclusion: reflective discussion

This chapter has provided a critical review of some of the central issues involved in debates on HRM and sustainability. We have shown that the concept of SHRM – often drawing on stakeholder theory – has emerged as an alternative to the more shareholder-oriented HR function associated with strategic HRM. As we have illustrated, strategic HRM is commonly understood as an attempt to increase the influence and legitimacy of the HR function in organizations. Efforts to move beyond this role may hence raise some concern pertaining to the legitimacy of HR going forward. However, Marchington (2015) argues that such worries are unwarranted, and that the opposite is in fact the case: it is when HR – by focusing on those functions for which marketing and finance departments tend to be better equipped – does not contribute on the basis of its *own* unique areas of competence that its long-term legitimacy is threatened. The broader frame of SHRM may thus provide new perspectives around which to formulate a legitimate role for HR, which he argues '[. . .] has forgotten that offering something different from other functions is critical to its contribution to long-term organisational sustainability [. . .]' (Marchington, 2015: 177). A similar argument is raised by Wright and Snell:

> We seek to be business partners, but if we take the shortcut by sacrificing our values and integrity for a 'seat at the table,' we may actually end up playing a significant role in the demise of our organizations [. . .] This is not blue-sky idealism. Although competitive realities require that HR organizations are business-oriented, HR leaders must distinguish between decisions that are driven *by* the business and decisions driven *for* the business. (2005: 181)

Focusing on what is good for business in the long term may hence in the perspective of SHRM imply the return to a more 'traditional' HR role, constituting a buffer between management and workers, and in so doing making sure that employees are willing and able to remain in employment. Adding to this role an increasing focus on environmental issues does not appear to present a particularly insoluble challenge, as we have illustrated that HR does possess some efficient tools to be utilized in enhancing environmental performance. The point is that this role is not justified on account of being 'morally' superior, but as an important aspect of the long-term survival of organizations. This chapter has also presented an analogous argument applied to the same issues on a more general level, with particular reference to Polanyi. Streeck, drawing on Polanyi, argues:

> Social systems thrive on internal heterogeneity, on a pluralism of organizing principles protecting them from dedicating themselves entirely to a single purpose, crowding out other goals that must also be attended to if the system is to be sustainable. Capitalism as we know it has benefited greatly from the rise of counter-movements against the rule of profit and of the market. (2016: 60)

Consequently, this chapter has argued that there is no natural balance or equilibrium between the different sustainability dimensions, which is a principal paradox of the very concept of sustainability: each dimension is in itself the single most important one, and they often simultaneously presuppose and contradict each other. For example, we noted above that raising the Swedish retirement age is presented as a necessary means to carry the costs of the pension system; *economically* sustainable public social expenditure here presupposes a *socially* sustainable working life. We also referred to a tension between economic efficiency on the one hand and employee well-being on the other – manifested in the competing loyalties of HR – but, equally, employees have an interest in the competitiveness and survival of their companies. Hence unions sometimes oppose environmental regulation in order to defend the jobs of their members. More generally, issues of 'social progress' pursued by organized labour tend to be coupled with economic growth serving as a means for resource distribution and general material improvement. In turn, however, economic growth is sometimes argued to conflict with many goals related to environmental sustainability. Reconciliation of these often conflicting goals is a matter of constant negotiation and contestation, within organizations as well as in broader society.

The stakeholder perspective provides a frame of reference within which to understand the plurality of forces and interests affecting the behavior of organizations and the resulting balance between the sustainability dimensions. Here, HR can be responsive to and point to the stakeholders affecting and being affected by their organizations. We have shown and contended that the HR function has a role to play when it comes to sustainability, a political and societal issue of principal concern, the importance of which is only going to be exacerbated in the coming decades.

Reflective questions

1. Which are the three dimensions of sustainability? Can you think of ways in which they complement each other? Can you think of ways in which they contradict each other?
2. What are some of the tensions between strategic HRM and Sustainable HRM?
3. The section on social sustainability points to a tension between efficiency and competitiveness on the one hand and the long-term wellbeing of the employees on the other. Who are the most important stakeholders affecting this balance?
4. Companies are presented with the challenge of finding a balance between economic expansion and environmental sustainability. Can such a balance be achieved, and if so, how? Applying the stakeholder perspective, who are some of the most important stakeholders in this regard? Name some HR practices that can contribute to the environmental performance of organizations.

Recommended readings

- Lyon, Thomas P. and Montgomery, A. Wren (2015) 'The means and end of greenwash'. *Organization and Environment*, 28(2): 223–49. DOI: 10.1177/108602 6615575332
- Malm, Andreas (2012) 'China as chimney of the world: The fossil capital hypothesis'. *Organization and Environment*, 25(2): 146–77. DOI: 10.1177/1086026 612449338
- Tomassetti, Paolo (2020) 'From treadmill of production to just transition and beyond'. *European Journal of Industrial Relations*, 26(4): 439–57. DOI: 10.1177/0959680120951701

References

Aiman-Smith, Lynda, Bauer, Talya N. and Cable, Daniel M. (2001) 'Are you attracted? Do YOU intend to pursue? A recruiting policy-capturing study'. *Journal of Business and Psychology*, 16(2): 219–37.

App, Stefanie, Merk, Janina and Büttgen, Marion (2012) 'Employer branding: Sustainable HRM as a competitive advantage in the market for high-quality employees'. *Management Revue*, 23(3): 262–78.

Bombiak, E. (2019) 'Green human resource management – the latest trend or strategic necessity?' *Entrepreneurship and Sustainability Issues*, 6(4): 1647–62. DOI: 10.9770/jesi.2019.6.4(7)

Bowen, Howard R. (1953) *Social Responsibilities of the Businessman*. New York: Harper & Bros.

Crippa, M., Guizzardi, D., Muntean, M., Schaaf, E., Solazzo, E., Monforti-Ferrario, F., Olivier, J. G. J. and Vignati, E. (2020) *Fossil CO_2 Emissions of All World Countries – 2020 Report*, EUR 30358 EN. Luxembourg: Publications Office of the European Union.

Dundon, Tony and Rafferty, Anthony (2018) 'The (potential) demise of HRM?' *Human Resource Management Journal*, 28(3): 377–91. DOI: 10.1111/1748-8583.12195

Ehnert, Ina (2009) *Sustainable Human Resource Management: A Conceptual and Exploratory Analysis from a Paradox Perspective*. Heidelberg: Springer.

Ehnert, Ina and Harry, Wes (2012) 'Recent developments and future prospects on sustainable human resource management: Introduction to the special issue'. *Management Revue*, 23(3): 221–38.

Ehnert, Ina, Harry, Wes and Zink, Klaus J. (2014) 'Sustainability and HRM'. In I. Ehnert, W. Harry and K. J. Zink (eds), *Sustainability and Human Resource Management: Developing Sustainable Business Organizations*. Berlin and Heidelberg: Springer, pp. 3–32.

Ehnert, Ina, Parsa, Sepideh, Roper, Ian, Marcus, Wagner and Muller-Camen, Michael (2016) 'Reporting on sustainability and HRM: A comparative study of sustainability reporting practices by the world's largest companies'. *International Journal of Human Resource Management*, 27(1): 88–108. DOI: 10.1080/09585192.2015.1024157

Elkington, J. (2013) 'Enter the triple bottom line'. In A. Henriques and J. Richardson (eds), *The Triple Bottom Line: Does It All Add Up?* Abingdon and New York: Taylor & Francis, pp. 1–16.

Eurofound (2012) *Sustainable Work and the Ageing Workforce: A Report Based on the Fifth European Working Conditions Survey*. Luxembourg: Publications Office of the European Union.

Foster, John Bellamy and Clark, Brett (2020) *The Robbery of Nature : Capitalism and the Ecological Rift*. New York: Monthly Review Press.

Fraser, Nancy (2014) 'Can society be commodities all the way down? Post-Polanyian reflections on capitalist crisis'. *Economy and Society*, 43(4): 541–58.

Freeman, R. Edward (1984) *Strategic Management: A Stakeholder Approach*. Boston, MA: Pitman.

Freeman, Richard B. and Medoff, James L. (1984) *What Do Unions Do?* New York: Basic Books.

Gerber, Jean-David and Gerber Julien-François (2017) 'Decommodification as a foundation for ecological economics'. *Ecological Economics*, 131: 551–6. DOI: 10.1016/j.ecolecon.2016.08.030

Gonäs, Lena and Larsson, Patrik (2014) 'Employment regimes and personnel work in Sweden'. In B. E. Kaufman (ed.), *The Development of Human Resource Management Across Nations*. Cheltenham: Edward Elgar, pp. 410–36.

Guerci, Marco, Longoni, Annachiara and Luzzini, Davide (2016) 'Translating stakeholder pressures into environmental performance – the mediating role of green HRM practices'. *International Journal of Human Resource Management*, 27(2): 262–89. DOI: 10.1080/09585192.2015.1065431

Guerci, Marco, Montanari, Fabrizio, Scapolan, Annachiara and Epifanio, Antonella (2016) 'Green and nongreen recruitment practices for attracting job applicants: exploring independent and interactive effects'. *International Journal of Human Resource Management*, 27(2): 129–50. DOI: 10.1080/09585192.2015.1062040

Gully, Stanley M., Phillips, Jean M., Castellano, William G., Han, Kyongji and Kim, Andrea (2013) 'A mediated moderation model of recruiting socially and environmentally responsible job applicants'. *Personnel Psychology*, 66(4): 935–73. DOI: 10.1111/peps.12033

Hall, Peter A. and Soskice, David (eds) (2001) *Varieties of Capitalism: The Institutional Foundations of Comparative Advantage*. Oxford: Oxford University Press.

Jabbour, Charbel José Chiappetta, César Almada Santos, Fernando and Nagano, Marcelo Seido (2010) 'Contributions of HRM throughout the stages of environmental management: Methodological triangulation applied to companies in Brazil'. *International Journal of Human Resource Management*, 21(7): 1049–89. DOI: 10.1080/09585191003783512

Kapp, K. William (1950) *The Social Costs of Private Enterprise*. Cambridge, MA: Harvard University Press.

Kassinis, George and Vafeas, Nikos (2006) 'Stakeholder pressures and environmental performance'. *Academy of Management Journal*, 49(1): 145–59. DOI: 10.2307/20159751

Kaufman, Bruce E. (2014) 'The development of human resource management across nations: History and its lessons for international and comparative HRM'. In B. E. Kaufman (ed.), *The Development of Human Resource Management Across Nations*. Cheltenham: Edward Elgar, pp. 1–20.

Kramar, Robin (2014) 'Beyond strategic human resource management: Is sustainable human resource management the next approach?' *International Journal of Human Resource Management*, 25(8): 1069–89. DOI: 10.1080/09585192.2013.816863

Lag & Avtal (2020) 'Kommunal ser höjd pensionsålder som svek'. *Lag & Avtal*, retrieved 8 July 2020. Available at: www.lag-avtal.se/avtalsrorelsen/kommunal-ser-hojd-pension-salder-som-svek-6983936

Lengnick-Hall, Mark L., Lengnick-Hall, Cynthia A., Andrade, Leticia S. and Drake, Brian (2009) 'Strategic human resource management: The evolution of the field'. *Human Resource Management Review*, 19(2): 64–85. DOI: 10.1016/j.hrmr.2009.01.002

Lyon, Thomas P. and Montgomery, A. Wren (2015) 'The means and end of greenwash'. *Organization and Environment*, 28(2): 223–49. DOI: 10.1177/1086026615575332

Macke, Janaina and Genari, Denise (2019) 'Systematic literature review on sustainable human resource management'. *Journal of Cleaner Production*, 208: 806–15. DOI: 10.1016/j.jclepro.2018.10.091

Maley, Jane (2014) 'Sustainability: The missing element in performance management'. *Asia-Pacific Journal of Business Administration*, 6(3): 190–205. DOI: 10.1108/APJBA-03-2014-0040

Malm, Andreas (2012) 'China as chimney of the world: The fossil capital hypothesis'. *Organization and Environment*, 25(2): 146–77. DOI: 10.1177/1086026612449338

Marchington, M. (2015) 'Human resource management (HRM): Too busy looking up to see where it is going longer term?' *Human Resource Management Review* 25(2): 176–87. DOI: 10.1016/j.hrmr.2015.01.007

Memili, Esra, 'Chevy' Fang, Hanqing, Koç, Burcu, Yildirim-Öktem, Özlem and Sonmez, Sevil (2018) 'Sustainability practices of family firms: The interplay between family ownership and long-term orientation'. *Journal of Sustainable Tourism*, 26(1): 9–28. DOI: 10.1080/09669582.2017.1308371

Pagell, Mark and Zhaohui, Wu (2009) 'Building a more complete theory of sustainable supply chain management using case studies of 10 exemplars'. *Journal of Supply Chain Management*, 45(2): 37–56. DOI: 10.1111/j.1745-493X.2009.03162.x

Polanyi, Karl [1944] (2001) *The Great Transformation: The Political and Economic Origins of Our Time*. Boston, MA: Beacon Press.

Räthzel, Nora and Uzzell, David (2011) 'Trade unions and climate change: The jobs versus environment dilemma'. *Global Environmental Change*, 21(4): 1215–23. DOI: 10.1016/j.gloenvcha.2011.07.010

Räthzel, Nora and Uzzell, David L. (eds) (2013) *Trade Unions in the Green Economy: Working for the Environment*. New York: Routledge.

Richards, James (2020) 'Putting employees at the centre of sustainable HRM: A review, map and research agenda'. *Employee Relations: The International Journal* (ahead of print). DOI: 10.1108/ER-01-2019-0037

Ringqvist, Josef (2021) 'Union membership and the willingness to prioritize environmental protection above growth and jobs: A multi-level analysis covering 22 European countries'. *British Journal of Industrial Relations* (ahead of print). DOI: 10.1111/bjir.12654

Silver, Beverly J. (2003) *Forces of Labor: Workers' Movements and Globalization since 1870*. Cambridge: Cambridge University Press.

Streeck, Wolfgang (2016) *How Will Capitalism End?* London: Verso.

Thomas, Adrienand Doerflinger, Nadja (2020) 'Trade union strategies on climate change mitigation: Between opposition, hedging and support'. *European Journal of Industrial Relations*, 26(4): 383–99. DOI: 10.1177/0959680120951700

Thompson, Paul (2003) 'Disconnected capitalism: Or why employers can't keep their side of the bargain'. *Work, Employment and Society*, 17(2): 359–78. DOI: 10.1177/0950017003017002007

Tomassetti, Paolo (2020) 'From treadmill of production to just transition and beyond'. *European Journal of Industrial Relations*, 26(4): 439–57. DOI: 10.1177/0959680120951701

Touboulic, Anne and Walker, Helen (2015) 'Theories in sustainable supply chain management: A structured literature review'. *International Journal of Physical Distribution and Logistics Management*, 45(1/2): 16–42. DOI: 10.1108/IJPDLM-05-2013-0106

Vidal-Salazar, María Dolores, Cordón-Pozo, Eulogio and Ferrón-Vilchez, Vera (2012) 'Human resource management and developing proactive environmental strategies: The influence of environmental training and organizational learning'. *Human Resource Management*, 51(6): 905–34.

WCED (The World Commission on Environment and Development) (1987) *Our Common Future*. Oxford: Oxford University Press.

Wright, Patrick M. and Snell, Scott A. (2005) 'Partner or guardian? HR's challenge in balancing value and values'. *Human Resource Management*, 44(2): 177–82. DOI: 10.1002/hrm.20061

Ybema, Jan Fekke, van Vuuren, Tinka and van Dam, Karen (2020) 'HR practices for enhancing sustainable employability: Implementation, use, and outcomes'. *International Journal of Human Resource Management*, 31(7): 886–907. DOI: 10.1080/09585192.2017.1387865

Zink, Klaus J. (2014) 'Social sustainability and quality of working life'. *Sustainability and Human Resource Management*. In I. Ehnert, H. Wes and K. J. Zink (eds), *Sustainability and Human Resource Management: Developing Sustainable Business Organziations*. Heidelburg and Berlin: Springer, pp. 35–55.

Index